# CARIBBEAN TOURISM

# CARIBBEAN TOURISM:
## MORE THAN SUN, SAND AND SEA

Edited by
Chandana Jayawardena

Ian Randle Publishers
Kingston • Miami

First published in Jamaica, 2007 by
Ian Randle Publishers
11 Cunningham Avenue
Box 686, Kingston 6
www.ianrandlepublishers.com

NATIONAL LIBRARY OF JAMAICA CATALOGUING IN PUBLICATION
DATA

Caribbean Tourism : More than Sun, Sand and Sea/ edited by Chandana
   Jayawardena

p.;   cm. – (Caribbean tourism ; book 3)

Bibliography : p.   .-Includes index
ISBN 976-637-178-4

I. Jayawardena, Chandana        II. Series

1. Tourism  – Caribbean Area    2. Ecotourism– Caribbean Area 3. Heritage
tourism – Caribbean Area        4. Sports and tourism – Caribbean Area

338.4791729           dc 21

Book and Cover design by Ian Randle Publishers
Printed in the United States of America

# TABLE OF CONTENTS

## SECTION 1: COMMUNITY & ECOTOURISM

## SECTION 2: AGRO-TOURISM

# FOREWORD

There is a discernible trend which will shape the future development of the tourist industry. In common with most industries throughout the world the tourist industry has been forced to specialise. Specialty tourism is the child of this process. Underlying this process is a greater environmental sensitivity globally, greater health consciousness and a growing preference by tourists to experience the effect of a pristine environment. Coupled with this trend is an awareness that the standard tourist package emphasising other natural endowments over the traditional sand and sea has taken root. Specialised Tourism is an attractive growing point of the industry.

This is the third volume on the Caribbean Tourist Industry that Dr Jayawardena has edited and offered to the public for scrutiny. This particular book has for its subject the specialised areas of the tourist industry such as ecotourism, agro-tourism and festival tourism. In each of these areas there is scope for the Caribbean to create a niche market which has the potential for substantial development.

In recent times festival tourism in particular has attracted considerable attention. And this is one area in which the Caribbean can be quite strong; for this Region possesses a powerful cultural tool in the form of its unique music, such as Reggae and Calypso. There is no doubt the infectious rhythms of the Caribbean music, giving rise as they have done to particular cultural forms of expression, have contributed to its attraction as a tourist destination. In other parts of the world where the Caribbean disaspora is quite strong, as in the case of Great Britain and North America, Caribbean music and other forms of cultural expression have been transformed into instruments of substantial commercial and economic value.

The new trends in the tourist industry also opens up possibilities for those countries that do not possess the traditional natural endowments, such as sand and sea. Guyana, for example, has been able to embark on a fledgling programme of ecotourism mainly because of the conceptual shift of what tourism represents today. Guyana and other countries with a similar environmental makeup can break into the Tourist Industry because the value of such places resides not in beaches and sand but rather in their appeal of possessing a pristine habitats. There is a great opportunity here for diversifying out of a narrow mode of production into a more general economic development.

What I have found of particular interest in all of Dr Jayawardena's books is a bold attempt to marry analysis to practical ends. I have noted that in this specific volume there is a section on making tourism a part of the school curriculum. This is an important development as it will be essential that our young people who might opt for a career in the Tourist Industry to begin to understand as early as possible the value of educating themselves to be dynamic and visionary entrepreneurs. The business culture, so much a part of our age and our time, must inform the approach to these specialised areas of tourism as it must other areas of Caribbean life.

This volume is as welcomed as the others that Dr Jayawardena has edited and placed in the public domain. He has done the Region a notable service by bringing analysis, debate and insight to an important area of growth for the economies of many states of the Caribbean Community.

Professor Kenneth O. Hall
Pro Vice Chancellor and Principal
Mona Campus
Jamaica

# PREFACE

This series of three books on 'Caribbean Tourism' aims to provide current thoughts and recent research findings on social, economic, and developmental issues in the tourism sector within the Caribbean region. It is hoped that these books will be considered as a milestone in research on Caribbean tourism. The series taps into the vast knowledge on tourism that exist within the Caribbean as well as in regions closer to the Caribbean. It is common in similar books to attract all or most contributions from academic or researchers. This series attempts to balance contributions from academics as well as practising industry experts. In fact, approximately 50 per cent of the contributing authors fall into the latter category. There are also a few chapters jointly authored by practitioners and academics.

This series was initiated with a simple e-invitation sent to some 128 potential authors. After six months the manuscript of three books with 48 chapters contributed by 81 authors from 27 countries were ready and submitted for publication. The pace at which the project was completed is a reflection of the commitment of experts on tourism-related areas in the Caribbean to share their knowledge, research findings and thoughts.

Only 20 per cent of the contributors are directly involved in tourism and hospitality education and research. This group includes eight former or current Heads of University Departments or Directors of Tourism/Hospitality Schools in the Caribbean. Thirty-three per cent of the contributors are academics and researchers from disciplines other than tourism and hospitality. This, itself, is an indication of the importance of a multi-disciplinary approach to tourism research which is an extremely complex area of study. This group also includes two pro vice chancellors from the University of the West Indies and a past president of the Caribbean Studies Association.

Twenty-two per cent of the contributors are from the private sector. This group includes the chairman of a leading hotel corporation in the Caribbean, two hotel general managers, a chief executive officer of an attractions management company and executives from airlines, restaurants and catering companies. Fourteen per cent of the contributors are from the public sector of Caribbean tourism including the secretary general of the Caribbean Tourism Organisation, a national director of Tourism and a few other senior officers. The remaining 11 per cent are consultants and other experts involved in the tourist industry.

The series is divided into three books with the following sub titles:

- Vision, Missions and Challenges.
- People, Service and Hospitality.
- Special Interests and Communities.

Special interest tourism covers many facets of the tourism industry, usually not related to mass tourism. Based on this, one can imagine that special interest tourism looks at niche markets which are much smaller than mass tourism segments attracted mainly for sun, sea, and sand elements.

In this context, it is highly unlikely that the special interest tourists will outnumber the mass tourists travelling to leading destinations in the Caribbean such as the Dominican Republic, Puerto Rico, Cancun, Cuba, The Bahamas, Jamaica, Aruba, US Virgin Islands, Barbados, Bermuda et cetera in the near future. Mass tourism, by and large, has been and will be the main contributor to the economies of such countries for a long time.

This is not an attempt to downplay the growing importance of special interest tourism to the Caribbean, but to be realistic in analysing the strategic options for the future of tourism in the region. Without doubt, the potential market share, significance, contribution to the Caribbean economies from special interest tourism will increase in the future.

Guyana, Suriname, Belize, Trinidad & Tobago, and Dominica entered the tourism arena much later than their neighbours because of different or a collection of political, social and geographical reasons. Due to the lateness of their entry and their geographical features, such countries are focusing mainly on special interest tourism and ecotourism. The World Travel Awards, which represent the highest accolade in the global travel industry awarded the 'World's Leading Ecotourism Destination' award to Tobago in November 2003. Most of the other Caribbean destinations are looking at developing special interest tourism and ecotourism to increase their chances for future tourism growth. This is commendable as special interest tourism and ecotourism provide better opportunities for local communities to participate and enjoy the benefits of tourism more directly than conventional mass tourism.

This book looks at some relevant issues on special interest tourism and ecotourism. It has 19 chapters and is sub-divided into the following four sections:

- Community and Ecotourism        -        7 chapters
- Agro-tourism                            -        3 chapters
- Heritage & Cultural Tourism       -        6 chapters
- Events & Sports Tourism            -        3 chapters

In addition to the above topics, adventure tourism and health tourism are also grouped under special interest tourism. The focus on special interest tourism is indicated in figure 1.

## Figure 1
## Special Interest Tourism (SIT) Flower

## COMMUNITY & ECOTOURISM

This volume begins with a discussion by Jayawardena on the importance of the community as an essential component in the tourist industry. The chapter also explores the importance and impact of a community-based approach to tourism development, particularly because tourism is the lifeblood of the Caribbean region. The author suggests a strategic approach to the development and diversification of the tourism product by increasing the involvement of all stakeholders in the industry. Jayawardena et al then examine ecotourism in the context of Caribbean tourism. The authors explore the different definitions of tourism around the region and examine the efforts made by countries such as Belize, Costa Rica, Dominica and Guyana. In chapter 3, Gordon explores the ecotourism and sustainable tourism movements in Trinidad and Tobago. An underlying assumption of this study is that tourism policies, like all aspects of the development dialogue, involve political as well as technical issues and that battles over scarce resources, economic gains, and environmental protection and conservation, are not easily resolved. The principal finding of this study is that Trinidad and Tobago, because of its previous history of nature tourism and relative late start in expanding the tourist sector overall, may enjoy advantages not shared by other Caribbean states. In chapter 4, Huntley explores the possibility of adopting a community-based approach to ecotourism development in Guyana, another new entrant in the tourism arena. The author proposes a marriage between the two concepts in an effort to sustainably develop the tourist industry. This would also ensure that local communities begin deriving benefits from ecotourism ventures in the country. Hoosein and Watkins then explore the role of the Iwokrama International Centre for Rain Forest Conservation and Development (Guyana) in providing education and training for resource management and conservation. The authors also discuss efforts made to develop ecotourism at Iwokrama and other successes of the Iwokrama programme. Boxill follows with am examination of tourism development in Belize. The author suggests that, because of Belize's unique environmental and cultural characteristics, the country should pursue a form of tourism that is would protect the integrity of the destination. He also suggests that alternative tourism ventures could be developed with collaboration from sister CARICOM states. Abel, in chapter 6, uses a form of ecological economics known as emergy analysis is used to evaluate recent ecotourism development on the island of Bonaire, Netherlands Antilles. Emergy is an alternative, donor currency that places all products of world ecosystems on one scale, based on the human-ecological work that contributed to the production of that product. The intensity of ecotourism development on Bonaire is also calculated and compared with other economic sectors. Boxill follows with an examination of tourism development in Belize. The author suggests that, alternative tourism initiatives that compliment the country's environmental and cultural characteristics should be pursued. He also suggests alternative ventures in collaboration with sister states of CARICOM.

## AGRO-TOURISM

In this chapter Phillips and Graham examine the findings of a conference on agro-tourism organised around the theme 'Agro-Tourism: A Sustainable Approach to Economic Growth'. Issues such as, the micro and macro-economic dimensions of agro-tourism, human and social dimensions, role of the environment in agro-tourism and an institutional framework for agro-tourism are explored and the requirements of an enabling environment for agro-tourism are assessed, with particular emphasis on the role of the community and a sustained natural resources base in fostering agritourism development. Mason and Milne then examine successful agritourism initiatives and present a model for developing agro-tourism initiatives. The authors caution that while the model will not guarantee a winning formulation for every situation, it does guarantee to throw up multiple viable possible projects. In chapter 10, McDavid et al explore a strategic approach to agro-tourism in the region. Agro-tourism is viewed as a viable means of diversifying the tourism industry while resuscitating the regional agriculture industry that has experience consistent stagnation in the past decade.

## HERITAGE AND CULTURAL TOURISM

This section begins with Sinclair who explores the issue of myths, nostalgia and reality in the indigenous tourism experience. The author proposes that emphasis should be placed on presenting the reality of the indigenous experience instead of romanticising this experience for visitors. Ajagunna then examines the current stage of tourism development and the challenges that are faced by the tourism administration in developing heritage tourism in Jamaica. Suggestions are then made towards achieving sustainability in the future. An important part of the suggestions made is the need for cooperation and collaboration among the stakeholders in the Jamaican tourist industry. In chapter 13, Thomas-Hope discusses the implications of developing heritage tourism in the Cock Pit country, Jamaica, which is inhabited by the Maroons, the descendants of runaway slaves, who secured treaty rights to land from the colonial authorities in the eighteenth century and were able to retain better their cultural traditions because of their inaccessibility. The author raises questions about the manner in which this unique aspect of Jamaica's cultural and environmental heritage is to be exploited. Walsh-Stoddard and Cornwell then present an analysis of how the ruins of former sugar plantations, especially windmills, reflect national identity in such societies as Barbados, Cuba, St. Kitts, and Tobago. The authors propose that since Caribbean plantation production was enmeshed in an early form of globalisation, its history should be of interest to visitors from all those societies that have evolved its matrix of economic relations, including West Africa, Asia, Europe, and the Americas. Care should also be taken to showcase the heritage of the Caribbean people from their perspective instead of from the perspective of the plantation owners. In chapter 15, Cooper examines reggae as a key element of Jamaican culture. The author also examines the success of reggae as a heritage tourism attraction and recognises the contributions of Bob Marley and a number of festivals in making reggae internationally accepted. Nurse closes this section with an examination of the contribution of the arts and entertainment to the field of tourism. The author also highlights the role of festivals as a demand-pull for the tourist industry as well as the ways in which tourism generates markets for the arts. The case for festival tourism is made in an economic assessment of the Trinidad Carnival, which is the largest festival in the Caribbean region.

## EVENTS & SPORTS TOURISM

Gooden et al focus on how special events are organised and marketed in chapter 17. The authors present a compilation of the best practices and make recommendations that can be used as a guide by amateur organisers and planners in organising and marketing special events. Beckles then examines the psychology of the English cricket fan in the West Indies. Special emphasis is placed on the 1994 Test Match between England and the West Indies at Kensington Oval, Barbados. The author explores the views and reactions of both the 'locals' and the 'foreigners' to this event and its implication in the postcolonial Caribbean society. Yearwood concludes this section by determining the benefits of sports events to the stakeholders in the Barbados tourist industry. Sports tourism was developed as a means of diversifying the island's tourism product and providing greater benefits for the stakeholder. The author finds, however, that the level of benefit received differ among stakeholders and were not considered to be significant.

This book has attempted to shed some light on relevant issues in Caribbean tourism. This publication by no means addresses all issues on the subject matter. It is evident that further and continued research is needed for the Caribbean region to optimise the benefits from tourism in a sustainable manner whilst balancing and satisfying the needs of communities, tourists, investors, operators, policy makers and the governments of the Caribbean.

# ACKNOWLEDGEMENTS

This would not have been possible without the dedication and hard work of many professionals. I am deeply indebted to the authors for their contributions and Ian Randle Publishers for publishing the book, along with the other two books on Caribbean Tourism I edited. I thank Professor Kenneth O. Hall, the principal of the Mona Campus and the pro vice chancellor of the University of the West Indies (UWI) for writing the foreword. I also thank Professor Alvin Wint, former head of the Department of Management Studies, UWI, Mona Campus, Jamaica, and my colleagues, for their support and encouragement during this book project.

My very special thanks are due to, and I am indebted to, Ms Eritha Huntley for her patience and hard work without which this text would not have become a reality. Eritha was dedicated to the timely completion of this book as well as the other two books of this series. She worked around the clock to complete the project before the very optimistic target I had set for both of us.

My special thanks are due to Mrs Allison Atkinson and my friends Mr Samuel Bandara and Dr Hilton McDavid for providing project support. I am also grateful to Professor Anthony Clayton, Professor Richard Kotas and Professor Richard Teare for their professional inputs as project advisers.

Chandana Jayawardena
Kingston, Jamaica.

# ACRONYMS AND ABBREVIATIONS

| | |
|---|---|
| ADB | Agricultural Development Bank |
| AIT | Alliance Internationale de Tourisme |
| AWNC | Asa Wright Nature Centre, Trinidad & Tobago |
| BCA | Barbados Cricket Association |
| BHTA | Barbados Hotel & Tourism Association |
| BTA | Barbados Tourism Authority |
| BWIA | British West Indies Airways Limited |
| CARDI | Caribbean Agricultural Research & Development Institute |
| CARICOM | Caribbean Community |
| CAST | Caribbean Action for Sustainable Tourism |
| CBD | Centre for Biological Diversity |
| CDC | Carnival Development Committee |
| CHA | Caribbean Hotel Association |
| CTO | Caribbean Tourism Organisation |
| CW | Caribbean World |
| CXC | Caribbean Examination Council |
| ECLAC | Economic Commission for Latin America & the Caribbean |
| EIU | Economist Intelligence Unit |
| EMA | Environmental Management Agency, Trinidad & Tobago |
| EMS | Environmental Management System |
| EU | European Union |
| FTAA | Free Trade Area of the Americas |
| GDC | Guyana Development Corporation |
| GDP | Gross Domestic Product |
| GEF | Global Environmental Facility |
| GIS | Geographical Information System |
| GUYMINE | Guyana Mining Enterprise Limited |
| IICA | Inter-American Institute for Co-operation on Agriculture |
| IMF | International Monetary Fund |
| JAMPRO | Jamaica Promotions Company |
| JCDC | Jamaica Cultural Development Commission |
| JTB | Jamaica Tourist Board |
| MALMR | Ministry of Agriculture, Land & Marine Resources, Trinidad & Tobago |
| MTTI | Ministry of Trade, Tourism & Industry, Guyana |

| | |
|---|---|
| NCDC | National Carnival Development Committee, St Vincent & The Grenadines |
| NGOs | Non-Government Organisations |
| OAS | Organisation of American States |
| POTS | Pyramid of Tourism Segmentation |
| SET | Strategic Eco-Tourism Model |
| STEA | South Trelawny Environmental Agency, Jamaica |
| TIDCO | Tourism & Industrial Development Corporation, Trinidad & Tobago |
| THA | Tobago House of Assembly |
| THAG | Tourism & Hospitality Association of Guyana |
| UNEP | United Nations Environmental Programme |
| UNESCO | United Nations Educational, Scientific & Cultural Organisation |
| UN/FAO | United Nations' Food & Agricultural Organisation |
| UWI | University of the West Indies |
| VFR | Visiting Friends & Relatives |
| WCED | World Commission on Environment & Development |
| WICBC | West Indies Cricket Board of Control |
| WTO | World Tourism Organisation |
| WTTC | World Travel and Tourism Council |

# SECTION 1
# COMMUNITY
# &
# ECOTOURISM

# CARIBBEAN TOURISM FOR TODAY AND TOMORROW

Chandana Jayawardena

## ABSTRACT

*The community represents an essential component in the development of the tourist industry and enhances the visitor experience. Yet the traditional sun, sea and sand tourism, for which the Caribbean is famous, has never really sought nor incorporated the input of community members in its operational plans, though often times the structure(s) and operations affect not only the physical community, but the lives and livelihood of the residents. Given the indication of world trends towards a growing interest in alternative tourism, the various stakeholders ought to take heed as they are increasing calls for greater levels of local inclusion and participation in tourism enterprises. This would require a new paradigm for tourism development in the Caribbean. One option which could be explored is that of community tourism and to validate this approach, the Pyramid of Tourism Segmentation (POTS) model is introduced and explained in this chapter. The chapter also explores the importance and impact of a community-based approach to tourism development, particularly because tourism is the lifeblood of the Caribbean region. By taking a strategic approach to the development and diversification of the tourism product, the region will be better positioned to manage the growth, shape, and control of the direction of the industry.*

## INTRODUCTION

The Caribbean region is the most tourism dependent region in the world. In general terms, the benefits of the industry continue to increase faster than all other regions in terms of revenue and employment. This success, however, was not a planned strategic option in most Caribbean countries. The industry is at times faced with challenges such as crime and tourist harassment. This arises mainly from the lack of community involvement and the low levels of benefits to the communities close to the resort tourist areas. Problems such as tourist harassment are more frequent and more serious in resort areas surrounded by poorer neighbourhoods.

The need for planned sustainable development is, therefore, essential for the future of tourism in the Caribbean. Efforts have been made by countries such as Belize, Dominica, Guyana, Suriname, and Trinidad & Tobago to develop alternative forms of tourism such as ecotourism, agro-tourism and community tourism to address concerns that have arisen as a result of conventional mass tourism activities. These countries, which are entering the tourism arena in the Caribbean relatively late have a great advantage of learning from the strengths as well as the mistakes made by regional tourist destinations now reaching the mature stage of the destination life cycle.

This chapter begins with an examination of tourism internationally and within the Caribbean. The author predicts that by 2010 Cuba will be the top tourist destination in the Caribbean again and explains his reasons for this prediction. The Pyramid of Tourism Segmentation (POTS) model is explained and the development of special interest tourism is advocated. The term 'community' in the context of the tourism sector is redefined and divided into broad segments. Community tourism and community involvement in tourism are identified as essential in the process of sustainable tourism development. The chapter also calls for the inclusion of all stakeholders in the process of tourism development as traditional models for tourism development often excluded communities and other stakeholders for various reasons.

If the industry is to develop sustainably there is, the need for a paradigm shift in the way in which planning, managing, controlling, reviewing and decision-making are done. Such challenges faced in developing tourism sustainably are not limited to the Caribbean region. Similar challenges are noted around the world, particularly in other developing regions. These challenges are examined and recommendations and suggestions are made to advance the cause of community involvement and participation, and to achieve the ultimate goal of sustainable tourism.

## TOURISM IN THE WORLD

A properly planned, developed and controlled tourist industry will positively affect the society and the economy. Enrichment of the tourist industry with national characteristics is vital for the healthy development of tourism (Jayawardena 1993). Travel and tourism – encompassing transport, accommodations, catering, recreation and services for travellers – is the world's largest industry. Today the worldwide tourist industry directly or indirectly employs around 231 million people representing 10 per cent of the world's workforce and contributes around 11.5 per cent, directly or indirectly, to the Gross Domestic Product (GDP) of the world economy. The World Travel and Tourism Council (WTTC) predicts that by the year 2010, the tourism contribution to GDP will increase to 12.5 per cent and the direct, and indirect tourism employees will increase to some 328 million worldwide (WTTC 1998). The growth of international tourist arrivals has been phenomenal as indicated below:

- 25 million in 1950
- 69 million in 1960
- 160 million in 1970
- 286 million in 1980
- 459 million in 1990
- 673 million in 2000 (estimate)

During the last 50 years annual tourist arrivals have increased 27 fold (Jayawardena 2001b).

International tourism, perhaps because of its enormous quantitative growth, finds itself in a phase of radical change, technologically, economically, ecologically and morally. In 1998, the Alliance Internationale de Tourisme (AIT), a parent company of more than 130 automobile and touring clubs, motorbike, bicycle, camping and hiking associations, looked into the 'future trends of tourism' on its 100th anniversary. AIT organised a Delphi study with 223 selected international experts from 64 countries with questions on the expected tourism development during the next 5–15 years.

In concluding, these experts identified a new 'Trend signpost' which is termed 4 E's of Tourism. Four E's predict the main reason for future growth in travel. This is summarised as:

- Educational Tourism, Culture and History
- Event and Mega-Event related Tourism
- Entertainment and Fun
- Environment and Clean Nature (Obermair 1999).

The world's top five destinations, in terms of tourist receipts are

1. United States
2. Italy
3. France
4. Spain
5. United Kingdom

The Caribbean, as a single destination, usually ranks sixth in the world in terms of tourist receipts. In 1999, the Caribbean attracted 3.1 per cent of tourist arrivals in the world.

# TOURISM IN THE CARIBBEAN
## The Region

The Caribbean is a fascinating and unique region. An archipelago of sunny, tropical islands naturally endowed with exotic flora and fauna, surrounded by blue sea and caressed by gentle breezes, is the general impression of the region in the minds of most visitors. This is true in most areas within the region. In fact, it is the main reason for the image it has enjoyed for over 50 year and continues to enjoy, in spite of the increasing competition from similar regions. This image made the Caribbean the most sought after region for romantic holidays and honeymoons in the world. But the Caribbean has much more to offer the millions of tourists and cruise passengers visiting the region year after year.

For convenience, the term 'Caribbean' is used in this chapter to identify 34 destinations that are members of the umbrella organisation of the region's tourism industry, the Caribbean Tourism Organisation (CTO). In this definition, the Caribbean region includes a few countries/regions on the mainland in South America and Central America. The area between the south of Florida in the USA, Cancun in Mexico, Belize in Central America, Venezuela, and Suriname in South America, is now referred to as the Caribbean. Although in the Atlantic Ocean the islands of The Bahamas and Bermuda are treated as Caribbean countries by the CTO for statistical purposes.

The population of the Caribbean is approximately 60.4 million with the five largest jurisdictions (Venezuela, Cuba, Dominican Republic, Haiti and Puerto Rico) accounting for approximately 86 per cent of the total population (KPMG 2000). These countries vary tremendously in terrain, size, population, culture and economic prosperity. It is noteworthy that four of these are Spanish-speaking countries and Haiti is a French-speaking country. In other words, the English-speaking West Indies is a significantly small part of the Caribbean.

## The Tourism Sector

The tourism sector in the Caribbean has assumed prominence as a result of consistent stagnation in the traditional economic sectors. As such, the region is often referred to as the most tourism dependent region in the world. Tourism earnings account for approximately 25 per cent of the region's Gross Domestic Product (GDP). In 1999, the Caribbean region recorded US$17,733 million in tourism receipts with 20.32 million tourist arrivals and 12.1 million cruise passenger arrivals (CTO 2001).

Based on the latest arrival figures issued by most of the Caribbean countries and reasonable estimates, the total arrivals for the year 2000, too, should be around US$20 million. The benefits of tourism are not, however, evenly distributed among the 34 countries and destinations in the Caribbean. The success of a country's industry cannot be judged by the number of tourists it attracts, the number of nights guest spent there or by the total amount of dollars spent by tourists. A more meaningful measurement will be to look at the net tourism receipts (gross profit calculated by deducting all expenditure directly related to tourism and foreign exchange leakage) and then analysing the per capita net tourism receipts. Unfortunately, this is not possible at the present time. As is seen in many other countries in the world, the Caribbean countries have not yet developed a system to quantify the actual foreign exchange leakage from tourism. In the absence of this data, the author has used the total tourism receipts to rank the top 10 tourist destinations in the Caribbean.

**Table 1.**
**Visitor Expenditure of Top 10 Caribbean Destinations in US$ Millions**

| DESTINATION | 1995 TOURISM RECEIPTS | 1999 TOURISM RECEIPTS | INCREASE % | 1995 RANK | 1999 RANK |
|---|---|---|---|---|---|
| Dominican Republic | 1,568 | 2,483 | 58.35 | 2 | 1 |
| Puerto Rico | 1,842 | 2,326 | 26.28 | 1 | 2 |
| Cancun | 1,371 | 2,144 | 56.38 | 3 | 3 |
| Cuba | 977 | 1,714 | 75.43 | 6 | 4 |
| The Bahamas | 1,346 | 1,583 | 17.61 | 4 | 5 |
| Jamaica | 1,068 | 1,279 | 19.76 | 5 | 6 |
| US Virgin Islands | 822 | 955 | 16.18 | 7 | 7 |
| Aruba | 521 | 773 | 48.37 | 9 | 8 |
| Barbados | 612 | 677 | 10.62 | 8 | 9 |
| Bermuda | 488 | 479 | (1.84) | 10 | 10 |
| Total of Top 10 Destinations | 10,615 | 14,413 | 35.78 | - | - |
| Total of Other 24 Destinations | 3,258 | 3,320 | 1.90 | - | - |
| Total of all 34 Destinations | 13,873 | 17,733 | 27.82 | - | - |
| % of Top 10 Destinations | 76.52 | 81.29 | - | - | - |

In 1999 the top 10 destinations in the Caribbean accounted for over 81 per cent of the tourism receipts in the region. Four years ago, these 10 countries accounted for 77 per cent of total tourism receipts in the region (Jayawardena 2001a). Phenomenal growth in tourism receipts over the last four years in Cuba (75 per cent), Dominican Republic (58 per cent), Cancun (56 per cent) and Aruba (48 per cent) have contributed to the increase of the market share of the top 10 Caribbean destinations as shown in table 1.

An important aspect shown in the table 1 is that 34 destinations in total have grown its tourist receipts by 28 per cent during the last four years. The top 10 destinations in total grew by 36 per cent and has significantly influenced the overall increase percentage to be impressive. But, what is not reflected in regional statistical analysis is that the overall picture is quite bleak for most of the other 24 countries. The overall increase recorded by these countries during the last four years has been less than 2 per cent and far behind the world average. This is bad news for a majority of Caribbean countries.

The same 10 destinations have remained in the top 10 list over the last four years. However, slight changes in the ranking have been observed over the five-year period. Barbados, Jamaica, The Bahamas, and Puerto Rico have slid one position each. Cancun, US Virgin Islands and Bermuda remain in the same position held in 1995. Dominican Republic and Aruba have advanced one position. Cuba is the only country in the top 10 that has advanced by two positions.

## Partnerships for Development

In many parts of the Caribbean tourism education and training by both the public and private sectors has never been adequate. In addition to national programmes, the Caribbean Tourism Organisation and the Caribbean Hotel Association have delivered programmes in tourism education and training. Both have had their successes and the CTO has benefited from significant EU funding in this area over the years. Both the CTO and the CHA continue, however, to suffer from lack of human and financial resources to establish a sustained and affordable programme covering the many areas needed (Holder 2001).

The need for partnership, co-operation and collaboration between the main stakeholders in the industry such as local communities, universities and the academic community, the private sector Caribbean Hotel Association (CHA), the public sector Caribbean Tourism Organisation (CTO) and CARICOM has never been greater (Jayawardena 2000). The local community must be the main focus of tourism development to ensure sustainability. Critical areas such as destination marketing, product promotion, customer service and guest safety and security are also areas that should be addressed. Nevertheless, the successful future of Caribbean tourism lies ultimately in teamwork, communication and a united effort by all main stakeholders. A solid foundation of social partnership and a clear understanding of the needs of the main segments of visitors to the Caribbean are urgently required.

Owing to the different political system, Cuba's needs for partnerships in tourism development seems different. Cuba has successfully entered into a few, but important partnerships with a few well established European hotel corporations as well as leading Jamaican hotel corporations, SuperClubs and Sandals, who manage hotels in the island. Most of the investment in these hotel projects in Cuba have been from the government with at times, 5–10 per cent investment from the hotel corporations. Melia of Spain now manages over 20 hotels in Cuba.

## THE CUBAN FACTOR

Considering the governmental focus and attention to rapid development of tourism in Cuba, the author predicts that by 2010 Cuba will be elevated to the number one position in Caribbean tourism, with or without a change in the policy of the USA towards Cuba. Another reason for this prediction is the current drive to develop the human resources needed for Cuba's tourism sector. As an example, in the year 2000 Cuba had 19 hospitality schools, which employed 1,000 professors and issued some 20,000 certificates. By and far, Cuba has the most educated community within the Caribbean today. Now Cuba is using that significant ingredient to choose and train employees for tourism.

It is observed in Cuba that, in many instances, managers from other sectors with excellent academic qualifications and professional experiences are attracted to the tourism sector, particularly the hotel industry, as this is seen as a quick and easy way to earn foreign exchange and receive a much higher income than in other sectors. FORMATUR, the national training and education agency for the tourism and hospitality sector in Cuba, has introduced a rapid one year education programme to convert such managers from other fields into assistant managers levels of hotels.

In general terms, the internal weaknesses and external threats are overshadowed by the internal strengths and external opportunities of tourism in Cuba. The growth of tourist receipts and arrivals to Cuba during the last few years has been amazing. Cuba attracted 762,666 tourists in 1995, passed the magical one million mark in 1996 and recorded nearly 1.8 million (including 76,898 tourists from USA) arrivals in 2000. As a result, the optimism for the potential for tomorrow by the Cuban government is very high. During a recent two-hour interview in Havana, the Director of Tourism Development, Ministry of Tourism, Cuba informed the author that between 5 to 7 million tourist arrivals (nearly 20 per cent of arrivals in the region) are anticipated by 2010 and all developmental issues pertaining to human resources, infrastructure, resorts and hotels are done with that target in mind. He further stated that it is generally expected and accepted that these targets will double as and when the relationship with USA eventually improves.

The author feels that these predictions are too optimistic, but based on his research, he is comfortable in predicting that Cuba will become the top tourist destination in the Caribbean, in terms of revenue and arrivals within the next 10 years. The main reasons for this prediction are:

- The size of the island and the population (highest in the region)
- The extra ordinary natural beauty of the island which includes, undisputedly, the best beach in the Caribbean (Varadero).
- The best airport in the Caribbean (Havana) and a total of nine international airports.
- The colourfulness of well-known personalities and legends such as Fidel Castro, Che Guvera, Ernest Hemmingway and even the American Mafia godfathers who controlled tourism in Cuba up to 1959.
- The mystique of the revolution and the sense of adventure in visiting Cuba (especially for those US citizens who defy federal warnings to travel to Cuba).
- Richness of art and culture.
- Richness of the heritage and architecture simply unmatched by any other Caribbean nation. In Old Havana alone there are some 1,640 old heritage buildings. Up to early 1990s most of these were badly maintained. But the ambitious restoration project initiated and led by the city historian of Havana is changing this most commendably.
- Focus and attention given by the government to sustainable tourism development.
- Support given by governments and private sectors of Canada and some European countries to infrastructure and tourism development.
- High level of education. It is claimed that over 20 per cent of workers in tourism sector have Bachelors degrees, a claim unprecedented by any other country in the world.
- Friendliness and politeness of most Cubans.
- Current level of general discipline which provides a very high level of safety to tourists. Harassment of tourists which seems to be a major problem in many Caribbean countries is, generally, not noticed in Cuba. With a potential change of the political system, one can anticipate that the situation may change.

Obviously, there are problems related to tourism in Cuba. Most parts of Havana for example, are badly maintained and have no running tap water. Water, air and noise pollution too are very high in cities. Prostitution is one such problem in which attempts by the state to control have failed in the past. However, in considering the identified positives, which out number the negatives, Cuba is on track to once again become the number one tourist destination in the Caribbean. This will have some implications for some of the Caribbean nations. But, in general terms, the region will benefit from the further growth of tourism in Cuba. Those who believe in the potential for multi-destination marketing in the Caribbean should consider Cuba as a prime destination, particularly for the European market.

# PYRAMID OF TOURISM SEGMENTATION (POTS) MODEL

The idea of marketing the Caribbean under one umbrella brand has resurfaced. Both the CTO and CHA believe that this is the correct path to take to increase the market share of the region in world tourism. As a first step it is important that the failure of such initiatives in the past are analysed. It is also essential to segment the target market for the Caribbean since the offerings of the region are diverse and many may appeal to a number of different segments. The total market for future Caribbean tourism can be broadly grouped into five segments, with the first three segments usually branded as 'mass' tourism. The five segments are:

- **Cruise Ship Passengers**

The first segment is the cruise line passengers, who spend the least (per capita) but is a large market segment. This sector is frequently criticised by others involved in tourism for creating lower than potential income for host destinations. On the other hand, it is viewed alternatively as a captive audience, which can produce future stay-over tourists. This sector represents 37 per cent of total visitor arrivals and 10 per cent of visitor expenditure in the Caribbean. Forty-five per cent of the total cruise ship berths out of the US are for Caribbean cruises. Ten years ago this share was 57 per cent.

- **All-inclusive Tourists**

Not all Caribbean destinations have seen investment in developing this category of hotels. Although there may be exceptions, a typical all-inclusive hotel guest may spend very little time visiting attractions, meeting local people, taking tours and experiencing the local culture. Often all-inclusive hotels will package the 'tasting of local elements' in their products within the limits, or within the walls of these hotels.

According to Paris & Zona-Paris (1999), 48 of the best 100 all-inclusive hotels are in the Caribbean. Out of these, 17 are in Jamaica, which is not surprising (Issa & Jayawardena 2002). The original concept of the French company 'Club Med' was borrowed, refined and introduced to the Caribbean by the Jamaican hotelier John Issa in 1976 and the world renowned hotel company Sandals was launched by Jamaican entrepreneur Gordon 'Butch' Stewart in 1982.

- **'Sun-lust' Tourists**

The third segment is tourists attracted to other beach resorts and inns in the Caribbean. A new wave of tourism in the Caribbean started with this segment after World War II with the leaders being Cuba, Jamaica, Bermuda, Puerto Rico, and The Bahamas.

- **Special Interest Tourists**

While research on this type of travel is comparatively limited, international trends are signalling that more people want action and the opportunity to experience new activities with a sense of personal adventure in a safe environment. As travellers mature in age and gain experience in travelling, they are more likely to become interested in special interest travel. Mass-market tourism will continue to be important to the Caribbean and is expected to grow when it is considered that most North Americans are yet to travel to another country. At the same time, special interest tourism is increasingly capturing the attention of more seasoned travellers.

- **Ecotourists**

This segment is still very small in comparison to the other segments and is often seen as a niche market. In general, hardcore eco-tourists are more educated, well read and often have more disposable income than the other segments. Ecotourism is often described as 'responsible travel to natural areas that concerns the environment and improves the welfare of the local people'. Ecotourism has the potential of receiving greater support from local people even in countries where institutions geared towards developing tourism often face hostility, cultural barriers, challenges and objections.

These segments can be grouped in a pyramid and lines of maturity, and the graduation to higher, but smaller segments can be identified (Jayawardena & McDavid 2000). This new (POTS) model is summed up in figure 1.

**Figure 1: Pyramid of Tourism Segmentation (POTS)**

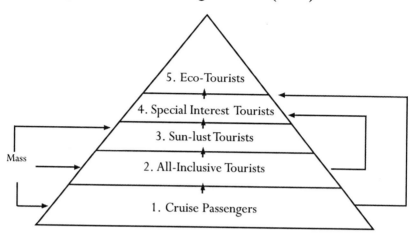

It is not essential that all visitors must graduate from level 1 to level 2 and so on. Some will remain in their respective levels throughout, as they will not be attracted to the products designed for tourists at other levels. Some may by-pass a level or two in the graduating process. At the same time, it is unlikely that a mass tourist will overnight develop a desire to become a hard-core eco-tourist. Some tourists of level 5 may eventually graduate to level 1. Special interest tourists are similar to the middle class of a country. It is the backbone of the future of tourism. On reaching this level, it is unlikely that most special interest tourists return to become mass tourists. Countries such as Belize, Dominica, Guyana, Suriname, and Trinidad and Tobago, are attempting to attract more eco-tourists. These countries should look at the potential increase of special interest tourists as an initial strategic step. Having that segment of special interest tourists will strengthen the structure and lay a good foundation for the growth of ecotourism in a strategic sense. Usually community involvement in tourism is high in special interest tourism and ecotourism. Hence, another valid reason to plan for these segments in the Caribbean to ensure the sustainability of the tourism sector.

## SPECIAL INTEREST TOURISM

Special interest tourism can, therefore, be sub-divided into five main sections:

- Cultural / Heritage tourism
- Adventure tourism
- Community-based tourism
- Health tourism
- Agro (or agri)–tourism

Each of these sections can be placed very close to ecotourism. In some cases overlapping areas can be identified. It is also possible to combine two or more of these sub-sections in tourism development. As such, a community-based approach to tourism development is becoming increasingly popular, especially in developing countries where local citizenry have often been left out of the planning and development process. The promotion of small-scale tourism is intuitively perceived as a suitable form of economic development in rural areas. However, its impact is controversial and not always obvious (Fleischer & Felsenstein 2000). This form of tourism should ideally serve as a catalyst for the sustainable development of the tourism industry. It also ensures that locals maximise the benefits received from tourism since community decisions should ultimately decide the type of tourism development within the community.

In agricultural communities, for example, a community-based approach to agro-tourism provides excellent opportunities for locals to bring about a marriage between the agricultural industry and the tourist industry. It provides a unique experience for tourists who may wish to experience rural life and meet and interact with the local people. Agro-tourism also emphasises and encourages respect for local cultures through education and organised encounters. In addition, effort is placed on the preservation and protection of the resource base, which is fundamental to tourism itself (KPMG 1996).

Following are a few examples of Agro-tourism activities from different parts of the world which result in tangible benefits to the local communities:

- Spending a day with rice farmers in China.
- Staying a night at a tea factory in Sri Lanka.
- Visiting a vineyard and taking part in the wine production process in France.
- Visiting a cheese farm in the Netherlands.
- Dining with a farming family and using the farmhouse sauna in Finland.
- Visiting an apple farm in Canada.
- Visiting an orange farm in Florida, USA.
- Spending a weekend on a cattle farm in the Rupununi area in Guyana.
- Spending a weekend at a sugar plantation in St. Kitts & Nevis.
- Spending a weekend in a Blue Mountain coffee estate in Jamaica.

The central theme in these experiences is the local community. It is important to understand the concept of community and the dynamics of communities, especially those that are directly or indirectly involved in all tourism sub-sectors. Special Interest Tourism can be used as a main tool to ensure that local communities:

- Benefit from tourism.
- Appreciate the importance of tourism.

- Support initiatives for tourism development.
- Play important roles in future tourism development.

# COMMUNITY

The term 'community' may mean different things to different people (Jayawardena 2001c). In the context of the Caribbean, the tourism-related communities can be categorised into four broad segments based on the nature of their involvement in the industry.

## *Communities Investing in Tourism*

This group typically involves leading businesspersons as well as small entrepreneurs. Communities possess indigenous knowledge and expertise that are often critical to the sustainable development of the industry. In most parts of Jamaica, along the south coast of Barbados and around St. Georges Basin in Grenada, a high degree of local ownership within the industry seems to contribute to the overall development of these economies. Even though these local entities have occasionally been accused of actions contributing to the degradation of the environment, the success of such companies is sometimes accompanied by a demonstration of social and environmental responsibility and respect for the environment.

## *Communities of Workers Directly Employed in Tourism*

Maintaining a strong community of interest among employees involves giving high levels of motivation, this being of poignant relevance as any form of community tourism will depend on the confidence level, training and cohesiveness of the employees and managers. It is worthy to note that, one of the primary factors affecting motivation in the workforce is the relationship between management and workers, which in the region is often authoritarian, a carry over from colonialism. One of the manifestations of this management style is an outbreak of conflicts such as strikes, 'go-slows', 'sit-ins' and 'sick-outs' that have had a serious impact on the sensitive hotel industry. Measures to diminish these outbreaks normally take the form of union prevention, paternalism or collaboration with the union (Jayawardena & Crick 2000).

## *Communities Indirectly Involved but Benefiting from Tourism*

The degree of indirect benefit received by communities is related to the level of linkage between tourism and other sectors of the economy though many governments find it difficult to quantify, categorise and capture the 'real' earnings from tourism. Through the multiplier effect, however, the benefits from tourism usually filter into many communities due to its pervasive and invasive nature. A case in point is the importance of vending as a source of income for a large number on people in the formal and informal sectors. In some instances, smaller hotels in the region contribute more to the indirect flow of benefits to these communities as they depend more readily on local agricultural communities for their food items. Quality of the produce provided is a primary concern but can be remedied via support and technical expertise from the hotel and tourism sector, as well as from the government, to assist in upgrading their standards, increasing the quality of their product and strengthening the network of suppliers. This once again illustrates the need for a holistic approach to servicing the industry.

### Other Communities

According to Boxill (2000) there is a relationship between perceived economic opportunities and internal migration, as well as between migration and squatting. Invariably, these tourism centres foster squatter settlements within or near to them resulting in negative attitudes and practices such as harassment. Often recipients of little or no direct or indirect benefits from the industry, these pockets seed resentment and even hostility. As a constant policy goal, it is important and instructive, therefore, to evaluate each community's sensitivity to the industry as a first step in planning sustainable tourism, the central lesson of this chapter.

## COMMUNITY TOURISM

Community tourism is essentially a collection of businesses that sell a variety of goods and services to visitors but are operated by local people. Community-based tourism development, therefore, not only supports community initiatives, but allows direct tourist dollars to flow into and stay in local communities. Community tourism may take many forms, from the provision of bed and breakfast accommodation in homes in less favoured tourism areas to ecotourism projects (McHardy 2001). It is a form of tourism that has inclusiveness as it primary goal. It requires that residents be involved throughout the tourism planning process in a two-way exchange of information and views. Community tourism should also provide local residents with ongoing control over tourism development. The primary reasons for communities becoming involved in tourism are to create more jobs, for general community development and for increased revenue (Severin 2001). However, community tourism is not a very lucrative enterprise, but provides a means of supplementing the income of locals. It also provides a means of ensuring that the benefits of tourism are shared equitably among the stakeholders in the industry.

It is important to note that community tourism exists only when there is participation by locals in tourism development (Hayle, 2000). While community participation in tourism development is very desirable there seems to be formidable operational, structural and cultural limitations to this approach to tourism development in many countries. Some of these are as a result of centralised decision-making and administration for the tourism industry; lack of co-operation and co-ordination between agencies and sectors; inadequate financial and human resources and the domination of community ventures by the elite members of the said community (Tosun, 2000). These challenges are not insurmountable. Instead the success of community tourism ventures is dependent on four primary features, namely:

## 1. Empowerment

Members of the community should be part of the decision-making process and also have a share in the rewards of the business.

## 2. Protection of stakeholders interests

Stakeholders should be clearly identified and their interests protected by legal and policy statements. Stakeholders would normally include community members and/or 'outside' private or government investors.

## 3. Accountability

Mechanisms should be in place to ensure that decisions taken in the interest of the businesses do not create problems for the wider community. Also that the interests of the tourists are served and that those responsible for taking decisions which run counter to the benefits of the community are identified and are dealt with satisfactorily.

## 4. Monitoring/ evaluation

There should be continuous assessment of the product in correcting negative impacts in the community and the product (Boxill 2000).

Severin (2001) describes empowerment as an action instead of a process, and it is facilitated by participation or genuine partnership, knowledge, access to resources, training and education and social services. Empowerment is also an improvement in the ability of people to design and participate in the processes and events that shape their lives (UNDP, 1994). McHardy (2001) further states that while it is important that the concept and management of tourism projects be generated within the community, it is important that locals are provided with technical and financial assistance from government in an effort to help co-ordinate their ideas for projects.

The importance of community inclusion in the tourism sector has been recognised by the Jamaican government and tourism administration. In the recently released *Ten Year Master Plan for Sustainable Tourism Development* (2001) the Ministry of Tourism and Sport in Jamaica identified a number of 'building blocks' for 'an inclusive industry'. These included:

1.  Increasing the supply of agricultural produce to tourism – letting farmers and traders know what is needed and helping them to meet the needs on a consistent basis.
2.  Supporting the development of arts and crafts by upgrading the skills of producers and vendors; assisting with access to loans; and by providing marketing support for authentic work of good quality.

Additionally, the industry was identified as a vehicle for the social upliftment of the Jamaican people. This is accomplished through activities such as community development projects and community heritage preservation and development projects. There are also plans to:

1.  Make the Resort Boards more representative;
2.  Establish a Community Support Unit to work in collaboration with the Resort Boards and Parish Development Committees to ensure that tourism planning is in keeping with local concerns and hopes
3.  Improve visitor-community relations.

## CHALLENGES TO TOURISM DEVELOPMENT IN THE CARIBBEAN

Significant increases in the contribution of tourism to regional economies are clearly evident. But, tourism as a viable industry received less than its fair share of attention in the past from politicians, public sector policy makers, planners, managers, researchers and academics in most of the Caribbean countries. There is a lack of a consistent definition of tourism as an economic sector. There is also a lack of appreciation by some of the region's governments of the need for an overall strategic plan and a well-co-ordinated approach to ensure the sustainability of tourism. CTO's predictions for the future appear to be optimistic as shown in the table 2.

The future of tourism in the Caribbean will depend largely on the ability of the region to deliver a high quality product that corresponds to the changing tastes, needs, wants and demands of the international traveller. Careful segmentation and niche marketing strategies may result in market broadening and growth. This will contribute towards the optimisation of income from tourism, and thereby economic growth. Greater attention will be required in the planning of overall infrastructure

**Table 2.**

**World and Caribbean Tourist Arrivals 1997 – 2010 (in millions)**

|  | 1997 | 2000 | 2010 | Average Annual Growth |
|---|---|---|---|---|
| World Tourist Arrivals | 612.0 | 673.0 | 1,045.0 | 4.2% |
| Caribbean Tourist Arrivals | 18.9 | 22.5 | 37.9 | 5.5% |
| Caribbean Cruise Passengers | 11.9 | 13.9 | 26.3 | 6.6% |
| Total Caribbean Visitors | 30.8 | 36.4 | 64.2 | 5.8% |
| % Caribbean Share (tourists only) | 3.1% | 3.3% | 3.6% | |

and logistics for resort cities and villages chosen for hotel development projects. This has to be adequate for expanding local communities, additional tourists, as well as increasing numbers of direct and indirect tourism employees. As an example, the largest hotel in the Caribbean, the 2,400 room Atlantis located on the Paradise Island, The Bahamas created 6,000 new jobs. Most of these employees, coming from other areas of The Bahamas, had to find accommodation in the areas closer to the hotel.

Public sector authorities also have to be fully focused on assessing the carrying capacity for each tourist attraction near these expanding and new resort areas. More importantly, they must take appropriate action to ensure the sustainability of such attractions for the benefit of current and future generations of local populations as external factors will have a significant influence on the future of the tourist industry in the Caribbean. Sound environmental management systems, globally accepted quality assurance systems, growing customer expectations and demands for better value for money will be some of the major challenges for the future. There is also the need to reduce the continued over dependency on North American feeder markets. Many Caribbean destinations will therefore, have to find creative ways to increase arrivals mainly from Europe, Latin America as well as the Caribbean intra-regional market. More importantly, they will have to devise creative and innovative ways of getting local communities involved within the sector.

# CONCLUSION

The future economic survival of the Caribbean region seems to depend largely on the development of a sustainable tourist industry, a concept that marries two conflicting ideas: development and sustainability. Achieving a balance is therefore, an important strategic goal, which requires moderation, control and co-ordination. Sustainability is often addressed from an environmental perspective. Less frequently this is coupled with socio-cultural and community concerns. The preservation of the environment, though a necessary condition; is not sufficient for the sustainability of tourism (Jayawardena 2000). In achieving sustainability the needs and hopes of local communities need to be considered. It is imperative that they be integrated within the tourist industry. Communities, villagers living near hotels, employees of tourist establishments should be educated about the benefits of tourism as well as the different cultures that tourists come from. Without the support of employees and the local community, it is difficult to ensure the satisfaction of the needs of tourists in keeping with their expectations.

Tourism in the Caribbean has been characterised as an industry that excludes locals through the creation of tourism enclaves. This is evident with the proliferation of the all-inclusive resorts that reduce the level of contact between tourists and the host population, as well as the amount of benefits that the locals receive from the industry. Such developments have at times resulted in resentment on the part of locals for the industry. The industry's success, however, is ultimately dependent on how the community culture enhances the tourists' experience. Industry operators have to realise that tourists are not attracted to a destination because of spacious hotel rooms and public areas. It is, in fact, the culture of the people and the opportunity to experience life in another part of the world that serves as a major pull factor to many destinations.

In addition to mass tourism, which primarily depends on the sun, sea and sand elements of the tourism product, the Caribbean needs to develop and market other types of tourism in a strategic manner. Ecotourism and special interest tourism, which includes sub sectors such as agro-tourism, adventure tourism, sports tourism, heritage tourism, health tourism and community tourism, may have key roles to play in this strategic approach. The tourist industry depends largely on the region's ability to maintain product quality, ensure profitability, promote effectively, provide air access, ensure safety, ensure acceptance of the local population, strengthen linkages between tourism and other economic sectors, and combine regional efforts to create a competitive force (Holder 1996). The enrichment of the tourist industry is vital for a healthy and sustainable tourism development. To achieve this all stakeholders, including governments as well as community leaders need to meet on a common platform and plan the future of the Caribbean tourist industry.

# REFERENCES

Boxill I. 2000. 'Overcoming Social Problems in the Jamaican Tourism Industry'. In *Tourism in the Caribbean*, eds. I. Boxill and J. Maerk, J. Mexico: Plaza y Valdex.

CTO. 2001 Caribbean Tourism Statistical Report 1999-2000. Caribbean Tourism Organisation. Barbados.

Economist. 1999. *Pocket World in Figures*. London, Profile Books.

Fleischer, A. and D. Felsenstein. 2000. 'Support for Rural Tourism: Does it make a Difference?' *Annals of Tourism Research* 27, no. 4.

Hall, K. O., J.S. Holder, J. S. and C. Jayawardena. 2005. 'Caribbean Tourism and the Role of the UWI in Management Education'. In *Caribbean Tourism: Visions, Missons and Challenges* ed. C Jayawardena. Kingston: Ian Randle Publishers.

Hayle, C. 2000. 'Community Tourism in Jamaica'. In *Tourism in the Caribbean*, eds. I. Boxill and J. Maerk. Mexico: Plaza y Valdex.

Holder, J. 1996. 'Marketing Competitiveness in a New World Order: Regional Solutions to Caribbean Tourism Sustainability Problems'. In *Practising Responsible Tourism* eds. L. C. Harrison and W. Husbands, 145-173. Toronto: Wiley.

Holder, J. 2000. 'Island Improvement'. *World Travel & Tourism Development, Association Report*.

————. 2001. Some Ideas For Tourism Change in a Changing World. Caribbean Tourism Organisation, Barbados.

Issa, J, and C. Jayawardena. 2002. 'All-Inclusive Business in the Caribbean'. In *Caribbean Tourism: People, Service and Hospitality*, ed. C. Jayawardena. Kingston: Ian Randle Publishers.

Jayawardena, C. 1993. 'Harmonising the Tourist Needs and Country's Expectations from Tourism Industry'. In *Tourism, Hoteliering and Hospitality Education,* ed. C. Jayawardena, 28-31. Sri Lanka: Vijeya Publications Ltd.

————. 2000. 'An Analysis of Tourism in the Caribbean'. *Worldwide Hospitality And Tourism Trends* 1, no. 3.

————. 'Tourism and Hospitality Education and Training in the Caribbean: An Analysis of Recent Initiatives'. A paper presented at the Pan-American Confederation of Hospitality and Tourism Schools [CONPEHT] Conference, Cuba, 2001.

————. 'Tourism vs. Community: Direction, Purpose and Challenges of Caribbean Tourism'. Paper presented at the 26th Annual Conference of the Caribbean Studies Association, St Maarten, 2001.

————. 2001. 'Community Tourism: Applying the Lessons in the Caribbean'. In *People and Tourism: Issues and Attitudes in the Jamaican Hospitality Industry* eds. H. Dunn and L. Dunn. Kingston: Arawak Publishers.

Jayawardena, C. and H. McDavid. 2000. 'Implications of Agro-tourism in the Caribbean'. In *Agro-tourism — A Sustainable Approach to Economic Growth*, ed. P. Collins, 119-135. Inter-American Institute for Co-operation on Agriculture, Trinidad and Tobago.

Jayawardena, C. and A. Crick. 2000. 'Human Resource Management in Jamaica Responding to Challenging Times'. In *International Human Resource Management in the Hospitality Industry*, eds. S.M. Hofmann, C. Johnson and M.M. Lefever, 113-128. Educational Institute, USA.

KPMG Management Consultants. 2000. *Intra-Regional Travel Market Study*. Caribbean Tourism Organisation, Barbados.

KPMG Management Consultants. 1996. *An Agro-Tourism Strategy for Nova Scotia*, Nova Scotia Agriculture and Marketing, Canada.

McHardy, P. 2001. 'Planning for Sustainable Tourism Development'. Paper presented at the Second Annual Educators Forum of the Caribbean Tourism Human Resource Council, Antigua.

Ministry of Tourism and Sport. 2001. *The Ten Year Master Plan for Sustainable Tourism Development*, Jamaica.

Obermair, K. 1999. *Future Trends in Tourism*. Austria: University of Vienna.

Paris, J. and C. Zona-Paris. 1999. *100 Best All-Inclusive Resorts of the World*. The Globe Pequot Press, USA.

Patullo, P. 1996. *The Last Resorts, The Cost of Tourism in the Caribbean*. UK: Cassell.

Severin, F. O. 2001. 'Community Development'. Paper presented to the students of M.Sc. Tourism & Hospitality Management. UWI, Jamaica.

Sproule, K. W. 1995. *Community-based Ecotourism Development: Identifying Partners in the Process*. Wildlife Preservation Trust International.

Tosun, C. 2000. 'Limits to Community Participation in the Tourism Development Process in Developing Countries'. *Tourism Management* Vol. 21, (2000).

UNDP. 1994. *Human Development Report*. United Nations Development Programme.

WTTC. 1998. APEC Tourism Working Group. 'The Economic Impact of Travel and Tourism Development', *World Travel and Tourism Council*, UK, (1998) p.1.

# 2

# REDEFINING ECOTOURISM IN THE CONTEXT OF THE CARIBBEAN

Chandana Jayawardena, Hilton McDavid and Tricia Spence

## ABSTRACT

*The traditional approach to tourism in the Caribbean has been that of the 3S type: Sun, Sea and Sand. While, yielding positive financial returns, it threatens the very 'goose that lays the golden egg', a non-sustainable path the region can ill afford to trod. Diversifying the tourism product in sustainable directions then becomes an option the Caribbean cannot ignore, especially in the face of a rapidly changing competitive landscape. This chapter, examines the new phenomena of ecotourism, seeking to deepen an understanding of the concept by drawing on the prolific works of experts on the issue, weighs the pros and cons and suggests ways in which all the stakeholders can play a part to ensure its viability. It notes that whilst ecotourism cannot replace the traditional 3S tourism in the Caribbean, its addition would not only reduce the potential damage to natural resources but add a different dimension to the overall package. Essentially, a strategic as well as practical approach must be taken in order for ecotourism to contribute meaningfully to the Caribbean economies. The authors conclude by introducing a new concept termed 'The Strategic Ecotourism (SET) Model'.*

## INTRODUCTION

The Caribbean is world renown for 3S (sand, sea and sun) tourism, attracting many northern sun worshipers who often flock to its shores searching for a paradise in the sun. However, Horwich et al (1993) pointedly notes that despite the attractiveness of tourism as a low cost, high-profit venture, mass tourism can have far-reaching, negative consequences for native peoples and the environment. Environmental degradation, manifested in the form of water pollution, coral bleaching, deforestation and the destruction of natural flora and fauna, is a major concern.

The increasing concerns for the environment, dissatisfaction with over development and congestion of traditional tourism, the desire for new experiences, and the belief that many natural environments are in danger of being degraded have increased interest in ecotourism. An increasing number of today's travellers want vacations that will allow them to experience intimately the people, places and culture that they visit. More importantly, they have become more environmentally conscious and sensitive.

There is an urgent need for the Caribbean to develop and market other types of tourism in a strategic manner, in addition to mass tourism, which primarily depends on sun, sea and sand elements of the tourism product. Governments must ensure responsible and sustainable tourism, which, among other benefits, promotes sustained use and protection of natural and cultural resources and is economically and architecturally responsible whilst supportive of local economies. Ecotourism and special interest tourism, which includes sub-sectors such as agro-tourism, adventure tourism, sports tourism, heritage tourism, health tourism, and community tourism, have a key role to play in this strategic approach.

This chapter seeks to clarify the concept of ecotourism, highlights the negatives and positives of such an alternative, and recommends ways in which the various stakeholders can participate in order to minimise the downsides to this type of tourism. A united stand is needed instead of individual stands and hopefully, at the end of this chapter, a clearer understanding of the 'ecotourism' concept will be grasped. The chapter also seeks to re-define success in ecotourism in a business sense.

## ECOTOURISM: AN OVERVIEW

The term 'Ecotourism' has been used in a rather lax fashion, with the goal posts for its definition so widely spaced that anyone can kick out a definition and score. Clarification of the concept is needed. Jayawardena (2001a) captures the essence of a few graduate student research papers on ecotourism presented in the year 2000 at the University of the West Indies (UWI). The research done by these students provide a meaningful basis for a debate on aspects of ecotourism. In 'Ecotourism – Myth or Reality', Hernandez et al. (2000), explore the concept of ecotourism, examine the recent ecotourism thrust and attempt to bring to the fore concerns surrounding the ecotourism debate by providing realistic options. In 'The Potential of Ecotourism in Jamaica', Golding (2000) assesses Jamaica's potential to embrace ecotourism. This was seen as a possible means of diversifying the industry.

Ecotourism could generate much needed revenue while serving as an impetus for private conservation efforts. Hernandez (2000), in 'An Analysis of the Strategies for Ecotourism Development in the Dominican Republic', states that changing tourist tastes have resulted in the demand for nature and adventures. The researcher explores the strategies and policies of the Dominican Republic government and the private sector to protect the integrity of the destination while ensuring benefits for local communities. Additionally, in '*Social Marketing – A Strategy for Ecotourism Development in Jamaica*', White (2000), identifies social marketing as a means of changing attitudes and behaviours towards the tourist industry. Social marketing provides the framework for analysing the needs, motivations, and also the barriers to better co-operation between the industry and local populations which is an essential pre-requisite for ecotourism to be successful. Yearwood (2000) explores *the role of* education and training in Belize's tourism sector, which is developing with an emphasis on ecotourism. The need for human resources development is critical to its success.

Seeking to find a purposeful and useful definition has its benefits, which includes the following:

- The facilitation of standard setting;
- Allowance for across the board comparisons;
- Making possible the measurement of growth and identification of trends;
- Enabling the development of compliance ratings;
- Permitting the differentiation of products;
- Aiding in planning and strategy development, and
- Making ecotourism more of a philosophy and not a marketing ploy or a buzzword.

In short, having a transparent definition will strengthen the power of the concept and prevent the misuse and the exploitation of the precious natural resources. Once standards can be established travellers can make rational choices among 'eco-service' providers, supporting the doctrine, 'take nothing but photographs, leave nothing but footprints'.

To ignore the impact of man's action and existence upon the fragility of nature and the damaging effects of constant abuse is tantamount to killing the goose that lays the golden egg. Mass tourism in many Caribbean islands has typically overloaded infrastructure, prohibited beach access for locals, carries high importation costs, fosters tourist ghettos and is a major source of pollution, especially from cruise ships to which the Caribbean is a popular host.

Clearly, an ecosystem approach to tourism is an interdisciplinary, balanced, comprehensive and inclusive process that requires economic, social and environmental structure and the interests of communities to work together to plan and implement development strategies, as non-commitment of any of the parties would only impede progress.

Governments, by leading through example and adopting a more environmental focus, should share in the responsibilities for ecotourism development. This can be done by developing strategies and standards, considering the issue of carrying capacity, providing training and education for locals on standards, and including tourism in land use planning by involving all ministries in sustainable development efforts.

Originally promoted by members of the World Wildlife Fund, ecotourism was seen as a way to preserve the flora and fauna while still deriving some economic benefit. One of the primary tenets of this philosophy was that revenues earned from the use of eco-sites would be reinvested into the venture to ensure sustainability, as a way of giving back to the community and provide security. Increased usage of the term has come about as improvements in telecommunications, technology and transport has acted as catalysts for increased knowledge of the dangers of short sightedness in damaging the environment. This has caused travellers not only to become more aware, but more sophisticated.

Today ecotourism forms a part of a growing segment of the industry also known as nature tourism. Estimates by the WTO are that nature tourism generates 7 per cent of all international travel expenditure. Overall, tourism has been growing at 4 per cent per annum whilst nature travel has been growing at a yearly rate in the range of 10 per cent to 30 per cent (Reingold, 1993). While mass tourism cannot be done away with, there must be protection and conservation for tourism to be successful. A first step towards this goal is the need for clarity of the concept. By giving perspectives from varied sources, the next section should lead to a somewhat clearer understanding.

## DEFINING ECOTOURISM

Crouch and Wood (2001) suggests that ecotourism encompasses a broad range of nature, wildlife, and adventure tourism. A rather wide definition by any measure. Critical to the measurement of growth is the ability to pinpoint what exactly the concept embodies so that parameters can be set enabling numeration.

By eliminating the 'wear and tear' on a site that conventional tourism encompasses, McDonald and Zieger (1997) proffer that ecotourism is concerned with the preservation of such natural habitats and archaeological areas. According to some, ecotourism is concerned with making money, but only in an environmentally friendly manner. This will pose a great challenge to many Caribbean states, as prevailing attitudes do not seem to support this behaviour. Tourism is prompted by a profit motive, hardly immeasurable long-term environmental gains.

Berle (1990) states, 'Ecotourism is big business. It can provide foreign exchange and economic reward for the preservation of natural systems and wildlife. But ecotourism also threatens to destroy the resources on which it depends'. Additionally, leakages are a realities that affect maintenance, upkeep and reduce the multiplier effect. The inability to control leakages can lead to resentment by the local populace, making them feel used and cheap, as re-investment lags behind destruction; an outcome of this could be the resurrection of the sentiment often heard during the period of the Black Power Movement, 'tourism is whorism'.

In an attempt to gain a definition of the concept other than that usually given by theorists and environmentalists, Sirakaya, Sasidharan and Sonmez (1999) sought to ascertain the perspectives of 282 US-based eco-tour operators. In summarising the results of the respondents they came up with the following: 'Ecotourism is a new form of non-consumptive, educational, and romantic tourism to relatively undisturbed and under-visited areas of immense natural beauty, and cultural and historical importance for the purposes of understanding and appreciating the natural and socio-cultural history of the host destination'. While this might serve as a comprehensive definition to an often ill-defined concept, can it be realistically applied to the Caribbean where there is the blatant misuse and abuse by the very inhabitants of the important natural resource base critical to tourism? To counter this problem a serious educational drive would be necessary as well as the institutionalising of viable economic substitutes to replace some of the destructive practices common in the Caribbean, such as slash and burn.

The common thread that seems to run through most of the definitions seem to centre on low impact activities to areas of geographical and ecological interest which allow visitors to absorb the culture of the inhabitants without intentional destruction of the natural surroundings while the community still reaps some economic benefit. Despite the myriad variations on the meaning of the concept, presently in the Caribbean there has evolved three versions of ecotourism.

- *Eco-sensitive tourism* – here the basic nature of the product is maintained, but principles of sustainable development are incorporated in the operations and management of an entity such as a tourist resort.
- *Soft ecotourism* – here opportunities are made available to visitors whose primary motives remain more conventional.
- *Hardcore ecotourism* – usually happens in a situation where beach tourism may be impractical or impossible; destinations might instead cater to nature-specific tourists.

In analysing key market segments in Caribbean tourism, Jayawardena (2001b) refers to eco-tourists as a segment that is still very small in comparison to the other segments and which is often seen as a niche market. In general, hard-core eco-tourists are more educated, well read and often have more disposable income than the other segments. Ecotourism is often described as 'responsible travel to natural areas that concerns the environment and improves the welfare of the local people'. Ecotourism has the potential of receiving greater support from local people even in countries where institutions geared towards developing tourism often face hostility, cultural barriers, challenges and objections.

# ECOTOURISM INITIATIVES IN THE CARIBBEAN

In recent years three distinct categories of ecotourism have been identified within the Insular Caribbean. The first form involved the incorporation of sustainable development principles to the traditional 3S product. In essence, the core 3S product was not changed but improvements made so that less environmental damage occurred. This greening of the product was further encouraged by the Caribbean Tourism Organisation, which has initiated Caribbean Action for Sustainable Tourism (CAST) Programme to help hoteliers effectively manage environmental resources (Waldrop Bay 1998). Seminars conducted by the Caribbean Hotel Association (CHA) to assist in the formulation of environmentally safe and sound standards for hotels have been launched, vis-à-vis, their 'Greening of Your Hotel' seminars. Cresser (2002) discusses this project in a study that demonstrates the importance of becoming an environmentally friendly hotel through the adoption of an Environmental Management System (EMS). He also identifies new opportunities for hospitality education and training in the Caribbean region by incorporating environmental 'best practices' into the training curricula of education and training institutes.

The Bahamas has changed its slogan to 'one country seven islands' giving visitors different avenues for escape. Many of the all-inclusive resorts in Jamaica endorse the greening of the hotel concept as well. Jamaica has embraced the soft tourism concept warmly, with many of the all-inclusive hotels offering visits to natural sites and setting up aviaries on property. Other islands such as Cuba, Bonaire and the Dominican Republic have also gone this route as the average traveller has become more sophisticated and aware of the importance of protecting the environment for future generations.

Puerto Rico's US$14 million El Portal Visitor Centre at El Yunque Rainforest and Aruba's plan to protect the island's culture, wildlife and natural resources are a few of the thrusts taking place in the Caribbean to introduce this type of ecotourism (Waldrop Bay 1998). Grenada, realising that ecotourism is more compatible with the environment and involves long staying and low density type of tourism, has viewed this type of tourism as an alternative. Three components of ecotourism that would demonstrate the extent to which the Grenadian government has embraced tourism are small-scaled, locally-owned activities and environmental conservation.

In Trinidad and Tobago, the Asa Wright Nature Centre (AWNC) promotes the recycling, reuse and sustainable use of water, cutlery and crockery. There is restricted access with guests utilising only 10 per cent of the land area. Prevention of poaching (hunting) and agricultural squatting on the reserve are some of the key measures taken. It has served as a model for ecotourism development for other local operators as it has a strong conservation ethic, balancing human needs for economic gain with that of the conservation and preservation of natural resources.

The most prolific example of the third type of ecotourism in the Caribbean is the island of Dominica. Endowed with mountainous terrain, heavy forest cover and a lack of white sand beaches, this island considered pursuing the traditional marketing of the Caribbean a useless effort. Seeing the opportunity of its distinct status, Dominica, on a gradual basis, chose to develop a small scale, nature based tourism product. Emphasis was place upon local foods and preservation of architectural traditions. Even the Turks and Caicos Islands are benefiting from the new class of tourist. Eco-tourists account for about 20 per cent of their international visitors.

Others islands in the Caribbean are catching on to the philosophy and have even gone so far as to change their slogans. Montserratt's slogan is now 'The Way the Caribbean Used to Be'. The British Virgin Islands captures the thrust best with its slogan of 'Nature's Best Kept Secret'. Hopefully, the other islands can achieve a share of the growing eco-tourist market in a more sustainable way, allowing their natural resources to renew, while obtaining economic benefit. 'Eco AdVenture', the soft adventure magazine of Trinidad and Tobago is a good example of a journalistic approach in promoting ecotourism in the Caribbean, with the slogan 'Essential reading for eco-tourists, soft adventure travellers, birders and even traditional vacationers', it has features on adventure holidays, beautiful birds, diving, turtles, flora and fauna as well as community tourism. This magazine contributes significantly to Trinidad and Tobago's ecotourism drive (Quesnel and Inglefield, 1999).

Despite having a more extensive and diverse offering than the islands in the Caribbean, the mainland countries concentrate primarily on soft-tourism. In Central America, Lake Atitlán (Guatemala) and Poás National Park (Costa Rica) are examples that come to mind. Bentick (1997) reports that in Guyana, there are attempts afoot to harmonise environmental protection with sustainable tourism development as demonstrated by the Kaieteur National Park Development Plan, the Iwokrama International Rainforest Project and National Protected Area System. The Iwokrama International Rainforest Project, integral to the creation of a National Protected Area and comprising of 360,000 hectares of rainforest, was donated to the Commonwealth for research into the sustainable use of the rainforest, the conservation of biological resources and the promotion of ecotourism. Interestingly, the framework has provisions to protect the rights of and involves the community's inhabitants in the decision making and management process. Then there is the Kaieteur National Park which is the only legally protected area in Guyana, home to the majestic 741 foot waterfall of the same name, and central to the development of the tourism master plan. The latter, which outlines the management approach for the Park, would assist in the aims of sustainable tourism development.

In Central America there is The Monarch Butterfly Reserve in Mexico which reflects the country's attempt to protect, promote and conserve the natural richness of the country. The International Biosphere Reserve La Fraternidad (Guatemala/Honduras/El Salvador), and Bosawas/Río Plátano Reserve (Nicaragua/Honduras) through bilateral and multilateral projects symbolise moves by Central American States to protect and preserve their natural resources. These are just a few of the efforts in Central America to sustainably control their natural resource endowment, even though ecotourism is not very significant contributor to tourism revenues.

Mader (1999) states that, ecotourism can be successful only if it can balance environmental conservation with tourism. How that is achieved while minimising damage or failure is a germane issue. The next section addresses the pros and the cons of venturing into this type of tourism and highlights ways in which the various stakeholders can help to make it more sustainable.

## IMPLICATIONS

### Positives

Incentive travel, which caters to the personalisation of travel packages to the interests of the traveller, has been one of the key impacts. Eco-sensitive properties such as Hotel Mocking Bird Hill, which offer tours and programmes on botany and marine biology, are becoming a feature on the Jamaican tourism landscape.

Ecotourism acts as a counter balance as it encourages the preservation of traditional architecture, crafts, dialect and culture. In Central America, for example, Mayan sites and natural areas in Mexico, Guatemala, Belize, El Salvador and Honduras are being promoted by the governments and conservation groups.

Strengthening of community links through the multiplier effect to the community from revenues and collaborative efforts by stakeholders is another of the benefit to be gained from engaging in the eco thrust.

The first country to embrace ecotourism in the mainland Caribbean is Costa Rica. Three factors are responsible for its success, first, it is a relatively stable and prosperous country. Secondly, for its size it is highly bio diverse, it is home to about 1,260 and 1,500 species of trees (Hall 1985; Rovinski 1991), 205 mammals, 849 birds, 160 amphibians, and at least 9,000 vascular plants, representing 4 per cent of the global total (Boza 1988). Thirdly, the various stakeholders instituted a comprehensive system of public and private protected areas and engaged in extensive marketing and promotions of these sites. Perhaps the rest of the Caribbean could learn a lesson from the latter.

### Negatives

Notwithstanding the aforementioned, Costa Rica still has not been able to eliminate some of the negative environmental impacts. There are problems related to water pollution, trail erosion, over crowding and changes in wild life behaviour. The environmental dilemma is one which all promoters of ecotourism face. How well it is handled depends on the preparedness and strategic planning, which went into the framework and the contribution of the stakeholders.

The lack of clarity of the concept makes it difficult to measure the economic benefits accruing from ecotourism. If the owner of privately run eco-tourist resorts cannot see the benefits on the balance sheet, chances are that activities that yield more tangible benefits will be pursued. No owner can be compelled to maintain a resource that is working to the owner's financial detriment. Moreover, companies do not necessarily have a vested commercial interest in sponsoring the safeguards required for a country or region's heritage resources. It was found by Sherman and Dixon (1991) that 'The eco-tourist who visits one natural wonder may be tempted to repeat the experience elsewhere'.

Tourism is a major foreign exchange earner, even though in many cases a large percentage of the monies is repatriated. Leakage of funds from the small island state is an issue that is often faced and minimising this is critical if nations are to prosper. In traditional mass tourism, it was found that the Caribbean (WTO 1999) experienced a leakage rate of 80 per cent. Eco-tourist destinations cannot support such leakage rates as reinvestment of funds is a necessary requirement for the preservation of the site and the surrounding community.

Western (1993) argues that ecotourism is about creating and satisfying a hunger for nature, about exploiting tourism's potential for conservation and development, and about averting its negative impact on ecology, culture and aesthetics. Finding the balance between conservation and tourism is a necessary goal. Failure to do so will only result in negative consequences. For one, the issue of carrying capacity must be considered. Carrying capacity is defined by McDonald and Zieger (1997) as 'the maximal population size of a given species that an area can support without reducing its ability to support the same species in the future'. Unplanned tourist development that proceeds with due consideration of carrying capacity will place unbearable pressure of the environment and its ability to renew. This goes against the grain of ecotourism, but is often overlooked. Air pollution from increased vehicular traffic to formerly inaccessible or remote areas can also be damaging. Uncontrolled visit rates can affect animal behaviour as some creatures do not enjoy being scrutinised. Sea lions on Isla Lobos (Ecuador) seem to become increasingly nervous and aggressive towards tourists. Some 'chase' after tourists who get too close taking pictures (Boo, 1990). Water pollution from the use by a large amount of visitors is also another problem. Dunn River Falls in Jamaica had to close off visits to the falls for a while so that the ecosystem could regenerate. In Dominica pollution of rivers and springs has arisen because of soap use.

There is a real danger that ecotourism may merely replicate the economic, social and physical problems already associated with conventional tourism. The only difference is that often previously undeveloped areas with delicately balanced physical and cultural environments are being brought into the locus of international tourism.

Fennell (1999) notes that the impact of tourism on traditional values is the demonstration effect, where local patterns of consumption change to imitate those of the tourists, even though local people only get to see a side of tourists that is often not representative of their values displayed at home. According to Crouch and Wood (2001) the process of commercialisation and commodification may ultimately erode the local goodwill and authenticity of products and the true culture of an area may devolve into a simplified and glamorised parody of that culture.

The Caribbean is a major transhipment point for drugs entering North America, so the presence of drugs money and direct outcome of money laundering is rife in the Caribbean with Belize being a case in point. Duffy (2000) stressed that the existence of shadow links between the private sector, the public sector and criminal elements makes enforcement of environmental legislation there problematic.

## MINIMISING IMPACT
### The Role of Government

Governments are agents of the populace. Leadership by example and the construction of a framework designed to improve the quality of life of the citizens of a nation are responsibilities that ought be undertaken by any government. Myopic vision on the part of many governments and vestiges from the colonial past have served only to impact negatively on the environment upon which tourism is dependent. Governments can no longer allow their resources to be plundered mercilessly because of the implications for future growth in the industry. The following are ways in which Government can play a part in mitigating against further environmental destruction:

- Collaborating with regional and international agencies concerned with environmental protection in the design of research, training and educational programmes;
- Passing environmental legislation and enforcing compliance;
- Instituting more comprehensive tourism policies that cover issues such as preservation of resources;
- Incorporating environmental education in school syllabuses;
- Fostering a culture of environmentally respectful citizens through the support of entrepreneurial activities that do not destroy the environment. Low interest accessible loans should be provided along with some level of training;
- Improving collections of nationally designated protected areas so that funds can be reinvested to aid in upkeep of the facilities;
- Using social marketing (defined by Andreasen, 1995, as the application of commercial marketing technologies to the analysis, planning, execution and evaluation of programmes designed to influence the voluntary behaviour

of target audiences in order to improve their personal welfare and that of their society) to make going 'eco' more of a philosophy than a marketing ploy is vital.

The above are by no means exhaustive of the measures that governments can take to attenuate environmental damage.

## Role of Non-Governmental Organisations (NGO's)

Often times the link between government and its citizens is weakened due to the numerous responsibilities placed upon its resources and the bureaucratic structure which reduces the pace at which decisions are made. This is where the role of the NGOs become critical. More often than not they can harness a better and closer working relationship with communities. The value of this is that it makes for a more profound and lasting impact when training and educational programmes have to be implemented.

The implementation of a tiering system should be effected so that locals and senior citizens can find it affordable to experience and support eco-sites.

## Role of the Community

Today when one speaks of 'community' in the context of the tourism sector, often reference is made in a narrow sense to a rural 'community' located in an area attracting tourists. However, the term 'community' may mean different things to different people. In the context of ecotourism, 'community' may mean: a group of local people living together in a location attracting eco-tourists or a group of local people living together and sharing common ownership of an eco-tourist attraction, such as the Amerindian peoples in the Guyanese rainforest (Jayawardena 2001).

Rather than blame the cow, citizens need to become more proactive in their approach to forming community groups to, not only explore the natural resources that can be utilised to their economic benefit, but also educate community members and users of the area's resources of the repercussions of environmental abuse, engage in clean ups, re-invest energy to maintain and preserve the natural environment, and penalise members not respectful of the earth.

Communities should also engage visitors in the exchange of 'exposable' elements of their cultural traditions in order to extend knowledge of the local culture. Oftentimes, however, deep rooted 'mystic' cultural elements and customs of indigenous people may not be available for exposure to the eco-tourists. The visitors' understanding and appreciation of such socially sensitive issues are critical for a meaningful and sustainable development of ecotourism in the Caribbean.

## CONCLUSION

Wahab and Pigram (1997) states that the 1992 Earth Summit gave rise to a worldwide increase in awareness of the links between ecologically sustainable development and environmental management. In the world of tourism this has been translated into growing endorsement of sustainability as an essential element in the development and operation of tourist facilities.

The 3S tourism has made the Caribbean world renown, however the time has come to explore other ways of harnessing this blessing while minimising its systemic degradation. Nature based tourism is an option, but it is not without its impact. Therefore, measures to minimise any negative effects upon the natural resources, which are the revenue generating centres for Ecotourism ought to be effected.

No longer can environmental protection be thought of as being mutually exclusive of tourism development. They work in tandem and must be the course to follow in order to continue attracting of tourists to the region. The use of social marketing, increasing the role of NGOs and government and involving community members are, but a few of the ways in which the socioeconomic, sociocultural and environmental costs can be attenuated.

By increasing awareness of not only the local population to be affected but the nation as a whole, thought processes and responses can be altered to see the merit of environmental preservation, hence, leading to actions that result in decreased destruction. The involvement of locals is based on the premise that this would limit the extent of leakage and would also ensure that the needs of locals are taken care of.

The development of ecotourism should not be viewed as a replacement for traditional 3S tourism in the Caribbean, but as a way of diversifying and enhancing the tourism package. For ecotourism to be successful, focus should be on long-term benefits instead of on short-term profits. Vision and not just sight, is needed along with the involvement of the various stakeholders. This strategic approach in planning and development of ecotourism is a prerequisite in ensuring long-term profits and sustainability in the business of tourism. A new model 'SET' reflects this concept and is given as figure 1.

Successful development of ecotourism largely depends on strategic planning. Success can be determined by measuring long-term profits to the investors as ecotourism has to be treated as a business. At the same time, local communities directly, or indirectly, involved must enjoy the benefits from the ecotourism ventures. The business of ecotourism cannot be sustained unless both investors and communities are satisfied with the mutual benefits derived from the business in the long-run. The SET Model suggests that an appropriate part of the profits must be re-invested in the same geographical area. At the same time, enhanced knowledge from the ecotourism experience of the past and the present must be utilised to better conserve and preserve those eco-areas which attract tourists. This, in return, will heighten the overall quality of ecotourism. The SET Model is a cycle and therefore the next step is reviewing the original strategic plan and continuing with the development of ecotourism in a more sustainable fashion.

**Figure 1: Strategic Eco-Tourism (Set) Model**

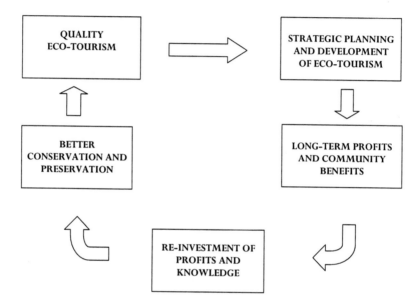

# REFERENCES

Andreason, A. R. 1995. *Marketing Social Change: Changing Behaviour to Promote Health, Social Development and Environment*. San Francisco: Jossey-Bass.

Bentick, K. 1997. 'Sustainable Tourism in Guyana: New Initiatives'. Proceedings of the First Conference on Sustainable Tourism Development, Caribbean Tourism Organisation. Barbados.

Berle, Peter A. A. 1990. 'Two Faces of Ecotourism'. *Audubon* 92, no. 2 (1990): 6.

Boo, E. 1990. *Ecotourism: The Potentials and Pitfalls*. Vol. 2 World Wildlife Fund Publications, 1990).

Boza, M. 1998. *Costa Rica National Parks*. San José: Fundación Neotropica.

Cresser, H. 2002. 'Environmental Management: A New Dimension to Tourism Training'. In *Tourism and Hospitality Education and Training in the Caribbean*, ed. C. Jayawardena. Kingston: UWI Press.

Crouch, G. H. and S. L. Wood 'Ecotourism 101', *Business and Economic Review* 47, no 2 (2001): 19–21.

Duffy, R. 'Shadow players: Ecotourism development, corruption and state politics in Belize', *Third World Quarterly* 21, no. 3 (2000): 549–565.

Fennel, D.A. 1999. *Ecotourism: An Introduction*. London: Routledge.

Golding, S. 2000. *The Potential of Ecotourism in Jamaica*. M.Sc thesis, UWI, Jamaica.

Gould, K. A.,'Tactical Tourism', *Organisation & Environment*, 12:3 (1999) pp. 245 – 262.

Hernandez, G. 2000. 'An Analysis of the Strategies for Ecotourism Development in the Dominican Republic'. M.Sc thesis, UWI, Jamaica.

Hernandez, G., B. 2000. Watson, D. White, and S. Yearwood. 'Ecotourism – Myth or Reality?' M.Sc thesis, UWI, Jamaica.

Holder, J. S. 1987. 'The Pattern and Impact of Tourism on the Environment'. In *Environmentally Sound Tourism Development in the Caribbean*. The University of Calgary Press.

Horwich, R. H., D. Murray, E. Saqui, J. Lyon and D. Godfrey. 1993. 'Ecotourism and Community Development: A View from Belize'. In *Ecotourism: A Guide for Planners and Managers*. Vermont: The Ecotourism Society.

Jayawardena, C. 'Strategic Planning and Management in the Caribbean Tourism: Recent Research by Graduate Students'. *Journal of Education and Development in the Caribbean* 5, no1: 2001.

Jayawardena, C. 2001. 'Tourism vs. Community: Direction, purpose and Challenges of Caribbean Tourism'. Paper presented at the 26th Annual Conference, Caribbean Studies Association, St. Maarten.

Jayawardena, C. 2001. 'Tourism and the Community: Challenges in the Caribbean'. In *People and Tourism: Issues and Attitudes in the Jamaican Hospitality Industry*, eds. H. Dunn and L. Dunn. Jamaica: Arawak Publishers.

Mader, R. 1997. 'Ecotourism Research and promotion on the Web: experiences and Insights', *International Journal of Hospitality Management* 11, no 2 & 3 (2001): 78–79.

McDonald, D. and J. B. Zeiger. 'Ecotourism: Wave of the future', *Parks & Recreation* 32, no. 9 (1997): 84–92.

Quesnel and Inglefield. 1999. 'Trinidad and Tobago: Eco Ad Venture'.

Reingold, L. 1993. 'Identifying the elusive eco-tourist'. In *Going Green*, a supplement to *Tour and Travel News*, (October 1993): 36–37.

Rovinski, Y. 1991. 'Private reserves, parks and ecotourism in Costa Rica'. In *Nature tourism: managing for the environment*, ed. T. Whelan, 39-57. Washington DC: Island Press.

Sherman, P. B. and J. A. Dixon. 1991. 'The economics of nature tourism: determining if it pays', in *Nature Tourism: Managing for the Environment* ed. T. Whelan. Washington DC: Island Press.

Shores, John N. 1999. 'The Challenge of Ecotourism: A Call for Higher Standards'. *www.planeta.com*.

Sirakaya, E., V. Sasidharan, and S. Sonmez. 1999. 'Redefining ecotourism: The need for a supply-side view'. *Journal of Travel Research* 38, no. 2 (1999): 168–172.

Wahab S. and J. J. Pigram. 1997. *Tourism Development and Growth: The Challenge of Sustainability*. New York: Routeledge.

Waldrop Bay, H. 'Greening the Caribbean'. *Successful Meetings* 47, no. 1 (1998): 107–108

Weaver, D. 'Alternative to Mass Tourism in Dominica'. *Annals of Tourism Research* 18, (1991): 414–432.

Western, D. 1993. 'Defining ecotourism'. In *Ecotourism: A Guide for Planners and Managers*, eds. K. Lindberg and D. E. Hawkins. North Bennington, BT: The Ecotourism Society.

White, D. 2000. 'Social Marketing: A Strategy for Ecotourism Development in Jamaica'. MSc thesis, UWI, Jamaica.

*www.ecotourism.org*. Ecotourism Statistical Fact Sheet.

*www.tourismconcern.org.uk*, Tourism Statistics, WTO (1999).

Yearwood, S. 2000. 'The Role of Education and Training in Ecotourism in Belize'. MSc thesis, UWI, Jamaica.

# 3

# THE PROMISES AND PERILS OF ECOTOURISM IN TRINIDAD AND TOBAGO

Dennis R. Gordon

Kelly Warren served as research assistant on this project. Edward Rooks, Kamau Aliki, Gerard Ramswak, Prof. Leslie Gray, and Prof. Janice Edgerly-Rooks have provided important insights on the topic. Financial assistance was provided by The of College of Arts and Sciences and International Programs at Santa Clara University.

## ABSTRACT

*The passage from exclusive dependence on primary product extraction and agriculture to a strategy, which emphasises tourism, is a common story in the Caribbean. The impact of tourism on both humans and the natural setting has led to diverse initiatives to establish global and regional regimes governing sustainable tourism and ecotourism. This chapter explores the ecotourism and sustainable tourism movements in Trinidad and Tobago. An underlying assumption of this study is that tourism policies, like all aspects of the development dialogue, involve political as well as technical issues, and that battles over scarce resources, economic gains, and environmental protection and conservation, are not easily resolved. Based upon an examination of government policies and interviews with local community members, the principal finding of this study is that Trinidad and Tobago, because of its previous history of nature tourism and relative late start in expanding the tourist sector overall, may enjoy advantages not shared by other Caribbean states.*

*The vacation industry is clearly here to stay. But the question which we dare not ignore is whether we, the Caribbean People, are going to have the wit and the will to make it the servant of our needs. If we do not, it will become our master, dispensing pleasure on a curve of diminishing returns while it exacerbates social divisions and widens that legacy of colonialism;*

*the gap between small, comfortable minorities and large majorities barely surviving at the social margin.*

Michael Manley

*Travel into the deep, cool canopy of lush green forest . . . Get in tune with nature, unspoiled and modest in its beauty. Qualified guides ensure that the integrity of the landscape is preserved for future generations.*

Tourism Brochure, Trinidad & Tobago

## INTRODUCTION

The passage from exclusive dependence on primary product extraction and agriculture to a diversified strategy which includes an important role for tourism is a common story in the Caribbean. Indeed, many nations are now heavily reliant on tourism as a fundamental sector of the economy and earner of foreign exchange. Globally, tourism is matched in size only by the oil industry and is said to be the world's single largest employer (Honey 1999). The effects of tourism have been the object of extensive examination by scholars seeking to understand its economic, political, and social impact on a nation. While there are many opinions about the benefits of tourism, it is safe to say that it is seen as a mixed blessing for many nations. Although tourism may earn foreign exchange and create local jobs, it can lead to continued dependence on unreliable and fickle foreign markets, encourage significant imported inputs to satisfy the tastes of international visitors, and bring cultural conflict both between guests and locals and between locals themselves.

In recent years an additional dimension has been added to the traditional sun, surf, and sand destinations as more visitors have come seeking to observe and experience first hand the flora and fauna which the diverse ecology of tropical islands offer. This nature or adventure tourism has emerged more or less simultaneously with a growing awareness of the irreversible changes to the environment produced by human development. While concern about the social and environmental impact of tourism originally came from nature-seeking visitors, along with local and international interest groups, today governments and a variety of regional and global governmental and non-governmental organisations have initiated programmes designed to protect rainforests, beaches, reefs, and indigenous cultures.

The recognition of the impact of tourism on both humans and the natural setting has launched diverse initiatives to establish global and regional regimes governing sustainable tourism and ecotourism. As with other efforts to create international norms and enforcement mechanisms, there are significant disagreements about how to define the problem and choose from competing solutions. This chapter explores tourism, the sustainable tourism movement, and the promotion of ecotourism in Trinidad and Tobago, a relative newcomer to the tourism market in the Caribbean. An underlying assumption of this study is that tourism policies, like all aspects of the development dialogue, involve political as well as technical issues and that battles over scarce resources, economic gain, and environmental protection and conservation, are not easily resolved.

## TOURISM IN TRINIDAD AND TOBAGO

Traditionally, Trinidad and Tobago, like other islands in the Caribbean, based their economy on extractive industries and agricultural products. First sugar, then oil and gas provided the basis for the twin-island republic's economy. With independence, Trinidad and Tobago sought to diversify into import substitution and export-led growth in manufacturing and offshore assembly operations. More recently, like other Caribbean states, Trinidad's governing elite has embraced neo-liberal models of free trade and aggressively sought foreign investment (Pattullo 1996).

Trinidad and Tobago represent somewhat of a special case in that the overall scope of tourism in the economy is comparatively small. At the turn of the century, tourism accounted for less than 4 per cent of Trinidad and Tobago's GDP. In Barbados, on the other hand, tourism provided over 40 per cent of GDP and nearly 60 per cent of export earnings. In Jamaica, more comparable in size to Trinidad and Tobago, tourism contributed over 25 per cent of GDP and 35 per cent of export earnings. In overall numerical terms, the scope of tourism in Trinidad and Tobago can be appreciated by a comparison with tiny St. Martin. St. Martin, in 2000, received approximately 1.5 million visitors whereas Trinidad and Tobago hosted less than 370,000. While the overall size of the tourist sector in Trinidad and Tobago is comparatively small, it grew at a rate of 38.1 per cent during the period 1995 to 1999 according to government figures released in May 2001, a pace which exceeded virtually all of its Caribbean neighbours. Table 1 shows tourist arrivals for Trinidad and Tobago for the period 1987 to 1999.

**Table 1.**
**Trinidad and Tobago Tourist Arrivals - Thousands**

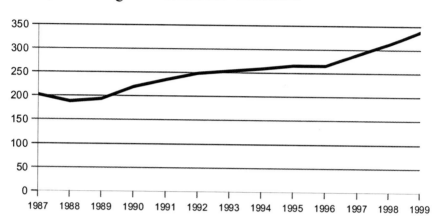

Source: Organisation of American States/Government Figures

Tourism in Trinidad and Tobago differs not only in overall size when compared to its Caribbean neighbours, but also in the purpose of the visit. According to the Organisation of American States, 54 per cent of visitors in 1996 came on a private holiday whereas 14 per cent were on a hotel-based visit. Hotel-based tourism, however, has played a larger role in Tobago, and the traditional small hotels and guest houses have been joined by larger establishments, especially in Crown Point and adjacent areas. Although real occupancy rates in 2001, especially in Tobago, challenge the government's optimism, the government's draft National Tourism Policy, released in May 2001, envisions 10 per cent growth in the tourism sector annually through 2010.

Growth in cruise ship arrivals has proven inconsistent in recent years, dropping from 50,952 visitors in 1996 to 31,880 in 1997. Growth returned in 1998 with 43,188 arriving passengers and 63,251 in 1999. Another area of important growth, especially in Trinidad, has been in hosting yachting events and pleasure boat maintenance. Trinidad's location offers reduced insurance rates during hurricane season and boaters now come for longer stays and for repair and maintenance offered by the growing number of boat yards. Yacht arrivals grew by 366 per cent from 637 arrivals in 1990 to 2,970 in 1999 (TIDCO 2000).

With the completion of the Tourism Master Plan in 1995 and the release of a draft National Tourism Policy in 2001, the government began to examine, in a systematic way, what role tourism might play in the twin island republic:

Given the tourism sector's ability to create employment, establish linkages and generate foreign exchange, the tumultuous fortunes of the petroleum sector have catalysed this effort to diversify the economy, with the development of tourism as a primary strategy. Indeed, the petroleum sector's sharp decline in 1998 (twice in fifteen years) reinforces the need to develop effectively and expeditiously the Tourism Sector.

According to the draft National Tourism Policy, the government's vision and objectives for tourism include:

1. To develop a high quality, internationally competitive and sustainable tourism product
2. To maximise the contribution of the industry to the economy — employment, foreign exchange, investment and sectoral linkages
3. To enhance, protect and preserve the natural and social environment
4. To enhance the national quality of life for the benefit of citizens and visitors.

The goals of sustainability and protection of the natural and social environment stand out as key economic and political issues which result from an increased emphasis on tourism. Indeed, the overall expansion of tourism in Trinidad and Tobago has taken place concurrently with a growing environmental awareness globally, regionally, and nationally. A review of some of the basic principles and issues involved in sustainable and ecotourism will provide a context for the issues which surround Trinidad and Tobago's tourism goals.

## SUSTAINABLE TOURISM AND ECOTOURISM

The movement to define and implement policies aimed at sustainable tourism gained momentum globally throughout the decade of the 1990s. A 1995 survey by the Travel Industry Association of America showed that 83 per cent of tourists supported some form of green or sustainable tourism and that they were willing to pay more for their holiday to promote environmental protection (Honey 1999). The tourism industry and its allies in governments around the world observed the growing public demand for sustainable practices and nature-based holiday experiences. The policy process included a variety of actors ranging from the private sector, inter-governmental organisations (IGO) and non-governmental (NGO) organisations. As with any discussion of development in the Caribbean, a vast array of interests, points of view, and socio-cultural perspectives have been represented. While it is impossible to catalogue all of the major players here, a brief listing of representative forces would include at the inter-governmental organisation level includes The Organisation of American States, the Inter-American Travel Congress, the World Tourism Organisation, The United Nations Environmental Programme, and The United Nations Economic and Social Council.

In the aftermath of the 1992 United Nations Conference on Environment and Development (Rio Earth Summit), The World Tourism Organisation, the World Travel & Tourism Council, and the Earth Council joined to launch 'Agenda 21 for the Travel & Tourism Industry: Towards Environmentally Sustainable Development.' This document was designed to aid the public and private sector in implementing and monitoring sustainable tourism practices for local implementation. At the non-governmental level organisations represent a variety of sectors including firms linked to the tourism industry and conservation groups. A good example of the importance now attached to the environmental and social consequences of tourism is the creation of high profile private sector organisations such as Green Globe. Green Globe was established by the World Travel and Tourism Council in 1994 to promote environmental awareness and to develop a private sector certification process recognising practices consistent with the industry's definition of sustainable tourism (which includes practices 'that make use of our environment without damaging it [and] ways that allow all local people to benefit from tourism without destroying their culture' (Green Globe 2001).

In the Caribbean region, the Caribbean Hotel Association established the Caribbean Action for Sustainable Tourism (CAST). CAST offers a variety of services including technical assistance to local enterprises supporting sustainability and 'overview maintenance of minimum Green Globe Caribbean criteria and award certification.' The list of CAST members includes:

- American Airlines
- Cable & Wireless
- Holiday Inn
- Bacardi
- American Express
- Caribbean Tourism Organisation
- Green Globe
- Texaco Caribbean
- Scotiabank

The private sector organisations advocating that their members adhere to sustainable tourism practices have tried hard to catch the travelling public's eye. Critics contend that Green Globe is concerned primarily with publicity and offering a set of goals rather than strict enforcement of meaningful standards. Questioning the ultimate utility of industry self-regulation, Martha Honey states that accepting, in principle, environmental standards is enough to earn a business Green Globe certification. Lacking an objective and independent verification of compliance, in Honey's opinion, renders Green Globe 'little more than a marketing ploy' (Honey 1999).

Other NGO actors include advocacy groups from many perspectives. NGOs operating globally including the World Wildlife Fund, World Conservation Union, and the Nature Conservancy. These organisations have set standards, established research programmes, and offer tours based on sustainable practices. The activities offered by these groups have been funded by various IGOs and national governments, including the United States Agency for International Development. In the Caribbean, the region-wide list includes the Caribbean Conservation Association and a host of NGO groups. Needless to say, there are many different definitions of sustainability given the array of interests and political perspectives surrounding tourism. For the most part, those active in the pursuit of sustainable tourism share the assumption that mass tourism will remain a path to increased economic activity. In this regard, the sustainable tourism perspective shares much with the general pursuit of sustainable development. As such, its proponents favour growth and development, but with the goal of avoiding 'killing the golden goose' through environmental damage, over crowding, and trampling of local cultural values. In 1988, the World Tourism Organisation stated that sustainable tourism is 'envisaged as leading to management of all resources in such a way that economic, social, and aesthetic needs can be fulfilled while maintaining cultural integrity, essential ecological processes, biological diversity and life support systems' (United Nations Environment Programme 2001).

Virtually all Caribbean governments, either in their rhetoric, through legislation or policy initiatives, have embraced sustainable tourism. There are, of course, many gaps between stated policy and the resources available for enforcement and the infrastructure to cope with water pollution, coastal erosion, poaching, and other harmful practices. It is beyond the scope of this study to examine all aspects of sustainable tourism initiatives in the Caribbean. If sustainable tourism faces obstacles to implementation, what of ecotourism which entails an even more demanding set of standards?

It is important to understand that sustainable tourism, while being embraced by many sectors of society, is not the same as ecotourism either in its practices or in its impact on a nation's overall development strategy. The United Nations Environment Programme, in proclaiming 2002 as the International Year of Ecotourism stated:

A clear distinction should be made between the concepts of ecotourism and sustainable tourism: the term ecotourism itself refers to a segment within the tourism sector, while the sustainability principles should apply to all types of tourism activities, operations, establishments and projects, including conventional and alternative forms.

## Ecotourism

The term *ecotourism* has been widely applied to a variety of activities and enterprises. Until recently little effort has been made to establish a definition. An exhaustive study conducted under the auspices of the Organisation of American States and the University of Idaho found that 'no single definition of ecotourism dominates the Americas. Instead, a range of definitions was identified across the governmental tourism agencies studied and the majority are 'homegrown definitions.' Of the 53 agencies contacted in Latin America and the Caribbean, the study's authors found that 25 provided a written definition of ecotourism and that 21 of the 25 definitions were 'homegrown' (Edwards, et. al. 1998).

Ecotourism involves a much more complex set of standards and activities than popularly conceived notions of nature or adventure tourism. It goes without saying that, lacking clear standards or certification authorities, many tour operators play upon the public's desire to take in the local natural sights. Indeed, promotion of supposed eco-tourist sites has become ubiquitous in public and private promotions of Caribbean tourism. In going beyond sustainable, nature, and adventure tourism, common components of most definitions of ecotourism include:

1. Nature-based tourism in which the main motivation of the tourist is the observation and appreciation of nature as well as the traditional cultures prevailing in natural areas.
2. Tourism which contains educational and interpretation features.
3. Tourism which is usually but not exclusively organised for small groups by small locally owned businesses and/or community groups.
4. Tourism which minimises negative impacts upon the natural and socio-cultural environment.
5. Tourism which supports the protection of natural areas by:

    * generating economic benefits for local host communities, organisations and authorities charged with managing natural areas
    * increasing awareness towards conservation of the natural setting and cultural protection both among locals and visitors.
    * providing employment and income opportunities for local communities distinct from existing pursuits which threaten the environment and reduce the sustainability of tourism and other occupations (United Nations Environmental Programme 2001).

Some organisations and individuals add more overtly political criteria in defining ecotourism. While the WTO states that a positive side effect of tourism will be increased awareness of respect for human rights, others contend that support for human rights and democratic movements is essential to real ecotourism, not a beneficial bi-product. 'Mass tourism', in Martha Honey's view, 'typically pays scant attention to the political system of the host country or struggles within it . . . Eco-tourists therefore need to be sensitive to the host country's political environment and social climate and need to consider the merits of international boycotts called for by those supporting democratic reforms . . .' (Honey 1999).

The inclusion of a specific political criteria to the already significant social and economic requirements of ecotourism increases the potential for disagreements over an already volatile subject. Most governments, including that of Trinidad and Tobago, which have a tradition of generally respecting human rights are not fond of being lectured by visitors from North America or Europe about their internal political relations. Leaving aside the overt conflicts resulting from linking human rights criteria, what general outcomes can be expected from promoting ecotourism based on the characteristics listed above in Trinidad and Tobago?

## SUSTAINABLE AND ECOTOURISM IN TRINIDAD AND TOBAGO

While somewhat of a late-comer overall to tourism, Trinidad and Tobago have long attracted visitors interested in nature. Thanks to the overall beauty of the islands, along with wide diversity of birds, butterflies, and other wildlife, Trinidad and Tobago years ago developed a small nature tourism industry. The rainforests of Trinidad's Northern Range are home to the Asa Wright Nature Centre, a nature-based lodge which, in some people's view, has been hosting eco-tourists long before the term was developed.

The Asa Wright Nature Centre opened its doors to guests in 1967 and since then thousands of visitors have walked its trails, learned about the rainforest environment, sampled local foods grown on the former coco estate, and been hosted by residents of the surrounding community. Over the years, the Centre has received numerous awards and attracted global attention for its approach to nature tourism. Foreign visitors to Asa Wright have increased steadily, growing from 1,571 in 1997 to 2,400 in 1999. The Centre also receives over 8,000 day visitors per year, many of whom are school children. Many observers agree that the Asa Wright Centre's success has encouraged other nature oriented tourism projects in Trinidad and Tobago.

The economic potential of tourism, including nature and ecotourism, has not been lost on the government nor private investors in Trinidad and Tobago. In 1995, the government's Tourism Master Plan was formulated to 'capitalise on tourism's potential for economic growth and diversification.' The plan calls for a number of initiatives including protecting the islands' resource base, linking tourism to the nation's social objectives, improving infrastructure and training, emphasising cultural events, and creating and enhancing natural and cultural attractions in designated tourism development areas.

The Tourism and Industrial Development Corporation (TIDCO), is charged with promoting tourism within a context of the Master Plan as elaborated in the National Tourism Policy document. Cognisant of their position in the highly competitive global tourism market, TIDCO has developed a niche marketing strategy designed to exploit each island's unique attractions. The 'Terrific Trinidad' campaign emphasises culture and events, hosting cruise ships, while 'Tranquil Tobago' concentrates on promotion and development of the dive sector, weddings and honeymoons, and golf holidays. Both islands promote hosting conventions and meetings, game fishing, and what TIDCO labels 'Eco/Soft Adventure' tourism. Promotions focusing on Eco/Soft tourism have included co-operation with the Asa Wright Nature Centre and Pax Guesthouse to attract the global birding community, participation in horticultural shows, and using the media to expand upon the publicity the nation received by being featured in David Attenborough's television series 'The Life of Birds'.

The development of a tourism plan and the inclusion of environmental concerns and ecotourism principles in the nation's development strategy was not, of course, due solely to the foresight of government officials. Along with Asa Wright, a number of other projects have proved successful in recent years. The Matura Turtle Co-operative is an example of a grassroots community effort to protect an endangered species while creating a tourism-based source of employment for locals. Some advocates of ecotourism argue that the Matura Turtle Co-operative, initiated with the support of forward thinking staff at the Wildlife Division of the Ministry of Agriculture, Land, and Marine Resources, represents the best example of community-based tourism project in Trinidad and Tobago. The Pax Guesthouse, which has long served as a retreat and holiday refuge away from the bustle of nearby Port of Spain, is transforming itself into a birding and nature centre. A new private initiative to build a model eco-tourist centre is being undertaken by the Paria Springs Trust in Trinidad's Northern Range while private citizens are turning their homes into bed and breakfast facilities and offering guide services to local attractions. The interaction of locals with the Trinidadian founders of the Paria Springs Trust provides an example of the social and political aspects of tourism, which warrants further study.

Sustainable and ecotourism projects have proceeded against a backdrop of increased politicisation of environmental issues. In recent years there have been significant public organisations to prevent development or outright destruction of natural areas. Examples of popular mobilisation around environmental issues includes the Nariva Swamp, Toco on the North East Coast, and Caroni Swamp to name a few. On Tobago, citizen action has focused on a variety of development projects, including the highly controversial Four Seasons resort. The NGO Environment Tobago pursues a multi-faceted strategy involving public education, technical studies, and direct advocacy.

Local communities are increasingly aware of the promise and peril of tourism and the potential advantages of managed interaction with visitors under the rubric of ecotourism. The Toco Foundation states that tourism can be a very important factor in the development of the North East Coast providing it results from a consultative process which produces self-reliance, productive jobs, family or community-based hotels, and a balance between the local population, natural resources, and the capacity of the environment to tolerate visitors (Eastern Voice 1999).

In order to assess local views of tourism's potential impact on their community a survey of residents of the Northern Range community of Brasso Seco was conducted in March 2001. The results indicate guarded optimism about the benefits of ecotourism. Nineteen of 21 residents contacted agreed that tourism was on the rise in the district. While 17 of the 21 respondents felt that local households were benefiting from hosting visitors, the positive responses were qualified with statements such as 'some, but not all', or only a 'small minority'. Figure 1 depicts popular opinions about the government's ability to provide support services for tourism and Figure 2 shows views of the benefits of having an Asa Wright style centre bordering on the community of Brasso Seco.

The results from Figure 1 are not surprising and may reflect the public's general scepticism about the government's ability to deliver services to a remote mountain community. Respondents' biggest concern was whether the Paria Springs eco-lodge would compete with or complement village lodging, guide, and other services. Many respondents cautioned that while they were optimistic, benefits would only come if the tourism project is 'geared toward the community and have the community at heart.' One resident, fearing that the tourists would change the village's way of life, commented 'when tourists come in they will stop us from doing our hunting that we do for eating and as a lifestyle and that is a bad thing.'

**Figure 1.**
**Community Trust of Government Tourism Promotion**

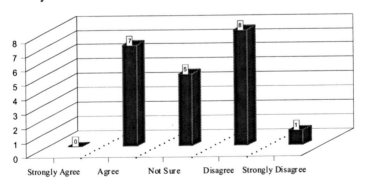

The government and TIDCO are concerned about local people ? March 2001, N=21

**Figure 2.**
**Benefit of Ecotourism**

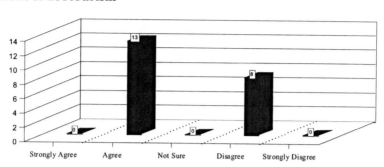

"Community will benefit from Asa Wright-style project," March 2001, N=21

## CONTRIBUTION OF ECOTOURISM

Beyond the local effects of Eco/Soft projects, two key questions remain about ecotourism in Trinidad and Tobago: 1) will ecotourism prove sustainable and afford protection for fragile scenic areas, habitat, and species, and 2) will ecotourism provide a level of economic development consistent with public and government needs and expectations?

Question 1, the sustainability of ecotourism is a matter of technical solutions and political will. While there remains much scientific work to be done to survey and catalogue Trinidad and Tobago's natural endowment, the largest areas of concern—urban encroachment, unauthorised farming and destructive agricultural practices, squatting, water pollution, wetland and reef destruction, poaching, and erosion—are well known and the subject of increased public debate. The infrastructure to provide water treatment facilities for the isolated communities fronting some of Tobago's most beautiful bays, for example, will be very costly and technically difficult. Discharge from private yachts and cruise ships is a growing regulatory problem. While proposed regulations will place controls on cruise ship discharge, the fine of US$5,000 is minuscule compared with other nations. The thousands of people coming to Asa Wright each year, moreover, pose threats as well as income opportunities. The single road leading to the centre must carry thousands of vehicles. Illegal farming, squatting, and a nearby quarry all reflect the conflicting activities and priorities that the government and public hold.

Institutionally, the National Environmental Policy commits the government to conserve biodiversity, use renewable resources in a sustainable manner, conserve non-renewable resources, preserve the ecological systems that maintain clean air and water, educate to change personal attitudes and empower communities to care

*49*

for their own environments. In theory, The Environmental Management Agency (EMA), under the auspices of the 1995 Environmental Management Act, is responsible for implementing the nation's overall environmental policy. Since 1995, the EMA has faced a variety of obstacles, including the lack of effective adjudication and enforcement mechanisms. The government's draft National Tourism Policy mandates a more direct role for the EMA in assessing proposed tourism projects. Under frameworks provided by the Tourism Development Act of 2000, projects within the coastal zone and other ecologically critical areas will be required to submit an Environmental Assessment Impact Report.

Like many other governments, actual oversight of environment related issues in Trinidad and Tobago is conducted by a variety of agencies. The Ministry of Agriculture, Land, and Marine Resources has a formidable portfolio. Its subsidiary agencies, including the Forestry Divisions' Wildlife and National Parks sections, and the Fisheries Division are spread thin and operate under what may be a conflicting mandate of both expanding utilisation and protecting natural resources. Local authorities in Tobago, operating under the Tobago House of Assembly, include the Forestry and Fishing Departments.

The government has attempted to create a funding base to support sustainable tourism through taxes such as the Green Fund Environmental Tax on business. In this regard, it is important to remember that Trinidad and Tobago, for all intents and purposes, lacks a system of national parks and preserves. The application of user fees for major tourist attractions is still only a proposal. Promotion of the active participation of local citizens and stakeholders, based in part on the model developed by the Matura Turtle Co-operative, is being pursued through an Honorary Game Warden System. As with other areas of national life, however, there are significant gaps between environmental policy and enforcement. Staff from the Forestry Division report a dire lack of resources in dealing with poaching, squatting, and other environmental threats. Staff often feel figuratively, if not literally, outgunned by poachers and others illegally using public lands. Citizen groups accuse the government of repeatedly turning a blind eye to violations committed by influential persons. The Caroni Swamp, whose proximity to both Port of Spain and Piarco Airport should make it the centrepiece of Trinidad's Eco/Soft tourism campaign, is seriously threatened. '. . . the problems that beset Caroni Swamp,' according to local guides, 'are a reflection of what is happening throughout Trinidad and Tobago: an ecological and tourism time-bomb born of mismanagement, misguided priorities, over-stretched resources, pollution, poaching, and public ignorance and indifference' (Meredith, 2000).

The Tourism Master Plan, while it has been given more of a specific focus through the draft National Tourism Policy, may well be contradictory in regards to both sustainable and ecotourism. In the case of Tobago, for example, emphasising traditional tourist attractions such as game fishing, the dive sector, and golf while simultaneously trying to protect fragile reefs and bays will require detailed planning and oversight which may be beyond the resources the government or private sector are willing or able to commit. The continued controversy over a large-scale project in Tobago involving a golf course and marina created tension which spread to the highest levels of government. While this controversy was more about longstanding conflicts between the nation's dominant political personalities, it nonetheless raised a variety of issues about local versus national priorities and the environment. Indeed, the ongoing friction between the central government in Port of Spain and the Tobago House of Assembly, which extends far beyond the issue of tourism, is a crucial dimension of ecotourism and the development dialogue in the twin island republic.

The public is increasingly aware of the importance of environmental issues overall and informed about specific controversies. Large-scale illegal rice cultivation in the Nariva Swamp, road construction on the north coast, and a proposed shipping terminal near the village of Toco produced significant public opposition and mobilisation. The forces which challenge environmental protection and sustainable tourism, however, are complex. Along with the trade-offs between short term economic gain and long range protection faced by many nations, local practices in Trinidad and Tobago, such as the domestic and export exotic bird and fish trade, the harvesting of plants for medicinal and ceremonial purposes, hunting, timber felling for furniture and handicrafts, may involve a cultural as well as an economic dimension.

Assuming, for the moment, that the major technical and political impediments to environmental protection are overcome, the question of ecotourism's contribution to the nation's economic goals remain. In nations such as Barbados or Cuba where tourism is seen as a major component of development strategy, projects which meet ecotourism standards are not likely to be major foreign exchange producers. Ecotourism, by its very nature, involves small-scale operations. While this may be partially offset by the high price of ecotourism holidays compared with large scale super resorts, the overall economic benefits of eco-tourist enterprises will not expand dramatically beyond the local community. For nations expecting tourism to provide a significant portion of the gross domestic product, the temptation to offer sham eco-tourist sites therefore will be great.

In Trinidad and Tobago, where the economy does not rise or fall on the tourist dollar, ecotourism sites may carve out a niche which will aid local communities while enhancing the nation's overall international image as a destination for visitors interested in nature. The government, acting through various agencies, has utilised the international reputation of Asa Wright and other destinations to attract visitors. Venerable members of the tourism sector, from Man-of-War Bay Cottages in the north of Tobago to Pax Guesthouse in Trinidad, have moved to adopt sustainable practices. There is significant evidence that ecotourism will create economic opportunities for the local community.

In considering the ability of tourism to stimulate agricultural production in the Caribbean, Janet Henshall Momsen found that while large scale enterprises tended to rely on imported food, ecotourism represented a new form of consumerism 'which demands healthy natural food produced by a sustainable agriculture that does not damage the environment' (Momsen 1998). Trinidad and Tobago's cultural diversity, as reflected in local cuisine, is one of the attractions of Brasso Seco and its other ecotourism centres. Emphasising locally grown and prepared dishes creates opportunities for both local farmers and cooks to develop new sources of income.

As a complement to ecotourism, the draft National Tourism Policy for Trinidad & Tobago offers a sophisticated appreciation of the latest regional and global thinking. The document envisions broad economic spread effects from growing tourism to include 'non-traditional manufacturing based on cultural traditions, marine industry, scientific research, steelpan research and manufacture, clean energy research, festivals management, cultural diversity training and the development . . .' The proposed tourism policy also stresses the importance of the participation of the local population and the need to revive 'dying traditions , art culture, build national pride, expose and record endangered historical facts . . . and build a more environmentally conscious population, who are stakeholders in clean, aesthetically pleasing, healthy surroundings.'

## CONCLUSIONS

As with the overall question of economic development in the Caribbean, the need for sustainability has become the watch word in the tourism sector. A variety of public and private initiatives, standards, and oversight programmes have emerged. In many ways, the pursuit of sustainable tourism faces the same pressures from the contradictions of growth-based and profit-oriented 21st Century neo-liberalism as other economic sectors. Caribbean tourism, especially ecotourism, faces the added pressure of needing to not only sustain output, but to preserve and conserve both the natural setting and the local culture. Given the growing popular interest in nature, adventure, and ecotourism, the temptation to 'make a fast buck' will continue to challenge the various international regimes and local actors seeking to set standards and provide enforcement. The embracing of sustainable tourism by the industry itself is welcomed in some quarters but seen as little more than a marketing gimmick by critics. While the efforts to set and enforce standards will not satisfy strict conservationists or bio-regionalists who believe that humans ought not to interject themselves into every corner of the earth, ecotourism does offer alternative livelihoods which will sustain local communities while reducing gross destruction of the environment.

Trinidad and Tobago, less dependent on tourism overall, may well be able to sustain eco-tourist projects which serve both local and national needs. A strategy which vigorously supports the creation of tourist attractions that meet the definition of ecotourism offered here can solidify Trinidad and Tobago's growing reputation as a nature tourism destination. A well-deserved global reputation for ecotourism, in turn, may provide the marketing base to attract large numbers of visitors to larger facilities and all-inclusive destinations. Applying sustainable tourism principles to the large facilities, while protecting traditional sites such as those in the Northern Range, might build an enduring marketing niche for Trinidad and Tobago consistent with sustainable and ecotourism concepts. In other words, strictly enforced sustainable practices for traditional mass tourist facilities, combined with genuine ecotourism at appropriate sites, might allow Trinidad and Tobago to succeed where others have failed.

There is little doubt that some form of sophisticated environmental protection regime is essential if tourism is going to make the sustained economic contribution envisioned by the government of Trinidad and Tobago. The risks of providing lofty policy statements but inconsistent and under-funded enforcement and planning are clear from the experiences of other nations. Butler's 1980 study 'The Concept of the Tourist Area Cycle of Evolution . . .' described the stages that tourism passes through from discovery to rapid expansion and international recognition, then to a plateau of maturity, and ultimately into decline as visitor tastes change and the once attractive site becomes over saturated and despoiled (Butler 1980). One of the most obvious accelerators to the cycle described by Butler is environmental degradation. Speaking specifically of the Caribbean, McElroy and de Albuquerque observed that 'the high-volume mass-market style tourism currently in practice in the region is nonsustainable; it inevitably damages both the amenity base from which it derives and marginalises domestic agriculture/fishing in this process' (McElroy and de Albuquerque 1992).

Significant questions remain, however, as to the overall commitment of important public and private interests in putting off short-term gains to establish enforceable ecotourism and related environmental protection standards in Trinidad and Tobago. Ultimately, a great deal of confusion remains about ecotourism, its economic potential, and its role in preserving fragile natural resources. This confusion, which stems from the global to the local level, is reflected in the opinions of the people of Brasso Seco, who when asked 'What does the word ecotourism mean to you?' offered the following replies:

- ecotourism is awareness of your surroundings . . . increased appreciation of all you are born and grow with.
- ecotourism is living in a natural setting, protection, conservation . . . keeping the place as it is with tourism as a part . . . the community also being stewards of the environment.
- I don't know

- ecotourism means that tourists will be coming in
- ecotourism is a good thing to put us in business
- enhancing the natural environment and preserving it for tourists to come in
- tourists . . . spending their money and we profit from that
- I don't know
- going into small business
- ecotourism equals success

## REFERENCES

Butler, R.W. 1980. 'The Concept of the Tourist Area Cycle of Evolution: Implications for the Management of Resources'. *Canadian Geographer* no. 24: 5-12.

Crick, M. 1989. 'Representations of International Tourism in The Social Sciences,' *Annual Review of Anthropology* vol. 18.

Eastern Voice. 1999. 'Obtain Sustainable Development through Environmental Protection' 2, no 2.

Edwards, S.N. *et. al.* 1998. *Comparative Study of Ecotourism Policy in the Americas-1998*, 1.1998, (University of Idaho, 1998).

Green Globe. 2001. 'Green Globe21-About Us'. *www.greenglobe21.com.*

Honey, M. 1999. *Ecotourism and Sustainable Development.* Washington: Island Press.

McElroy, J. L. and K. de Albuquerque. 1992. 'An Integrated Sustainable Ecotourism for Small Caribbean Islands'. Indiana Centre on Global Change and World Peace, Occasional Paper no. 8.

Meredith, M. 2000. 'Sorry Tales From the Swamp'. *Sunday Express*, section 2:4.

Momsen, J. Henshall. 1998. 'Caribbean Tourism and Agriculture: New Linkages in the Global Era'. In *Globalization and Neoliberalism: The Caribbean Context*, ed. Thomas Klak. Lanham, Maryland: Rowman & Littlefield.

Pattullo, P. 1996. *Last Resorts*. London: Cassell.

TIDCO. *Corporate Report. www.tidco.co.tt/corporate/report/tourism.*

United Nations Environment Programme. 'International Year of Ecotourism'. *www.world-tourism.org.*

# 4

# THE POTENTIAL FOR COMMUNITY-BASED ECOTOURISM IN GUYANA

Eritha O. Huntley

## ABSTRACT

*This chapter is an exploratory study that seeks to assess the potential for employing a community-based approach to ecotourism development in Guyana. A combination of primary and secondary data were used to inform this study. The author conducted interviews with members of the public sector and the private sector of Guyana, and issued questionnaires to members of the public to ascertain their views on the subject of this chapter. The findings of this research are analysed and discussed. The chapter concludes with recommendations for the private sector and the public sector that would assist in developing a sustainable tourist industry.*

## INTRODUCTION

The purpose of this chapter is to examine and analyse the prospect of adopting a community-based approach to tourism development in Guyana. It does not propose a choice between ecotourism and community tourism. Instead, it proposes a marriage between the two concepts, considering that they both embrace the common objective of ensuring that locals derive maximum benefits from the tourist industry.

Located on the northern tip of the South American continent, Guyana occupies a total land area of approximately 216,000 square kilometres (approximately the size of England). It is bounded on the north by the Atlantic Ocean; on the southwest by Brazil; on the east by Suriname and on the west by Venezuela and is the only English-speaking country on the continent. Guyana is well endowed with natural beauty comprising waterfalls, mountain ranges, a multiplicity of islands, diverse flora and fauna and dense tropical rainforest. These resources greatly increase Guyana's attractiveness as a nature tourism and ecotourism destination.

Guyana was chosen for the study because of its relatively 'new' tourism industry with a focus on ecotourism and nature-based tourism, and because it has a growing indigenous population that stand to be affected, either positively or negatively by tourism development in the hinterland region. A number of other segments of Guyanese society have also demonstrated an interest in becoming involved in the industry. Most of these enterprises are small-scaled, locally owned operations. There have, however, been complaints by local communities (especially Amerindians groups) of their being excluded from making meaningful contributions to these enterprises that have affected them both positively and negatively. This study will, therefore, obtain the following:

- Explore the concept of community tourism.
- Assess Guyana's potential to embrace this approach to tourism development.
- Identify factors that would facilitate or hinder this process.
- Discuss the current level of local participation and involvement in the industry.
- Make recommendations that would assist in the development of community-based tourism in Guyana.

## METHODOLOGY

### Study Area

The size and relative inaccessibility of the interior regions of Guyana resulted in the narrowing of the study area to the areas in and around Georgetown, the Berbice Coast and the Essequibo Coast. With the use of the telephone, however, the researcher made contact with a number of the indigenous peoples who inhabit the areas in the extreme south of the country.

### Data Collection

Primary and secondary data were used to inform this research. A review of relevant literature is presented with the aim of identifying and defining the research topic. The researcher also collected primary data on a trip to the area of study. A questionnaire and formal, structured interview were used to achieve this purpose.

### Selection of Sample

The researcher conducted structured interviews with ten (10) individuals within the tourism sector in Guyana who were thought to hold well-articulated views on the research topic. These persons are hereafter referred to as the 'interviewees'. Open-ended questions allowed them the opportunity to freely express their opinions on the research topic. The list of interviewees comprises the coordinator of the Tourism Studies Unit, University of Guyana, the assistant director of Tourism, the president of the Tourism and Hospitality Association of Guyana (THAG), tour operators, hotel managers and community group leaders.

The researcher felt that if a community-based approach to tourism development was to be adopted it was vitally important to determine the view of community members on the tourism industry. As such, one hundred (100) questionnaires, comprising a number of close ended and open-ended questions, were administered to determine their view of the tourism industry, tourists and the role that they could play within the industry. These were administered based on the premise that the members of the sample chosen were unfamiliar with the research topic specifically, and tourism in general. These persons are hereafter referred as the 'respondents'. There was a 98 per cent response rate.

## TOURISM DEVELOPMENT IN GUYANA

There are no official reports that recount the development of the tourist industry in Guyana. It is recorded however, that prior to the 1970s the sector was thriving. Foreign-owned companies such as Guyana Mining Enterprise Limited (GUYMINE), the bauxite company, as well as the government constructed resorts and guesthouses in Guyana's interior where senior staff members retreated for rest and relaxation in areas such as Lake Mainstay, Rockstone, Dadanawa and Karanambo. The industry, at that time was organised and managed by the Guyana Development Corporation (GDC) which devised policies that led to the construction of the Guyana Pegasus (now Le Meridien Pegasus), the only international hotel in the country, and a number of other hotels and resorts (Benjamin-Trotman 1996).

The post-independence period of the 1970s saw a shift in government's economic policies amidst sweeping changes in the public sector orchestrated by the Burnham administration. Under his leadership, which ended with his death in 1985, Guyana boldly embraced an ideology of 'co-operative socialism' which was characterised by the nationalisation of the country's main industries and the silencing of the private sector; restrictions on trade; the rigid controlling of the Guyana dollar; and the inculcation of anti-tourism and anti-tourist feeling. It was commonly felt that, though the benefits of tourism were desirable, the costs to society were too high — especially in the area of 'cultural imperialism' (Brotherson 1990).

The results of this policy were devastating and led to the deterioration of infrastructure, a decline in social services and a decline in the growth of the tourism industry. According to Brotherson (1990) by 1988 one tour operator declared that the tourist industry 'was dead'. In 1978 the said operator recorded 1,750 bookings for his Overland Tour Company and in 1988 this number had reduced drastically to only 15. In the 1986 budget speech however, national interest in the tourism sector re-emerged with the industry being identified for development (Benjamin-Trotman 1996). This represented a radical shift in government policy. Ecotourism has been the segment of choice for the Guyanese government because of the country's natural beauty.

Today Guyana is a parliamentary democracy on the road to economic recovery. The government openly recognises the benefits that tourism could bring to the economy vis-à-vis foreign revenue that would help in alleviating incidents of persistent poverty, coupled by staggering international debt and fiscal imbalances. As such, the Guyana government has identified six tourist zones for development, namely, Georgetown, Imbamadai, Mabura, Kaieteur, Orinduik and the Rupununi, because of their natural beauty and attractiveness (Ganga 1996). The Ministry of Trade Tourism and Industry (MTTI), Department of Tourism (DOT) have also invested in substantial public relations campaigns geared at influencing the public attitudes towards tourism to secure their commitment and support in order to ensure that the industry develops sustainably.

## COMMUNITY TOURISM
### Defining 'Community'

There are varying definitions for community tourism, it is important however, to understand the concept of *community* before committing to a definition. According to the Oxford Dictionary, a community is *'a body of people living in one place or country and considered as a whole'*. It also goes on further to define community as *'a group with common interest or origin'*. Sproule (1995) states, however, that communities may be complex, comprising separate interest groups and should not be thought of as one homogeneous group. As such, members of the community with disadvantages such as landlessness and insufficient income are usually excluded from participation in developmental enterprises.

### What is Community Tourism?

Community tourism is, therefore, tourism developed by the people, for the people and run by the people (*www.interconnection.org*). It involves various individuals and groups, small business owners and entrepreneurs as well as government officials interested in developing tourism in innovative ways. The community tourism industry is simply a collection of businesses that create and sell a variety of goods and services to visitors (*www.interconnection.org*). It encompasses several sub-sectors such as attractions, car rentals, bars and restaurants and several other support systems which facilitate the primary tourism offerings (Hayle, 2001). The development of this form of tourism is usually in response to the opportunities inherent in the tourism industry, or in response to threats posed by the tourism industry. Environmental degradation, the alienation and marginalisation of local communities and the disruption to indigenous culture have accompanied traditional tourism. Thus, community tourism is an alternative, cooperative approach to tourism development.

Community tourism however, is not synonymous with rural tourism or ecotourism. Ecotourism for instance, is defined as,

> the purposeful travel to natural areas to understand the culture and natural history of the environment, taking care not to alter the integrity of the ecosystem, while producing economic opportunities that make the conservation of natural resources beneficial to local people (*www.greenbuilder.com*).

Rural tourism, on other hand, is defined as,

> tourism which provides diverse opportunities for visitors to experience novel attractions and hospitality services through activities and services which are centred around a real or perceived non-urban way of life: occurring through the travel to a specific non-urban area or attraction, or travel through a non-urban area as part of an itinerary between other destination points (Messerli 1990, quoted by Pigram 1993).

The need for a community-based approach to tourism development arises as traditional communities have often been left out of development decisions (Hayle 2001) and have received few benefits from the tourism industry. They have had little control over the way in which the industry developed, as they are primarily unable to match financial resources with that of external investors (Munt & Mowforth 1998).

## The Benefits of Community Tourism

This alternative approach to tourism development, therefore, addresses the question of 'who benefits' (deKadt 1990). In Guyana, for example, the tourism sector has been identified as one which presents the Amerindians of Guyana the opportunity to build an indigenous industry that would provide benefits for the local communities because of it's labour intensive nature (NDS 1999).

Contrary to popular belief, community tourism is not a very lucrative enterprise. Instead, revenues made from this form of tourism simply supplements that of the host community. It offers an added economic option that assists in sustaining the livelihood of communities. The success of these ventures, lies in the community's ability to be creative and innovative (Pigram 1993).

Tourism development is often defined by the culture within which the industry is developed. The enclave nature in which some all-inclusive resorts developed for instance, may have little or no influence on a community and may reduce community involvement in the industry to the provision of 'low-skilled minimum wage jobs'. Further, because of incidents of crime, violence and poverty some industry operatives attempt to 'protect' tourists from the negative realities of a destination by limiting their contact with local communities (www.interconnection.org). Conversely, in examining community tourism in Jamaica, a destination whose image has been affected because of reported incidents of harassment and crime, McIntyre-Pike (1999) states that community tourism *will* assist in alleviating harassment, social problems, crime and the present perception in communities that tourism is only for the hotels, resort areas and 'the big man'.

Community tourism could, therefore, serve as a catalyst for sustainable tourism development in that it promotes the respect and appreciation for diverse cultures which lends themselves to the overall tourism product (Holder, 1995). In Manyallaluk community in Australia, for example, visitors are attracted primarily by the opportunity to interact with aboriginals to learn of their life and culture (*www.interconnection.org*).

McIntyre-Pike (1999) reiterates this point by stating that 'through visitor/community interaction respective cultures are explored, ideas and information are exchanged and new friends are made.'

## COMMUNITY TOURISM AND SUSTAINABILITY

As an alternative form of tourism, community tourism presents a more 'people-centred' approach to tourism development that necessitates 'a relocation of decision-making and a rearrangement of the locus of power' (deKadt 1990). Such an approach embodies the basic elements of sustainable development, which is defined as 'development that meets the needs of the present without compromising the ability of future generations to meet their own needs' (WCED 1987).

Owen et al (1993, quoted by Eagles, 1995) has identified several key principles of sustainable tourism development. These include:

- Tourism should be part of a balanced economy.
- The use of the environment should allow for the long-term preservation and for the use of the environment.
- Tourism should respect the character of an area.
- Tourism must provide long-term economic benefits.
- Tourism should be sensitive to the needs of the host population.

As such, community tourism must be socially sustainable (*www.interconnection.org*) to ensure that the 'needs' of the local populace are met and this can only be achieved if there is local inclusion in tourism schemes (Munt & Mowforth 1998). In examining the challenges to ecotourism development in Dominica, Poon (1997) describes local involvement as 'the primary function of sustainable tourism development'. This point was reiterated by McIntyre-Pike (1999) who stated that 'sustainable tourism cannot be successful without the participation of communities in the development and management'. The concept of sustainability also gives consideration to posterity, a move which deKadt, (1990) describes as 'intergenerational justice'.

## PARTICIPATION AND DECISION-MAKING

Inclusion of local communities in the decision-making process is crucial for the sustainable development of the tourism sector but local populations are often left out of planning, decision-making and operations of tourism schemes (Munt and Mowforth 1998). This point is reiterated by McCool, (1995) who intimated that decisions, once made, are often irreversible and may change the 'character' of communities so that they may eventually lose features that were attractive and distinctive to non-residents.

The call for 'local involvement' and 'community-based participation' are becoming popular rhetoric but the only patterns of local participation that are likely to break existing patterns of power and unequal development are those that originate from within local communities themselves (Munt & Mowforth, 1998). Citing research work such as Doxey's Tourist Host Index and Butler's Tourist Area Lifecycle model, Simmons (1994) states that there are usually high levels of community involvement and acceptance of tourism in the initial stages, but then residents begin to appraise and take action on the negative changes brought by tourism development.

The inclusion of local communities in decision-making and planning may not always be practical because of a potentially poor knowledge of tourism and how it evolves in local destination areas, but with considerable promotional input and facilitative efforts locals can be convinced that their input is necessary (Simmons, 1996). As such, the level of partnership may vary depending on the community. Hayle (2001) states that participation could be 'full or limited'. Petty (1995, quoted by Munt & Mowforth, 1998) presents an interesting typology of participation which ranges from 'manipulative' in which virtually all power and control over the development lie with people or groups from outside of the community, to 'self-mobilisation' in which development is by local initiative, with power and authority resting with the local community. The typology is given as table 1.

# Table 1:
# Typology of Community Participation

| Typology | Characteristics of each type |
|---|---|
| Manipulative participation | Participation is simply a pretence: 'peoples'' representative on official board, but they are un-elected and have no power. |
| Passive participation | People participate by being told what has been decided or has happened already: involves unilateral announcements by project management without any listening to people'' responses; information shared belong to external group. |
| Participation by consultation | People participate by being consulted or by answering questions: external agents define problems and information gathering processes, and so control analysis; process does not concede any share of decision-making. |
| Participation for material incentives | People participate by contributing resources (e.g. labour) in return for food, cash and other material incentive; this is commonly called participation, yet the people have no stake in prolonging technologies or practices when the incentives end. |
| Functional participation | Participation is seen by external agencies as a means to achieve project goals, especially reduced costs: people may participate by forming groups to meet project objectives; involvement may be interactive and may involve sharing decision-making, but tends to arise only after major decisions have been made by external agents. |
| Interactive participation | People participate in joint analysis, development of action plans and strengthening of local institutions: participation is seen as a right, not just the means to achieve project goals. As groups take control of local decision-making and determine how available resources are to be used, so they have a stake in maintaining structures and practices. |
| Self-mobilisation | People participate by taking initiatives independently of external institutions to change systems: they develop contacts with external institutions for resources and technical advice they need, but retain control over resource use; self-mobilisation can spread if government and NGOs provide an enabling framework of support. Self-mobilisation may or may not challenge existing distributions of wealth and power. |

Source: Petty, 1995, quoted in Munt and Mowforth, 1998

# ANALYSIS OF FINDINGS
## Potential And Possibilities

All (100 per cent) of the persons interviewed for this research expressed a basic understanding of the concept of community tourism with all of them stating that Guyana possessed great potential for venturing into tourism, especially community tourism. They further stated that the key features that would enhance this potential include both the culture of the people and the natural beauty of the country.

From the questionnaires distributed, 94 per cent of the respondents stated that they were aware of the fact that Guyana was developing its tourism industry. Contrary to responses obtained from personal interviews with members of the public and private sector, only 68 per cent respondents felt that the country had the resources necessary to engage in tourism development as shown in figure 1. Additionally, when asked to rate the responses of the Guyanese people to tourists, 47 per cent stated that Guyanese were 'friendly' while 37 per cent recorded that they were 'very friendly' as against 15 per cent who stated that Guyanese were 'tolerant' of tourists. The question and answers are given as figure 1.

## Figure 1:

## Do you think that at its current stage of development Guyana has the necessary resources to engage in tourism development?

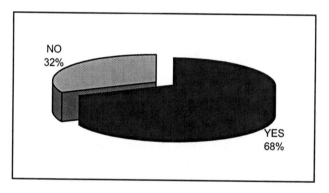

One hundred percent (100 per cent) of the persons interviewed stated, however, that the potential for community tourism lies in the hinterland region and remote communities. Thirty per cent of the interviewees also identified the coastal region as having this potential. The culture of the indigenous peoples, inclusive of arts and craft and music that have been retained despite contact with western society, were identified as contributing to this potential. Further, the Chairman of the Lethem Tourism Committee, in the extreme south of Guyana, revealed that efforts were currently underway 'to preserve these cultures while keeping up with development'. An interviewee from a locally based tour company remarked, however, that though the potential was there for developing community tourism, this should be a controlled process that prevented the influx of tourists into communities since this could have serious consequences, particularly for Amerindian communities.

The former president of THAG and owner of Roraima Airways felt that while the potential for adopting a community-based approach to tourism development existed, an economic impact study should be carried out to clearly identify the benefits that could be had from this form of tourism development. The president of the Linden Tourism Committee agreed and also stated that, based on his experience, a reward system is important to encourage locals to become involved in the industry because of the prevailing economic situation in his town.

Moreover, another respondent from the Iwokrama Centre for Rainforest Conservation and Development called for the development of a strategy geared at identifying and developing products both in the hinterland and on the coast of Guyana, with potential for community-based tourism development.

The coordinator of the Caribbean and Tourism Studies Unit, University of Guyana cautioned that since community-based tourism would only be applicable to select communities, its usefulness as a model for tourism development is limited to individual, specific communities. He stated, however, that community-based tourism initiatives would be enhanced if there were greater 'policy impetus from the Tourism Directorate, higher levels of community awareness and a greater awareness at the national level of the meaning of tourism, its benefits and the roles of communities in its development'.

## Hindrances To Community-Based Tourism
### The need for tourism education and awareness

The interviewees unanimously agreed that the lack of tourism education and awareness at the national, regional and community levels was the main hindrance to the adoption of a community-based approach to tourism development. In a public opinion survey undertaken this point was underscored since, when asked to identify who a tourist was, only fifty-nine per cent (59 per cent) of the respondents chose the correct response. A surprising thirty-eight per cent (38 per cent) did not perceive Guyanese travelling within the country as tourists. Instead, they identified a tourist as a traveller from any country outside of Guyana.

An official of the Amerindian Affairs Ministry therefore, noted that because tourism was 'a new thing' in Guyana education will be necessary before venturing into the industry, especially where the Amerindian people are concerned. Such an approach the respondent felt, would move them from being 'the affected to being the involved', and would assist in guarding against the negative effects of (spontaneous) tourism development. Moreover, the findings revealed that in many of the hinterland communities there were few secondary schools, with education going up to the primary level, in some instances. In Lethem, for example, secondary education is available, but there is a shortage of teachers.

One resort owner noted that there is the need for locals to 'orient their outlook' in terms of the tourist industry through tourism education. In supporting this view, The former president of THAG stated that THAG, along with the Department of Tourism, was in the process of getting tourism education into the schools' curricula. Similarly, the chairman of the Lethem Tourism Committee added that education should not just be directed to the people in the local communities, but to all Guyanese, and also to tourists desirous of visiting these communities. She further stressed the importance of learning to respect the culture of the local people.

## Lack of government support

The former president of THAG stated that even though local entrepreneurs had the motivation and desire to venture into the industry, the Guyana government needed to be more proactive in its approach to tourism development to make this successful. Similar sentiments were also expressed by 50 per cent of the persons interviewed. One tour operator disclosed that the government was adopting a 'top down' (bureaucratic) approach to the development of the industry. Such an approach it was said, served to frustrate the local entrepreneurs that are currently involved in tourism.

## The need for supporting policies

There are currently no approved policies to guide the tourism sector in Guyana. One of the interviewees stated, however, that the draft alludes to the development of policies geared to encourage community involvement and participation in the sector. He further expressed the view that there was 'limited enunciation and articulation of policy guidelines regarding community-based tourism'. Sixty per cent of the persons interviewed reiterated this point, 20 per cent of whom stated that there is 'a lot of talk' in terms of community participation, but that there was 'little walk' in this regard.

## Involvement and Participation

One hundred per cent of the participants interviewed stated that local involvement and participation in the tourism sector was minimal. They also felt people were interested in getting involved in tourism but the necessary skills had to be taught and further developed. Respondents to the questionnaire confirmed this point. Twenty-two per cent of these respondents were involved, directly or indirectly, in the tourism sector. Of the 78 per cent who stated that they were not involved in the industry, 70 per cent expressed a desire to do so. A number of reasons were given for this decision. Table 2 presents the most popular reasons given.

## Table 2:
## Why would you want to be involved in the tourism industry?

| Positive | Negative |
|---|---|
| ❑ To assist in the improvement and development of Guyana. | ❑ Respondents had no interest in the tourism industry. |
| ❑ To learn more about the country. | ❑ Respondents gainfully employed in another sector of the economy. |
| ❑ To secure employment | |
| ❑ To meet people from different countries. | |
| ❑ Respondents felt that all Guyanese should be given a chance to become involved in tourism. | |
| To assist in the conservation and preservation of the environment. | |

Another interviewee from the Iwokrama Centre for Rainforest Conservation and Development and former vice president of THAG, shared that the current level of participation and involvement is limited to a number of local businesspersons involved in the sector. As such, there were no civic groups that focussed on tourism development in any meaningful way other than THAG.

Further, an official from the Amerindian Affairs Ministry stated that though the Amerindian inhabited the prime ecotourism areas, these communities were usually 'informed' about developmental activities in their region. He stated, however, that if the government was serious about employing a collaborative, consultative and participatory approach to tourism development, Amerindians should not just be informed, but should be involved in decision-making and the formulation of regulation. The view was also shared that a dictatorial approach was currently being taken to tourism development. Another interviewee, therefore, stated that the only way community tourism would be successful was if the initiative came from within the community. 'They [the local communities] have to want community tourism for it to be successful'.

The former president of THAG also stated that his company was integrally involved with the communities with which they interface. Santa Mission, an Amerindian community located on the Pokerero River, was said to be in partnership with his company. As a result, the school in the village has been 'adopted' and there are plans underway to construct a library for the students. The people of the community also benefit from this relationship.

Conversely, the official from the Amerindian Affairs Ministry revealed that the relationship that existed between tour operators and the local communities were not very good. Instead, he called for the creation of (meaningful) partnerships between members of the private sector, the government and these communities so that the Amerindian people could be given a chance to participate. In the Rupununi region, for example, 30 per cent of the interviewees shared that, because of incidents of high unemployment, community tourism would be welcomed. One of these respondents cautioned, however, that though the potential for this form of tourism existed in the region, the prospect would be challenging for the community and would require education and training for the people in the area.

## *Facilitative Measures*

As such, a number of areas were identified that needed to be dealt with before adopting a community-based approach to tourism development. These areas are given as table 3.

## Table 3:
## Measures that could be taken to facilitate the process of community tourism development

1. Generic promotion, advertising and marketing to make the international tourist market aware of Guyana as a destination.
2. Identification and communication of an appropriate image to the market, dispelling misconceptions held about Guyana.
3. The introduction of safety standards and regulations. Two tour operators who felt this would assist in protecting the image of the destination called for stricter safety standards.
4. Making flight to the hinterland more affordable for locals as well as international tourists since the rates currently charged were too high.
5. Information should be provided for domestic and international tourists before they visit destinations.
6. The development of infrastructure and the accommodation sector to facilitate the flow of visitors.
7. The need for greater collaboration between the public sector and the private sector.

It was agreed unanimously, however, that the local people should be allowed the opportunity to become involved in the planning and development of tourism enterprises. One interviewee further added that guidance should be given to young entrepreneurs to guarantee the sustainability of community tourism ventures. The need for the empowering the people to take actions for development was also identified by interviewees.

## DISCUSSION OF FINDINGS

Based on the findings of this research, Guyana, unarguably, has the potential to encourage community tourism. According to the persons interviewed this potential is attributed to the natural beauty of the country and the culture that exists there. The identified potential needs to be coupled with the knowledge, vision and resources (financial and human) to make community tourism a sustainable option (*www.greenbuilder.com*). Additionally, the Tourism Directorate and industry operatives need a clearer understanding of the concept of community tourism. With this understanding should come the knowledge that community tourism is not confined to any one community or region. Instead, it comprises a series of activities and interactions, which make up an experience (Hayle, 2001) that could occur in any part of Guyana.

Community tourism, therefore, is far more complex than simply allowing tour operators and tourists into a remote community to view an attraction or experience the culture of a community as with rural tourism or ecotourism. It entails meaningful interactions between locals and tourists, both domestic and international. As such, while much was said of the benefits that could be received from adopting a community-based approach to tourism development there are also a number of risks that accompany such ventures. The call for the sensitising of visitors about community norms and customs is, therefore, a critical point to be considered in this process since community tourism has as one of its main components interaction between locals and tourists. Although the tourism industry has not had any significant impact on the society and culture in Guyana, the potential for negative impact to occur exists, especially in remote communities that were identified as primary candidates for community tourism development.

Since most of the communities in the interior of Guyana are faced with severe economic problems, encouraging tourists to visit and share in community life while contributing to the economic and socio-cultural development of these areas is a very viable prospect. It would, however, necessitate the creation of appropriate machinery that would ensure that the communities benefit not only today, but have sustained benefits economically, socially and culturally. This would include technical and financial assistance from the government and local NGOs should be able to provide training, technical expertise and funds necessary for infrastructural development in these areas in order to ensure that visitors' experiences are enhanced and rewarding.

Additionally, consideration should be given to the dynamics within a community to guard against situations in which only one faction of the community derives maximum benefits from the industry. The ability to communicate with each other, build satisfactory relationships and operate effectively and efficiently as a group are key elements in administering community-based businesses (*www.greenbuilder.com*). Community members therefore, have to be competent enough for any venture to succeed.

The findings have also revealed that the lack of tourism education and awareness was a major hindrance to embracing this form of tourism. Again, this area needs to be addressed if steps are to be taken to successfully develop community-based tourism enterprises. The pending plan to introduce tourism education into the curricula at schools while commendable, may only realise its objectives in a number of years. Additionally, in many communities that were identified as having 'potential' to develop community tourism the findings revealed that there was a dearth of facilities offering higher education, as well as teachers to assist in the education process. It is, therefore, doubtful that these communities will effectively benefit from this programme when implemented.

As such, a more active approach needs to be taken to correct the persistent problems of ignorance in the area of tourism. Alleviating this problem will necessitate close collaboration between the tourism ministry, THAG, local NGOs and community groups that are interested in venturing into the industry. This would, in effect, prevent insouciant tourism development by communities that are ill prepared and ill equipped to do so. Such occurrences may possibly result in poor visitor experiences that could effectively damage the image of the destination.

Further, because there is an expressed desire by the interviewees as well as the respondents to the questionnaires to become more actively involved in the tourist industry, the Guyana government has a very important role to play in addressing the hindrances identified in the findings. The onus for solutions to these problems should not, however, be left totally to the government. Instead, through a process of collaboration and consultation with local community and the private sector, solutions to these problems may be realised. This should result in the tourist ministry adopting the role of policy-maker and legislator, while creating supporting policies and legislation to encourage private sector involvement and participation in tourism.

One commentator on the state of tourism in Guyana expressed feelings commensurate with those of the interviewees when he stated that 'the MTTI appears to exist principally to bureaucratise an industry best left in the hands of the private sector' (*Guyana Review*, 1998). The establishment of the long awaited Guyana Tourism Authority which is vested with responsibility for the creation of a marketing strategy to advertise and promote the country generically; promoting an image of the country that is commensurate with the experiences that can be had in Guyana, is welcomed.

During an address made to the delegates at the Caribbean Tourism Organisation Conference on Sustainable Tourism Development in Georgetown, Guyana, Mr. Bharrat Jagdeo, president of Guyana, reported that G$20 million had been put aside for the formation of the Tourism Authority (*Stabroek News*, 24/5/00). The Tourism Authority will, hopefully, assist in the process of decentralising decision-making since it comprises representatives from both the public and private sector.

Moreover, there exists a draft policy document that gives attention to the issue of local involvement and participation in the industry. The broad objective identified was 'to encourage and facilitate the involvement and participation of local communities at all levels of tourism development'. So far, no efforts have been made to realise the above-mentioned policy objectives. It is hoped, however, that the necessary energy will be expended to bring about a realisation of these policies which could effectively enhance the chances of local communities becoming more involved in the industry.

The most rewarding forms of tourism are those that involve both residents and tourists. Community tourism ventures should, therefore, be rewarding both in terms of the visitor and resident experiences and the economic viability of the community tourism businesses. The need for greater levels of facilitatory input by policy makers should also be stressed since community interest and tourism must work together for any chance of long-term success.

## RECOMMENDATIONS

It is very crucial that the local people are given a chance to become fully involved in this industry if any consideration is to be given to community tourism. This, however, will not happen without a number of changes in the policies and practices that currently exist within the sector. As such, there is the need for a holistic approach to tourism development with all key stakeholders involved in and benefiting from the process. Responsibility for such action lies not just at the national level, but also at the regional and community levels. The following are, therefore, some recommendations:

### National and Regional Levels

- The Tourism Directorate needs to examine their existing objectives to determine if the current objectives could serve the purpose of promoting greater levels of involvement and participation by the local citizenry. Policy objectives should reflect the desire of a large segment of the population to become directly or indirectly involved in the sector,
- Existing policies should be revisited, reviewed and revised in collaboration with local communities, particularly indigenous groups, to ensure that they

become meaningful participants in the process of tourism growth and development. Additionally, these should be designed to:

- Recognise and strengthen local cultures.
- Encourage the development of national pride by cultivating the 'Guyaneseness' of the destination.
- Strengthen efforts that are being made to preserve socio-cultural values and beliefs.

- The tourism ministry should also take more active steps for public education on tourism issues. Education is one of the prerequisites for the development of community tourism, especially if this segment is to be developed sustainably. This requirement should therefore, be fulfilled with collaboration with local community groups, the Ministry of Education, the University of Guyana and vocational schools. A possible approach that could be taken to remedy this problem is to identify individuals from within communities, who wish to venture into community tourism, for extensive tourism education and training. They should then be vested with the responsibility to share the knowledge acquired with the other members of their community. Workshops, seminars and community meetings could also serve as excellent fora at which local communities could be educated in tourism issues.

- A public awareness and sensitisation programme is also necessary to correct some of the opinions that exist in terms of the tourism sector. This programme, which should serve as a complement to the tourism education programme, should also have as its main aim the reformation of positive public attitudes towards tourists and the industry. The campaign against bad manners is a start in the right direction.

## Community Level

There is a desire at the community level to become more meaningfully involved in the sector. As such, a strategic approach to the development of community tourism is proposed. These recommendations speak to the establishment of a framework within which community tourism could be integrated into community life. The following is suggested:

- Identify the goals and objectives of the community. These should state what it is that the community is hoping to accomplish from the tourism venture, how they intend to accomplish this, and what factors are necessary to attain these objectives. All members of the community should have a stake in this phase of the planning process.
- Forming groups with identified members of the community who understand what community tourism entails and have the vision to make such an approach

to tourism development work. The committee should be democratically appointed with the full support of the local community and vested with the responsibility to plan the activities of the community in accordance with pre-established objectives.

- An analysis of the community's strengths and weaknesses should then be done to determine if the community has the resources necessary to encourage community tourism and the level to which the community will be involved in the venture. A number of serious questions will need to be addressed such as; what does the community have to offer? Does it have the resources necessary to successfully undertake the venture without external assistance? How do the members of the community feel about the prospect of venturing into community tourism? Is their support guaranteed in the long run? How will they benefit from this venture? What role will they play in the process? The community will also need to establish clear limits to the amount of visitors they will allow, the periods at which they will be welcomed into the community and the extent of the interaction. The community will also need to identify possible competitors with whom they could form alliances or benchmark successful practices that may be identifiable, along with possible opportunities and threats that could impede the success of community-based tourism ventures.
- A strategic plan should then be devised and designed that captures the goals and objectives of the community. It should be flexible yet comprehensive, including the following:
  - Clearly established policy of conduct to which community members should adhere. This should be defined and determined by the members of the community.
  - How the venture will be financed, by community members, with assistance from the government or local NGOs or with assistance from local tour operators.
  - Identifying target markets for their offerings.
  - The possibility of forming partnerships with local NGOs, the government or other communities for technical support.
  - Contingency plans in anticipation of changes in the internal and external environment.
- A time frame will have to be established stating the period within which the community-based venture is to be successfully implemented.
- Allowances will also have to be made for adjustments in the plan that may result from feedback from community members.

# CONCLUSION

The concept of community tourism, though subject to varying interpretations has at its core the involvement of local communities in the process of tourism development in a manner in which they could contribute meaningfully to the development of the sector and also to national development. It is a 'bottom up' approach to the management and organising of tourism, with local communities having the opportunity to gain a greater measure of control over the manner in which the industry develops and in so doing, minimising the impact it may have on their society. As such, this form of tourism finds applicability in Guyana where existing patterns of tourism development are often criticised for being dictated by the government or by external forces.

Adopting a community-based approach would challenge the current system within which the industry is managed, resulting in a paradigm shift and a change in the current mode of operation. The success of such a venture could, however, be hampered by a number of hindrances that should be overcome with cooperation from the private sector, the public sector and local communities. To accomplish this, a holistic approach to tourism development that is compatible with the aims of sustainable development is needed, especially if sustainable tourism development is to be obtained.

Further, the benefits inherent in community tourism offer great opportunities for national development since it promotes involvement by all in meaningful enterprises that would generate income and foreign exchange, create a greater awareness of their society and culture, while encouraging meaningful interactions between host communities and visitors.

# REFERENCES

Benjamin-Trotman, L. 1996. 'Seminar on Comprehensive Tourism II in Fiscal Year 1996, Country Paper'. Guyana: Ministry of Trade Tourism and Industry.

Brotherson, F. 1990. 'The Politics of Tourism in a Caribbean Authoritarian State: Cooperative Republic of Guyana'. *Caribbean Affairs* vol. 3 (second quarter), no. 2: 38-55.

de Kadt, E. 1990. *Making the Alternative Sustainable: A Lesson From Development For Tourism*. Institute of Development Studies, Discussion Paper, No. 272. Brighton.

Eagles, P. F. 1995. 'Understanding the Market for Sustainable Tourism'.

Ganga, G. 1994. *Ecotourism In Guyana: Implications for Sustainable Development,* (Institute of Development Studies, University of Guyana, Working Paper No. 12, 1994).

Guyana Review, November, 1998.

Hayle, C. 2001. 'Community Tourism'. In *Tourism in the Caribbean* eds. J. Maerk and I. Boxill. Plaza Y Valdes, S.A. de C.V., 2000.

Holder, J. 'Regional Solutions to Caribbean Sustainability Problems'. Presented at the Caribbean Conference on Sustainable Tourism, Punta Cana Beach Resort, Dominican Republic, November 29 - December 2, 1995.

McCool, S. 1995. 'Linking Tourism, the Environment, and the Concept of Sustainability: Setting the Stage'. *www.ecotourism.org.*

McIntyre-Pike, D. 1999. 'CountryStyle CommunityTourism'. *Jamaica Profile.* Tourism Product Development Company.

Munt, I. and M. Mowforth. 1998. *Tourism And Sustainability: New Tourism in the Third World.* Routledge, London & NewYork.

NDS. 1999. National Development Strategy For Guyana - Shared Development Through Participatory Economy. Chapter 37 - Tourism Policies.

Oxford Dictionary and Thesaurus. United Kingdon: Oxford University Press.

Pigram, John. 1993. *Tourism Research: Critiques And Challenges.* D. Pearce and R. Butler, (eds.), (University Gronnga of the Netherlands, Routledge, 1993).

Poon, A. 1997. 'Addressing the Challenges — Towards a European Union Program of Support to the Dominica Ecotourism Sector'. Proceedings of the First Annual Sustainable Tourism Development Conference, Dominica.

Simmons, D. G. 1994. 'Community Participation in Tourism Planning', *Tourism Management* 15, no.2: 98-107.

Sinclair, D., *et al* 1999. Tourism Policy. Division of Caribbean and Tourism Studies, University of Guyana.

Sproule, K.W. 1995. 'Community-Based Ecotourism Development: Identifying Partners In The Process'. Wildlife Preservation Trust International.

Stabroek News Editorial. 2000. 'Promoting Tourism'. May 23rd.

WCED. 1987. *Our Common Future.* United Nations World Commission on Environment and Development.

www.campfire-zimbabwe.org.

www.greenbuilder.com.

www.interconnection.org.

www.kiskeya-alternative.org.

www.planeta.com.

# 5

# NATURAL AND CULTURAL HISTORY TOURISM AT IWOKRAMA: THE ROLE OF FIELD TRAINING

Macsood Hoosein and Graham Watkins

## ABSTRACT

*The Iwokrama International Centre for Rain Forest Conservation and Development is an integrated enterprise involving research, training, education, outreach, ecotourism, and other sustainable business ventures. The Centre offers technician-level training for rangers and environmental interpreters, a guide training course, and international short courses. The Centre's hands-on training approach in a naturally and culturally rich environment has played a central role in defining the high quality of rangers and guides graduating from Iwokrama, and its concomitant ecotourism and scientific tourism products. The Iwokrama example indicates that good field training can play a major role in improving interpretation and ecotourism services in the Caribbean. World-class training in this area is good for the region, but is severely challenged by a scarcity of resource persons, declining interest from the private and public sectors, and what it perceived as the high cost of offering a programme of such standard.*

## INTRODUCTION

The Caribbean region is remarkably rich in cultural history for an area of its population and geographic size. It has a rich history linked to the arrival and establishment of Africans, Amerindians, Chinese, East Indians, Europeans, Javanese, Portuguese, and other peoples in various territories. Linked to the diversity introduced by the arrival of these groups is a richly diverse political history of colonial governance, involving imperial powers such as the Dutch, English, French, and Spanish. The composition of the region is significantly diverse as a result, with significant diversity in the ethnic, linguistic, culinary, and architectural tapestry, to list but a few areas.

The Caribbean region also has a significantly rich natural history. It accounts for an extensive marine seascape consisting of a variety of ecosystems and species, islands of both sedimentary and volcanic origins, island and continental terrestrial ecosystems, and a significant part of the Guiana Shield, one of the world's oldest geological formations. The region therefore accounts for a high level of biological and physical diversity covering marine, freshwater, and terrestrial habitats, together with significant biological endemism.

With settlement of its diverse populations in these habitats for more than a decade, close associations have developed between the cultural and natural diversity. It is true, in fact, that there is a reinforcing relationship between the cultural and natural diversity of the region.

Over the past few decades, the natural resources of the region have come up against very significant challenges and threats. As the twenty-first century advances these challenges continue to bear on the region. The changes in both natural and cultural resources, and the consequent challenges for sustainable development of the region are too complex to be comprehensively listed here. However, key among the changes in the area of cultural history are population increase, threats of cultural assimilation and decline, high emigration, and a growing recognition of the importance of cultural diversity to areas of economic activity such as tourism, and to sustainable development as a whole. In the natural history dimension, increasing demands on natural resources due to population and industrial expansion, ecological changes occurring in natural habitats, and the recognition that effective natural resource management requires the support of well trained personnel and an educated populace, are some of the changes. The opportunity is present, nevertheless, for the region to promote the conservation of its ever-threatened natural (and cultural) assets and for capturing more of their economic potential by positioning itself to benefit from the development internationally of a new tourism ethos called 'ecotourism' (see Ganga, 1996 and Poon and Poon, 1994 on the economic opportunity presented by ecotourism).

## Education and Training for Resource Management

The important role of training and education in natural resource management and sustainable development has been well documented. For example, the United Nations Convention on Biological Diversity acknowledges not only the relationship between cultural and natural diversity, but calls for research, training, education and awareness in these areas of living diversity (UNEP/CBD 1994).

Glowka et al (1994) point to a shortage of trained personnel that 'is decidedly greater in developing countries' than in developed nations. This shortage of trained personnel constrains development. While it is recognized that effective natural resource management requires good management and well trained field personnel, in Central America and the Caribbean, educational opportunities for young people that would help them become more able to solve pressing conservation problems are largely nonexistent (Acosta, 2000).

Training for resource management in developing nations has been concentrated on more formal, academic education and there is greater need for trained technical personnel who can implement field activities. This capacity may be most efficiently achieved through the combining of formal training with practice or skills-oriented training (IUCN, WWF and UNEP, 1980). The role of training in influencing the quality of tourism experience in a natural environment has been repeatedly indicated (Lugo and Ford, 1986; Countryside Commission, 1991; Wallace, 1993; Ceballos-Lascuráin, 1996; Toole, 1997).

The authors subscribe to the view that resource management is as much a social as a technical issue and that sustainable development is linked to the conservation of both natural and cultural diversity. In this chapter, they address the issue of training in natural and cultural history and its role in the development of tourism in the Caribbean region. They use the work of the Iwokrama International Centre as a case study to demonstrate the capacity to provide this training within the region, and to identify some lessons learned and experiences. Iwokrama is not only a regional centre of excellence for research and training in natural resources, it is also located in a country with one of the highest levels of cultural and natural diversity in the Caribbean.

The researchers' argument is that hands-on training of technical, field personnel in natural and cultural history is an effective strategy for improving the tourism product and promoting the development of the nature and heritage tourism sub-sectors. Indeed, the trend internationally is that the traveling public, and especially eco-tourists, are looking for experiences that combine a greater awareness of the 'social' and 'physical' environment, and expect at high quality of interpretation of this environment (Coathup, 2000; Cooperative Republic of Guyana, 1997). Interpretation personnel are a fundamental component of the management of parks and natural areas, yet in the majority of cases in Latin America and the Caribbean the persons discharging these functions lack much of the specific training required for interpreting the environment (Miranda, 1992). It is therefore important for guiding personnel in the Caribbean to have sufficient knowledge and skills in the natural and cultural history of the physical and social environment they will be interpreting to visitors.

For the purpose of this chapter, training is defined as a process of facilitating the acquisition of knowledge and skills, while interpretation is a process of explaining to visitors the nature of the natural and cultural resources of an area in ways that encourage interest and motivate action.

# WHAT AND WHERE IS IWOKRAMA?

The Iwokrama International Centre for Rain Forest Conservation and Development (Iwokrama) is an international research and development partnership sited in Guyana. The site consists of a pristine natural area of 360,000 ha that integrates a multitude of resources including several forest types, rivers, mountains, a segment of the road corridor that connects Guyana's capital city to Brazil in the south, indigenous Amerindians, and a host of archaeological sites.

The Centre is situated in central Guyana, at the northern periphery of the Rupununi sub-region (Fig. 1). The North Rupununi borders the Iwokrama Forest on the south and consists of 13 communities. The population of the sub-region is mainly from the following Amerindian groups; Makushi (81 per cent), but there are also Wapishana (12 per cent), Arawak (4 per cent) along with 'Coastlander' (2 per cent), Brazilian, and other ethnicities making up the population (unpublished data[1]).

The Centre is currently focused (Iwokrama 2002) on the following six programme areas:

### Thematic Programme Areas:
1. Conservation and use of Forests and Biodiversity
2. Business Development
3. Human Resources Development

### Cross-cutting Programme Areas:
1. Research, Monitoring and Evaluation
2. Information and Communication
3. Stakeholder Processes and Governance

# TOURISM AT IWOKRAMA

Tourism, specifically ecotourism development and management, is one of the activities under the Business Development programme at Iwokrama. The Centre is a destination in itself, but is also linked with local communities and private tourism operatives to define a diverse regional tourism product featuring nature, cultural heritage, and adventure. Its programme in community ecotourism development seeks to increase awareness of tourism and develop tourism management capacity within the surrounding communities. Iwokrama carries out training, awareness building, micro credit venture support, and general capacity building in support of tourism development in the surrounding communities and Iwokrama itself. Its programme in Business Development aims to establish partnerships — with the private sector and local communities — for the launching and development of tourism business ventures.

**Figure 1:**

## Map showing location of Iwokrama Forest and surrounding North Rupununi Amerindian communities.

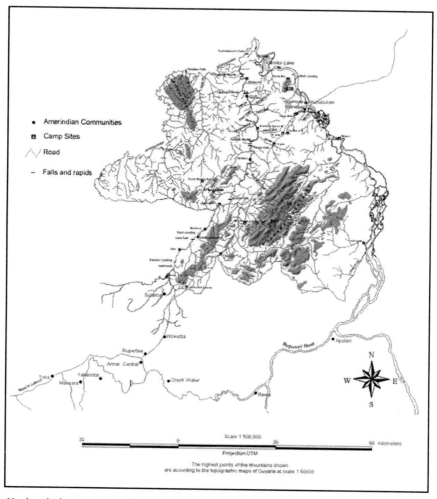

Used with the permission of the North Rupununi District Development Board

An ecotourism study at Iwokrama (Gruin and Thorne, n.d.) describes Iwokrama as 'a unique resource of natural and human communities with extraordinary scientific and global conservation value, with a combination of attractive elements that have tremendous appeal to potential visitors interested in natural history, social anthropology and conservation, and with great potential for education, interpretation and demonstration'. Iwokrama's tourism strategy is to offer a kind of tourism that is fundamentally an educational and interpretive experience, in addition to providing entertainment and recreational value (Iwokrama, 1998). A further dimension of the tourism strategy (Iwokrama, 2002) is aimed at developing private sector-community-Iwokrama partnerships. Iwokrama already has significant infrastructure (see later in this chapter) which forms a central part of its tourism development programme. It presently attracts three major groups of visitors:

- **Educational groups** of between 20 and 30 staying between one and three weeks
- **Adventure visitors** of groups of up to 30 youths staying up to three months; using Iwokrama as a basis for traveling through South America
- **High end nature tourists** in groups of up to eight staying from three to eight days

In addition, the Centre is targeting the following groups of visitors in smaller numbers:

- International volunteers and researchers
- Guyanese and expatriates traveling along the Georgetown-Lethem road
- Local community members including wildlife clubs and school groups

The strategy is for Iwokrama to provide visitor services and facilities at its sites and facilitate or carry out research that provides information leading to product development. Iwokrama will partner with the private sector, local communities, or private-community joint ventures that will lease ecotourism on a concession basis. The partners will provide investment, human resources, management capacities, marketing, and quality control.

In practice, visitors to Iwokrama travel to a number of natural sites and participate in interpretive and recreational activities or visit archaeological sites and the Amerindian village within the forest. This visit is often preceded or followed by separate itineraries to Amerindian villages in the savannahs south of the Forest.

Iwokrama, as a site, presents a number of themes for interpretation to visitors. Some of these are geology and geomorphology (Guiana Shield, dykes, et cetera); Amazonian fish biology; rare birds; giant plants and animals; plant endemism; economic botany; cultural history; traditional knowledge; archaeology; the history of the Kurupukari crossing and road to Brazil; the history behind the name 'Iwokrama'; a stellar night sky; and climatology (El Nino, wildfires, et cetera). There are also opportunities for interpreting within a larger geographical, cultural and political context, for example cultural diversity within the Caribbean; the origins of indigenous peoples of the Caribbean; Guyana, CARICOM, and the Commonwealth; and boat building.

## RESEARCH AT IWOKRAMA

Research is one of the core activities at Iwokrama. Research is conducted by both third parties (researchers and students) and Iwokrama (management-oriented, monitoring, et cetera). Research has played a fundamental role in planning and management at Iwokrama, not only in tourism development, but in all aspects of resource management. Extensive bio-physical and social inventory and mapping work has played a key role in land use planning, the location of tourism and other infrastructure, the development of conservation priorities, and the identification of strategic business opportunities for Iwokrama. This research has been carried out over a period of several years and the yield from these efforts indicates a high degree of biological, cultural, and physical resources present within and surrounding the Iwokrama Forest. Such research has made Iwokrama one of the best studied sites in the Caribbean.

Information is collected through both conventional methods in the physical and social sciences and local traditional knowledge. The availability of this information has made a large input into both the training and tourism programmes at Iwokrama. Rangers, community environmental workers, and guides have benefited in a significant way from the availability of this information in refining their knowledge and skills for tour guiding work, interpretation, and environmental education. Not only is there a close relationship between scientific tourism and ecotourism (Wallace 1993), but at Iwokrama there is an interconnectedness between research, training and tourism that has impacted positively upon the development of ecotourism. Research findings and activities are part of what is interesting about Iwokrama to those from outside of the Centre.

## TRAINING AT IWOKRAMA

Training at Iwokrama straddles both the core areas of human resources development and business development. It is a vehicle for information and communication, and is a basic tool for all other core areas. As an example, training is important in sustainable ecotourism development because it is necessary for developing technical and administrative capacity among local communities, and likewise for increasing and enhancing the specialized skills and knowledge required of rangers and tour guides.

Iwokrama aims at delivering world-standard training, utilizing state of the art technology and capitalizing on recent information from research and experience generated at Iwokrama and elsewhere. Facilitators are out-sourced from among local, national, and international experts or drawn from Iwokrama staff to meet the requirements for learning in the comprehensive range of subject areas in which Iwokrama has capability.

## FEATURES OF TRAINING AT IWOKRAMA

The majority of the training at Iwokrama is carried out *in-situ* and by living on location, participants derive the attending benefits from this arrangement. The immersion environment provides a multitude of direct and collateral opportunities to experience many of the facilities, phenomena, problems, interventions, and other realities relating to the physical and social resources present in a real-life environment. This describes the experiential context within which Iwokrama carries out its largely hands-on training to ensure the highest degree of learning of functional skills and knowledge. This latter is further enhanced by the employment of an array of teaching methods and an extensive stock of equipment and teaching materials (discussed later).

The multiple resources and opportunities at Iwokrama mean that the Centre is able to offer a comprehensive curriculum to facilitate significant breadth in learning. Though comprehensive overall, the training retains an intensive focus, capitalizing on the resource-rich environment and the live-in presence of participants to obtain significant depth in the respective subject areas.

## TRAINING FOR TOURISM AND INTERPRETATION

Interpretation personnel play a vital role in tourism and interpretation programmes, being the source transmitting notions of how natural and historic processes function, using local examples to illustrate fascinating stories, and explaining the basic dynamic of the environment (Wagar, 1978). (Miller, 1973) contends that a guide should have the following skills and attributes:

- Secondary or technical education
- Leadership skills
- Survival, emergency and rescue skills
- First aid skills
- Knowledge of, and application of laws and rules
- Knowledge of problems and techniques of patrolling
- Skills to receive and attend to the public
- Skills in interpretation
- Communication and audio-visual presentation skills

# IWOKRAMA CERTIFICATE PROGRAMMES

The Certificate Programme at Iwokrama is a one-year, residential programme. So far, Iwokrama has twice mounted the Ranger Certificate Programme, which provides the broadest possible preparation in natural and cultural history, resource management, and many other ancillary skills that are useful not only for resource management, but for tourism management. The programme meets and surpasses the requirements for training and certifying as ranger/warden/guard, professional guide, or interpreter. It is built around the following nine modules:

1. **Communication Skills**
   Oral Communication; Writing Skills; Personal and Interpersonal Skills; Computer Skills; Still and Digital Cameras; and Camcorders and Video Production.

2. **Travel Skills**
   White Water Canoeing; Handling and Maintenance of Outboard Motors; Riding and Maintenance of Trail Bikes.

3. **Survival Skills**
   Wilderness First Aid; Wilderness Survival; Camp Cooking and Catering; Astronomy, Meteorology and Hydrology.

4. **History and Traditional Skills**
   History, Political Organization and Governance; and Concepts and Methods in Archaeology.

5. **Law and Enforcement**

6. **Fish and Wildlife Biology**
   Biology of Fish; Field Biology of Reptiles and Amphibians; Field Biology of Birds; Field Biology of Mammals; and Concepts in Natural Resource Management.

7. **Forest Identification**
   Geology and Soils; Field Botany; Forest Entomology; and Field Mycology.

8. **Forest Practices**
   Mapping and Surveying; Reduced Impact Logging; Operation and Maintenance of Chain Saws; Low Impact Board Milling; Shingle Making; Fire Prevention and Control (optional).

### 9. Ecotourism and Wildland Management
Concepts and Practices in Wildland Management; Group Leadership and Guiding Skills; Environmental Interpretation (optional); Tour Planning and Operation; and Community Ecotourism Planning.

Graduates of this programme have been employed at Iwokrama in areas of facilities maintenance, inventory work, field research, tour guiding, outreach, and patrolling.

From 2004, Iwokrama plans to offer a further upgraded certificate programme with three options:

- Ranger Certificate
- Forest Technician Certificate
- Certificate in Environmental Communication and Interpretation

Participants training under these options benefit from both the breadth and depth available through the Iwokrama curriculum and the flexibility to choose coursework that best needs their needs. The last of the three options mentioned is especially suited to persons who are desirous of specializing at the professional level in the area of recreation, tourism, and tour guiding.

The Certificate programme is a qualification that enables graduates to either enter university, or to supplement theoretical knowledge already gained at university with a range of practical skills. The Centre is working on the option of allowing university graduates to take the certificate programme as a post-graduate diploma.

## GUIDE TRAINING PROGRAMME

In 2003, Iwokrama introduced the Guide Training Programme for persons seeking to start a career in tour guiding without requiring competency in other related areas such as outreach, wildlife, forestry, or administration. The programme has an intensive integrated five week curriculum consisting of a more basic range of subject areas. It is also residential and adopts the same hands-on learning approach, though not of the same depth as the certificate options. During the programme, each participant completes a field project as part of the requirement of the programme. External certification and licensing to carry out guiding work is provided by the tourism private sector.

## SHORT TRAINING

The Centre also offers opportunities for in-service training and customized training for persons from the tourism and hospitality industry. It can design and mount programmes to meet the needs of clients not met by the Certificate or Guide Training programme. In addition, individual courses that make up each module in the Certificate curriculum could be taken as stand-alone courses or under the International Short Courses option.

# FACILITIES AND RESOURCES FOR TRAINING AND TOURISM

## *Physical Resources*

Iwokrama has significant infrastructure to support training and tourism activities. These include a field station, several satellite camps, a canopy walkway, and a developing trail system. At the field station are a Learning Centre with open-hall space for classes and group activities, a computer lab, wet and dry laboratories, a medical centre, a kitchen, and HF radios. The computers at the Field Station are networked, with access to the Internet, and there will soon be a satellite phone facility. There is also a weather station on site. The stock of equipment is extensive, covering audio-visual equipment and instruments for hydrology, ichthyology, mammalogy, ornithology, herpetology, soil science, geology, botany, and forestry.

There is a significant library holding in the Information and Communications Unit consisting of books, journals, Iwokrama publications, colour slides, educational CDs, video documentaries, a public access computer connected to the Internet, various audio-visual equipment, and a seminar room. Further, Iwokrama has a geographic information systems (GIS) laboratory.

For transport, Iwokrama has a Bedford high-bed truck, and fleets of Land Cruisers, outboard-powered boats, and aluminium canoes.

## *Resource Persons*

Through linkages with individuals and institutions in Guyana and overseas, the Centre accesses professional expertise in a variety of subject areas. Resource persons who have so far been involved in training at Iwokrama include Amerindian experts, professionals (both Guyanese and non-Guyanese) in Guyana, the University of Guyana, local hotel personnel, the Guyana Defence Force, universities and museums in Canada and the USA, and Wilderness Medical Associates (USA).

# SOME LESSONS FROM IWOKRAMA

Iwokrama is an international centre combining research, training and management relating to biological, social, and managerial problems relevant to the natural environment. It is one of the few providers within the Caribbean region of hands-on field training for rangers, environmental interpreters, forestry and wildlife technicians, and tour guides. Over the years of testing and application of new training and tourism interventions many lessons and conclusions have emerged. In relation to field training in natural and cultural history, the following emerged:

1. The use of a natural field setting with the presence of various active resource use programmes and local communities is a powerfully demonstrative and enriching environment for developing knowledge and skills in natural and cultural history.

2. People from local communities have significant knowledge of the local culture and environment. Many also have significant dexterity that enables rapid learning, development of skills requiring hand or body, and interpretive demonstrations. With relevant training, they can become highly resourceful guides and rangers.

3. Individuals who attained secondary qualifications (whether from local communities or otherwise) were better able to benefit from the more mentally demanding subject areas, were generally more confident and competent with leadership and administrative responsibilities, and better able to undertake the difficult task of interpreting and explaining complex scientific concepts. Completion of secondary education was therefore an additional success factor in training for leadership responsibility in interpretation and tour guiding.

4. People who did not have a hinterland background showed significant learning ability in identifying, understanding and explaining new species, natural phenomena, indigenous cultural traditions, and the significance of these under the training regime provided. In short, the training strategy is generally effective and is not limited to local community members.

5. Rangers, trained under the comprehensive curriculum at Iwokrama, turned out to be very capable research assistants. Rangers played leading roles in assisting researchers in locating research objects in the field, in identifying species, and in turn learned new information and methods from researchers with relative ease. Ranger graduates can therefore play an important role in support of field research and in scientific tourism.

6. Repeated testimonials from national, regional and international visitors to Iwokrama commended the knowledge and skills of ranger graduates in the natural environment, local culture, and inter-personal communication. The ranger training programme is therefore well suited to the development of professional, career-oriented interpretation professionals giving guiding services to tourists, researchers, and other visitors.

7. Rural intonation and grammatical idiosyncrasies of guides did not seem to be of importance to visitors; rather knowledge, interpersonal skills, and the

interpretation of the environment seemed to matter more in determining the quality of experience of visitors.

8. The development and success of ecotourism at Iwokrama is not predicated on the spectacular or charismatic as exclusive attractions. The experience of rangers acting as guides at Iwokrama suggests that good interpretation of the flora and local history are as important in shaping the experience of a visitor as the presence of charismatic wildlife or spectacular physical features.

9. Well trained guides make a large difference to the quality of experience of an ecotourist and can serve as a major ingredient in marketing a destination. Investment in implementing international-standard, field-based, hands-on training as a strategy for attaining this is, however, severely challenged by a lack of expertise locally and regionally in certain subject areas, and the high cost of putting together such a programme.

## REFERENCES

Acosta, C.A. 2000. 'International conservation education'. *Conservation Biology* 14, no. 4: 924.

Ceballos-Lascuráin, H. 1996. *Tourism, ecotourism, and protected areas*. Switzerland: IUCN.

Coathup, D. 2000. *The North Rupununi: an approach to sustainable development and natural resource management*. Unpublished report prepared for WWF, Guianas.

Countryside Commission. 1991. *Tourism in National Parks. A guide to good practice*. Countryside Commission/English Tourist Board/Wales Tourist Board, UK.

Ganga, G. N. 1996. *Ecotourism in Guyana*. Working Paper Series no. 17. Mona: UWI Centre for Environment and Development.

Glowka, L., F. Burhenne-Guilmin and H. Synge. 1994. *A guide to the Convention on Biological Diversity*. Environmental Policy and Law Paper no. 30, IUCN, Gland.

Gruin, M. R. and A. G. Thorne. (n.d.). *Ecotourism Study*. Georgetown: Iwokrama International Centre for Rain Forest Conservation and Development.

Iwokrama. 1998. *Operational Plan 1998-2002*. Georgetown: Iwokrama International Centre for Rain Forest Conservation and Development.

Iwokrama. 2002. *Five Year Framework 2003-2007*. Georgetown: Iwokrama International Centre for Rain Forest Conservation and Development.

IUCN, WWF and UNEP. 1980. *World Conservation Strategy: living resources conservation for sustainable development*. Gland, Switzerland: World Conservation Union.

Lugo, A., E. and L. B. Ford eds. 1987. 'Forest recreation in the Caribbean islands'. Proceedings of the Third Meeting of Caribbean Foresters, May 19-23, 1986. Puerto Rico: Institute of Tropical Forestry, Southern Forest Experiment Station.

Miranda, J., M. 1992. *Manual para la interpretación ambiental de las áreas silvestres protegidas*. Chile: Oficina Regional de la FAO para América Latina y el Caribe.

Poon, A. and R. Poon. 1994. 'The Ecotourism opportunity in the Caribbean'. Working Paper Series no. 5. Mona: UWI Centre for Environment and Development.

Toole, L. 1997. 'Ecotourism – potential for enhancing conservation'. In: Workshop on Ecotourism in Protected Areas of the Amazonian Region, February 4-11, 1996, Work Document Series 3, SURAPA, Bogotá.

UNEP/CBD. 1994. *Convention on Biological Diversity – text and annexes.* Interim Secretariat of the Convention on Biological Diversity, Geneva, Switzerland.

Wallace, G., N. 1993. 'Visitor management: lessons from Galápagos National Park'. In *Ecotourism - a guide for planners and managers* eds. K. Lindberg and D.E. Hawkins. Vermont: The Ecotourism Society.

# 6

# EVALUATING ECOTOURISM WITH ECOLOGICAL ECONOMICS: A CASE STUDY FROM BONAIRE

Thomas Abel

## ABSTRACT

*A form of ecological economics known as emergy analysis is used to evaluate recent ecotourism development on the island of Bonaire, Netherlands Antilles. Emergy is an alternative, donor currency that places all products of world ecosystems on one scale, based on the human-ecological work that contributed to the production of that product. The intensity of ecotourism development on Bonaire is calculated and compared with other economic sectors. It is argued that weak sustainability can be achieved if development intensity is appropriate to the original economic context. Ecotourism development on Bonaire in the last 15 years has been more intense than prior development on the island, though not dramatically so, with some resulting ecological economic transformations. Detailed intensity measurements were made for five hotels, and a hotel size appropriate to the island context is recommended.*

## INTRODUCTION

Wherever economic 'development' occurs, ecological economic impacts will follow. Development transforms people and nature simultaneously at multiple spatial and temporal scales. It invariably captures the natural production and mineral resources of less-developed countries and funnels them into the global economy. What do they get in return? How does development ripple through an economy (and ecology), transforming the economic strategies of people and their relationships with nature? Ecological economics is a quantitative alternative to economic analysis that can address these questions. It aims to locate economic behaviour within its ecological context, incorporating environmental limits and multi-scaled impacts.

Emergy analysis is a form of ecological economics that provides the means to evaluate national economies and natural systems with quantitative measures (Odum,

1996). Emergy is an alternative, *donor* currency that places all products of world ecosystems on one scale, based on the human-ecological work that contributed to the production of that product (Brown and Ulgiati, 1999). Emergy is a single currency that can represent flows or storages of energy, materials, goods or services. Emergy is foremost a systems concept, which was constructed from the systems principles of self-organization, hierarchy, scale, pulsing, and others.

This chapter is one component of dissertation research that addressed the nested, multiple-scaled effects of ecotourism development on the island of Bonaire in the Netherlands Antilles (Abel 2000). There were three spatial scales of analysis in the dissertation: the island-international scale, the inter-island economic scale, and the household-farm scale. The ecotourism analysis presented in this chapter is one component within the inter-island economic scale. This chapter will focus primarily on the emergent ecotourism sector itself, and will not address in detail the other social-economic transformations that accompanied development. That analysis can be found in Abel (2000).

## WEB OF SOCIAL ECONOMIC PRODUCTION

The human presence on Bonaire is manifest in a web of market and non-market production subsystems. Figure 1 depicts the unique nature of the Bonaire web of social-economic production subsystems.

Bonaire does not possess every conceivable economic production subsystem. As a small island with few mineral resources, Bonaire has very little primary economic production. There are no fuel or metal sources mined locally. There is also no heavy industry. These vital ingredients to Bonaire's system are imported, represented by the 'Fuels' and 'Mnfd Goods' shown coming from outside the boundaries of figure 1. This drawing provides a way to depict the production subsystems that do exist on Bonaire, and how they are related to one another.

The ecological-economy of Bonaire is driven by emergy sources of many types (yellow circles). Natural renewable sources enter from the left. Non-renewable fuels and manufactured goods and services are emergy sources that enter from the top and right. These sources together drive the human-ecosystems of the island, which are aggregated as the single production symbol 'Environment'. Storages of 'Stone', 'Water', and 'Soil' contribute to natural production and human economic production. Bonaire's unique suite of economic production subsystems forms a hierarchy or web. 'Household Subsystems' produce labour that feeds into each.

In figure 1, the subsystems are arranged in the web (or hierarchy) in accordance with the emergy analyses conducted on each (Abel, 2000). These analyses produce a web that is analogous to an ecosystem food web. Lower trophic levels of an ecosystem contain numerous individual organisms that attract a small percentage of available emergy inflows individually, but together process great quantities of available emergy, concentrating it, and making it available to higher trophic levels. In an

## Figure 1:

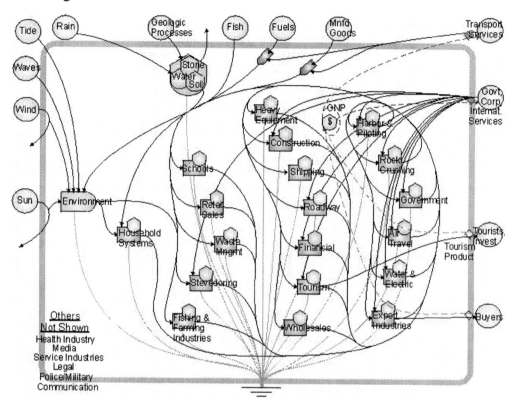

economy, production subsystems on the left of the diagram capture dispersed resources and concentrate them. Production systems on the right have larger storages of assets with slower turnover times, and have bigger feedback effects when applied to other subsystems of Bonaire society.

Wage labour should be understood to feed into each of the subsystems. Wage labourers are reproduced within a Household Production subsystem that is linked to market and non-market sources.

Figure 1 also shows each production subsystem connected to every other subsystem. This is a hypothesised relationship, and may not hold in fact. It is, however, important to expect a high degree of interconnectedness between subsystems as they self-organise.

Foreign Owners, Lenders, and Governments are important sources of resources in the creation and support of Bonaire production subsystems. They are represented by the symbol to the right (Govt., Corporate, International Services), with flows of goods and services leading to many subsystems. This suggests Bonaire's high degree of dependency on the will of outsiders, and the feedback control that outsiders can levy on Bonaire. The broken line leading out to these sources represents the flow of money that is returned for those goods and services in the form of taxes, loan payments and interest, and profits.

Bonaire's several export industries are shown with a flow leaving Bonaire and going to 'Buyers'. These export industries are eclectic and weakly integrated into the rest of the Bonaire social-economic system. They include an oil transhipment terminal, a rice processing facility, a salt production facility, and two large relay-antenna farms. In return for these exported goods, some money enters the Bonaire system and is shown leaving the system for the purchase of Fuels and Goods and for payments of taxes and debt.

One final important source of cash to Bonaire is Tourism. It is depicted here as another 'export' industry, with goods and services leaving Bonaire and going to 'Tourists' and with tourist money entering the system and adding to the island money supply. This is a convention that was chosen here, but is not uncommon in discussions of the tourism industry. Most of the direct 'product' of tourism is 'consumed' by foreign tourists, just as export goods are consumed by foreign buyers. The difference is that the buyers travel to Bonaire to consume the goods.

## ECOTOURISM

Ecotourism has been the engine of development for Bonaire since the mid-eighties. Ecotourism on Bonaire has spurred expansions in support industries, especially construction and trade. At the same time, tourism on Bonaire has been facilitated by infrastructure (water, electricity, airport, roads, harbour) that was funded by the Dutch and Antillean governments (themselves fuelled by the energy dividends of Dutch natural gas and island refineries, respectively). In the mid nineteen-eighties ecotourism boomed on Bonaire. This occurred simultaneously with a groundswell of international interest in ecologically sensitive travel, and with growing popularity for dive tourism. This is shown in figure 2.

The S-shape of this curve is one of the most common in nature. It is a logistic growth curve, which can be produced easily in simulation by an auto-catalytic growth model. In that model, a storage is gradually built by a linear flow of assets, as when infrastructure improvements like airport expansion or water / electric networks gradually improve the tourism product (1955–1985). Suddenly at some critical point, the existing storage begins to feedback and amplifies the production of itself (1985–95). Growth can continue until new limits are reached that constrain expansion. This process is intuitively understood by planners and developers, who know that tourism development can unexpectedly 'take-off' after years of slow, incremental expansion, and fortunate positioning in the tourism market, after which it plateaus (Abel, 2000).

Ecotourism can take many forms. Indeed, there is no single definition for the phenomenon. Resource conservation, cultural heritage protection, biodiversity

**Figure 2:**

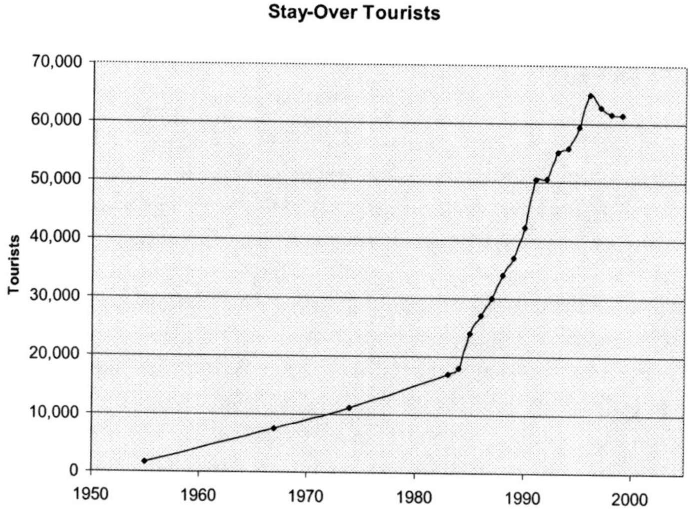


conservation, sustainable development, green management, environmental education, income sharing, local development, community-based initiatives, among others, are touted as benefits of ecotourism by some. The conservation component is described by Brandon and Margoluis (1996):

> The major underlying assumption of ecotourism is that visitors can provide the necessary economic incentives to achieve local conservation and development. In theory, ecotourism generates revenue which will be used to protect and conserve the biodiversity and natural resources that draw visitors to a particular site.

The cultural heritage component is included in Wallace's (1996) definition:

> Ecotourism is travel to relatively undisturbed natural areas for study, enjoyment or volunteer assistance. It is travel that concerns itself with the flora, fauna, geology, and ecosystems of an area as well as the people (caretakers) who live nearby, their needs, their culture and their relationship to the land.

Community-based ecotourism is defined by Sproule (1996) as:

> ...ecotourism enterprises that are owned and managed by the community [which imply] that a community is taking care of its natural resources in order to gain income through operating a tourism enterprise and using that income to better the lives of its members.

# GROWTH LIMITS AND TOURISM POLICY

The mission statement of the National Tourism Policy of Bonaire captures many of these intentions:

> The overall objective for the development of tourism in Bonaire is to enable the people of Bonaire to benefit from the promotion and development of tourism by providing an optimum level of economic contribution consistent with the overall protection of Bonaire's environmental assets, cultural heritage, human resources and lifestyle (TCB 1995).

The National Tourism Policy is a comprehensive plan for managing development, which attempts to limit lodging, foreign labour and natural resource exploitation (specifically coral reef contact with scuba divers). Growth limitation is a well-reasoned strategy for ecotourism destinations as shown in table 1. However, popular consensus for limits can wane as growth slows. For that reason it is essential that the local population has been included in the benefits of growth, at all levels including ownership and management positions. In addition, the population should be informed and included in policy debates and decisions.

# Table 1:
# Growth Limits

| Limits On: | Achieved With: |
|---|---|
| 1) New lodging | 1) Unit caps and a new construction moratorium |
| 2) Lodging size | 2) Restrictions on large developments and incentives for small businesses |
| 3) Sprawl | 3) Zoning and land use planning |
| 4) Environmental impact | 4) Required impact studies for new lodging |
| 5) Coastal development | 5) A moratorium on new construction on the coast |
| 6) Diving | 6) Monitored reefs and dive limits if necessary |
| 7) Park excursions | 7) Limited park visitation if necessary |
| 8) Dive shops | 8) Restricted permitting for shops |
| 9) Tourist types | 9) Tourism policy that promotes high-end market segments like scuba, birding, windsurfing, etc. |
| 10) Fast-food chains | 10) Policy that excludes multinational fast-food chains and promotes local and gourmet ethnic restaurants |
| 11) Cruise ships | 11) Low promotion for cruise and strict rules to limit cruise impact |
| 12) Yacht moorings | 12) Restrictions to constructed mooring sites |
| 13) Foreigner residents | 13) Strict policies for foreign labor and residence, which also limits the rate of population growth for the island as a whole. |

Empirical research can contribute to the popular discourse and negotiation of limits. One of the goals of the dissertation (Abel, 2000) was to provide environmental education that can infuse the democratic and economic discourse, which is lively and productive on Bonaire.

The National Tourism Policy for Bonaire is an exceptional set of guidelines to manage economic development. The policies are given in table 2. Summarised in general terms, the Policy has two main goals,

1.  to control, to restrict, to limit development growth in various ways, and
2.  to assure the inclusion of Bonairians in the economic benefits of development.

## Table 2:
## Policies that Promote the Inclusion of Bonairians in Development

| Policy Directive: | Achieved With: |
|---|---|
| 1) Investment incentives for Bonairians | 1) Small capital loans and technical advice for Bonairians who will invest in local tourism developments |
| 2) Tax holidays for Bonairians | 2) Exemptions for import duties and property taxes for Bonairian investors |
| 3) Building linkages | 3) Policy to promote links to other island industries, particularly agriculture, fisheries, handicrafts and other services |
| 4) Foreign labour limits | 4) Visa time limits, and restrictions to services that cannot be filled by Bonairians |
| 5) Training and education | 5) Training services for tourism jobs for all positions including management, and with education in primary and secondary schools directed toward the tourism industry. |

If there is something negative to say about the ecotourism policy on Bonaire, it is that it was not in place early enough. Ecotourism growth in the mid-eighties began without sound policy direction. As is all too common in economic growth around the world, impact studies are often conducted only after an intense period of rapid construction. In 1990, a Structure Plan was produced to provide 'a development framework suitable to a small-island economy with a fragile physical and socioeconomic environment (Island Government, 1990)'. The Structure Plan was followed in the early 1990s by the Pourier Report (1992), and the National Tourism Policy.

# INCLUSION POLICIES AND EMPLOYMENT

Inclusion is a very important issue to Bonairians, and it deserves special attention. The National Tourism Policy includes some strong and probably controversial statements about employment and emigration. It is a stated goal to:

> Maximize job opportunities for Bonaireans and other qualified Antilleans at all levels of skill and responsibilities in the tourism sector by expanding training opportunities for nationals already working in, or potentially interested in entering the tourism industry and by limiting the validity of work permits of expatriates in cases where suitable qualified Antilleans are not available to such reasonable periods of time as are required for the training of local counterparts. Bonaire's labour policies should seek to encourage Bonaireans and other qualified Antilleans living elsewhere, to consider taking up job positions in Bonaire...

> ...Application for work permits for expatriates will not be entertained in cases where suitably qualified Bonaireans or Antilleans are available to fill the vacant positions. Where applications for work permits are granted they will be limited to the periods of time required for the training and succession of local counterparts.

These provisions are critical if Bonairians are to be given a chance to grow expertise locally, and therefore participate fully in the benefits of tourism development.

Does the present tourism industry offer desirable employment opportunities for Bonairians? It is well recognised that management positions in foreign-owned hotels around the world are often not available to the native-born. One tourism textbook makes this general statement:

> Another concern among host countries has been that a foreign-owned hotel allows limited opportunity for local employees to reach positions of responsibility. International hotel chains usually have a core expatriate management team of three in a 100-room hotel, five in a 250-room hotel, and eight in a 350-room hotel. Some management contracts will stipulate that within, say, three to five years the management team must be made up of locals (Mill and Morrison 1985).

Furthermore, the hotel industry produces many jobs that are undesirable or demeaning to many Bonairians, such as housekeeping. This leaves some hotels even less integrated into the island social-economics, with foreigners hired at both ends of the pay scale, and Bonairians occupying the middle.

# EMERGY AND THE ECOTOURISM PRODUCT

It is not uncommon to view tourism as an export good. As other exports, tourism generates foreign currency earnings. In fact, it is the major source of foreign currency for the Bonaire economy. From the perspective of emergy accounting, this view is especially appropriate. Goods and services purchased from a tourism host country are purchased by foreigners who use the hotel facilities, eat the restaurant food, and take the goods with them. From that standpoint, the material products of tourism are consumed by foreigners, who happen to travel to the tourism destination to consume them.

What is the tourism product exported on the global market? Is it a T-shirt? Is it an hour diving on a reef? From the perspective of emergy accounting, the tourism product includes energy, materials, environmental goods, manufactured goods, and human services. These are components of the tourism product that is exported. Emergy accounting provides methods to identify the full inputs to an economic activity, and to calculate their contribution to work in that subsystem with the single currency of emergy. Unlike economic analyses, an emergy evaluation will include the irreplaceable contribution from nature. The emergy of the tourism product that is exported is equal to the total input emergies. The exported emergy is the sum of the inputs, both environmental inputs and human-made. Figure 3 shows the inputs to the tourism sector on Bonaire.

## Figure 3:
## Inputs to the Tourism Sector

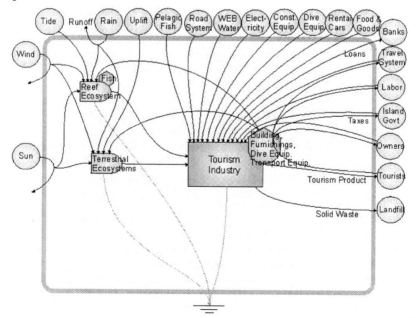

Ecotourism on Bonaire depends on many inputs of emergy (circle *sources*). Some are environmental, but many are purchased from the international economy. Each of the input flows in this diagram has been calculated (see (Abel, 2000) for detailed analysis). Relative percentages are calculated and graphed in figure 4.

**Figure 4:**
**Tourism Energy**

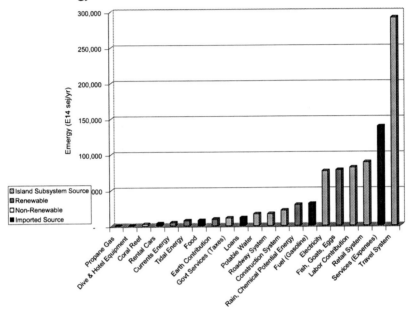

Important emergy inflows to ecotourism are many and varied (figure 4 and [Abel, 2000]).

1. Obviously 'Travel' is an essential ingredient, and this value was estimated as 40 per cent of emergy from the island airport.
2. 'Services' is an estimate of all expenses for (mostly foreign) goods and services to maintain and promote the hotels. 'Services' also includes the expenses paid to foreign airlines and tour operators. Money for these services goes out, but the emergy of the services is an input to the subsystem.
3. Imported goods (which include the emergy of shipping) are represented in the emergy inflows from the 'Retail' subsystem.
4. Tourism has a large labour force and the emergy inflow from 'Labour' is substantial. There are many important emergy inflows to the ecotourism subsystem (Abel, 2000). Uncounted or undercounted by economic

analysis, many essential ingredients are natural, renewable resources. Others are non-renewable resources from nature (fossil fuels or minerals). On Bonaire especially, many of the inflows to ecotourism are imported flows of goods and services. Finally, some sources to tourism are the outputs of other production subsystems on Bonaire, which themselves use renewable, non-renewable, and imported sources.

5. Several important environmental inputs enter ecotourism, rainfall, earth, tide, and currents, and additionally fish, goats, and eggs. The 'Fish' input is surprisingly large, and signifies an important input for tourism and loss to the local economy. Rain, earth, tide, and currents are the emergy sources for the terrestrial and marine ecosystems. They are calculated on an aerial basis. In other words, the larger the area associated with tourism, the larger the environmental basis. Before the Marine Park, Bonairians fished from boats directly on the reefs, but this is no longer legal. The production of fish on the reef has therefore been captured by the tourism industry. Part of the marine environment has also been captured by shipping from the harbour, the salt works, and the oil terminal. Part is still captured by households as they fish from the rocks, or otherwise use the coasts. It was estimated that half of the environmental emergies of the marine ecosystems should be included in the tourism total.

6. The high 'Electricity' and 'Gasoline' inputs to Bonaire's tourism industry indicate the 'developed' nature of the ecotourism product.

7. Other obvious and important inputs are 'Construction', the 'Roads' used by tourists and establishments, 'Fresh Water', 'Loans', and the 'Island' and 'Central Governments' that assure private property.

The sum of these emergy inputs is a total, which represents the emergy in the tourism export good. In other words, it is the emergy quantity that is exported when tourism is consumed by foreign tourists. This total leaves the island in return for foreign currency. It is 970,586 E14 sej/yr, which is the highest total for all export industries (Abel, 2000).

On a per establishment basis, however, tourism emergy inflows and storages are not high. Unlike the other export industries, there are many establishments that compose the tourism industry. Ranked among all production subsystems on Bonaire, tourism lies somewhere in the middle. This places tourism in the centre of the 'web' drawing of production hierarchy on Bonaire (Figure 1).

## TOURISM INTENSITY AND SUSTAINABILITY

In emergy analysis, the intensity of development is a calculated measure that can be compared to alternative development choices in order to estimate the impacts that a development choice is likely to have on an economy and ecology. This type of approach was applied by Brown and Murphy (1993) in evaluating ecotourism at resorts in Papua New Guinea and Mexico:

> If a development's intensity is much greater than that which is characteristic of the surrounding landscape, the development has greater capacity to disrupt existing social, economic, and ecologic patterns (Brown and McClanahan 1992). If it is similar in intensity it is more easily integrated into existing patterns. For example, in the Papua New Guinea and Mexico comparison already mentioned, the initial differences between a heavily urbanized area and an undeveloped wilderness area led Brown and Murphy to recommend very different appropriate intensities of development for each area (Brown and Murphy 1993).

This intensity measure has implications for so-called '*weak* sustainability' (Bryner, 2001). In human history, human activity has been supported by the fluctuating use of renewable and slow-renewable resources. In recent human times, human society has been subsidized by the capture and use of non-renewable resources (specifically fossil fuels and metals). If sustainability refers to an economy supported solely by renewable and slow-renewable resources (so-called '*strong* sustainability'), then human activity on Bonaire would need to return to pre-contact densities of less than 1,200 people, living as horticulturists. On the time-scale of millennia, this is the 'sustainable' human pattern. However, in the time-scale of the 150-year fossil fuel pulse that we are now riding, sustainability can have a different measure. In this context, it can usefully refer to human activity that does not further tax existing ecosystems, and/or threaten the renewable and slow-renewable resources upon which we also depend (such as fresh water, topsoil, forests, and coral reefs). This *weak* sustainability position can guide development to appropriate intensities.

Subsystem intensity ratios are defined here as the ratios of subsystem emergy inputs divided by the total environmental emergies entering the island. This places each subsystem on an equal environmental basis. In other words, it is assumed that the numbers of establishments have self-organised to be appropriate for the spatial and environmental scale of Bonaire, and thus each subsystem (species, niche) is supported by the total system environmental emergy. Figure 5 depicts the intensity ratios for the production subsystems on Bonaire.

Ecotourism on Bonaire combines reef eco-management with luxury accommodations for higher-end dive tourists. This brand of ecotourism obviously requires a substantial construction industry, and significant water, electric, and waste management. Ecotourism of this sort has a relatively high subsystem intensity ratio. However, as discussed, intensity ratios are used as relative measures. Investment that matches an existing intensity of development, in principle, will not disrupt existing social-economic systems. Intensity ratios must always be considered in this context of existing intensity.

**Figure 5:**
**Subsystem Intensity Ratios**

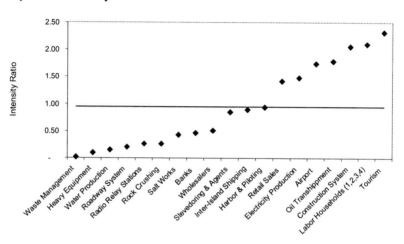

Intensity ratios measure the ratio of economic subsystem emergy inflows to the inflows of environmental sources. The average ratio is the solid line at 0.94. The related industries of tourism and construction are the highest intensity subsystems. These are relative and not absolute measures that can compare, for instance, the entire construction subsystem with the single oil transhipment terminal, and find that their intensities are similar. The average intensity ratio (0.94) can be used as a guideline for the approval of future establishments that are intended to minimise environmental stress (Abel 2000).

Figure 5 displays a range of intensity ratios. While the related industries of tourism and construction are high, this is only in a relative sense that draws comparisons with other subsystems on the island. For instance, perhaps obviously, the intensity ratio for the oil refinery on Curacao would be far greater than these numbers. The intensity ratios for Bonaire permit comparisons between diverse production subsystems (like tourism or construction) with single site industries (like the salt works or transhipment terminal).

The value of these ratios is in providing guidelines for the approval of new establishments. If such indices were calculated before tourism development had begun, they could have been used to guide development to a lower intensity, with perhaps less disruption. As it is, tourism development still ranks close to other existing industries. However, there are probably few Bonairians who would say that tourism has not transformed the island along at least a few dimensions, that is, congestion, crime, inflation, or others. It is suggested here that if tourism development had been managed to match existing intensities that existed prior to development, these few negative effects would not have been felt.

As stated in the quotation above from Brown and Murphy, 'If a development's intensity is much greater than that which is characteristic of the surrounding landscape, the development has greater capacity to disrupt existing social, economic, and ecologic patterns'. Obviously this is a relative measurement, one that places establishments within the context of the existing system. For example, a 1,000-room hotel in New York City would not be disruptive to the existing ecological-economic system, but the same hotel on Bonaire would dramatically transform the existing environmental-economic relationships that currently exists. If one professed goal of ecotourism is to minimize the impacts of development activity, then development should match a scale appropriate to the extant host site. The next section will compare five existing hotels on Bonaire and use these principles to suggest an appropriate scale for hotel establishments.

## FIVE HOTELS COMPARISON

Five anonymous hotels were extensively interviewed and compared. Emergy inputs were calculated for each. There is a range of hotels on Bonaire, from small to large. An attempt was made to interview hotels near both ends of this continuum, and in-between. Figure 6 compares the hotels on utility emergies, which are among the largest emergy inputs to the hotels.

**Figure 6:**

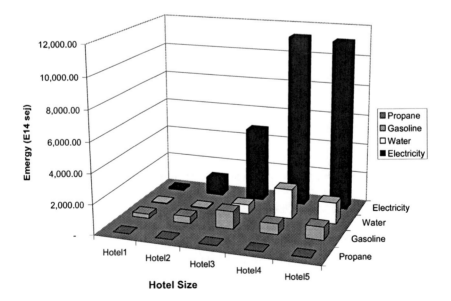

Figure 7 displays the intensity ratios for five hotels. The intensity ratios show an obvious pattern of increase with hotel size. Recall that the subsystem intensity ratio compares the contribution of purchased goods and services to the contribution of natural, domestic ecosystems. Intensity ratios can suggest a development size that is appropriate for an existing economy. The average intensity ratio for production subsystems on Bonaire is the solid line at 0.94, and for the total tourism subsystem it is the solid line at 2.32.

## Figure 7:
## Hotel Intensities

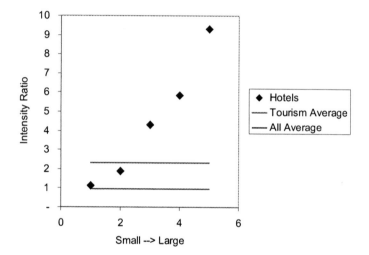

Electricity is the largest utilities input for large hotels. However, gasoline is the largest emergy inflow for smaller dive-oriented hotels. Recognise that these are emergy and not money inputs, and therefore indicate the relative work that each contributes to the tourism product. Electricity is a higher-transformity energy source, because it is produced by combining fuels with high-technology generators. The output electric power is a very flexible and versatile form of energy, appropriately matched to urban settings. Fresh water normally has a high emergy value because it is the product of the work of natural systems to evaporate seawater and converge rainfall into usable concentrations. Fresh water on Bonaire is especially valuable because it is instead a fossil fuel product, manufactured in the desalination plant.

As stated above, one goal of ecotourism should be to match the scale of new development to the existing intensity of development, a rainforest in some contexts, or an urbanizing tropical desert island in another. In the case of ecotourism on Bonaire, therefore, hotels with intensity ratios of approximately 2.32 or less would be appropriate. This suggests that any future developments should be somewhere between Hotel 1 and Hotel 2 in scale.

Intensity Ratios were calculated for the five hotels interviewed. Intensity ratio might suggest an ideal or appropriate hotel size for hotel developments on the island. 'All Average' is the average intensity ratio for all subsystems on Bonaire (0.94). Values are calculated in (Abel 2000).

Many Bonairians have a sense of the desirable scale for development on Bonaire, which is remarkably similar to the results of my analysis. They can also give concrete examples of the unforeseen costs of over-scaled development, such as lost access to swimming areas for kids. Many people spoke of their desire that Bonaire not change too much, that the tranquillity of the island not be lost, as many have seen from travels to Curacao, Aruba or St. Maarten. Many are wary of mass tourism, which is a tempting option for some of the existing, larger hotels that are having financial difficulty in the dive tourism market. Others, however, simply believe that tourism growth is a common good. An often heard slogan is 'the more tourists the better' ('mas turista, mas mihó').

## CONCLUSIONS

Given the remarkably strong policy positions taken in Bonaire's many policy statements towards growth limits and local labour inclusion, Bonaire may be a relatively successful story of ecotourism management at appropriate intensities. Threats to this success however are many. As a systems principle, feedback and maintenance must always follow rapid growth if a system is to persist. Maintenance of the tourism product on Bonaire will require investment (feedback) from production systems (including the tourism industry itself and government) to the natural and household systems of the island. Obvious needs are waste management, education, and a vigilant determination to defend the labour inclusion policy. Another threat is population growth, which increases the intensity of the human presence, and therefore stress on existing natural systems, which is the lure for ecotourists on Bonaire. Perhaps the greatest threat to the expressed policy preference for 'sustainable' ecotourism development is the slippery slope of mass tourism. There are some forces tugging Bonaire in that direction. It is the hope that studies such as this will add quantitative measure and therefore support for well-intentioned and reasoned political policy for managed development.

## REFERENCES

Abel, T. 2000. *Ecosystems, Sociocultural Systems, and Ecological-Economics for Understanding Development: The Case of Ecotourism on the Island of Bonaire.* FL: University of Florida.

Brandon, K. and R. Margoluis. 1996. In *The Ecotourism Equation: Measuring the Impacts* 99. New Haven: Yale University.

Brown, M.T. and T.R. McClanahan. 1992. Centre for Wetlands and Water Resources, Gainesville, 1992).

Brown, M.T. and R.C. Murphy. In *Emergy Synthesis Perspectives, Sustainable Development, and Public Policy Options for Papua New Guinea* eds. S.J. Doherty and M.T. Brown. Final Report to the Cousteau Society. Gainesville, Fl: Centre for Wetlands, University of Florida, 3D1-3D27.

Brown, M.T. and S. Ulgiati. 1999. *Ambio,* 28: 486-493.

Bryner, G. C. 2001. *Gaia's Wager: Environmental Movements and the Challenge of Sustainability*. Lanham: Rowman and Littlefield.

Island Government, B. 1990. Netherlands Antilles Department for Development Cooperation; Island Government of Bonaire Executive Council.

Mill, R. C. and A.M. Morrison. 1985. *The Tourism System: An Introductory Text*. Englewood Cliffs, NJ: Prentice-Hall.

Odum, H.T. 1996. *Environmental Accounting: Emergy and Decision Making*. New York: John Wiley.

Pourier, M. 1992. Bestuurscollege van het Eilandgebied Bonaire en de Regeringen van de Nederlandse Antille en Nederland, Kralenkijk.

Sproule, K. W. 1996. In *The Ecotourism Equation: Measuring the Impacts* 99. New Haven: Yale University.

TCB. 1995. Tourism Corporation Bonaire. Bonaire.

Wallace, G. N. 1996. In *The Ecotourism Equation: Measuring the Impacts* 99 New Haven: Yale University.

# 7

# CHALLENGES AND PROSPECTS FOR TOURISM DEVELOPMENT IN BELIZE[1]

Ian Boxill

## ABSTRACT

*In this chapter the author argues that tourism development in Belize should avoid going the traditional mass tourism route taken by most Caribbean destinations. He suggests that Belize should forge an alternative model, which draws and builds on its geographical location, history, culture and ecology. The author identifies a number of limiting and facilitating factors to tourism development. These facilitating factors recommend an alternative model that includes nature, education and community tourism; and a type of cruise tourism that is linked to education and culture. For this effort to succeed, the chapter recommends that the government and civil society work together and develop a sustainable tourism industry in Belize.*

## INTRODUCTION

Like many Caribbean countries, Belize is a small open economy which is largely impacted by changes in the global economy. Although possessing an abundance of natural resources, the Belize economy is based largely on agriculture, agro-industry and merchandising. Sugar is the chief crop, accounting for almost half of all exports, however bananas is the largest employer of labour (*http://www.1uptravel.com/ international/centralamerica/belize/economy.html*, p.1). As with many countries in the Caribbean basin, the past decade has been difficult for the country as an economic downturn has resulted in growing trade deficit and widespread unemployment. At the same time Belize has also witnessed an large influx of immigrants from neighbouring Guatemala, a phenomenon that has change the country's demographic make-up from being largely African/Creole to Mestizo.

One response to the continuous economic problems faced by the country was for government to place greater emphasis on the tourism industry. Writing in the early 1990s, Cutlack (1993) observed:

> *Tourism is Belize's newest industry with the greatest international impact.... It is the country's fastest growing sector and potentially her biggest winner.... (p. 30)*

During the late 1990s the tourism industry contributed significantly to the growth in the economy. Estimates for Belize suggest that tourism now contributes about 20 per cent of GDP (Belize Travel and Tourism Statistics, 2001). At the moment, it would appear that the Belize government is using tourism as its main instrument of economic development (Belize Travel and Tourism Statistics, 2001). Based on arrival statistics, the country seems to be moving away from its traditional ecotourism model to embrace mass tourism. This apparent change in model raises questions of the appropriateness and sustainability of the industry. In this chapter it is argued that this change is not good for Belize and it concludes by pointing to an alternative tourism development path for the country.

## TOURISM IN THE CARIBBEAN AND BELIZE

There is enough evidence to indicate that tourism is the world's largest industry and that it makes a significant contribution to the GDP of Caribbean countries (Jayawardena, 2002). Tourism is growing in its importance to the Caribbean and Central American nation of Belize. For the Caribbean, tourism's contribution ranges between 5 per cent and 80 per cent.

Now, while stayover arrivals in Belize are not as high as for destinations such as Cancun, the Dominican Republic, Barbados, Puerto Rico, The Bahamas, and Jamaica, Belize compares favourably with countries such as Antigua and the Cayman islands. However, Belize has one of the lowest cruise ship arrivals in the entire region (Belize Travel and Tourism Statistics, 2001); although this year's arrivals have increased dramatically. Belize is still a moderate to low density destination, even though revenues earned from the industry are relatively high (Table 1).

## Table 1:

## Key sociocultural and socioeconomic indicators for Barbados, The Bahamas and Jamaica and Belize (1999)

| Indicator | Barbados | The Bahamas | Jamaica | Belize |
|---|---|---|---|---|
| Tourist arrivals per thousand of the population | 1936 | 5205 | 484 | 1344 |
| Rooms per thousand population | 21 | 49 (1998) | 9 | 16 |
| Visitor expenditure per capita (US dollars) | 2490 | 5224 | 496 | 459 |
| Tourism penetration ratio | 54 | 77 | 14 | 25* |
| Visitor expenditure as a percentage of GDP | 32.20 | 32.87 (1998) | 21.40 | 16.19 |

*estimated

Still there has been growth in the industry. Tourism has grown in its importance to the Belize economy over the last ten years. Between 1987 and 1999 stay-over tourist arrivals to Belize grew by more than 200 per cent, from 99,300 to 326,600 (Caribbean Tourism Statistical Report, 1999–2000).

During the past five years, arrivals by cruise ships have grown significantly. Three years of remarkable growth ended with a 17.2 per cent decrease in 2001 (Belize Travel and Tourism Statistics, 2001). However, it should be noted that this year has seen a significant recovery from previous years — over 300 per cent increase over last year.

Even though the arrival numbers are relatively small compared to the more established destinations, the dramatic increase in tourist arrivals for a country which has recently started to market itself as a low density/nature-based tourism destination has resulted in some important social impacts. These impacts are visible in larger resort areas, such as San Pedro, and to a lesser extent, in the smaller communities such as Hopkins and Dangriga (Boxill and Castillo, 2002). As can be seen from Table 2, the level of direct impacts from tourism on these two communities is low to moderate. It is Hopkins that exhibits some very moderate impacts. Now, while most of these impacts are positive and have to do with the creation of opportunities in employment and business, there are some negative and potentially negative impacts.

## Table 2:

## Summary of main social impacts and their intensity in Gangriga and Hopkins

| Type of impact | Dangriga | Hopkins |
|---|---|---|
| Employment creation | Low | Moderate |
| Development of community infrastructure | Low | Low |
| Sociocultural conflicts | Low | Low |
| Community business creation | Low | Moderate |
| Hotel density in or near communities | Low | Moderate |

Source: Boxill I. and P. Castillo (2002) 'Socio-economic Impact of Tourism in Dangriga and Hopkins, Belize' in *Tourism, Development and Natural Resources in the Caribbean* edited by A. Periera, I. Boxill and J. Maerk. Mexico City: Plaza y Valdez.

Now, it should be understood that even though the current impacts are minimal, the changing situation in these two communities is of concern for policy makers and residents alike. For example, in Dangriga there is some male prostitution and the sale of illegal drugs. The extent of this problem is very small and there are very few persons in the community involved in these illicit activities. However, there is a distinct possibility that growth in tourism could lead to an increase in the number of persons involved. To arrive at an idea of what the future might hold for these communities in, say, the next ten to 20 years, a cross-impact matrix was used. This matrix was used to generate various scenarios given assumptions about the conditions in relation to tourism development in the two communities. There were both positive and negative outcomes. The following conditions were assumed:

1. An increase in hotel density.
2. An increase in tourist arrivals.
3. More real estate development along coastal areas.
4. Sale of property in Hopkins to outsiders.

Possible positive scenarios generated from this situation include:

1. A rapid reduction in unemployment as hotels expand.
2. The growth in community-owned businesses.
3. Improvement in physical infrastructure.
4. Reduction in the poverty levels of communities.

5. Increased training of community members in tourism and related services.

6. More educational institutions in the communities.

7. The growth of service related jobs in the communities.

8. Rapid expansion of the community and the emergence of a town in Hopkins.

Possible negative scenarios generated include:

1. An increase in land prices, especially in Hopkins.

2. Increased crime and sociocultural conflicts from a growth in tourist density.

3. Possible alienation of land from communities as hotels and investors might try to buy out coastal areas from the community in Hopkins, in particular.

4. A rise in prostitution and drug peddling, especially in Dangriga.

5. Greater violence and alienation.

6. Destruction of Garifuna culture.

7. Migration of Garifuna people to other parts of Belize and the end to Garifuna communities as other people compete in the communities for work.

8. Greater emphasis on and hybridization of the Garifuna culture in response to outside culture.

9. Increase in population as people from other parts of the country and neighbouring countries come in search of jobs.

Of these potential impacts, the possibility of the community in Hopkins losing its land to foreign investors seems very real. Many poor persons in Hopkins may be persuaded to sell their beachfront property to the growing number of American investors in search of new investment opportunities in Belize. Already some persons in the community have agreed to sell their property, in the hope of receiving enough money so that they can start a new life in other parts of Belize or overseas. If this process of selling land to foreigners continues, it is quite possible that the traditional and unique Garifuna way of life may disappear with the break-up of the community. At the very least, this process will certainly lead to contradictions between Garifuna life and a new leisure lifestyle of people who come from industrialized countries.

The tourism industry is in its early stage of development in both Dangriga and Hopkins. For this reason, and also because the density of tourists is extremely low, there are no significant and immediately visible impacts on the two communities. However, things are likely to change in the near future if tourism development continues. These changes may be largely positive or largely negative. It all depends on how the development of tourism is managed.

There is an upside to tourism in these communities. What is emphasized is the need for careful planning of tourism involving members of the various communities.

There is much that can be learned about how not develop tourism from the examples of countries throughout the Caribbean. From Cancun to Jamaica to

Barbados, there are studies which show the social and environmental impacts of unmonitored mass tourism on the ecology and the lives of the people (Patullo 1996; Maerk and Boxill 2000; Periera et al 2002 ).

Therefore, Belize should be careful about the way in which it develops its tourism industry. It should eschew the sudden embrace of the traditional sea, sand and mass cruise ship model that most countries of the Caribbean are pursuing. Belize should place greater emphasis on the quality of the visitor rather than the quantity. It should also bring more stakeholders into the process, including the communities and educational institutions. In other words, Belize should adopt an alternative path to that pursued by the majority of the major Caribbean destinations.

## ALTERNATIVES FOR BELIZE

Now, obviously there are both limiting and facilitating factors to any type of development. These variables are not necessarily inherent, but are contingent upon a broad philosophical orientation of development.

Tourism development is simply one dimension of a set of development policies that may be pursued by a country. Belize would be better off with a development process, or a tourism development policy, which respects people's ways of life, engages them in a way which is psychologically, intellectually and economically beneficial; and sustains ecological systems without which we cannot hope to survive for very long. Of course this type of tourism should ideally help to bring about economic transformation and must be sustainable. Given its stage of development and its assets, Belize is the one country in the Caribbean region that is best suited to undertake this type of tourism development. What are the reasons for this? In other words, what are the facilitating factors? They are as follows:

1. Belize is a low density tourism destination. Both the land to visitor density and the tourism penetration ratios are relatively low.
2. Belize is a country with an abundance of natural beauty, and has an ecological system which is the envy of most of the Caribbean.
3. Belize is located in strategically in Central America but is also washed by the Caribbean Sea and therefore enjoys best of both worlds. Proximity to the U.S. may also be seen as an advantage.
4. Belize has a diverse culture which incorporates the major cultures of the Americas: indigenous (Maya, Garifuna), African/Creole, European (Spanish and English); Hispanic and Asian.

Nonetheless, one must be mindful of some limiting factors. These include:

1. Competition from other destinations in the region in the mass market; especially now from the rise of Cuban tourism, which is the fastest growing in the region.
2. Social and cultural conflicts which are likely to arise from significant growths in arrivals – particularly as it relates to mass tourism.
3. The relative softening of traditional destinations of the U.S and Europe, due to rising local crime and the threat of global terrorism.
4. Potential environmental problems associated with all types of tourism, especially mass and cruise tourism. Many of these impacts have been detailed in the studies of the Anglophone Caribbean and Cancun.
5. The present and potential problem of airlift due to the financial difficulties associated with the airline industry.

Belize should continue on a path of low to moderate density tourism, with some minor elements of sea and sand/mass variety where possible. The country should adopt a well planned, highly regulated tourism with a strong focus on developing the cultural and ecological gifts of the country. Belize should try to differentiate itself from the pack by focusing on high end tourism and by being more adventurous and courageous. Thinking out of the box is what we need at this moment. But, what are some of the elements of this alternative?

## ELEMENTS OF THE ALTERNATIVE
### Education and cultural tourism

With the imminence of the Free Trade Area of the Americas (FTAA), there is a great deal of potential for training in languages and cultures across the region. As a member of Caribbean Community (CARICOM), Belize should develop institutions to train English speakers in Spanish and, Spanish speakers in English. The University of Belize (UB), along with the University of the West Indies (UWI) could spearhead an initiative aimed at the development of institutions to train people in languages, both short-term and long term. These should be well run, well marketed and well organized bodies which will attract some of the brightest and the best minds in the country.

The Cubans have been developing a tourism education sector, with little competition from other Caribbean destinations (see Jayawardena, forthcoming). In the case of Belize, it should be possible to link the established educational institutions to those aimed at the study of Creole languages in the Caribbean. The target market should be Latin Americans, Caribbean people and U.S, and European colleges and education institutions. There are millions of Caribbean people in and outside the Caribbean who look for places to go on vacation, study and explore every year. There is a critical mass of Caribbean people with quite a bit of disposable income.

Relatedly, there is the possibility for the development of a festival type tourism, which draws on the culture of the country. The Belize annual Garifuna festival on November 19 is an example of festival tourism, but there are many others which can draw on the history of all peoples in the country. These festivals should be carefully managed or they can backfire, leading to the commercialization of sensitive aspects of people's cultures. There is the possibility to link these festivals to the educational institutions thereby consolidating their presence and preserving their authenticity.

The Mundo Maya project of Central America is in this tradition, but it needs to incorporate more aspects of the educational type tourism, thus bringing in a different segment of the tourism market.

## Cruise tourism

In relation to cruise tourism, there are questions about its long term benefits to the Caribbean as currently constituted. Cruise tourism often results in a considerable amount of environmental problems for the income which is earned (Patullo 1996; Periera et al 2002). Still it remains an option, which may be pursued but if properly managed. However, there is an alternative or complement to the status quo of cruise tourism.

This approach to tourism, which is based on collaboration of regional countries rather than competition among them, is well suited for CARICOM, especially in light of the FTAA. This new approach is based on a paper presented by Ian Boxill to the Caribbean Maritime Institute and the University of the West Indies (UWI) in March 2002. The project, entitled the 'Caribbean World' (CW), is an attempt to build upon the rich cultural history of the region, using the sea as a mode of transportation, to create a new tourism industry in the region. More specifically, the CW is an idea that draws on the rich history and human resources of the Caribbean region to integrate and further enhance the development of the region by the promotion of alternative education opportunities, alternative tourism and training. This can be accomplished by using ships to sail around the region and calling at ports according to the objectives of the particular journey. The basic idea is to develop a cruise ship experience that involves people traveling throughout the Caribbean and learning about the history and culture of the Caribbean. These ships should be owned and operated by organizations in the region, in the interest of the region. Four important aspects our history are critical here: Amerindian settlement and history; European colonization; slavery; and East Indian indentureship.

The specific objectives of this type of tourism should include:

1. The development of a destination for regional and international tourists similar to the 'Mundo Maya' project in Central America.

2. To link the islands and landmasses of the Caribbean through travel.
3. To generate revenue for the good of the countries.
4. To provide an alternative educational experience for regional and international students.
5. To foster closer regional cooperation and integration.

Here is another way of picturing this proposal. Imagine sailing the Caribbean in a ship with the comforts of a medium-size cruise liner, manned by staff and students of the Caribbean Maritime Institute, beginning in Belize taking in Maya ruins, then on to Jamaica stopping at Port Royal, then to Haiti for two days to see the Citadel, and then in St Kitts to tour one of the region's greatest military forts. On board are staff and students of the hospitality programme of the UWI and the UB, managing the cuisine and provision of services that are second to none offered in a five-star hotel. Or imagine being on board a ship, with a group/class comprising students from the UWI and other institutions across the world. Students who filter in and out of the large library on board; students who would not only learn about the Maroons of Jamaica or the Caribs of Dominica, but also get a chance to interact with them, and help in one of the many excavations being run by the UWI's archaeological department. On the way, they will get a glimpse of the famous Bussa Statue in Barbados and learn about his slave rebellion.

Later, they will stop at one of the famous markets in St Vincent and take in a lecture on the history of the steel pan in Trinidad and Tobago, as part of an assignment in cultural studies.

This is an option that could be spearheaded by Belize. Belize could use its knowledge and infrastructure from the Mundo Maya project and lead this process. This type of tourism is consistent with the low density, eco/heritage tourism which the country is well known for..

## Community tourism

Then of course there is community tourism. Here is where communities can gain greater control and benefit from tourism by having more cooperative ventures. The community organizations need to play an integral role in the development of properties and the creation of regulations which protect the communities from exploitation by foreign investors. There is need for the training of community members in management and entrepreneurial skills. Government officials need to provide incentives for locals to get involved in the industry as owners of properties rather than as suppliers of cheap labour. Above all, there is the need for a healthy respect for the way of life in communities, in view of the changes that will most certainly come with an expansion of tourism. The only way this will happen is if the community leaders take a proactive role in the development of tourism in their communities

## CONCLUSION

What is needed for this alternative to succeed? To succeed, tourism planners in Belize need vision, will and confidence. Tourism is serious business which requires careful planning, evaluation and administration. The model which I propose means that governments would have to invest seriously in education at all levels. The UB and other educational institutions should be at the centre of this type of tourism development.

But, tourism should not be left up to governments or investors; this is a mistake which Caribbean societies are now realizing (Hayle, 2000). Tourism cannot survive in an environment of uncertainty, high crime, poor management and local resentment. On the other hand, people must be made to feel as though they benefit from the industry (Hayle, 2000). Belize is at a stage of its development where it can fashion a new tourism, and not make the mistakes of the more mature Caribbean destinations.

## REFERENCES

Belize Travel and Tourism Statistics. 2001. Belize City: The Belize Tourist Board.

Boxill, I. 2002. 'Caribbean World'. Paper prepared for the University of the West Indies and The Caribbean Maritime Institute.

Boxill, I. and Castillo, P. 2002. 'Socioeconomic Impact of Tourism in Dangriga and Hopkins, Belize'. In *Tourism, Development and Natural Resources in the Caribbean* eds. A. Periera, I. Boxill and J. Maerk. Mexico City: Plaza y Valdez.

Boxill, I. 2000. 'Overcoming social problems in the Jamaican tourism industry'. In *Tourism in the Caribbean* eds. by J. Maerk and I. Boxill. Mexico City: Plaza y Valdez.

CTO. 2001. Caribbean Tourism Organization Statistical Report 1999-2000. Barbados: Caribbean Tourism Organization.

Cutlack M. 1993. Belize: Ecotourism in Action. London: The MacMillan Press Ltd.

Hayle, C. 2001. 'Community Tourism in Jamaica'. In *Tourism in the Caribbean* eds. J. Maerk and I. Boxill. Mexico City: Plaza y Valdes.

*Http://www.1uptravel.com/international/centralamerica/belize/economy.html*

Jayawardena, C. 2002. 'Community Development and Caribbean Tourism'. In *Tourism, Development and Natural Resources in the Caribbean* eds. A. Periera, I. Boxill and J. Maerk. Mexico City: Plaza y Valdez.

Jayawardena, C. Forthcoming. 'Cuba: Crown Princess of Caribbean Tourism'. *IDEAZ* 2, no. 1.

Maerk J. and I. Boxill. 2000. *Tourism in the Caribbean*. Mexico City: Plaza y Valdez.

Patullo, P. 1996. *Last Resorts. The Cost of Tourism in the Caribbean*. London: Cassell.

Periera A., I. Boxill and J. Maerk., eds. 2002. *Tourism, Development and Natural Resources in the Caribbean*. Mexico City: Plaza y Valdez, Mexico City.

## NOTE

This chapter is based on an article by the author published in *the International Journal of Contemporary Hospitality Management* 15, no. 3 (2003): 147-150.

# SECTION 2
# - AGRO-TOURISM -

# 8

# ISSUES OF AGRO-TOURISM IN THE CARIBBEAN

Willard Phillips and L. Barbara Graham

## ABSTRACT

*In April 2000, some 95 delegates, industry specialists, researchers and other institutional leaders from 11 countries assembled at the Conference Centre of Mount Irvine Bay Hotel in Trinidad &Tobago for a three-day regional Conference on Agro-tourism. Organised around the theme 'Agro-Tourism: A sustainable Approach to Economic Growth', the participants engaged themselves in the exploration of issues such as the micro and macro-economic dimensions of agro-tourism, human and social dimensions, role of the environment in agro-tourism and an institutional framework for agro-tourism. Resulting from these issues, the requirements of an enabling environment for agro-tourism are assessed, with particular emphasis on the role of the community and a sustained natural resources base in fostering agro-tourism development. The special case of water as a critical resource is discussed, as is the imperative for the harmonised policy framework. The chapter concludes with some speculations on opportunities and the way forward for regional economies through agro-tourism.*

## INTRODUCTION

In April 2000, some 95 delegates, industry specialists, researchers and other institutional leaders from 11 countries, assembled at the Conference Centre of the Mount Irvine Bay Hotel in Tobago for a three-day regional conference on Agro-Tourism. This conference was first proposed by the Tobago House of Assembly (THA), (the local government agency in Tobago with responsibility for the management of specific aspects of the island's development), which subsequently sought the partnership of a number of national, regional and international agencies in organising the conference. Among such agencies were the Ministry of Agriculture,

Land and Marine Resources of Trinidad and Tobago (MALMR), the Inter-American Institute for Cooperation on Agriculture (IICA), and the Regional office of the Food and Agriculture Organisation of the United Nations (FAO), which participated as co-hosts with the THA. Other national and regional agencies included, the University of the West Indies (UWI), the Caribbean Agricultural Research and Development Institute (CARDI), the United Nations Economic Commission for Latin America and the Caribbean (ECLAC), the United Nations Development Programme (UNDP), the Agricultural Development Bank of Trinidad and Tobago (ADB), the Tourism and Industrial Corporation of Trinidad and Tobago (TIDCO), and CARONI (1975) Limited.

The three days of discussions were organised around the theme '*Agro-Tourism: A Sustainable Approach to Economic Growth*' and engaged participants in the exploration of issues such as:

- The Micro and Macro-Economic Dimensions of agro-tourism;
- Human and Social Dimensions;
- The Role of the Environment in Agro-tourism, and;
- The Institutional Framework for Agro-tourism.

This chapter presents a general perspective on the scope of these discussions, and explores important dimensions to be considered in the pursuit of a regional strategy for agro-tourism development. It begins by examining the question of why agro-tourism, and subsequently discusses important emerging issues from the conference. Resulting from these issues, the requirements of an enabling environment for agro-tourism are assessed, with particular emphasis on the role of the community, a sustained natural resource base in fostering agro-tourism development and a harmonised policy framework. The special case of water as a critical resource is discussed, and the chapter concludes with some speculation on opportunities, and the way forward for regional economies through agro-tourism development.

## WHY AGRO-TOURISM?

Cursory reflection on the current state of economic and social development in the Caribbean Region, as well as the prevailing regime of global change, offer some insights into the factors which motivate this discourse at this point in time. Perhaps, the principal development in this context is the stagnation and/or relative decline of the agriculture sector within the region over the past two decades. This decline, which first became evident in the early 1980s, was further exacerbated by the effects of the trade liberalisation process which began in the mid-1980s.

The conclusion of the Uruguay Round of Multinational Trade Negotiations in the mid-1990s with the emergence of World Trade Organisation (WTO) conditionalities for the conduct of global trade, found a regional agriculture sector which was largely ill-prepared to participate in this new global economy. The sector was geared towards the production of mainly traditional export crops such as sugar, bananas, citrus and spices, and faced structural rigidities such as low levels of production, and low factor productivity, declining competitiveness, and an inadequate internal and external policy framework. Moreover, while the sector has played a key role in the economic growth of the region, its viability was based ostensibly on preferential access to guaranteed markets, particularly in Europe. Needless to say therefore, the coming into being of the new global trade dispensation as contemplated under WTO, served to immediately undermine the viability of the primary agriculture sector, both by a reduction of market prices, and access. Table 1 compares share and growth indicators for the regional agriculture sector for the decade of the 1990s.

# Table 1:
# Share and Growth Indicators – Agriculture Sector, 1990s

| Real Prices % | Agriculture in GDP % | | Avg. Agri-GDP growth p.a | | GDP Growth p.a. | |
|---|---|---|---|---|---|---|
| annual average percentages | 1995 | 1999 | 1991-94 | 1995-99 | 1991-94 | 1995-99 |
| Trinidad & Tobago[1] | 3.53 | 3.20 | 1.86 | 0.85 | 0.79 | 4.44 |
| Jamaica | 7.92 | 7.38 | 7.56 | -1.63 | 1.47 | -0.69 |
| Guyana | 27.86 | 29.69 | 13.71 | 5.35 | 7.62 | 4.09 |
| Belize | 19.06 | 20.50 | 5.49 | 5.03 | 4.61 | 3.41 |
| Suriname | 11.67 | 11.84 | 2.58 | -2.50 | -2.74 | 7.75 |
| Antigua & Barbuda | 3.87 | 3.51 | 2.52 | 0.48 | 3.70 | 3.03 |
| Barbados[1] | 6.90 | 6.40 | -4.83 | 0.80 | -1.26 | 3.60 |
| Dominica | 20.27 | 18.91 | -0.51 | -1.32 | 2.22 | 2.00 |
| Grenada | 10.34 | 8.10 | -3.83 | 1.23 | 1.71 | 5.13 |
| St. Kitts & Nevis | 5.86 | 5.25 | 4.08 | 0.72 | 4.04 | 4.10 |
| St. Lucia | 9.38 | 7.76 | -6.21 | -1.95 | 2.08 | 2.26 |
| St. Vincent & Grenadines | 15.59 | 10.40 | -10.68 | 5.06 | 1.80 | 4.46 |

1: includes sugar manufacturing;
Source: Francis (2000) '*Socio-Economic Experiences of Caribbean Agriculture in the 1990s*', Publication Forthcoming.

Francis (1997) notes two additional factors could be regarded as key in explaining the decline of the agriculture sector over the last 20 years. Firstly, the region's past emphasis on a primary agriculture has not fostered a requisite policy framework for the sustainable development of the *non-traditional* agriculture sector, or for the evolution of significant *value-added* within the primary sector. Hence, with the faltering of the primary agriculture sector, the non-traditional sector is not now in a state of readiness to compensate for current sector decline.

The second factor is that in most of the region's economies, even where there has been no significant decline in agricultural output, low levels of growth, accompanied by more spectacular growth rates in the non-agriculture sectors, has resulted in a *relative* decline of the agriculture sector in the region. These non-agriculture sectors include, mining (as in the case of Jamaica and Trinidad and Tobago), services (Barbados, Antigua and Barbuda), and manufacturing (Trinidad and Tobago, Jamaica, Dominican Republic). Growth in these sectors has had the effect of shifting the internal terms of trade against agricultural products, thereby rendering the sector even more incapable of competing for domestic production factors such as a land, and labour. The economic sector which perhaps has experienced the most spectacular growth in the region since the early 1980s is the tourism sector, and it is this sector which has had the most significant impact on the agriculture sector in terms of competition for resources. This competition is evident in the use of resources such as land, water, and labour. Additionally, inter-sectoral competition is also apparent in the region's allocation of public sector investment and trade promotion resources, as well as the development of human talent, and entrepreneurship.

According to Jayawardena (2000), in 1998 the Caribbean region attracted 31.8 million visitors, of which some 12.3 million arrived by cruise ship. Additionally, over the past decade, the region's tourism sector enjoyed an average annual growth rate of 5.5 per cent which exceeded the world average for the same period by approximately 0.6 per cent. In terms of importance, tourism has come to play an even more significant role in Caribbean economies when compared to other global tourism centres. Considering employment for instance, roughly 25 per cent of the region's workforce is directly or indirectly engaged in some type of tourism-related enterprise. Total sector earnings for the region (including all Caribbean Basin countries) is estimated at over $US17, 900 millions, which in 1998 exceeded the tourism sector earnings of major centres such as Germany, Austria and China.

Within the CARICOM sub-region, the role of the tourist economy is even more significant, with per capita earnings from tourism being approximately 61 per cent greater than per capita earnings for the region as a whole (Jayawardena, 2000). Table 2 profiles the growth of visitor expenditure for the selected destinations during the last decade.

These developments notwithstanding, tourism has not created the type of linkages that could enhance the long-term sustainability of itself, or other economic sectors in the region. That this limitation exists is borne out by a high regional import bill for goods and services, especially food, and is regarded as one of the distinctive features of the Caribbean tourism industry (Pattullo, 1996).

Additionally, emerging trends in the global tourism industry suggest that the attractiveness of the region based solely on the concept of a romantic island holiday is not likely to be a sustained over the long term. Hence, there is the need to embark on a process of diversification of the region's tourism product in order to remain

## Table 2:
## Estimates of Visitors' Expenditure (US$ millions)

| Destination | 1994 | 1995 | 1996 | 1997 | 1998 |
|---|---|---|---|---|---|
| Antigua and Barbuda[1] | 293.4 | 246.7 | 257.9 | 269.4 | 255.6 |
| British Virgin Islands | 197.7 | 205.4 | 267.6 | 210.2 | 232.0 |
| Saint Lucia | ʳ224.1 | ʳ267.8 | 268.5 | 283.7 | 291.3 |
| Bahamas | 1,332.6 | 1,346.2 | 1,450.0 | 1,415.9 | 1,402.8 |
| Barbados | 597.6 | 611.8 | ʳ632.9 | ʳ657.2 | 703.0 |
| Jamaica | 973.0 | 1,068.5 | 1,100.0 | 1,131.0 | 1,197.0 |
| Trinidad and Tobago[1] | 87.3 | 72.6 | 108.1 | 192.6 | 201.2 |
| Curacao[1] | 186.5 | 175.4 | 185.5 | 200.5 | 261.1 |
| Martinique | 378.9 | 414.8 | 410.6 | 397.0 | 415.0 |
| Puerto Rico | 1,782.3 | 1,842.1 | 1,930.2 | 2,125.0 | ᵉ2,155.6 |
| Cancun (Mexico) | 1,339.0 | 1,370.6 | 1,704.6 | 2,051.8 | 2,430.0 |
| Dominican Republic[1] | 1,147.5 | 1,568.4 | 1,765.5 | 2,099.4 | 2,141.7 |

globally competitive, and to respond to an ever-changing travelling public. Agro-tourism is considered to be one such strategy that could be employed towards achieving this objective.

The implications of attaining a successful agro-tourism strategy are many. Firstly, the production of traditional export crops such as bananas, cocoa and citrus, evolved important socio-institutional linkages with the economy, the value of which often exceeded economic worth measured solely in terms of export earnings. Hence, where agriculture is declining, there arises an imperative for alternative and emerging sub-sectors to establish similar linkages so as to engender more meaningful benefits to the wider society. This is particularly important in the context of the current evolving nature of the regional tourism towards exclusivity viz. the phenomenon of *all inclusives*. There is clearly a role for an agro-tourism strategy in mitigating some of the social and economic effects of this type of development.

Secondly, and this is related to the first, is the question of the role of all social partners, in the evolution of the regional economy. Such partners include, women, and youth, whose needs are typically, not contemplated in the traditional development policy framework.

Finally, competition for, and wise use of natural resources is an issue that requires a joint examination of both sectors in context, in order to plot an optimal strategy for development. After all, both agriculture and tourism, utilise a common natural resource base (land, and water), and are now intimately engaged in competition for labour, a key factor of production in any economic enterprise.

Against this backdrop of a downward spiralling agriculture sector, alongside a burgeoning but insulated tourism sector, it should hardly be surprising that the issue of agro-tourism, and its scope for brokering intersectional linkages have now assumed an important place in the consciousness of many regional thinkers, policy makers, and entrepreneurs. The Regional Conference on Agro-tourism was, therefore, conceived as a forum for discussion, sharing and learning on this complex subject.

## THE EMERGING ISSUES

While the conference engaged participants in discussion and introspection on a wide range of issues, a number of key thematics consistently emerged during the three days of deliberations. From the onset, one such issue was an enduring definition and conceptualisation of agro-tourism, and many presenters opined on the subject. A second issue had to do with the historical antecedents and scope of agro-tourism globally, while the role of the community in brokering an agro-tourism development strategy evolved as a third discussion thematic. Each of these issues is addressed in turn below.

### Agro-Tourism: Towards a Definition

In attempting to fashion a concept and definition, it became readily apparent that the common view of agro-tourism was that of an inter-sectoral arrangement whereby the agriculture sector supplied food and drink, often in it's primary form, to the tourist sector. This idea is nevertheless quite limiting, in so far as it speaks primarily to the *linkages* aspect of agro-tourism. Many presenters, however, offered insights, which afforded a more profound and broadened notion of the topic. Thomas (2000) suggests that beyond the matter of linkages, agro-tourism involves the presentation of the existing agriculture itself as a part of the overall tourism product. In this regard, he contends that agro-tourism should involve direct interaction of the agricultural producer and his or her agricultural products, with tourists.

With this definitional schematic established, other presenters sought to add substance by citing a few additional properties. One of these is the property of locality in which agro-tourism, for it to be such, must take place within an agricultural region or environment. Indeed, it has been suggested that the idea of an agricultural region as a tourist destination is paramount to the understanding of the concept of agro-tourism (Graham B.L., 2000).

Charles (2000) also proposes another important property, which is the sharing of the intellectual legacy and heritage of the agricultural community with visitors in such a manner as to enhance understanding, and appreciation of the community. This heritage could include agricultural traditions, technologies and even folkways in the use of agricultural output. Hence the set of socioeconomic activities that take place in an agricultural region so as to link travel with products, services and experiences of the agricultural and food systems form the essentials of an agro-tourism economy.

Having added these elements of form to the definition of agro-tourism, the challenge of setting the boundaries for agro-tourism then emerged. Here, MacDonald (2000), supported by Thomas, argue an agro-tourism definition more from the standpoint of what it is *not* rather that what it is. Based on the tenets of an industrial strategy, MacDonald notes that agro-tourism is not *ecotourism* since agro-tourism allows for a process which transcends the normal limits imposed by the eco-system on both tourism and agriculture. As such, agro-tourism offers greater developmental scope to the extent that it seeks to solve agricultural problems, by exploiting the industrial potential of a dynamic tourism sector. It is presumed that the level of organisation and processes of the tourism sector makes it the more 'industrial sector', which could exert industrial influence on the agriculture sector in an agro-tourism context. In this way, *both* the tourism and agriculture sectors are transformed, by becoming more highly diversified and more sustainable. In a similar vein, Thomas posits that agro-tourism should not to be diffused into the notionally broader idea of *rural tourism*, but should be regarded as a well-defined segment of rural tourism in which the direct interaction of both sectors within the rural space, is emphasised.

Jayawardena (2000) offers a simple but effective contextual framework for agro-tourism, by classifying it as a sub-set of the broader group of *special-interest tourism*. Within this group is to be found *Adventure Tourism, Community-Tourism, Health Tourism,* and *Agro-tourism*. As shown in figure 1, agro-tourism involves some or all of these sub-sets, but attains currency through its emphasis on the interaction between the location-based agricultural products and services, and the tourism sector.

## Agro-Tourism: It's Not New!

The conference also offered participants an opportunity to learn of the historical and geographic scope of agro-tourism. It was noted quite repeatedly, that often times it was not the practice of agro-tourism itself which was lacking, but the recognition of an enterprise as an agro-tourism one which precluded our appreciation of this activity.

However, Thomas (2000) notes that the practice of agro-tourism has been with us for more than 100 years, with areas such as Ireland, USA, Australia and New Zealand having well-established agro-tourism industries. Even within the Caribbean, countries such as Barbados (Crop Over Festival), Saint Lucia (Mamiku Gardens,

**Figure 1:**

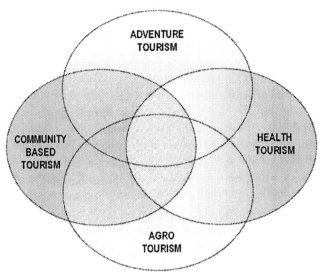

Coubaril Estate) and Jamaica (Yam Festival, Appleton Estate) have sought to at least embellish their tourism offerings by an appeal to some aspects of their agricultural legacy or practice. Today, countries such as Canada and Thailand have declared stated intentions to become global leaders in the agro-tourism industry. The conference noted that the recognition of the agro-tourism strategy as a relatively old one, provides both challenges and opportunities to the Caribbean region in terms of embarking on a similar strategy. With respect to opportunities, this means that there are already practising agro-tourism centres from whose experience the region could draw in developing and implementing an agro-tourism strategy. At the same time, the key challenge is to be able to act expeditiously, so as to fashion the required policy framework which could make the region a significant international player in this burgeoning sub-sector.

## *Agro-tourism: A Community Development Tool*

The importance of the community was recognised from at least two dimensions. One such dimension is the possibility for involving the *total* community in the development effort. This has distinctive implications for rural women and youth, for whom an expanded regime of economic and social activities could be brokered under an agro-tourism strategy. As noted by Kambon (2000), within the region, the share of youth unemployment exceeds 30 per cent in most countries, while it is higher still for *females*. Furthermore, women generally receive lower wages than men for the same work. An agro-tourism strategy for community development offers the prospect of enhanced utilisation of productive resources in the community.

A second dimension relates to the enhancement of the physical, social and economic infrastructure which takes place consequent upon the pursuit of an agro-tourism strategy. As suggested by MacDonald (2000), the synergy generated by both sectors becomes the driving force for economic activities not previously contemplated in the singular development of each sector. Such effects are perhaps best demonstrated in the experience from the *Rubano Project* in Brazil, as presented in figure 2.

## Figure 2:
## Dynamism of Agro-tourism: A Brazil Case Study

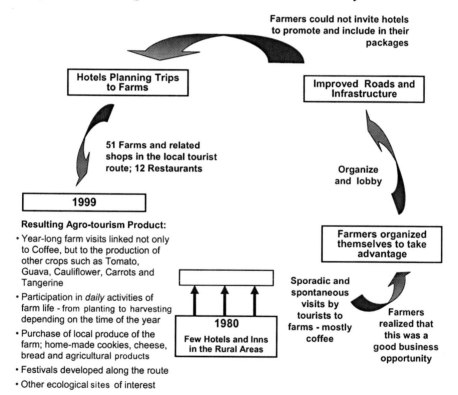

Source: Taken from Project Rubano

Based on figure 2, some time in the early 1980s coffee farmers began to observe that tourists from a nearby touristic sub-region were making sporadic visits to their farms. They soon realised that this offered a good business opportunity, and organised themselves so as to fully exploit this opportunity. The organisation process involved the formation of an active lobby to encourage the hotels to include farms on their tour agendas, as well as to bring about infrastructure improvements to support this type of activity in the farming region. By 1999, farm visits had mushroomed into a dynamic economic activity involving as many as 51 farms, 12 restaurants, related shops and other attractions along a well-defined rural route. Many of the activities became established as year-round activities, which complemented the seasonal nature of the farming enterprises. Moreover, this development expanded to include, not only coffee producers, but also other farming types as well as indigenous post-harvesting, processing and rural culinary activities.

Notwithstanding the positive Brazilian experience documented above, the achievement of a successful agro-tourism strategy could often be stymied by the potential for conflicts among stakeholders of the agro-tourism product. This aspect has been described by Mason and Milne (2000) as the 'ugly' side of the agro-tourism linkage experience, and has been documented throughout the world of international tourism. The case of tour operators exacerbating problems of local development in Madagascar; tension between local residents and international developers over land use at the Saint Lucia Jalousie Project (Pattullo 1997); and friction between resort operators and fisher-folk, with respect to beach access at Tobago's Club Pigeon Point are but some examples.

The issue is important in the context of the community and agro-tourism, since the prospects for reducing potential conflicts are greatest where the benefits of agro-tourism development are both demonstrable and tangible to all agents in the community. To achieve this, communication, participation, education and infrastructural support are but a few of the critical ingredients in planning a feasible policy framework for development (Mason and Milne, 2000).

## AN ENABLING ENVIRONMENT FOR FOSTERING AGRO-TOURISM REQUIRED

By the conclusion of the conference, it was abundantly clear that a requisite enabling environment is key to the development of a successful agro-tourism sub-sector. Such an environment must provide space for at least three key elements, these being community participation, eco-system sustainability, and, a harmonised institutional and policy framework. The first two of these elements have been found to be intimately related in a strategic context.

*Community Participation and Eco-system Sustainability*

Strategising an enabling environment for community participation in agro-tourism is a necessity for success, since this approach enhances the probability of attaining a sustainable link between preservation of cultural systems, ecological processes and social and economic development (Kersten, 1997; Brandon, 1993; Horwich, 1993).

According to Kersten (1997) citing Woodley (1973), a community approach to tourism suggests the development of a community as a core component of a tourism destination area or tourism product. At the same time it suggests some control by residents over tourism development and management. However, Kersten in his own writings on nature-based tourism, recognises the limited perspective of this approach in that it does not highlight the importance of the maintenance of the ecological processes. He proposes an approach that combines, ecological processes, tourism, socioeconomic development and cultural preservation. By adding the agriculture or farm component we would have defined the scope of the enabling environment for agro-tourism. In Kersten's own words *'a truly grand task'*.

Figure 3, below is a modification of Medar's (2000) concept of ecotourism and is an attempt to show the inter-relationships of the components for community

## Figure 3:
## Components of an Enabling Environment for Sustainable Agro-tourism

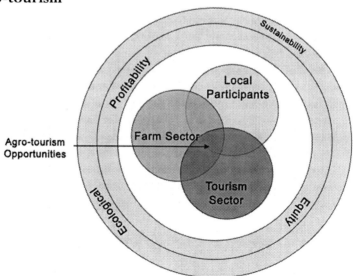

Source: Graham and Phillips, 2000 Dynamism of Agro-tourism: A Brazil Case Study

based agro-tourism. It suggests that while agro-tourism allows one to transcend *the normal limits* imposed by the ecosystem, ultimately, economic developments are constrained by considerations of ecological sustainability. Of paramount importance here, are local communities with the capacity to participate in sustainable development.

Because of the relevance of issues of ecological sustainability to agriculture and tourism they remain integral to the argument for a rational strategy towards agro-tourism development. Firstly, a large and significant part of the region's tourism is based on aspects of its ecosystem's biological diversity: habitats, plants and animals and ecological processes in the biosphere. Secondly, for a very long time yet, the success for agro-tourism will rely on a vibrant mass tourism sector, from which an adequate percentage of tourists with an interest in visiting agro-tourism sites would be necessary, to make it a viable form of tourism. Hence, those factors which impact on mass tourism, are likely to impact on visitorship to agro-tourism locations. In tourism circles these ecological processes translate into a commodity that comprises goods and services for health and recreation. Hence, practices that degrade and destroy these natural ecological processes and reduce the capacity of eco-systems' functioning will impact negatively on all tourism including agro-tourism.

Thomas (2000) and MacDonald (2000) remind us that agro-tourism transcends linkages between agriculture and tourism. There is no doubt that the sharpest evidence of this is the complex relationship with the natural resource base and the related ecological processes. All of the products of agriculture are dependent on the diversity and proper functioning of ecosystems. Sometimes they are the same ecosystems that serve mainstream tourism. For example, forests, other plant communities and ponds increase infiltration of rainwater and enhance soil water availability for agriculture. These same ecosystems also preserve habitats and the tropical greenery that attract visitors to the region.

Ecosystems and their processes also determine the culture and practices of agriculture in farming communities. Agro-tourism integrates all of these and brings into sharp focus the symbiotic relationship between agriculture and tourism.

The context of the Trinidad and Tobago conference did not allow for a comprehensive analysis and presentation on an enabling environment for ecological sustainability. However, the pervasive nature of freshwater reserves in issues of ecological sustainability makes the case of water resources management a suitable point of departure for demonstrating the value of an enabling environment for the development of the region's agro-tourism potential.

## Ecosystem Sustainability in Agro-tourism: The Case of Fresh Water

Requirements for water for tourism although not clearly defined within municipal water, is the most critical input in the region's tourism industry. With the bulk of visitors arriving during the dry season, water requirements are highest when volumes are lowest. Disruptions in municipal water supply are frequent experiences during this period. The tendency during these difficult supply periods is to give preference to those geographical areas which house visitor lodgings, and related facilities: restaurants, theme parks, swimming pools, lawns and golf courses. It is estimated that in Jamaica current requirements for potable water for the sector is 10 times that of potable water for residents (Lawrence, 1999), while in The Bahamas potable water for the sector is 3-5 times higher than the national average for residents (Weech, 1999).

## Table 3:
## Status of water resources for Caribbean states

| Island State | Water Availability Mcm/yr. | | Water Supply Mcm/yr. | | Future Use Mcm/yr. | Desal. Plants | Comments |
|---|---|---|---|---|---|---|---|
| | GW | SW | GW | SW | | | |
| Saint Kitts | 6.63 | 3. 32 | 5. 0 | | 8. 3 | - | High demand in tourist season. No irrigation. |
| Nevis | | 3. 02 | 1. 82 | | 2. 7 | - | Tourism expansion. |
| Grenada | 1.7 | 8 - 11.6 | 0. 8 | 8. 0 | - | 2 | Livestock watering sacrificed during dry season. |
| Saint Vincent | N/A | 95 est. (1971) | N/A | N/A | - | - | Rainwater harvesting common. Hotels use rain and Desal. Irrigation schemes planned. |
| Antigua & Barbuda | | 4. 6 | 4. 6 | | 5. 2 (2010) | 2 | Rainwater harvesting by law UFW high 40%. |
| Dominica | - | 26 | - | >16 | N/A | - | Exports water. Irrigation planned. |
| Haiti | | 0. 13 | 0. 013 | | 0.22 | - | |
| Saint Lucia | N/A | N/A | - | 9 | 15 (2025) | - | Tourism expansion Planned. |
| Suriname | N/A | N/A | - | 3153 | - | - | Over 85% for irrigation of rice. |
| Belize | N/A | N/A | - | 3.1 | - | - | Supply for citrus and banana irrigation. No data on domestic supply. |
| Bahamas | | 696 | 41 – 50 | | - | Several | GW, Desal and Barging |
| Guyana | | 2355 - 11775 | 65 | | - | - | Quality constraints on use. |
| Barbados | 76 | 6. 3 | > 76 | >6. 3 | - | 1 | 1 Mcm/yr. Available from the recycling of wastewater. |
| Jamaica | 3419 | 666 | 850 | 76 | 1684 (2015) | - | Irrigation use to increase. |

There could be little argument that there is a regional policy shift towards the promotion of tourism as the engine of growth. This means that the demand for water by tourism will increase in the short to medium term and perhaps significantly, with concomitant demand shortfalls for other economic sectors such as agriculture. The situation is rendered even more precarious, considering that the chance for sustainability is virtually unknown since most of the countries have not completed freshwater availability assessments and are consequently unaware of their current capacities to satisfy inter-sectoral demands for water.

It is, therefore, not surprising that based on the available data on the status of water resources management, the Conference was concerned that planned development and consumption of water resources in the region, is not now sustainable even for tourism and agriculture alone as shown in table 3.

Figure 4, illustrates the sources of water and the various sectoral demands that must be satisfied.

## Figure 4:
## Water Sources and Inter-Sectoral Demands

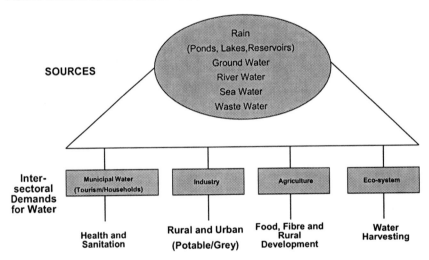

Source: Adapted from 'Proposal for Integrated Water Resources Management for the Caribbean" Second Joint Meeting of the Special Committees for the Protection and Conservation of the Environment and the Caribbean Sea and Natural Resources

Note that in reality much of municipal water/potable water is being used for agriculture, industry and recreation at the expense of potable water. However, any meaningful discourse on sustainable use of water must recognise that the freshwater reserves (ground water); habitats (wetlands, ponds, lakes, mangrove swamps, waterfalls, rivers, natural springs), forests and scrub-lands, biotic communities for butterflies and birds, as well as coastal and marine waters, are all part of an inter-dependent water cycle as presented in figure 5.

There is, therefore, really no escaping from the proper management of each of the ecological processes which contributes to the functioning of the water cycle if a successful agro-tourism development strategy is to be achieved. Any development action that degrades, destroys or places too much pressure on parts of this interdependent water cycle has the potential to reduce quality and quantity of freshwater over the long-term. In order to avoid unexpected limitations to development it is important that measures be put in place to ensure that projected rates of economic development is consistent with water demand.

## Figure 5:
## General Description of the Water Cycle (Shiklomanov, 1999)

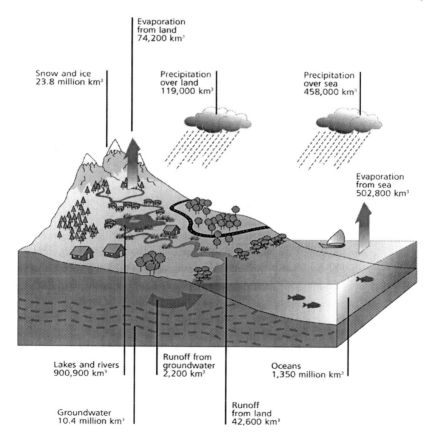

Against this background, it is only natural that a gathering on agro-tourism would immediately identify with the significance of wise ecosystem management. As noted earlier, agro-tourism is location based. It is also nature-based. The symbiotic nature of the agro-tourism product makes it totally dependent on the capacity of the agro-ecosystems in which the enterprise is located to continue to deliver those good and services which it promises over the long term. This water reserve in ecosystems, is critical to the integrity of agro-ecosystems on which the region's agro-tourism depends. Its primary attributes include: productive soils for agriculture, diversity in plants, fish and animals for diversity and higher levels of productivity in agriculture; as well as for scenic tours and hikes, fibre for traditional craft, habitats for animals, herbs and plants that support traditional practices, culture, and just plain greenery.

The case of water proved to be a good point of departure for emphasising the rationale for an enabling environment. While the subject was certainly not entirely explored, the information presented was sufficient to point to the urgency for an appropriate strategy that will facilitate development at a pace that is in tandem with the ecological processes. Failure, to do this in a timely manner will jeopardise long-term prosperity through the many goods and services of ecological processes and which make up the tourism product of the region.

At the same time, the adoption of the community-based approach in a framework of ecological sustainability requires a strategy that enables community building for community development and participation. It has implications for achieving a level of social organisation capability and social organisational culture. This approach is, therefore, strategic since it fosters the basic foundation for economic well being of the communities.

## *Harmonised Institutional and Policy Framework Critical*

An ecologically sustainable regime apart, a harmonised institutional framework for the implementation of any agro-tourism strategy is another critical element of a feasible enabling environment. In discussing this issue, Noel (2000) focuses on the local policy framework, and identified elements such as education and training, land-use, and the environment. Education and training were considered to be important since this would serve to inform relevant stakeholders of the opportunities and responsibilities which would be involved in pursuing an agro-tourism strategy. Land use policy, especially with respect to zoning was also identified, since the potential for conflicting land use activities between agriculture and tourism is real. Related to this was the issue of environmental policy, particularly in respect of water use, wastewater and sewerage disposal and possible impact of agricultural chemical run off on the natural environment. Policies, which establish common ground for dealing with the environment, by both sectors, were also deemed to be important.

In a regional context, however, Springer (2000) emphasises the value of a more holistic regional policy framework for agro-tourism development. Such a framework should be based on elements such as a smart partnership philosophy and practice, in which all the regional social partners share a common vision of national development. Based on this philosophy, any regional policy should aim at the attainment of global market access. To achieve this, an ordered approach to the generation of agro-tourism business projects, the engendering of a strong entrepreneurial culture, and good venture capital support and technical assistance is critical.

## AGRO-TOURISM: A NEW REGIME OF OPPORTUNITIES

The regime of new opportunities presented by community-based agro-tourism fall largely into four categories: economic, social, technological, and financial.

### *Economic Opportunities*

The economic opportunities are primarily the new and/or improved agri-enterprises. According to Anderson and Lieison (1980), exclusively agricultural households have lower incomes than households with farm and non-farm incomes. In the case of agro-tourism the multi-active farm household derives from the introduction of leisure services into the daily operations of a farm or agricultural region, without disrupting the productive farming operations of the farm or the region. Mostly it is achieved by identifying new activities for commercialisation of traditionally unused farm family time, better organisation of the farm operations in order to attract the curiosity of visitors, and the creative linking of off-farm activities to the agro-tourism product.

Project Rubano, described earlier in this chapter is a very good example of the dynamic nature of agro-tourism. Many other good examples of diversification within the agricultural enterprises and creating linkages are found in Latin America, Asia, and Europe in particular Spain. In promoting farm tourism (agro-tourism) in the Basque Country of Spain, farmers capitalise on the many mythological characters associated with the geography and culture of the area. Mythological characters such as Mori and Lamik are incorporated in farm presentations. Festivals, rural sports and the fresh or cooked foods of the area are worked into the product. Gastronomy is a major part of the goods and services provided. In the case of Mary Barlow a farmer in Michigan, the idea was to bridge the gap between young people and agriculture. She packaged her farm and educational tours for school children and found that parents and grandparents also came. In the words of Barlow as reported by Moses (1999) *the tourist is the newest cash crop.*

The capacity to identify enterprising opportunities in agro-tourism is not beyond our small farmers in the region. In December of 2000, the Ministry of Agriculture, Forestry and Fisheries in Saint Lucia collaborated with the Saint Lucia Heritage Tourism Limited and the IICA to host a *Agro-tourism Workshop for the Southern Micro-region.* At that workshop small farmers identified a range of new agro-tourism opportunities for the micro-region. The starting point was their main farming activities, the growing of vegetables, bananas, root crops, tree and fruit crops, husbandry of livestock (small ruminants, poultry, dairy and swine). They quickly identified leisure and service activities which incorporated the culture and productive activities of the micro-region. Animal presentations (poultry farms and animal interaction) and animal sports (goat racing, crab catching, racing and eating). Introduction of organic gardening using locally grown seaweed was also identified. Nature and heritage tours included the history of the agricultural area, of the crops and the traditional and current technologies linked to these crops. In fact the possibilities were quite exhaustive. Traditional cooking including classes and tasting, sale of fresh and processed products from the farm, trails and scenic tours from the farm into the scenic forests, folk music, traditional Indian weddings, festivals such as *Jounen Kweyol* were worked into the agro-tourism possibilities which the farmers presented.

Increased production of fresh food for hotels and production of raw materials for craft and souvenirs were also identified as opportunities. Hotels participating in the tours would naturally want to serve some of the fresh farm produce in their restaurants. Production of agricultural raw materials that can be the base for souvenirs was also an option.

Really new opportunities exist in concepts such as island nature games, which could foster networking among the island systems. The establishment of service malls in agricultural communities, showing off the agricultural practices and culture and encouraging interactions with the farming community are also possibilities.

The organisation of the heterogeneous goods and services that make up agro-tourism takes the farmer or the farming community into a new realm. It requires an enterprise approach, good organisational and management skills, reliability and timeliness in the delivery of services, knowledge of the technologies and processes of the farm, and compliance to standards. Agro-tourism therefore creates the opportunity to improve the way agriculture does business pushing the actors to a higher level of economic competitiveness. It has implications for modernisation as appropriate, good accounting (farm records), improved marketing strategies and profitability as a goal. It has real opportunities for raising the commitment to entrepreneurship among the farming communities and to change the growing perception of the sector as one which is important for its social benefits rather than its economic productivity.

## Social Opportunities

Agro-tourism brings with it a new level of social organisation and hence, opportunities for social development to the communities involved. This derives from the multifaceted nature of agro-tourism. It impacts on health services, education, training in hospitality, infrastructure (roads, communication, sanitation and hygiene, transportation) fire and security. It is, therefore, a good tool to facilitate the connection of all these aspects of social development within the communities concerned.

As seen in Project Rubano, with public sector support communities begin to appreciate the benefits of a collective or co-operative approach, and of consensus and goals in order to negotiate for the public sector benefits. Also, because agro-tourism is locally-based and locally managed, opportunities are created to foster leadership and public awareness and to empower communities to participate efficiently in the development issues that impact on their welfare.

Improvement in welfare of agricultural communities cannot be achieved only in modernisation of agriculture. Furthermore, there is a point at which communities, which are largely made up of small farmers, can no longer participate at another level of modernisation. Agro-tourism provides the opportunity of a process that fosters capacity building to explore in a rational and sustainable manner the potential benefits from diversification within and among the resources available to these communities.

## Technology Opportunities

Agro-tourism can be the vector for incorporating communities into the benefits of developing technologies that increase their ability to compete. Mason and Milne (2000) cite New Zealand's experience in the application of information technology (IT), as a very useful tool in contemporary agro-tourism for enhancing marketing, as well as brokering consensus among community stakeholders.

The case of the Golden Bay Region of Nelson, New Zealand demonstrates the application of Geographic Information Technologies (GIS) to gather critical information for planning a resources use strategy which is amenable to both local ecotourism operators, and aqua-culture producers. By gathering and analysing all relevant information, the process offers an opportunity for the involvement of all stakeholders, in ultimately designing a sustainable and harmonious plan for the use of the natural resources in the Golden Bay area.

A second application of IT technologies is that of *'Web Raising'* in which the Internet is exploited to engender capacity building within rural communities, by reducing provider isolation and more effectively utilising resources. In this way, rural tourism could better connect with international tourist flows. In many countries outside of the region, mapping of agro-tourism sites and the use of e-commerce have also brought to rural communities an appreciation for information management and speed of transmitting or receiving information in the competitive tourism sector. These modern methods of transforming knowledge into information and action will no doubt spill over into the normal day to day activities of regional agro-tourism, thereby building new capacities for competition among rural peoples.

Yet another exciting new opportunity for using technology well is by exploiting the concept of remote tourism. In this manner the agro-tourism product can be enjoyed millions of miles away from the agro-tourism location. There are good benefits in that it preserves the agro-tourism location, by reducing physical visitorship, while still providing the same level of pleasure to the user of the CD Rom or the website. It also extends the economic benefits of agro-tourism to rural communities that are still difficult to reach.

Agro-tourism can also impact on the application of modern production technologies on the farm. It presents a real opportunity to package and promote traditional technologies and practices as a commodity. For example, farmers in Jamaica have the opportunity of showing off the process in making the Blue Mountain Coffee, or of making the internationally desired jerk pork, or the traditional ways of firing Jamaican pottery. In Saint Lucia and Jamaica, opportunities exist to create a leisure enterprise from the technologies in cassava food processing. Traditional creole-bread making in Saint Lucia and the many traditional ways of making cane juice, across the region are also interesting technologies. The production technologies for the well known Antigua Black (pineapple) in Antigua and Barbuda, enjoyed by so many visitors, is another example of the technologies which could be packaged and marketed, thus changing the perception of them being rural and uncompetitive.

Similar ideas could be generated around the history of well-known names such as Jamaica Red and Jamaica Black cattle breeds or the Barbados Black Belly Sheep. There are also the water conservation and, energy-saving technologies and the history and processing of herbal medicines, all of which can be creatively packaged and presented as a good or leisure commodity. The activities listed here and many others already enjoy a level of curiosity either because of the myths surrounding them, their innovativeness or the longevity of their economic and cultural relevance.

There is a challenge in packaging the technologies in order for them to have the appeal of a tourism product, but this is not beyond the combined intellect of tourism and agriculture.

*Financial Opportunities*

Finally, there are many international non-governmental organisations with interest and the willingness to provide financial and institutional support to regions, which, by their actions, show commitment to proper management of natural resources. This is even more attractive when the actions are linked to human development. Debt swapping and its link to natural resources management has also been practised in the region. There are ways in which the region could position itself to benefit from such sources of funding. Agriculture or tourism on their own has not been able to access these sources of funding despite its link with the natural resources. Sources of financing such as GEF and the Ecotourism Society are very under-utilised in the region. A primary regional objective could be to put in place planning models to link agro-tourism, poverty alleviation and welfare and ecosystem sustainability.

## CONCLUSION: THE WAY FORWARD

According to FAO (internet sources - SARD) the prices of agricultural commodities exported by small island developing states are likely at best to rise only marginally as a result of the Uruguay Round Agreement on Agriculture. Already countries in the region which have benefited in the past from preferential access to developed markets are experiencing reductions in export earnings and reduced levels of rural employment in agriculture. The impact on rural households and increased poverty is already being felt in some countries. Invariably lower incomes or loss of incomes will result in a breakdown in social organisation and in increased environmental degradation.

Several writers, among them Graziano de Silva and Del Grossinn (2000); Kersten (1997) have demonstrated that agricultural households can sustain or increase their incomes by incorporating non-farm activities in their daily activities. Agro-tourism appears to be an alternative not only to maintaining economic activities, but also in embracing all the dimensions of sustainable development.

Barkin (1999) suggests that agricultural or rural communities are the most likely to be the losers in what could be a 'permanent economic olympics' fostered by new trading arrangements for agricultural commodities. Agro-tourism offers an opportunity to allow communities to diversify and produce new goods and services to an area of trade, which allows them to continue to participate in the global trading system in a sustainable manner. Furthermore, the actors can foster the integration of their traditional function as custodians of the natural resources into their development process. It therefore promotes sustainability and development.

Finally, it is clear that agro-tourism would have to be part of a broader regional or national strategy to seriously address some of the structural aspects of policy and institutions. What agro-tourism can do is to provide the framework and a process for field-testing the way forward for sustainable economic growth in the region.

# BIBLIOGRAPHY

Alexander, M. R. 1999. 'Farmer turns to Agro-tourism', *The Detroit News*.

Anderson, D. and M. Leiserson. 'Rural Non-Farmer Employment in Developing Countries', *Economic Development and Cultural Change* 28, no. 2 (1980): 227-248.

Barkin, D. 1996. *Ecotourism - A tool for Sustainable Development*.

Brandon, K. 1993. 'Basic steps towards encouraging local participation in nature tourism projects'. In *Ecotourism*, eds. Lindberg/Hawkins, 134-151.

Campanhold, C. and J. G. de Silva. 2000. 'Projecto Rubano - Tourism in the rural area: A new opportunity for small farmers' (internet source).

CEPAL. Summary of Economic Survey of Latin America and the Caribbean, 1998-1999.

Charles, H. 2000. 'Opening Address – Regional Agro-tourism Conference, Tobago'. Trinidad and Tobago: IICA Regional Agro-tourism Conference.

Fernandez B. P. Proposal for Integrated Water Resources Management for the Caribbean, Food Security and the Environment. World Food Summit, Rome, 13-17 November 1996.

Fernandez B. P. and L. B. Graham. 'Sustainable Economic Development Through Integrated Water Resources Management in the Caribbean'. Paper presented to the 11 Water Meeting, Montevideo, Uruguay, June 15 –18 1999.

———. 'Sustainable Economic Development through Integrated Water Resources Management in the Caribbean'. COMUNIICA no 14, (2000): 39-43.

Francis, D. 2000. 'Some Economic Experiences of Caribbean Agriculture in the 1990s', (2000). Publication Forthcoming.

Horwich, R. H. *et al*. 1993. 'Ecotourism and community development: A view from Belize'. In eds. Lindberg/Hawkins.

IICA 1999. 'Diversification of the Saint Lucian Agricultural Economy Through Agrotourism'. A joint endeavour of the Florida State University, The Florida Association of Voluntary Agencies for Caribbean Action and the Inter-American Institute for Cooperation on Agriculture.

———. 1999. 'A Synthesis of Country Reports on Water Resources Management in the Caribbean'. Inter-American Institute for Cooperation on Agriculture.

———. 1999. 'Performance and Prospects for Caribbean Agriculture', (Inter-American Institute for Cooperation on Agriculture.

IUCN-The World Conservation Union. 2000. 'Vision for Water and Nature. A World Strategy for Conservation and Sustainable Management of Water Resources in the 21st Century'. IUCN-The World Conservation Union.

Jayawardena, C. and H. McDavid. 2000. 'The Implications of Agro-tourism in the Caribbean'. Trinidad and Tobago: IICA Regional Agro-tourism Conference.

Kambon A. 2000. 'Placing Women and Youth Within the Framework of an Agro-tourism Strategy'. Trinidad and Tobago: IICA Regional Agro-tourism Conference.

Lawrence, S. 1999. 'Macro-economic conditions and sustainable agriculture and rural development'. *http://www.fao.org.sard*.

Lawrence, S. 1999. 'Agro-tourism, Farm Tourism in the Basque Country'. Internet Source.

Mac Donald, C. 2000. 'Agro-tourism – New Dimensions of Industrialisation in the Caribbean'. Trinidad and Tobago: IICA Regional Agro-tourism Conference.

McKercher, B. & Robbins, B., 'Developing Successful Nature-based Tourism Business: An Operator's Perspective' (1997).

Mader, R. 'Latin America New Ecotourism: What is it?'. *http://www.planeta.com.madder* (1999-2000).

Madramootoo C.A. 1999. 'From a Green to a Blue Planet. Brace Centre for Water Resources Management'. McGill University, Montreal, Canada, 1999).

Milne S., & Mason D. 2000. 'Linking Tourism and Agriculture: Innovative Information technology Solutions'. Trinidad and Tobago: IICA Regional Agro-tourism Conference.

Mwansa, B. J. 1999. 'The Impact of Tourism on Water Resources Management in Barbados'.

Noel C. 2000. 'Developing the Linkage Between the Tourism and Agricultural Sectors'. Trinidad and Tobago: IICA Regional Agro-tourism Conference.

Organisation of American States. 1984. Reference Guidelines for Enhancing the Positive Socio-cultural and Environmental Impact of Tourism. Washington, DC : volume 1.

International Fund for Agriculture Development. IFAD Technology Systems for Small Farmers-Issues and Options, (1994).

Pattullo P. 1998. *Cost of Tourism in the Caribbean, Last Resorts*. Kingston: Ian Randle Publishers.

Pattullo, P. 1996. *Last Resorts – The Cost of Tourism in the Caribbean*. London: Cassell.

Shiklomanov I.A. 1999. 'World water resources: modern assessment and outlook for the 21st century'. Federal Service of Russia for Hydrometeorology and Environmental Monitoring: State Hydrological Institute.

Socioeconomic Impact of Restructuring the Banana Industry in Saint Lucia. 'West Indian Commission-Time for Action'. Barbados, Overview of the Report of the WIC 1992.

Springer B. 2000. 'Towards a Regional Policy for Agro-tourism Linkages'. Trinidad and Tobago: IICA Regional Agro-tourism Conference.

The United Nations. 1998. University, Work in Progress. A Review of Research Activities of the United Nations University 15 no. 2. The United Nations University.

The World Conservation Union. 1999. Water for Food and Rural Development. The World Conservation Union.

The World Conservation Union, Water and Nature. 'Freshwater and Related Ecosystems-The Source of Life and the Responsibility of All'. November 25, 1999. The World Conservation Union.

Thomas, C. 2000. 'Product Innovation: Reflecting on the Prospects for Agro-tourism in the Caribbean'. Trinidad and Tobago: Proceedings, Regional Agro-tourism Conference, IICA.

USAID. 1999 Caribbean Regional Program-Assistance Strategy 2000-2005, 1999. Agency for International Development.

Weaver, D. 1998. *Ecotourism in the Less Developed World*. New York: CAB International.

Weech, P. 1999. Case Study Water Resources in The Bahamas. Water Resources in the context of the imperatives of Tourism Industry in The Bahamas.

Williams, P. 1994. Farm Based Tourism and Leisure: A Step Further. East Essex, UK: Nuffield Farming Scholarship Trust.

Wood, M. E. 1997. 'Ecotravelling into the Century'. Article from the Greenmoney Journal.

# 9

# GENERATING AGRO-TOURISM OPTIONS IN THE CARIBBEAN: A COST-EFFECTIVE MODEL

David Mason and Simon Milne

## ABSTRACT

*Agro-tourism can increase the earnings and quality of life of rural communities. While there are many examples of successful agro-tourism initiatives there are many examples of difficulties in maximising the links between tourism and agriculture. In part this reflects ambivalence as to what agro-tourism is, or should be, and a lack of a common definition. More importantly progress will only be made when all involved can learn to extract the potential that lies in every farm and village. This chapter demonstrates an orthogonal model, which works by systematically evaluating elements of rural assets and thus generates ideas for new tourism products. While this will not guarantee a winning formulation for every situation, it does guarantee to throw up multiple viable possible projects. The chapter shows how the model was used in three specific instances.*

## INTRODUCTION

Agriculture is often held up to be a sector that has much to gain from tourism development. Tourist-driven demand for a greater variety and higher quality of food encourages farmers to increase and diversify production. In many regions farms, and the rural lifestlye they sustain, also become an integral part of the broader tourism product.

There are numerous agro-tourism success stories. The Martinborough wine and food festival attracts over ten thousand visitors to one of the premier wine growing regions in New Zealand. The festival runs for two days just before the grape harvesting begins and offers a market, food stalls, open air entertainment, wine tasting and vineyard tours. Despite being forty kilometres over a twisty mountain road from the nearest large town, tickets are sold out within hours of going on advance sale.

During early spring in the North East USA and Canada thousands of visitors leave the cities to venture into maple syrup producing countryside for the well known 'sugaring-off' period. Visitors to small rural towns like Mont St Hilaire in Quebec are able to share in a hearty breakfasts of farm reared eggs and ham and are also encouraged to put fresh maple syrup, and to dip the syrup in large troughs of snow — to form instant maple syrup popsicles. For many small towns this represents a vital boost in income at a time of year when other sources of revenue are low.

A number of European nations have implemented national visitor schemes promoting 'agriculture' and farmstay programs (ETB, 1991). The French government, for example, promotes 'gites'. These are usually modest places, mostly conversions of old or disused farm buildings with government assistance. The government markets the gites internationally but lets the local owners, often pensioners, take the bookings and collect the monies. The scheme only applies in rural areas and puts visitors directly into farms and villages.

While there are many examples, particularly from the developed world, of successful agro-tourism product development and growing agriculture tourism linkages, much of the evidence from the developing world is less positive. In the Caribbean, for example, numerous studies note the failure of inter-sectoral linkages to develop and, in some cases stress that tourism can actually damage local agriculture (Bélisle, 1984; Patullo, 1996). The Caribbean is an area with a strong agricultural tradition and a bright tourism future. As such the region needs to examine how and where agro-tourism can be introduced. In this chapter we address some of the key issues raised in the literature on agro-tourism and then move on to outline a model that can enhance its development potential. We conclude with a series of case studies from the Caribbean, New Zealand and Canada that show how the model has generated new products, improved linkages and can be refined for use in very different cultural and environmental conditions.

## Agro-tourism

The authors deliberately take a broad-based approach to conceptualising agro-tourism in this chapter. The focus is on both agricultural tourism products and the linkage structures that exist between tourism and the agricultural sector. By products they mean tourism conducted on working farms (including aquaculture) and rural areas where the working environment forms part of the product from the perspective of the visitor. This definition is wider in scope than simple accommodation provision: covering attractions, activities and hospitality, plus mutually supportive combinations of product elements (CEC, 1990; Cox, 1991).

*143*

In terms of linkages, the authors step beyond a narrow focus on hotel food purchasing patterns and look at information flows, marketing and distribution mechanisms, demand for food as expressed by tourists, and infrastructure, production and farm-level constraints. They argue that agro-tourism involves understanding the relationships, mechanisms and interactions between the tourism industry, agricultural operations and intermediary (marketing and distribution) structures and human agents. They also draw on literature that focuses on both terrestrial and marine ecosystems and which also, on occasion, touches on the sustainable hunting of wildlife populations.

Thus, in an idealised setting, agro-tourism can be considered to be any agricultural activity that is related to tourism in some way (either directly or indirectly) and that mobilises the skills and resources of rural communities and spreads visitor expenditure through the local economy.

While several studies have advocated a similarly broad approach to defining agro-tourism (Denman and Denman, 1993; Lane, 1994) it is clear that the successful development of agro-tourism is not an easy goal to achieve. In fact there is a long history of the negative effects that come from introducing tourism into rural settings. The most commonly cited negative impacts include:

- competition for land resources (Dieke, 1993);
- inflated land values (Bélisle, 1984a);
- competition for labour resources (O'Ferral, 1991; Wilkinson, 1989);
- increased imports of food and foreign exchange leakages (Bélisle, 1983; Dieke, 1993; Taylor et al, 1991);
- increased local consumption of imported foods through the 'demonstration' effect (Gomes, 1993; Ryan, 1991);
- inflated food prices (Bélisle, 1984);
- changes in cropping patterns (Adams, 1992);
- decline in agricultural production (McElroy and Albuquerque, 1990); and
- deterioration of the natural resource base (West and Brechin, 1991).

There are also more subtle impacts associated with the links between tourism and agriculture. The inequitable distribution of tourism benefits (Freitag, 1996; Bookbinder et al, 1998) has led to community problems, such as loss of local control and damage to the social fabric of community life. Tourism can alter family structures or traditional gender-based division of labour and influence local production patterns. Migration to tourist areas can place pressure on local land and other resources, even to the extent that the areas that lose population may not have enough people to carry on with traditional rural activities (Torres, 1996).

The larger, chain-based operations that dominate accommodation in many nations tend to have fewer linkages with local agricultural producers than their smaller locally-owned counterparts. Recent work has shown that the 'all-inclusive' and cruise sectors often exhibit a limited ability to generate downstream benefits (Poon, 1998; Wilkinson, 1999; Wood, 2000).

However, none of this is inevitable. There are clear benefits from agro-tourism when properly implemented. Some of the positive outcomes of the links between tourism and agriculture that have been highlighted in the literature include:

- stimulation of new agricultural development (Cox et al, 1994; Tefler and Wall, 1996);
- increased profitability of agricultural production;
- creation of new market opportunities;
- the provision of increased or supplementary income for farmers;
- opportunities for economic diversification (O'Connor 1996; Oppermann 1997); and
- if used effectively local produce can provide a unique (and potentially cost effective) competitive advantage for hotels and restaurants (Midmore et al, 1996).

In some cases, there are clear benefits leading to increases in local employment, maintenance of rural landscapes, maintenance of local traditions and sense of place (ETB, 1991).

## THE IMPORTANCE OF PARTICIPATION

The literature points to a number of factors that limit the effectiveness of agro-tourism. Most of these centre on a lack of direct community/farmer participation in the planning and development process (Hudson, 1996; Fagence, 1998). The problems include difficulties in communication and understanding between the people involved, problems in monitoring market needs, lack of education, inadequate training opportunities, and poor infrastructure (Midmore et al, 1996; Drumm, 1998). Another factor related to participation is immediacy: unless residents receive tangible benefits from tourism and can exert some control over its development they may undermine the initiative — either covertly or overtly (Jenkins and Prin, 1997; Johnson et al, 1994).

For example, Campbell (1999) points to the fact that the limited benefits flowing to the community of Ostional in Costa Rica from tourism will remain so unless formalised planning and intervention take place — she argues for local control so that communities can have a vested interest in safeguarding wildlife habitats. Koch (1997) notes that tourism can only be used as a tool to reconstruct the rural economy if serious efforts are made to address obstacles that inhibit genuine community participation in these ventures — the importance of including local knowledge in the management of parks in particular.

*145*

Chambers (1997) has shown that participatory approaches have much to offer the policy-making process as they 'enable local people to share, enhance and analyse their knowledge of life and conditions and to plan, act, monitor and evaluate'. Local participation can generate important and often surprising insights producing policies more in tune with the needs of local residents and communities. More fundamentally, they can strengthen the understanding of those in authority and begin to change attitudes and agendas. Participation is not only one of the goals of social development, but an integral part of the social development process.

Patullo (1996) provides examples of successful Caribbean agro-tourism initiatives that have revolved around participatory approaches. In 1991 in Nevis the local growers association, livestock farmers co-op and Daly Farm (poultry) trading with a 200 room Four Seasons resort — set up under the guidance of the Caribbean Agricultural Research and Development Institute. In 1994 in Saint Lucia the Saint Lucia Hotel Association and the Ministry of Agriculture launched an 'adopt' a farmer pilot programme with two of the all-inclusives on the island (Sandals and Club Saint Lucia).

Midmore et al (1996), note some of the more common approaches adopted in attempts to improve linkages between the two sectors: product and service directories (public libraries etc), trade events where producers and hoteliers can meet, training courses, and market intelligence about shifting demand. There are opportunities for private sector action also, for example closer liaison between communities seeking to protect their resource base and way of life, and hotel managers using environmental marketing strategies (Olsen, 1997; Drumm, 1998).

## GENERATING AGRO-TOURISM OPPORTUNITIES

From the foregoing it is clear that there is no systemic barrier to agro-tourism, provided it is introduced with the full knowledge and support of those involved. If agro-tourism is to flourish, then local people have to be able to come up with viable and profitable ideas which suit their circumstances and needs. For people who are not active in the tourism industry this can be quite a daunting prospect.

In order to help people see the possibilities and to generate feasible schemes we have developed a framework for generating agro-tourism ideas. The framework consists of a three dimensional matrix which systematically evaluates each resource in combination with a set of visitor activities and patterns of visitation. The framework, given as table 1, does not guarantee to generate an award-winning tourism product, but with ten basic resources, multiplied by 14 potential activities involving that resource multiplied by three visitation durations, the resulting 300 or so possibilities are almost certain to present some viable ideas for discussion.

The model lists activities down the side and resources across the top. The third dimension refers to the duration of the visit. A *stop* is defined as a visit lasting less

**Table 1.**
**Framework for generating Agro-tourism ideas**

Stop | Visit | Stay

| | Land Buildings Produce Shelter History<br>Plants Animals Skills Technology Culture | | | | | | | | | | |
|---|---|---|---|---|---|---|---|---|---|---|---|
| Caring | | | | | | | | | | | |
| Drinking | | | | | | | | | | | |
| Eating | | | | | | | | | | | |
| Exercising | | | | | | | | | | | |
| Gathering | | | | | | | | | | | |
| Hunting | | | | | | | | | | | |
| Learning | | | | | | | | | | | |
| Making | | | | | | | | | | | |
| Participating | | | | | | | | | | | |
| Recording | | | | | | | | | | | |
| Relaxing | | | | | | | | | | | |
| Transport | | | | | | | | | | | |
| Watching | | | | | | | | | | | |
| Working | | | | | | | | | | | |

than one hour but more than simply a few minutes break in an otherwise continuous tour. A *visit* is defined as lasting more than an hour or two but not including an overnight stay. A *stay* is defined as any visit which includes overnight accommodation.

To use the model, take the first activity and consider how it can be applied to the first asset, then the second activity with the first asset, and so on, considering each activity in turn with that asset. Then repeat the exercise applying all activities to the second asset, then the third asset, and so on. The aim is to go through the combinations rapidly, to spark off ideas that can later be explored in depth.

## RESOURCES

The method uses common agriculture-based assets and systematically evaluates their tourism potential. Most potential agro-tourism operators will have resources of Animals, Buildings, Culture, Land, Plants, Produce, Technology, History, Skills and Crafts, and Shelter.

**Animals:** This resource can focus on the animals being reared for market, or the animals used for work such as horses or dogs, or the wild animals found in the area. Tourists are predominantly from urban backgrounds so any commonplace activity associated with animals can be an attraction. Domestic animals can be penned or stabled, or left free to roam among the visitors. Wild animals can be caged or be encouraged by feeding, or simply have their habitat conserved. Each stage of the cycle of animal husbandry can be used as an attraction. Horses can be shoed, sheep rounded up, goats milked, hens fed.

**Buildings:** These do not have to be old or magnificent. Visitors like seeing how other people live, and will happily tour ordinary domestic buildings. Farm buildings are of interest in explaining their role in the cycle of agriculture. Old, even decrepit, buildings can be of interest if they show changes in lifestyle. Disused granaries, dovecots, pens et cetera can be shown as is, or converted to museums or retail outlets. Former human habitations are of special interest such as slave quarters or tied cottages, or as illustrations of how life used to be. The domestic architecture of towns and villages can be of interest if the visitor is guided to show how they reflect the history of the area. Buildings for cultural purposes such as temples, jails, markets, cemeteries can all be pressed into service.

**Culture:** Most non-urban areas have a distinctive culture not found in towns, and this provides an ideal vehicle for hosting visitors. The country cycle of life is generally marked by festivals, markets, dancing, celebrations, and processions: each of these can be exploited as a visitor attraction. The range of cultural interests is endless. Carnivals, traditional dress, pageants, harvests, sports, religious events — all can be used as an attraction where appropriate.

**History:** Everything has a history and everyone is interested in history if it is interpreted appropriately. Agricultural history can deal with the crops, the land, the people, the rulers — any aspect can be featured for visitors. It can be supported by photographs, videos, museum displays, acting, guides or story telling.

**Land:** Land is the core of agriculture, but for tourism purposes can be used in many ways. Land is the basis of scenery, so it can be used to create viewing points for painting or photography, or camping and picnic spots. It can be used for exercise and exploration, especially parts not used for crops. Caves can be explored, sand dunes used for slides, hills for climbing. The land can also be used directly as in fossil hunting or archaeology. Wasteland can be used for trail biking or four wheel drive courses. Land includes water, marshes, scrub and forest. There is no feature of the land which cannot be used for something.

**Produce:** This includes crops, animals and their by-products. Most visitors only consume refined goods, and so know little about the varieties, stages and features of the raw product. These can be shown in their natural state as in rubber or coconut plantations, or in gardens demonstrating commercial varieties, or in museums showing the life cycle and pests and diseases. Almost any crop can be featured in a public festival, where it is eaten, feted, decorated, blessed or even destroyed.

**Skills and Crafts:** Farming has a unique set of skills. Ploughing, shearing, chopping and sawing can all be featured in competitions. Weaving, saddlery, tool making, knitting and other manual skills can be turned into exhibitions for tourists.

**Shelter:** Accommodation ranges from minimal to palatial. Campsites are cheap and simple. Old buildings can be converted to bunk houses for backpackers. Accommodation does not always mean overnight stays. It includes sun and wind shelters, huts for beaches, toilets, waiting rooms and bird watching hides.

**Technology:** Most tourists only see agricultural produce in its finished state so every stage of the processing cycle is interesting. When there is a manufacturing process involved this can be shown to tourists. Tea and coffee processing, cheese making, tanning, brewing, preserving have all been used as attractions, along with tasting and sales.

**Community Assets:** Potential resources can be privately held, or may be vested in the community such as market days and agricultural shows. This applies particularly to cultural and historic assets, (Clarke, 1999). There are thousands of events which fall into this category. Some large events like the Rio Carnival, the running of the bulls in Spain, and the blessing of the fleet in Azores are already major tourist attractions. Others of a smaller scale or more bizarre nature have real potential: goat racing in Tobago; cheese rolling in England and tomato fights in Spain.

## ACTIVITIES

The range of possible tourist activities is endless, but the model attempts to gather them under a few generic headings. The list of activities below is not exhaustive and other activities may apply in particular situations. Nor are they mutually exclusive. In general, the more of these activities that can be combined simultaneously, the better will be the visitor experience.

**Caring:** Visitors are strongly attracted to animals, birds and opportunities for grooming, petting and feeding. They are also interested in conservation of habitats and buildings, and can be encouraged to help local efforts.

**Drinking:** The normal expectation is the sampling or consumption of alcoholic drinks, but fruit juices and traditional drinks such as kava can be successfully used. This activity combines well with visitor education.

**Eating:** The scope for visitor participation covers the whole range of activities from harvesting, selecting, preparing, and cooking through to consuming. Visitor involvement can come through sampling in taste tests, through picnics, and can, of course, include complete waiter served meals. This can be combined with lessons in authentic cooking of local specialities.

**Exercising:** Walking is a major visitor interest, especially if guided, and visitor exercise can be extended to exploring and more strenuous activities such as sports, climbing and swimming.

**Gathering:** This involves the visitor seeking things in the agricultural context, usually after some training or education. Mushroom gathering, herb collection, flower picking and strawberries are well known. Tourists can also be encouraged to gather several elements of their own lunch or meal.

*149*

**Hunting.** This can be for the purposes of killing for food or prestige, or may be ecologically aware and involve catch and release programmes. It can also be applied to inanimate resources like gem searching, gold panning, or fossil hunting.

**Learning:** Education is a neglected element in tourism products. Education can be high-brow such as a presentation of the history of a building or region, or an explanation of interacting ecosystems. Or it can be quick and simple like showing how to catch and cook a fish.

**Making:** Visitors love to leave with something they made themselves so weaving, painting, carving, glass making and other craft exhibitions can be combined with participation and education to allow the visitor to have a little pride in ownership.

**Participating:** The opportunities for involving visitors in hands-on activities are probably greater in agro-tourism than in any other branch of tourism. Visitors can be encouraged to participate in cultural events such as processions and dancing, to help sow and harvest, to try country skills or tend animals.

**Recording:** Vast amounts are spent on photography and other ways of recording the visitor experience. Posing for photos, arranging photo opportunities and guiding to favoured spots are valued by the tourist. The same applies to certificates recording visits and activities and to a lesser extent, mementoes of visits.

**Relaxing:** This is ostensibly what tourists set out to do, but relaxation takes many forms. They range from lazing in the sun, playing with children, to watching sport, to learning craft skills, dancing and shopping. Some visitors actively seek solitude.

**Transport:** The tourist has to move around the property or area somehow, and this can be done on foot, by animal power, by machine power, or under human power. Animal power includes all kinds of carts and appliances pulled by animals, from bullocks to dogs. Riding ranges from donkeys to elephants. Mechanical power includes tractors, railways. Human power includes bicycles, canoes, and rickshaws.

**Watching:** This does not mean merely spectating, such as looking out of the window of a tour bus, but a directed activity which engages the visitor's intelligence. Common examples are bird watching, game watching, turtle hatching and so on. It can also be combined with other activities such as hiking, boating and relaxing.

**Working:** Paradoxically many tourists actually seek out hard work as a form of relaxation. Farm work is popular either for long periods, or just to help with harvesting or animal husbandry and live the farming lifestyle. It can be combined with accommodation and education activities.

## THE MODEL IN ACTION – CASE STUDIES

The model works best in a group situation where several people can work together to brainstorm ideas. This does not have to be in a formal setting, nor does it need any great preparation. It is best if the group has at least one person with some tourism experience or expertise in order to weed out the unfeasible.

There are a wide range of other tools, which can be used in the process of interviewing individuals or groups and fall under the same categories. The appropriateness of the methods used for doing research is based not only on the content of the project objectives, but furthermore on the context of the research agenda. There are a huge variety of examples in the literature of how those methods can be used, such as natural resource management, establishing land rights of people, development and planning, as well as negotiation and conflict management.

This approach is an interactive way of giving local people a means to participate in decision-making, which affects their quality of life. Although this planning might be time consuming and difficult in the long term it can avoid cost of resolving conflicts, because it can be build on the knowledge and capacities of the stakeholders.

The following cases are offered to illustrate the model in action.

## Case One: Sugar Inc. A large sugar processor in the Caribbean

This organisation wanted to get into tourism but could not see how to get started. The company has extensive cane fields, and buys in cane from other growers, processes the cane into sugar and packs and despatches it. By applying the model with a small number of management staff, several potential ways of starting tourism products were suggested and are being evaluated.

The process starts by considering the first activity and the first Resource - Caring and Land. Sugar cane is grown in large blocks on flat land there didn't seem to be much of interest in that particular combination. Drinking and land didn't bring anything to mind but eating did. The mental image of eating and cane fields raised the image of visitors trying raw sugar cane. Few overseas visitors would have seen sugar cane in its natural state so actually chewing the cane might be an interesting experience. This might also properly belong at Eating and Produce but an idea is valuable wherever it comes from. The notion of eating also raised the idea of some sort of picnic or rest area in the large clear spaces between blocks. The next activity, exercising, built on that. The blocks are not unlike a maze and some form of games, treasure hunts, orienteering might be feasible.

Gathering was not a productive avenue to pursue, since sugar cane is a monoculture, but hunting immediately suggested activities to do with the numerous reptiles and mammals which live in the cane fields. This process was continued through the other activities and the remaining resources.

The end result was a list of promising tourism ideas of which the most promising one was a packaged tour of the cane fields. The trip would cover the growing cycle, provide a demonstration of cane cutting (with a chance to try it out), a trip on the narrow gauge railway to a visitor centre where snakes, cane toads and rats are on show. A demonstration and tasting of the different types of cane products and the differences between coffee crystals, demerara, and granulated sugar would be provided along with the chance to taste raw sugar cane. Another exhibition chronicled the days of slave labour. The event would be serviced by local bus operators who would pay a per visitor fee to the company.

## Case Two: Independent Lodge - New Zealand

This family runs a subsistence small holding in a remote area of New Zealand. The farmlet has horses and chickens but no field crops. It is located on an ocean beach on the edge of inland hill-country. There are basic services such as telephone and electricity but very little else. The nearest shop is twelve miles away. The owner built a basic three-bedroom house, originally for sale, but then opted for lodging which sleeps up to twelve people. The challenge was to keep the operation filled year round with a limited advertising budget.

In the initial application of the model three resources stood out: land, vegetation and culture. Land in this instance meant the surrounding area as well. The position right on the seashore with hills and a river close by, and no built up area mean that there are a wide variety of habitats in close proximity. Although there is little vegetation of any note on the property itself, there is a pristine forest within walking distance. The cultural element had potential because the hostel was in the traditional Maori heartland, has Maori owners and the whole area has a rich history.

The generation session then concentrated on these resources, comparing each with each possible activity. Caring generated some discussion, but was inconclusive. Drinking and Eating didn't seem to offer much. Exercising had clear potential with a huge empty beach and lots of room for any sort of activity but the attraction was probably not enough on its own to draw people there. Gathering and Hunting were out, since the area is part of Maori communal land and much of it adjoins national park land. The next activity, Learning proved to be the most fruitful. The pristine nature of the area, the mixed habitats, the nearby conservation land and the absence of development all suggested that the area would be of interest to ecologists, conservationists and the 'green' market in general.

Since the hostel lies about 90 minutes from the nearest main road, brief visits and stopovers are not feasible. What kind of people would be keen to stay in minimal conditions to study nature for an extended length of time? Students fitted the requirements nicely. The isolation, the beach and forest would provide leisure time activities with scope for interaction with the Maori community as a bonus. A business plan was drawn up to establish a field centre to host university groups on rural/environmental field trips of a week or more.

## Case Three: Tourism and local food in Nunavut

Tourism to the eastern Arctic of Canada (Nunavut) has grown in recent decades as visitors seek to discover the unique flora and fauna of the region and strive to learn more of the Inuit way of life. Tourism also plays a particularly vital role in the local economy of Nunavut — supplementing public sector employment opportunities, subsistence hunting and government welfare payments. One key way for tourism to spread its economic benefits to the local community is for the industry to link more effectively with the local food producing sector — so called 'country food'.

By adopting the model outlined above, one hotel in the region has been able to achieve far higher use of local food on its menu than in the past. This is not because the local produce has suddenly appeared, it had always been there, rather new and innovative ways to use the produce have been explored.

In the early 1990s there was little if any local food on the menu of the case study hotel, a fact mirrored across the region with research revealing that on average less than 5 per cent of hotel food requirements were met by local produce (Grekin and Milne, 1998). The main reasons for a lack of local food on the menu were availability and a perceived lack of interest from visitors.

Research revealed, however, that visitors did want to try local food — some items like arctic char or caribou as main courses, others such as seal or whale as 'novelty' items in part of a broader menu. By working through the model it became possible to develop ways to make such products more interesting and palatable to visitors.

Menus could feature special Inuit sections that focused on the role played by the particular food in the traditional diet. Interpretation of the spiritual value of animals in the Inuit culture can also be presented. At the same time new forms of preparation can be used. For example, whale and seal can be presented in bite-sized novelty portions. This approach has been strengthened by government initiatives to encourage new recipes and cooking ideas through an annual contest.

The hotel in question has strengthened its local food offerings considerably in the past decade — with country food now accounting for 10-15 per cent of total food requirements. This provides the following benefits:

- hunting and fishing are part of the traditional economy. As tourism grows this is one important way that the industry can continue to directly benefit the country food producing sector. Opportunities in tourism need not take people away from subsistence hunting, but can act as an income supplement.
- purchases of local produce mean that money reaches the community and does not 'leak' out of the local economy. There is an opportunity to generate 'downstream' jobs and income in other related sectors of the economy.

- benefits also emerge in terms of cost savings for the local tourist industry: the cost of serving a pound of locally harvested caribou meat or Arctic char steaks is less than half that of serving an equivalent amount of 'imported' hamburger meat.

## CONCLUSION

The model presented here provides another tool to enhance performance in local economic development. However, it must be used in context. Agro-tourism can only succeed if trust, reciprocity and the will to succeed exist among key stakeholders. It also requires government or some other grouping to provide the right types of support and infrastructure to facilitate the development of successful agro-tourism. Agro-tourism holds great potential for the Caribbean. Food accounts for one third of tourist expenditures in the Caribbean and in many other parts of the world. Any reliance on imported food represents both a lost opportunity to local agriculture and a massive loss for the region of net benefits derived. Despite the weak linkages that now characterise the relationship between the tourism and agriculture sectors in many parts of the Caribbean there is significant potential to increase the share of locally produced agricultural products supplied to the tourism industry, and thus to reduce the need for imported foods. There is also great potential to take working agriculture and rural environments and add value to them by linking more effectively into new and existing tourism products.

Enhancing the linkages between tourism and agriculture is an effective way to stimulate the local economy and to improve the distribution of tourism benefits to rural people. By converting farmers and other rural participants into economic stakeholders in, and beneficiaries of, the tourism industry, the incentive to abandon farming and move to the city will be significantly reduced, at the same time rural landscapes and the heritage benefits attached to them may continue to survive.

# REFERENCES

Adams, V. 'Tourism and Sherpas, Nepal: Reconstruction of Reciprocity'. *Annals of Tourism Research* 19, (1992): 534-554.

Bélisle, F. J. 'Tourism and Food Production in the Caribbean'. *Annals of Tourism Research* 10, (1983): 497-513.

_____. 'The Significance and Structure of Hotel Food Supply in Jamaica'. *Caribbean Geography* 1, (1984): 219-233.

_____. 'Tourism and Food Imports: The Case of Jamaica'. *Economic Development and Cultural Change* 32, (1984a): 819-842.

Bookbinder, M.P., *et al.* 'Ecotourism's support of biodiversity conservation'. *Conservation Biology* 12, no. 6, (1998): 1399-1404.

Campbell, L. M., 'Ecotourism in rural developing communities', *Annals of Tourism Research* 26, no. 3, (1999): 534-553.

Chambers, R. 1993. *Challenging the Professions: Frontiers for Rural Development*. London: Intermediate Technology Publications.

_____. 1997. *Whose Reality Counts? Putting the first last*. London: Intermediate Technology Publications.

Clarke, J. 'Marketing structures for farm tourism: beyond the individual provider of rural tourism'. *JOST* 7, no.1, (1999): 26-47.

Commission of the European Communities. 1990. Community Action to promote Rural Tourism, Communication from the Commission. Brussels: CEC 90, 438.

Cox, L. J. and M. Fox. 'Agriculturally based leisure attractions'. *Journal of Tourism Studies* 2, no. 2, (1991): 18-28.

Cox, L. J. *et al.* 'Does Tourism Destroy Agriculture?' *Annals of Tourism Research* 22, (1994): 210-213.

Denman, R. M. and J. Denman. 1993. *The Farm Tourism Market: a Market Study of Farm Tourism in England*. London: English Tourist Board.

Devas, E. 'Hotels in the Caribbean'. *Travel and Tourism Analyst* 2, (1997): 57-76.

Dieke, P. 1993. 'Tourism and Development Policy in the Gambia'. *Annals of Tourism Research* 20, (1993): 423-449.

Drumm, A. 1998. 'New approaches to community-based ecotourism management, Learning from Ecuador'. In *Ecotourism: a guide for planners and managers* eds. K. Lindberg, M.E. Wood and D.J. Engelburn. Ecotourism Society, North Bennington.

English Tourist Board. 1991. *Tourism and the Environment. Maintaining the Balance*. London: ETB.

Fagence, M. 'Rural and village tourism in developing countries'. *Third World Planning Review* 20, no. 1, (1998): 107-118.

Freitag, T.G. 'Tourism and the transformation of a Dominican coastal community'. *Urban Anthropology* 25 no. 3, (1996): 225-258.

Gomes, A. J. 1993. 'Integrating Tourism and Agricultural Development'. In *Tourism Marketing and Management in the Caribbean* eds. D.J. Gayle and J.N. Goodrich. London and New York: Routledge.

Grekin, J and S. Milne. 1996. 'Community based tourism: the experience of Pond Inlet'. In *Tourism and Native Peoples* eds. R.W. Butler and T. Hinch. London: Thomson International.

Harrison, D. 1992. *Tourism and the Less Developed Countries*. London: Belhaven Press.

Hudson, B. 'Paradise lost: a planners view of Jamaican tourist development'. *Caribbean Quarterly* 42, no. 4, (1996): 22-31.

Jenkins, J.M. and E. Prin. 1997. 'Rural landholder attitudes: the case of public recreational access to "private" rural lands'. In *Tourism and Recreation in Rural Areas*, eds. R. Butler, C.M. Hall and J. Jenkins. Wiley: Chichester.

Johnson, D., J. Snepenger and S. Akis. 'Residents perceptions of tourism development'. *Annals of Tourism Research* 21, no. 3, (1994): 629-42.

Koch, E. 1997. 'Ecotourism and rural reconstruction in South Africa: reality or rhetoric?'. In *Social Change and Conservation: environmental policies and impacts of national parks and protected areas*, eds. K.B. Ghimire and M.P. Pimbert. London: Earthscan Publications.

Lane, B. 'Sustainable rural tourism strategies: a tool for development and conservation'. *JOST* 2, no. 1&2, (1994): 102-111.

McElroy, J. L. and K. de Albuquerque. 'Sustainable Small-Scale Agriculture in Small Caribbean Islands'. *Society and Natural Resources* 3, (1990): 109-129.

Midmore, P, N. Parrott and A. Sherwood. 1996. 'Integrating Agriculture and Tourism in South Pembrokeshire: a review of Marketing Opportunities'. Aberystwyth: University of Wales.

OAS/CTRC. 'Tourism and Agricultural Linkages in the Caribbean'. *Final Report OAS/CTRC Workshop.*

O'Connor, E. 1996. 'Rural tourism as a farm diversification option for small farmers'. In *Tourism on the Farm* ed. J. Feehan. University College, Dublin: Environment Institute.

O'Ferral, A.M. 'Tourism and Agriculture on the North Coast of the Dominican Republic'. *Revista Geográfica* 113, (1991): 171-191.

Olsen, B. 'Environmentally sustainable development and tourism, lessons from Negril, Jamaica'. *Human Organization* 56, no. 3, (1997): 285-93.

Oppermann, M. 1997. Farm tourism in New Zealand. In *Tourism and Recreation in Rural Areas* eds. R. Butler, C.M. Hall and J. Jenkins. Chichester: Wiley.

Patullo, P. 1996. *Last Resorts*. London: Latin America Bureau and Cassell.

Poon, A. 1998. 'All-inclusive resorts'. *Travel and Tourism Analyst no. 6*. London: EIU.

Ryan, C. 1991. *Recreational Tourism: A Social Science Perspective*. New York: Routledge.

Taylor, B.E., J.B. Morison and E.M. Fleming. 'The Economic Impact of Food Import Substitution in the Bahamas'. *Social and Economic Studies*. 40, no. 2, (1991): 45-62.

Tefler, D.J. and G. Wall. Linkages Between Tourism and Food Production. *Annals of Tourism Research* 23, no. 3, (1996): 635-653.

Torres, R. 1996. 'The Linkages Between Tourism and Agriculture in Quintana Roo, Mexico'. PhD proposal, Dept of Geography, University of California, 1996. *http://www.ntrnet.net/~skilli/dissert.htm.*

West, P. C. and S.R. Brechin. 1991. *Resident Peoples and National Parks: Social Dilemmas and Strategies in International Conservation*. Tucson: University of Arizona Press.

Wilkinson, P. F. 'Strategies for Tourism in Island Microstates'. *Annals of Tourism Research* 16, (1989): 153-177.

Wilkinson, P. F. Caribbean cruise tourism: delusion? Illusion? *Tourism Geographies,* 1 no. 3, (1999): 261-282.

Wood, R.E. 'Caribbean cruise tourism: globalisation at sea'. *Annals of Tourism Research* 27, no. 2 (2000): 345-370.

# 10

# A STRATEGIC APPROACH TO AGRO-TOURISM IN THE CARIBBEAN

Hilton McDavid, Chandana Jayawardena and Vindel Kerr

## ABSTRACT

*The millennium signifies the dawning of a new age, symbolic of change. Changes in paradigms, changes in the ways people work, changes in the way products are packaged. The trade rules have changed. This chapter explores the potential of a marriage of agriculture and tourism in the region. The Opportunities for Agro-tourism Strategies (OATS) Model is explained. Whilst diversification of the traditional tourism product is germane, the chapter concludes by noting that more primary research needs to be conducted to identify potential markets for agro-tourism in the Caribbean, and emphasises the importance of a team approach by the key players.*

## INTRODUCTION

'Agro-tourism' is a sub-sector, which combines two key sectors in the Caribbean. The current failures, in financial terms, are often noted in the historically and socially important agriculture sector in many Caribbean countries. Rising costs of sugar production in some Caribbean countries today are higher than the selling prices of sugar in many markets. By and large the banana industry in the Caribbean faces major threats from some non-Caribbean countries whose costs are much lower. Recent decisions taken by The World Trade Organisation (WTO) regarding the preferential terms (normally granted to Caribbean bananas by the European Union) only worsens matters.

On the other hand, the growth rates of tourism in the Caribbean usually surpass the world average growth rates for the sector. Most Caribbean countries are increasingly becoming more dependent on tourism as the engine of growth. In this context, can a marriage between the decreasing agriculture sector and the booming tourism sector be of mutual benefit to both sectors? Probably it will. But its success will largely depend on the manner in which agro-tourism is developed and marketed in the Caribbean. This chapter focuses on the importance of taking a strategic approach in developing agro-tourism in the Caribbean.

Mason and Milne (2000), states that 'while tourism and agriculture are vital components of most Caribbean economies, the two sectors have never been characterised by particularly harmonious relationships. Many commentators argue that economic linkages between these two sectors require further strengthening'. The introduction and development of agro-tourism would, therefore, provide opportunities to marry two sectors that are critical to the survival of the Caribbean region. There is a great deal of interest today in the concept of sustainable tourism, and there are now a number of initiatives in pursuit of this new goal. This process has been largely driven, to date, by the growing concern over environmental issues (Clayton, 2000). Tourism development needs to be sustainable if it is to bring about long-term environmental and social gains. To survive as a viable industry, tourism must be developed with the needs of the community and the environment in mind and in line with plans for the development of the region as a whole. Otherwise, there is a danger that long-term benefits and the sustainability of the industry can be sacrificed for short-term gains. Agro-tourism provides the opportunities for sustainability in development and cultural preservation. It also forges a relationship between the traditional tourist product and that being gravitated to by a growing class of nature seekers and adventurers.

## AGRO-TOURISM IN THE CARIBBEAN

Agro-tourism stresses the facilitation and improvement of contacts between hosts and guests. It is essentially small-scale, low density and dispersed in rural areas, and caters to special interest groups of people with mainly above average education and with natural, social and community values and allows both hosts and guests to enjoy positive and worthwhile interactions and shared experiences (KPMG, 1996). Arguably, the first recorded use of the term and an attempt at developing the concept in the Caribbean began in Cuba, shortly after the Cuban Revolution in 1959 when President Fidel Castro envisioned developing the agriculturally rich and breathtakingly beautiful important province of *Pinar del Rio* for what he called 'agro-tourism' (Honey, 1991). What is important in this approach is the link of conventional tourism with the agricultural sector as part of the tourist attraction. Agro-tourism as a concept or type, seeks to formalise the natural inquiry of man into how things are done or made into an added attraction to the tourist. However, it is important to recognise that this type of tourism is not new, but has existed in certain parts of Europe for hundreds of years (Bubsy & Rendle, 2000). Tourists have been visiting the historical sites in Europe and, as part of their tour, have visited the vineyards and olive orchards and observed how wine was made and olive oil produced. It is for us to satisfy this interest of man in learning and experiencing how products are made into extended stays in the Caribbean.

A good way to describe the concept of agro-tourism is to borrow Newfoundland's and Labrador's (Canada) interpretation,

> Agri-tourism is an economic activity that occurs when agricultural products, services and heritage are linked with travel markets. At its core are tourist product offerings and services and either take place on working farms or directly involve and benefit working farm families in venues such as agricultural fairs and festivals. Facilities which directly promote and interpret the agricultural industry to tourists such as heritage gardens, dedicated agricultural museums and food processing operations may also be considered part of the agro-tourism sector (D. W. Knight Associates, 1999).

There are many opportunities within the Caribbean region for agro-tourism, which is a growing trend, which merges the world of travel with the experiences of agriculture. In addition, increased demand for organic foods by a new and health-conscious middle class group is certainly paving the way for more creativity and specialisation at the farm level.

The agro-tourism marketing mix could be further enhanced by the following specific products and places as real Caribbean experience: spending a day with rice farmers in Guyana or Trinidad and Tobago; visiting and observing the picking of Sea Island cotton in Barbados and participating in 'Crop Over' — an annual national festivity (carnival) of both agricultural, historical and cultural significance; visiting a banana farm in the Windward Islands or Jamaica; spending a weekend on a cattle farm in the Rupununi area in Guyana; spending a weekend at a sugar plantation in Cuba; spending a weekend in a Blue Mountain coffee estate in Jamaica, or spending a weekend at an organic vegetable farm in Grenada.

The basis for a strategic marketing approach to agro-tourism in the Caribbean must be analysed from the perspective of the Opportunities for Agro-tourism Strategies (OATS) Model. This is a new model developed by the authors using sections of previous models (Cox & Fox, 1991, & KPMG, 1996). The 'OATS' model is presented as figure 1.

The model focuses on the agro-tourism product of the Caribbean and categorises the entire product scope and places.

Development of new tourism products and services in the Caribbean by using its natural resources to satisfy the needs of identified market segments whilst ensuring environmental and economic sustainability is required. The main perceived implication of agro-tourism in the Caribbean is that it should emphasise cultural sustainability and respect for the cultural realities experienced by the tourists through education and organised encounters. In addition, effort is being placed on the preservation and protection of the resource base that is fundamental to tourism itself.

# Figure 1.
# Opportunities for Agro-Tourism Strategies (OATS) Model

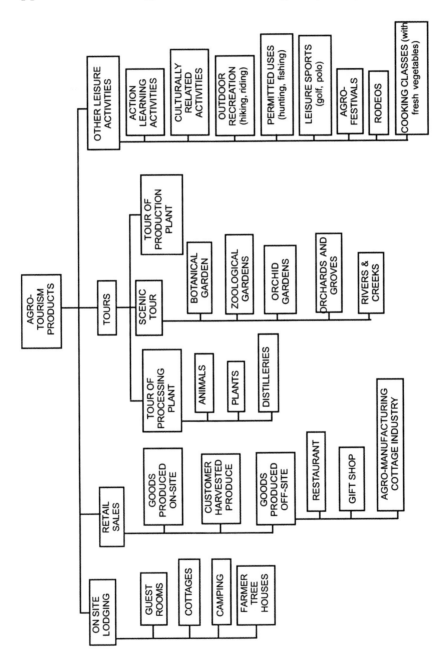

# ECONOMIES AND OPPORTUNITIES FROM AGRO-TOURISM

A major impact of agro-tourism would be to make marginal farms more profitable. Quite often, diversification is misinterpreted to mean the abundance of the original product or reduction in production. In Guyana, the state-owned Guyana Sugar Corporation, diversified by reducing acreage of sugar under cultivation and getting involved in cattle farming as well as rice cultivation. In most parts of the Caribbean, the fact that the agricultural areas are within easy reach of the beach is an added advantage as tourists can be accommodated on the farm and spend time on the beach, or vice versa. Tour packages can also be divided into stays on the beach as well as stays on the farm. In all the scenarios mentioned, there is not only the potential for attracting more tourists, but increasing the duration of visits. An average one-day extension of a 10-day stay to experience a taste of agro-tourism will increase present tourist earnings by 10 per cent.

Agro-tourism can have the following on-farm benefits:

- introduction of new consumers (tourists) to the farm;
- earnings can be attained from added attractions;
- income can be obtained from hospitality services provided; and
- farmers and small, local entrepreneurs can produce non-traditional products such as confectioneries from local fruits (sugar cakes, tamarind balls, fudges, jams, pickles, chips from plantains, bananas, yams and cassava) and craft items.

Agro-tourism also provides an excellent means of supporting rural communities and businesses. Tourists can provide income to local businesses that maintain farming communities. An added impact of agro-tourism is that it will increase agricultural awareness and agro-manufacturing education among the local population and promotion of domestic agricultural products. This is of particular importance to Caribbean economies as local fruits and vegetables are under heavy competition from foreign produce.

Bull (1991) reported that the multiplier ranged from 2.5 in Canada to 0.8 in Bermuda and The Bahamas. With the reduction of leakage, by emphasising the consumption of local products, the secondary income, that income that remains after 'leakage' will increase significantly and circulate successively throughout the economy creating indirect income and induced income. Agro-tourism will have a reduced outflow from the country and region and more of the initial tourist expenditure will remain to circulate through the economy. By definition, there should be much less reliance on imported resources outside of the Caribbean and the region. A major set back of conventional tourism in the Caribbean has been its dependence on human, physical and capital inflows from extra-regional sources.

The fact that the multiplier for Canada is greater than three times that of the two Caribbean countries mentioned illustrates the dependence of conventional tourism in the Caribbean on external resources. Added to this is the fact that much of the management control, direct ownership or franchising lies in the hands of external, multinational interests. No such state should be allowed to develop with agro-tourism.

Agro-tourism can provide opportunities to:

- Disperse visitor loads and spread the benefits of tourism across a variety of sites by developing recognised touring routes.
- Expand the economic base of a local area or region while bringing to the community a number of new skills and employment opportunities. It also has a regional economic multiplier effect as this additional income is spent be recipients. It also helps to increase the economic prosperity of a region by generating extra income from tourism, the circulation of which through the community can act as a buffer against the highs and lows of rural economies.
- Encourage the maintenance and enhancement of the cultural attributes of a community through the preservation, development, interpretation and promotion of traditional arts and crafts, heritage, rural industries and lifestyles. The development of agro-tourism may also encourage local to remain in rural areas, thus, contributing to community stability and sustainability (KPMG, 1996).

## STRATEGIC APPROACH

Tourism is predominantly a private sector activity that capitalises on a market for the purpose of making a profit. However, as discussed earlier, it represents a substantial percentage of the Gross Domestic Product (GDP) of many regional economies, hence governments concern about its sustainability as well as the maximising of efficiency through improvement of management and the streamlining of service systems. Government's role, therefore, should be that of a facilitator providing incentives for agro-tourism development, developing appropriate land-use philosophies, providing access to the public / tourist and helping to create an effective tie with the resource base.

The rise in ecotourism and special interest tourism has been attributed to the growth of the tourism sector. Agro-tourism is one area of special interest tourism that can be linked with conventional tourism, as well as ecotourism and other special interest tourism packages. For agro-tourism to be successful, a strategic marketing approach has to be taken for its development in the Caribbean.

Heskett (1986) identified four basic elements of service strategy:

(1) the targeting of market segments;
(2) the conceptualisation of how the service will be perceived by the consumer;
(3) the focusing on operation strategy; and
(4) the designing of an efficient service delivery system.

In adapting these elements to agro-tourism development one must inculcate the defining characteristics of the tourism and hospitality industry. These can be categorised as:

(1) high contact;
(2) tangible concepts;
(3) right to use;
(4) seasonal demand; and
(5) content of service package.

- High Contact: Service delivery and service consumption takes place simultaneously in time and space with an agricultural or farm environment.
- Tangible Concepts: Clients are quite sensitive to the tangible concepts in the service package. Both the tangibility and intangibility of agro-tourism has to be properly marketed. The intangible aspects can attract the tourist and the tangibles will assist in developing loyalty.
- Right to Use: The customer has the right to use accommodations and other facilities on the farm but do not possess the property.
- Seasonal Demand: Caribbean tourism demand is subject to the performance of economy external to the host country. However, there is a trend, which follows the climatic seasons of Europe and North America. Due to the educational nature of agro-tourism, local and regional demand can be created to fill excess capacity.
- Content of Service Package: The service package in most cases should be linked to other forms of tourism and attractions. For example, in Barbados sessions of the 'Jazz Blues Festival' are held in old plantations.

Key aspects of a strategic marketing approach to agro-tourism may be categorised as:

(1) marketing strategy;
(2) service and product strategy;
(3) operating strategy; and
(4) integrative elements.

Service strategy, operating strategy and integrative elements will support the overall marketing effort.

- **Marketing Strategy**

  The agro-tourism product is complex and requires different marketing approaches to successfully attract prime clients who are usually from diverse cultural and ethnic backgrounds. The agro-tourism product is no doubt a social product to a large extent requiring a social marketing approach. Social marketing is distinguished by its emphasis on so-called non-tangible products-ideas and practices, as opposed to the tangible products and services that are the focus of commercial marketing. Therefore, in positioning this product it is essential that those strategies most relevant to marketing a commercial product not be readily employed. Social marketing is more complex and can be less effective than commercial marketing. While for a commercial product, it is usually easier to sell its tangible beneficial effects, with agro-tourism, physical attributes are most easily used to promote the product but these physical attributes and symbols do not always reflect the reality of the emotional experience of the agro-tourism product.

  Therefore, emphasis must be placed on target marketing, understanding the needs of the different potential market segments and design promotional campaigns to appeal to the needs and wants of the captive segments. Pricing must be aimed at reaching and attracting the maximum number of target groups. A social product such as agro-tourism is expected to be priced at the higher end of the market given the clientele it attracts and its uniqueness. The market segmentation for agro-tourism must be synonymous with customer segmentation. Too often analyses treat the tourism product as a rigid, physical product, such as a car. One country can offer various forms of tourism and added attractions to a tourist on a single trip. The model developed earlier indicates the behaviour of tourists. Agro-tourism should be attractive to the increasing number of highly educated and environmentally sensitive tourists who are becoming increasingly bored of long stays on the sea and sand. A proper study of the market segments most suited to agro-tourism must be done and once identified, targeted. Segmentation may be based on geographic, demographic, psycho graphic or any other relevant basis. All key marketing activities such as market segmentation, adjustments to the elements of the marketing mix and marketing planning must be done with marketing research inputs as a strong foundation for the development of agro-tourism in the Caribbean.

- **Service and Product Strategy**

  It is crucial to recognise that agricultural environment provides service differentiation from other types of tourism. However, further differentiation can be achieved by emphasising supportive elements that would be difficult to duplicate. Human resources can also be used as an instrument of differentiation and a source of service excellence. In addition, tour guides should be well trained in the area of their expertise and be capable. They should also be able to defer specific technical questions to other competent staff members. This raises the issue of the proper scheduling of tours so as not to affect the operational efficiency of the production process. It should be noted that highly motivated and well-trained employees of both the agricultural production and tourism development sectors would provide high quality service or employee-customer interaction, thus, increasing both customer loyalty and systems efficiency. Of strategic marketing importance, each agro-tourism entity must define its tourism product, market, and opportunities, and with this in mind, must satisfy the expectations of the customer through proper delivery.

Each organisation involved in agro-tourism will have to develop its own service delivery system. The system should be designed to achieve maximum customer satisfaction and must include facilities and their layout, technology and equipment to be utilised in servicing the tourist, processes for delivering the service and those processes relating directly to the agro-industry that will be displayed, job descriptions for employees and the roles both employees and the tourist will play during an encounter. For example, it should be decided what aspects the tour guide will explain and when he/she will defer explanation.

At the macro-level policies and guidelines should be in place to assist the firm in identifying the important features of the service delivery system and how best they can be organised, paying special attention to capacity and quality standards.

- **Operating Strategy**
  The operating strategy is a set of strategies, plans and policies, which provide guidelines, and to some extent, direction for the firms that will be operating in the agro-tourism sub-sector. While operating strategy tends to be much broader than a marketing strategy, it plays a key role in bringing all other operating elements together. Critical amongst these other elements is that of marketing. From this the firm can derive their own operating strategy pertaining to operations, financing, marketing, development of human resources and controlling in order that it can bring its service or product concept to the customers.

  The operating strategy should be developed considering government's role particularly regarding: taxation, duties, import policy, government marketing effort, financing, particularly interest rates, education and training, tourism master plans and incentives.

- **Integrative Elements**
  The tourism aspect will incur cost in maintaining and operating the delivery system. Value is leveraged over cost when the perceived additional value in dollar terms far exceeds the cost of creating it. The differences between perceived value and cost of service can be maximised through standardisation; customisation and emphasising easily leveraged activities. At the level of the agro-tourism firm, certain integrative elements help the basic elements fit together for a consistent tourism strategy. They provide the guidelines for planning actions, implementing the strategic decisions including strategic market positioning and leveraging value of a cost and strategy system integration. The agro-tourism market is positioned to satisfy the customer's needs for knowledge while at the same time giving an opportunity for relaxation. For agro-tourism to be successful, the firms not only have to achieve consistency between the target market segment of the tourist population and service concept, but between service concept and operating strategy. Similarly, operating strategy must be consistent with the delivery system for this allocation to become a whole. In the agro-tourism sub-sector, consistency can be achieved between the operating system and service delivery system by carefully designing the hiring policies, service processes and facilities, and integrating these carefully with the agricultural production entity. In areas such as sugar production, advantage can be taken of the growing, harvesting and grinding seasons for re-deploying resources to the various aspects of the tourism service being offered. There is, however, great need for proper co-ordination of the tourist activities with the production process.

## CONCLUSION

Agro-tourism has the capacity to add significant value and uniqueness to products and services and play an integral role in the further development of Caribbean tourism. The comprehensive development of tourism in the region should include agro-tourism as part of its core cluster of any strategy. Giving the nature and content of agro-tourism as it presently stands, it deserves to be of strategic importance for priority development. To achieve this, government, private sector initiatives and other relevant third-parties should work collaboratively in identifying and developing community leadership as a medium for progressing the interests of rural tourism (industry associations, all spheres of governments, rural communities). Creating a separate section highlighting agro-tourism within the current travel guides may prove to be a useful strategy. An important strategy could be a highway signage programme to identify agro-tourism opportunities such as farm vacation sites and roadside markets.

The Caribbean Tourism Organisation should now encourage the provision of reliable data to be used for rural tourism development. They should also be asked to analyse their market segmentation data or gather more primary data from rural perspectives to identify potential markets for the rural tourism product.

Agro-tourism without a doubt provides new opportunity as well as a new challenge to the Caribbean region. It can succeed only if a strategic approach is taken. The potential benefits to be derived from the agro-tourism sub-sector of the Caribbean can best be realised with the full participation and involvement of public and private sector organisations, specialists and academics working as a team to achieving the greater end.

The role of key players in this new development should be focused on creating awareness and vision for agro-tourism in the Caribbean as the primary step forward. These agencies should then join hands in preparing a strategic master plan for agro-tourism in the Caribbean with inputs from potential consumers, tour operators, travel agents, airlines, ground transportation providers, investors, managers, researchers, consultants and above all, from local communities.

## REFERENCES

Bull, A. 1991. *The Economics of Travel and Tourism*. Pitman.

Busby, G. and S. Rendle 'The transition from tourism on farms to farm tourism'. *Tourism Management 21*, no. 6, (2000): 635–642.

Clayton, A. 'Sustainable Tourism: the agenda for the Caribbean'. *Worldwide Hospitality and Tourism Trends*, 1, no. 2, (2000): 60–78.

Cox, L. J. and M. Fox. 'Agriculturally based leisure attractions'. *The Journal of Tourism Studies 2*, no. 2, (1991): 18–26.

D. W. Knight Associates. 1999. 'A Study of Agri-Tourism in Newfoundland Labrador'. Canada: The Department of Forest Resource and Agri-foods, Canada.

Heskett, J. L. 1986. *Managing in the Scarce Economy*. Boston: HBS Press.

Honey, M. 1991. *Ecotourism and Sustainable Development*. Washington DC: Island Press.

Jayawardena, C. and H. McDavid. 2000. 'Implications of Agro-Tourism in the Caribbean'. In *Agro-tourism – A Sustainable Approach to Economic Growth* ed. P. Collins. Trinidad & Tobago Inter-American Institute for Co-operation on Agriculture.

Jayawardena, C. 1999. 'Tourism Trends in the World and the Caribbean'. Conference Paper presented at The Millennium Tourism Trends Conference. North – East of Finland: Centre for Adult Education.

KPMG. 1996 'An Agri-tourism Strategy for Nova Scotia'. Canada: Nova Scotia Agriculture and Marketing, Canada.

Mason, D. and S. Milne. 2000. 'Linking Tourism and Agriculture: Innovative Information Solutions Technology Solutions'. *In Agro-tourism – A Sustainable Approach to Economic Growth*, ed. P. Collings. Trinidad & Tobago Inter-American Institute for Co-operation on Agriculture.

# SECTION 3
# HERITAGE &
# CULTURAL TOURISM

# 11

# CHASING MYTHS, FINDING PEOPLE: DEFINING THE PRODUCT IN INDIGENOUS TOURISM IN THE GUIANAS[1]

Donald Sinclair

## ABSTRACT

*The product in indigenous tourism is often an equation that is as much myth as reality. When so much of tourism is itself concerned with the satisfaction and fulfillment of unconscious desires, indigenous tourism is even more a journey into some complex recesses of the unconscious. Visits to the people of the rainforest are framed by the language of the brochures as an ontological journey that is, for the tourists, both myth and magic. Indigenous tourism is presented as an encounter with the primitive that embraces two dominant myths — primitivism and nostalgia. Indigenous tourism on the ground cannot be confirmation of the myths of the brochures. The challenge for the experience providers is therefore to address and confront these myths and re-present the 'primitive' of the brochure as the 'indigenous' — real people on the ground.*

## INDIGENOUS TOURISM

Indigenous tourism has been defined simply as 'tourism activity in which indigenous people are directly involved either through control and/or by having their culture serve as the essence of the attraction' (Hinch and Butler, 1996). The substance of the experience has tended to centre more specifically on the forests, rivers, lands and lifestyles of the indigenous peoples. Lands and peoples are the *subject* of the experience of indigenous tourism, not the *object* of any coastal or Western configuration. This subject status of indigenous tourism counters a traditional Western discourse that has been nurtured by over five centuries of colonial history. In this discourse indigenous spaces are perceived as passive and docile objects of external manipulation, acted upon, imposed upon, conceived and configured as having value less in themselves than as balms or therapies for Western civilization.

The picture framed by the brochures is heavily influenced by the thematic of the (western) tourist who, driven by nostalgia (Rosaldo, 1989), visits an 'exotic' remote destination almost as a rite of passage (Selwyn, 1994). A mythology is created in the processes that romanticizes both the peoples and cultures visited, transforming the entire travel experience into an encounter with the primitive, and a satisfaction of that nostalgia for a simpler form of existence that indigenous communities are supposed to epitomize. The danger introduced by the brochures, and by experience providers who seek to translate and extend their messages, is a distortion of the reality of indigenous life. Subscription to mythology must therefore be contained by the quest for reality on the ground.

The quest for reality must not be interpreted as a suppression of the mystique that attaches to remote communities, peoples and cultures. Much travel writing does attest to a valid feeling of awe and mystery on the part of those who venture into regions far removed, both technologically and geographically, from modern urban-based societies. The sense of wonder is integral to tourism and adds much spiritual fulfilment to the experience of travel. Indigenous tourism as a travel experience is no laboratory analysis coldly concerned with the pursuit of empirical truths; the mystique holds as much value as the encounter with reality.

Interest in the lifestyles, lands and cultures of indigenous peoples has been nurtured by a convergence of events beginning even before the decade of the nineties in the twentieth century. Global concern for the health of the environment, the alarms that have been sounded about air, water and land pollution, concerns about deforestation, global warming and the general welfare of indigenous populations have all served to heighten interest, on a global scale, in the welfare of the world's forests and its denizens.

While at the political level there has been increased agitation in favour of indigenous peoples, evidenced by a number of treaties and declarations designed to enhance their living conditions and general well-being, at the level of tourism there has been a marked increase in the number of tours and tourism enterprises involving indigenous peoples. In the Caribbean the main indigenous tourism zones have been in Belize, Dominica, Guyana and Suriname, with smaller sites diffused throughout the insular Caribbean. The main area of concentration in this chapter will be on the South American territory of Guyana.

## INTERIOR TOURISM

The tourism product of Guyana is largely an interior product. Guyana is a country situated at roughly 6 degrees latitude south of the Equator, on the north-eastern shoulder of the continent of South America. Such location places that mainland territory south of the Caribbean blue-water chain and directly under the influence of the mighty Amazon river. The earliest ancestors of present-day Amerindian Peoples are believed to have entered Guyana through the Northwest about 11,000 years ago (Williams 1993). The seventeenth century began the era of contact between Europeans and Indigenous Peoples in both Guyana and Suriname. It was this period that ushered in the 'conditions of destruction, extinction and marginalisation' (Fox and Danns, 1993) that have dominated some perspectives on indigenous history. Since the indigenous peoples in both Guyana and Suriname are associated with settlements remote from the plantation enterprises that greatly influenced the course of Caribbean history, an important discourse of resistance now attaches to the narrative of those communities. The 'bush' in Guyana, as well as in neighbouring Suriname, as the principal home of Amerindian and Bush Negro communities, is as much a spiritual as a geographic entity. The 'bush' is a guarantee of economic independence of the plantation and later, the coastal, economic system. The 'bush' is a guarantee (though, as we shall see, not an absolute one) of cultural sovereignty.

Interior tourism as a travel experience on the ground entails visits to Indigenous communities for the purpose of observing the cultural forms and lifestyles of those communities; their distinctive modes of traditional dress, distinctive physiognomy, interior dwellings, religious and social rituals, myths and beliefs. Discussing the latter component in Aboriginal tourism Hollinshead (1996) remarks: ' ... this spiritual life is no esoteric or fragmentary part of indigenous culture, and ... the religious and sacred mysteries of the Dreamtime are vitally and centrally part of all things Aboriginal'.

## TWO PLATFORMS

The 'Indigenous question' in tourism seems to have spawned two main platforms in the literature. First there is a 'cautionary' (Jafari, 1990) platform. Forte (1993) concedes that tourism is not likely to make Amerindians suffer more than they already do at present. Williams (1993) giving essential support to the critiques of Mowforth (1993), Koch (1993) and Ziffer (1989), challenges the blithe assumption that generous tourism benefits automatically accrue to indigenous peoples. While Klautky (1994) is aware of the many perils that attend indigenous tourism, he is prepared to recommend a sustainable form of tourism that would respect and support the integrity of Arawak and Carib peoples visited by tourism in Guyana.

In the same 'cautionary' vein Andrew Garner (1993) perceptively discusses the power-relations operative in the establishment of a tourist resort in one Amerindian community. He analyses 'the images and myths (which) structure the relationship between the Amerindians, developers, tourists and majority population' (Garner, 1993). Hollinshead (1996) is a writer of a similar cautionary persuasion.

The other platform can be described as one of 'advocacy' (Jafari 1990). Valene Smith (1989) assesses both the promises and the pitfalls of the tourism experience and stresses that the latter 'has not been a significant agent of culture change'. McKean (1989) and Crystal (1989) adopt similar positive positions. Similarly, both

Altman and Finlayson (1993) and Mercer (1994) focus upon tourism as it affects Aboriginal Peoples and propose a concept of appropriate sustainable tourism in Aboriginal areas.

## TOURIST MYTHS

Promotional literature frequently presents the tourist journey as a quest for a world from which he has distanced himself. This quest for lost worlds usually entails a passion for nature, for the countryside, for remote spaces and peoples, for nature's children — 'the people of nature, once labeled Peasant and Primitive peoples and considered creatures of instinct' (Graburn, 1989). John Urry argues that this touristic 'appropriation' of the countryside, where the latter is treated as a 'spectacle' or 'theme' is essentially post-modern. On the same theme Dann comments 'Today a great deal of time and energy is dedicated to looking backwards, towards capturing a past which, in many ways, is considered superior to the chaotic present and the dreaded future. This world of yesteryear is a safe environment' (Dann, 1994).

For Erik Cohen the 'nostalgic yearning for our beginnings, for the roots or origins of our modern human existence, is... a powerful mythical and religious motif; it is also a potent touristic motivation of moderns, expressed in the quest for the primitive, and more extremely, the primitive savage' (Cohen, 1996). Sharing Cohen's view Dann notes that 'remote Third World villagers living for generations in one place would be baffled by nostalgia. It is the dislocated Western traveler of today who experiences nostalgia to the fullest and who, incidentally, travels precisely on account of such disorientation' (Dann, 1994).

The nostalgia myth in tourism has been debunked in the literature. Bruner (1991) dismisses this polemic as an essentially Western concept. Nichter (1992) observes that nostalgia 'entails a fair amount of romanticism' and ridicules those who, in the service of anthropology, assist in 'reproducing the ideology of imperialist nostalgia through a search for authentic cultural forms untainted by modernity' (Nichter, 1992).

In its most extreme strain nostalgia leads tourists not only beside the still waters and green pastures that restore the soul, but also into those remote, Conradian heartlands that they may encounter the 'primitive' (MacCannell, 1976; Torgovnick, 1990).

Closely related to nostalgia is the pursuit of authenticity. As a counterpoint to the accretion of artificiality and the profusion of pseudo experiences of post-modernity, contact with remote peoples and communities is framed as an encounter with the real, the natural and authentic. Supposedly, according to the myth, the indigenous world has remained relatively untouched by the forces of modernization. Hence those societies have managed to escape the clutches of artificiality and pseudo-experiences that now bedevil modern society. Tourism then becomes a quest for that order of authenticity, for a supposedly purer form of existence that pre-dates modern corrupting influences.

Much of the authenticity debate centres on performance — the 'staging' of cultural events that become the commodities of tourist consumption. Greenwood deplores the 'objectification of local culture via tourism' (Greenwood, 1989). The following prescription is apt: 'Given that the essence of authenticity is its cultural meaning, the bottom line must be that host communities determine what is meaningful to them...In other words, has the event any cultural meaning for the host community and the participants, or is it merely a commodity to be sold?' (Getz, 1994).

In countries possessing indigenous tourism attractions discussion has often centred on the most appropriate methodology for making visitors aware of indigenous cultural forms; a methodology that while providing material and economic benefit to the communities would at the same time be safeguarding the integrity of those cultural forms. In the Caribbean, for example, the propriety of Kumina rituals being performed in hotels in Jamaica in the 1960s has been discussed, so has the accessibility of voodoo rituals to visiting tourists in Haiti.

The third myth — the quest for the primitive is a key pursuit that is part of the thematic structure of the brochures. Cohen comments succinctly upon this quest in his discussion of hunter-gatherer tourism in Thailand. He remarks: 'The fulfilment of this quest (for the primitive) consists in meeting people who, while they represent the inversion of modern man, the 'Other,' also facilitate the realization by moderns of their own original nature' (Cohen, 1996). Concluding his discussion Cohen asserts: 'The metaphor of the 'human zoo' for the tourists' encounter is thus in a profound sense more appropriate for hunter-gatherer tourism...since it touches upon a deep-set general human theme: the desire to see man as he was before 'civilization' or even 'culture' (Cohen, 1996).

Marianna Torgovnick also offers an interesting insight into the subject of the primitive. She declares 'To study the primitive is thus to enter an exotic world which is also a familiar world. That world is structured by sets of images and ideas that have slipped from their original metaphoric status to control perceptions of primitives...primitives are our untamed selves, our id forces — libidinous, irrational, violent, dangerous. Primitives are mystics, in tune with nature, part of its harmonies' (Torgovnick, 1990).

The myths introduced in the foregoing discussion relate directly to the experience of indigenous tourism in Guyana. The lifestyles and cultural forms of Amerindians or Bush Negroes form the basis of an experience of indigenous tourism that is as mythogenic as the Thailand experience discussed by Cohen. References to nostalgia, primitivism and authenticity in promotional material will be seen to be integral to the marketing of indigenous tourism in Guyana.

## CHASING MYTHS

The engagement with myths begun as early as 1911 when Edith Browne published what is perhaps the earliest known piece of promotional literature based on the then British Guiana. In *British Guiana as a Holiday Resort,* Edith Browne describes the Amerindians of the interior: 'The majority of these primitive inhabitants of the primeval forests and remote savannahs are in ordinary parlance, savages' (Browne, 1911). The dark side primitivism unfolds even more stridently as she continues: 'Leathers, seeds, fibre, the teeth of wild animals, skins, wood, bark and natural dyes, are his raw materials, and with them he not only makes his fancy costume, but numerous gaily ornamental instruments which produce weird noises, fierce wild musical accompaniment to primitive revelry' (Browne, 1911).

That is an evocation of the consummate noble savage — primitive, wild, but one who, like the Caliban of Shakespeare's *Tempest,* has a passion and ear for music. She concludes her description by stating: 'If you have anything of the barbarian in you, any strain that sets your heart beating fast when you are brought into contact with untamed nature, you would consider yourself amply repaid for a visit to British Guiana if you experienced nothing but the sight of one of these children of the forest' (Browne, 1911).

More than eight decades later and almost in response to Edith Browne, one tourism scholar, writing from her own Yetholm gypsy background, bemoans the manifest injustice of the visited indigenous peoples and takes the brochures to task: 'Tour operators promote and package holidays, with emphasis being placed on exotica and brochures romanticize indigenous cultures. They are part of a process that turns indigenous groups into commodities to be exploited for profit' (Keefe, 1993).

The forested or savannah environment that typifies Amerindian settlements in Guyana has proved an almost inexhaustible fund for myths of nostalgia and excursions into the primitive. An extract from Robert Brown will be quoted and analysed:

> Guyana is almost unique in the world in having almost all of its tropical rainforest intact and undisturbed, and as such one of our greatest attractions is Ecotourism… The Tropical Forest stretches unbroken from the edges of Georgetown to the Rupununi Savannahs on the border with Brazil and the mist-shrouded peak of Mount Roraima… reputedly the inspiration for Conan Doyle's 'Lost World'. Although Roraima is not filled with the dinosaurs of Doyle's imagination it is a lost World in its own way, … (Brown, 1992)

In this excerpt Brown's reference to the ubiquity of the rainforest is but the prelude to his nostalgic invocation of the lost world motif, suggesting that Roraima is 'a lost world in its own way.' What this brochure does is to recreate a new mythology that centres upon the mysterious enchantments of the Roraima landscape. Brown continues in the same vein:

> The very fact that so much of the forest is still intact means that much of the countryside is still inaccessible, but lodges being built are now offering an opportunity to visit this tropical wonderland of wildlife. For the more adventurous Guyana offers an endless panorama of forest, rivers and waterfalls just waiting to be discovered. It is a unique opportunity to experience the primeval forest untouched by man as it has existed for millennia (Brown, 1992).

Brown continues to sustain and propagate his neo-mythology. The subject of nostalgia in this case embraces a distant, bygone era when some noble traveller would be planting his first footprint upon the floor of the ancient forest. The brochure appeals to the Adamic instincts in those adventurous tourists who have at their disposal the limitless vista of the primeval forest, hitherto untouched, spared of any prior human intervention.

Nostalgia is projected with equal force, if with less subtlety, in a Tropical Adventures brochure. One passage invites visitors to:

> Relive the days of the cowboy at Karanambu ranch, in the savannah of the Northern Rupununi on the banks of the Rupununi river. Enjoy the simple life of a bygone era and the unique accommodation of clay brick and thatched roof huts.

The (probably male) tourist is invited to undertake that nostalgic journey to the days of the cowboys, the frontier days when tough men rode tough steeds. The past life being invoked is, thematically, simpler than today's with its complexities. The brochure's thematic structure carefully fuses two sets of myths — nostalgia and authenticity. The desired 'simple life of a bygone era' is a muted repudiation of the accretion of artifice, ultimately, inauthenticity, that now defines modernity.

The final excerpt for analysis will be a newspaper advertisement which appeared in a Guyana daily newspaper. One of the country's most famous resorts — Timberhead Resort — ran an advertisement promoting its rainforest lodge that is situated up the Kamuni Creek in Demerara on lands leased from the Amerindian village of Santa Mission. One of the promotional lines read 'See the exotic Amerindians'. That statement explosively compresses into one meaning a complex of myths associated with Amerindian Peoples. This is Cohen's 'human zoo' (Cohen 1996) concept. In response to the challenge of introducing indigenous tourism into the marketplace Hollinshead asserts that there is need for 'an enlightened sensitivity by which over time, indigenous cultures should be introduced to the exigencies and realities of marketing practice' (Hollinshead, 1996).

Promotional writing treads a fine line between the evocation of the sense of wonder, the expression of tourist awe and the crude stereotyping of primal peoples.

Romanticisation of indigenous experience and peoples reduces the tourism encounter to a quest for the confirmation of the myths of the tourist imaginary. It would certainly a mistake to assert that the distortion of indigenous tourism experience occurs only at the level of promotional expression. The design of the experience of the ground can be just as potent an agent of debasement and distortion. The 'staging' of indigenous ritual and the celebration of ethnic stereotypes under the guise of purveying the 'primitive' are manoeuvres aimed at facile tourist consumption. That scenario substitutes indigenous tokenism for indigenous tourism. The latter as a product is delicate and sophisticated, demanding the utmost sensitivity on the part of the image-makers as well as the experience providers.

## THE INDIGENOUS TOURISM PRODUCT

The indigenous tourism product essentially comprises two elements — People and land. People are seminal to the indigenous tourism product. The People component embraces language, forms of dress and worship, cuisine, patterns of dwelling, physiognomic factors, customs, practices, traditions, belief systems, forms of social and political organization and technological capabilities. The People component encompasses the entire spectrum of responses to the external environment. Land encompasses all natural formations and creations in the environment in which indigenous peoples find themselves.

Evidence from promotional writing indicates that in indigenous tourism both components — People and land — are invested with aura and mystique. Often the land is projected as the ancient backdrop against which the 'exotica' of Indigenous life unfold. This excerpt from a *Tropical Adventures* brochure illustrates the narrative power of the land itself:

A journey along the Kamuni river – overhanging vegetation has stained the water a deeper black colour and the chill air is relieved by intermittent bursts of sunlight. This is Amerindian Reservation land and we're on route to Timberhead.

This is the evocation of a 'bush' aesthetic, introduced by enchanting black waters and sunless air. Indigenous tourism succeeds when the prospective traveler is drawn to an Indigenous community by some insight into its land and people. In the course of that stay the visitor gains a deeper appreciation and understanding of some aspects of the lifestyle and culture of the visited community and of the environment of which the community is an integral part. In addition, that visit should in some way contribute towards the improvement or enhancement of the well-being and condition of the host community. With that objective the indigenous tourism experience can be constituted along the following lines.

**Planning:**
Positive – Community must be involved at all phases of operation.
Negative – Developers decide independently of community input.

**Promotion:**
Positive – Promotional tools create an image that stimulates a sense of wonder.
Negative – Image romanticises and falsifies indigenous experience.

**Attractions:**
Positive – Community determines or endorses selection of attractions and visitor frequencies.
Negative – Tours and attractions chosen and conducted with no reference to community.

**Experiences:**
Positive – Presented as integral to religious life.
Negative – Presented as staged, theatrical experience.

## CONCLUSION

People are indispensable to 'product' in indigenous tourism. That form of tourism entails a culture-system in which people and land inter-relate in a symbiosis conceived ages ago. Different from mass or resort tourism, indigenous tourism defies its own nature if it omits people from its very nucleus and axis. It is possible for a tourist to visit an all-inclusive resort and enjoy experiences that bear little relation to any resident or contiguous community. Beach tourism is not designed to enlighten participants about ethnographic subtleties of a visited community. A beach vacation seldom defines itself in relation to any historical or cultural frame of reference, and experiences are often transferable to locales at different points of the global seaside international. Indigenous tourism, on the contrary, is place and culture-specific; with each experience a custom-made product of a unique culture-system.

The centrality of people in indigenous tourism commits the managers of the indigenous tourism experience to observing some sensitivities in the design, marketing and development of the indigenous tourism product. Product development that is not on terms determined or endorsed by Indigenous Peoples is unlikely to endear tourism to the community. In Guyana a period of friction and tension sullied relations between a resort developer and the Amerindian community of Whyaka. This was the undesirable outcome of a breakdown in communication between the two groups.

Marketing tools and promotional imagery that derive more from tourist fantasy than from indigenous reality will poorly represent, and do violence to, the practice of indigenous tourism.

## REFERENCES

Altman, J & Finlayson, J. 1993. 'Aborigines, Tourism and Sustainable Development'. *Journal of Tourism Studies* 4 no. 1: 38 – 48.

Brown, R. 1992. 'Guyana's Natural Treasures'. *Guyana Tourist Guide*. Georgetown: Hughes and Thorne.

Browne, E. 1911. *British Guiana as a Holiday Resort*. Georgetown: Sprostons Ltd.

Cohen, E. 1996. 'Hunter-gatherer tourism in Thailand'. In *Tourism and Indigenous Peoples* eds. T. Hinch & R. Butler. London: International Thomson Business Press.

Crystal, E. 1989. 'Tourism in Toraja (Sulawesi, Indonesia)'. In *Hosts and Guests: The Anthropology of Tourism* ed. V. Smith. 2nd. edn. Philadelphia: University of Pennsylvania Press.

Dann, G. 1994. 'Tourism: the Nostalgia Industry of the Future.' In *Global Tourism: the Next Decadee* ed. W. Theobald. Oxford: Butterworth-Heinemann.

Forte, J. 1993. *Amerindians and Tourism in Guyana*. Georgetown: University of Guyana.

Fox, D. and G. Danns. 1993. *The Indigenous Condition in Guyana: A Field Report on the Amerindians of Mabura*. Georgetown: University of Guyana.

Garner, A. 1993. 'Finding the Balance: Defining a Truly Beneficial and Sustainable Tourism in Guyana'. MA Thesis. Roehampton Institute, London.

Getz, D. 1994. 'Event Tourism and the Authenticity Dilemma'. In *Global Tourism: the Next Decade* ed. W. Theobald. Oxford: Butterwoth-Heinemann.

Greenwood, D. 1989. 'Culture by the Pound: An Anthropological Perspective on Tourism as Cultural Commoditization. In *Hosts and Guests: the Anthropology of Tourism* ed. V. Smith. 2nd edn. Philadelphia: University of Pennsylvania.

Graburn, N. 1989. 'Tourism: the Sacred Journey'. In *Hosts and Guests: the Anthropology of Tourism* ed. V. Smith. 2nd edn. Philadelphia: University of Pennsylvania.

Hinch, T. and R. Butler. 1996. 'Indigenous Tourism: a Common Ground for Discussion'. In *Tourism and Indigenous Peoples* eds. T. Hinch and R. Butler. London: International Thomson Business Press.

Hollinshead, K. (1996) "Marketing and Metaphysical Realism: The Disidentification of Aboriginal Life. In *Tourism and Indigenous Peoples* eds. T. Hinch and R. Butler. London: International Thomson Business Press.

Jafari, J. 1990. 'Sociocultural Dimensions of Tourism'. Paper presented at Caribbean Tourism Organisation Conference on 'Tourism and Sociocultural Change in the Caribbean'. Trinidad & Tobago.

Keefe, J. 1993. 'Tourism and Land Alienation'. In *Tourism in Focus* ed. T. Barnett. London: Tourism Concern.

Klautky, C. 1994. 'Position of Guyanese Organisation of Indigenous Peoples'. Draft presentation to Tourism Advisory Board.

Kotch, E. 1993. 'The Politics of Developing Ecotourism' In *Tourism in Focus* ed. T. Barnett. London: Tourism Concern.

MacCannell, D. 1976. *A New theory of the Leisure Class*. New York: Shocken.

McKean, P. 1989. 'Towards a Theoretical Analysis of Tourism: Economic Dualism and Cultural Involution in Bali'. In *Hosts and Guests: the Anthropology of Tourism* ed. V. Smith. 2nd edn. Philadelphia: University of Pennsylvania.

Mercer, D. 1994. 'Native Peoples and Tourism: Conflict and Compromise'. In *Global Tourism: the Next Decade* ed. W. Theobald. Oxford: Butterworth-Heinemann.

Mowforth, M. 1993. 'In Search of an Ecotourist'. In *Tourism in Focus* ed. T. Barnett. London: Tourism Concern.

Nichter, M. 1992. *Anthropological Approaches to the Study of Ethnomedicine*. Switzerland: Gordon and Breach.

Rosaldo, R. 1989. *Culture and Truth: the Remaking of Social Analysis*. Boston: Beacon Press.

Selwyn, T. 1994. 'Tourism as Religion'. In *Tourism in Focus* ed. T. Barnett. London: Tourism Concern.

Smith, V. 1989. 'Nascent Tourism in Non-Western Societies'. In *Hosts and Guests: the Anthropology of Tourism* ed. V. Smith. 2nd edn. Philadelphia: University of Pennsylvania.

Torgovnick, M. 1990. *Gone Primitive: Savage Intellects, Modern Lives*. Chicago: University of Chicago Press.

Williams, P. 1993. 'Whither Ecotourism?' Paper presented at First National Conference on Ecotourism in Guyana, Hotel Tower, Georgetown.

Ziffer, K. 1989. 'Ecotourism: The Uneasy Alliance'. Conservation International Ecotourism Series. Washington DC: Ernst & Young.

## NOTE

1. This chapter is partly based on an article by the author published in the International Journal of Contemporary Hospitality Management, Vol. 15, No. 3, 2003, pp. 140-146.

# 12

# PLANNING FOR SUSTAINABLE TOURISM DEVELOPMENT: JAMAICA HERITAGE DESTINATIONS APPROACH

Ibrahim Ajagunna

## ABSTRACT

*This chapter examines the concept of sustainable tourism development and how the concept could be translated to heritage tourism destinations in Jamaica. The first part of the chapter takes an in-depth look at what sustainable tourism is all about, its importance and why it is important to formulate objectives for sustainable development at the planning stage. The chapter goes on to examine the importance of policy for sustainable tourism development as well as what conditions must be met for effective policies to be achieved. Economic, environmental, social and political costs and benefits of sustainable tourism development at heritage destinations are examined in detail. The role and responsibilities of partnership in planning for success at heritage tourism destinations in Jamaica are further expatiated on, and the chapter is concluded by taking a look at some principles behind the approach to sustainable tourism policy and planning and how these principles could be successfully applied to Jamaica heritage tourism destinations.*

## INTRODUCTION

Among the essential fabric of Jamaica's economy is the tourism industry. In recent years, new dimensions such as the all-inclusive concept, the cruise shipping industry, community and heritage tourism have been added. While it is true that heritage is viewed as something to be shared by all, that is, by both locals and visitors alike, the focus should be how to conserve heritage resource assets from any form of erosion. Today, most destinations of the world, especially the first world countries, are putting their focus on sustainable tourism development. However, the question remains whether this idea has, in any way, been properly conceptualised by the

Jamaican government, the Tourism Product Development Company (TPDCo), the Jamaica Tourist Board (JTB), and other private tourism product developers.

Tourism, as defined by Jafari (1982:11) is 'the study of man away from his usual habitat, of the industry which responds to his needs, and of the impacts that both he and the industry have on the host's socio-economic and physical environment'. Because of the multitude of impacts of tourism on all aspects of life and environment, sustainable tourism development is now the order of the day. The World Commission on Environment and Development defines sustainable development as 'development that meets the needs of the present generation without compromising the ability of future generations to meet their own needs' (Owen, Witt and Gammon, 1993). This has been the focus of many heritage tourism destinations in Jamaica. A good example should have been the Port Royal Heritage Tourism Project. However, this concept may rather be considered a marketing strategy than a thing of reality. A plausible reason for this is that a large percentage of the Jamaican population currently lives below the poverty level and individuals tend to scramble for the little resources that are available and which are within their reach, amongst which is tourism products.

## TOURIST-HOST RELATIONS IN JAMAICA

Mathieson and Wall (1982) drawing upon Doxey's experience in the Barbados and Niagara-on-the-lake, studied that tourist destinations pass successfully through stages of euphoria, apathy, irritation and antagonism, and to the final stage in which people have forgotten what they cherished and the environment is destroyed. It may be argued, that the reality of Doxey's theory of irritation suggests that sustainable tourism development may be difficult to achieve based on the present state of Jamaica's economy. Evidence of these are apparent in most of the island's destinations, where tourist harassment has continually been on the increase. One viable option to this has been the all inclusive hotels. But then, for how long will people continue to be held in captivity to be entertained? Also, some members of the society may argue that the resorts patrol have been doing a good job in policing perpetrators of crime and harassment in some resort areas in Jamaica, then again is their presence not in a way creating some panic for the tourists? The tourists want to be free and hence a free and secure environment should be provided at all times.

While a large number of tourists may escape being victims of crime and violence, only a few escape harassment. Beach boys, street vendors, art and craft vendors, taxi operators and beggars have contact with tourists and they do sometimes harass them. Harassment of tourists in Jamaica is not a new phenomenon. Evidence is presented in a television documentary on Jamaica and Florida titled 'Dark Side of the Sun' by Yorkshire Television (1995). In the documentary, tourists to Jamaica were seriously warned about the level of harassment on the island. The tourists were advised to avoid downtown Kingston (if possible) as it is considered to be highly prone to crimes. This suggests that almost everyone visiting Jamaica is approached many times by a variety of characters, including street vendors, beach boys and a host of others.

The Jamaica scenario is similar to what Briguiglo, Butler, Harrison and Filho (1996) had associated with tourism in Barbados. Their contention was that many locals in Barbados try to make a living by entrepreneurial interaction with the tourists on the beach and in the street. Rather than these locals seeing this behaviour as unworthy, the perpetrators often see these approaches as simply those of hopeful salesmen looking for business.

## SUSTAINABLE TOURISM DEVELOPMENT

It is important to conceptualise sustainable development at the planning stage for community and heritage tourism destinations in Jamaica, in order to avoid what is presently plaguing most tourist destinations on the island. Whether development is a conventional system or an eco-system, there is a need for proper planning and management. Tourism planning is conceptualised by Rose (1984) as a multidimensional activity and seeks to be integrative. It embraces social, economic, political, psychological, anthropological and technological factors. It is concerned with the past, present and future. According to Mill (1992), consequences of unplanned development may include negative physical, human, marketing and organisational impacts. Most of these impacts are currently facing most tourism destinations in Jamaica, where crime and/or harassment have become serious social issues.

For heritage destinations in Jamaica, these consequences need to be anticipated and plans to deal with them should include proper education of the locals as to the importance of tourism to their community. Other plans should include provision of specialised skill training for the locals so that they can take up jobs in the tourism industry. These will effectively prevent outsiders from taking up all available jobs within the heritage centres.

## PLANNING FOR SUSTAINABILITY

The importance of planning for sustainability of a heritage destination should be to set in motion an extraordinary process of transforming the economic base of the community into a major international resort, while at the same time preserve the unique cultural elements and historical authenticity that have made the site attractive for development. According to Gunn (1994), historical societies have recognised the value of mounting campaigns to preserve historic sites and buildings.

But, in addition to protecting lands, and structures, they have rebuilt and modified structures to adapt them to tourism.

Successful development of heritage destinations should begin with goal setting, as goals are important during planning and development. Gunn (1994) emphasised that goals provide the framework for the identification of specific objectives. Gunn further emphasised four planning goals which include, enhancement of visitor satisfaction, improved economic and business success, protection of resources and assets, and community and area integration. It is an empirical matter to state that goals and objectives are important in planning for heritage tourism and it is necessary to put them in practice. Bramwell (1996) suggests some broad objectives in a local plan directed at developing sustainable tourism under three headings; these are social, environmental and economic.

Examples of social objectives are to enhance the well-being of visitors and local residents, to ensure that tourism brings benefits to local culture and traditions of the area, to promote forms of tourism which increase respect between visitors and local residents, to promote tourist activity which draws upon and celebrates the distinctive character of the culture and traditions of the local area and to involve the local community in decisions about the development of tourism in the local area.

Examples of environmental objectives are, to ensure that tourism benefits the environment by raising funds from tourism for environmental conservation work, to promote forms of tourism which lead to enhanced appreciation and understanding of local environment qualities and to develop tourist activities which draw upon the distinctive environmental features of the local area.

Examples of economic objectives are to maximise the economic benefits of tourism for local residents and businesses and to avoid leakages of tourist expenditure outside the local economy. There is urgent need to encourage tourists to respect the ways of making a living in the local area, ensure that tourism creates rewarding and well-paid jobs for local residents, ensure that tourism activities help support local services such as public transportation and retail shops, and to ensure that tourism does not dominate the local economy and that it helps diversify local employment and sources of income.

## IMPORTANCE OF SUSTAINABLE TOURISM POLICY

To guide against negative effects of tourism, planners of heritage tourism in Jamaica must develop policies and strategies that will guide against these effects. Amongst the policies should be to disallow illegal settlers or squatters in and around the heritage resort and to provide training opportunity for locals to work with the police in policing the heritage centres and its environs in order to discourage any form of illegal activity such as prostitution and sale of illicit drugs. This particular policy should help reduce crimes and harassment against the tourists, and subsequently create confidence in the tourists that the locals will candidly deal with them. It should also be the policy that a certain percentage of employees in tourism-related business be drawn from the heritage centres. This policy should aim at uplifting the quality of life of the people at the heritage centre, while at the same time improve the local economy and business success.

However, it may be argued that this type of policy may not be of interest to the general public and the government. This is because such a policy cannot remain independent of the political process within the region and it cannot be value free. While it is in the government's interest to commit substantial amounts of money to planning and development, the government also has responsibility for provision of employment to all her subjects, both within the heritage centre and outside the area for development.

Planning for heritage tourism in Jamaica should, from the onset, focus exclusively on economic, social, cultural and environmental issues. As tourism is expected to grow steadily in Jamaica, the aim for heritage tourism has been to expand it as an important economic sector. It is apparent that this expansion will result in increased pressure on the environment with negative impacts, (for example deforestation, mining of the hills for filling lowlands for building purposes et cetera), unless appropriate measures are taken by the government.

Because of the inseparability of tourism and the environment, heritage tourism developers must recognise the role and importance of the National Environment Planning Agency (NEPA) and the government as an agent that can enforce environmental protection. It is needless to say that, today, tourists globally are demanding that their environment be of high quality, pollution free as well as interesting. This, therefore, calls for proper environmental analysis and planning of the heritage centre before development is allowed to commence.

In addition to environmental analysis and planning, the developers must add the planning and design of tourist facilities. Inskeep (1987) asserts that environmental planning of tourist resorts, hotels and associated facilities is done at three levels. They are land use planning, site planning, and architectural, landscaping and engineering planning. Inskeep (1987) argues that the independence and the interdependence of these levels depend on whether the project is a small single-purpose or a large multi-purpose resort. Facilities and infrastructures which must be included on the drawing board to create comfort for the locals and tourists at heritage centres should include road network, disposal system, security, health services, housing, utilities, and good network communication system.

Because Jamaica is prone to and has witnessed disasters such as hurricane, flooding, land slides and earthquakes, environmental engineering design is of paramount importance. Engineering design is necessary for environmental hazards such as earthquakes, hurricanes, heavy rainfall and flooding, land erosion and land slides. This, therefore, calls for the inclusion of an organisation such as Office of

Disaster Preparedness and Evacuation Management (ODPEM) at the planning and development stage of any heritage centre. This will allow for daily monitoring and reporting on the environment for any disaster that is foreseen.

However, the question that remains in mind is: what form of maintenance and management is thought of for the environmental quality since tourists are increasingly seeking high quality destinations and are willing to pay a premium price for attractive pollution-free environments? The only alternative for heritage tourism developers in Jamaica is to aim towards sustainable development. Bramwell (1996) argues that there is increasing recognition of the importance of managing tourism so that it does not threaten the natural, social and cultural resources base on which the tourist industry and our environment and society depends. The options therefore seem to revolve around the fact that heritage tourism planning should focus on two extremes; on the one hand, to maximise the benefits of tourism while, on the other hand, minimise the negative impacts of tourism.

## COSTS AND BENEFITS OF SUSTAINABLE TOURISM DEVELOPMENT

Bramwell (1996) asserts that developing a more sustainable tourist industry is concerned with planning and management in a positive way which encourages the retention of as many benefits from tourism. His contention is that, benefits and costs are economic, environmental, social, cultural and political. Economic benefits include the injection of additional income and employment in local economies, the opportunity for economically marginal forms of businesses to diversify their activities and gain new sources of income and assistance in the economic diversification of declining old industrial areas and declining rural areas.

A practical example of this is Port Royal heritage tourism that was also targeted as a cruise shipping destination. Potential economic costs are that tourism may distort local employment patterns with more part-time and seasonal jobs, excessive leakage or expropriation of profits from local activities to outside business interest. These costs may be somehow difficult to abate in Jamaica today since most tourist consumables are imported rather than being produced locally; an evil which has long been perpetrated by the all inclusive hotels. There may also be a loss of local control over business as external transnational companies are now taking over the local tourist industry. Examples of these would be the Ritz Carlton and the Hilton, just to mention a few.

Environmental potential benefits are that tourism may protect ecosystems from encroachment by other economic activities and funding for conservation and research may be provided from tourism. Tourism may enhance public understanding of ecological issues, such as biodiversity and energy conservation. Potential environmental costs are that tourism can increase many types of pollution, marine and terrestrial habitual degradation ( such as the Kingston harbour) and contribution to worldwide environmental problems.

Social and cultural potential benefits include support for local services used by both tourists and local residents, increased cultural diversity and community pride and sense of identity through promotion and celebration of cultural differences, revitalising traditional festivals and other cultural and artistic activities. Potential social and cultural costs include, rising property prices and cost of living which can mean local residents cannot afford to live in the area. These may eventually lead to loss of cultural authenticity, open antagonism and crime specifically directed at tourists. In Jamaica today, these costs are endemic to many tourist destinations such as Ocho Rios, Montego Bay and Negril.

Political benefits are that tourism may reinforce regional and local identity and pride through the promotion of regional and local distinctiveness. It may empower the local community by involving local people in tourism planning. Also, it might be able to encourage the liberalisation of restrictive and oppressive regimes. Costs may include an increased influence of external, often transnational business which may lead to a loss of local community control and erosion of democratic processes and local accountability.

As stated earlier, achieving all the above require that effective policies be put in place during planning. Owen, Witt and Gammon (1993) are of the view that the concept of sustainable development is infiltrating the policy framework of many government organisations and agencies and that the challenges that face policy makers should not be underestimated. They suggest certain conditions which must be met for effective policies to be realised. These conditions include:

- Compromise, that is, striking a balance between growth and conservation. This calls for the present generation to make sacrifices in favour of a generation that is not yet born.
- Commitment, that is, recognise that sustainability requires deeds as well as fine words and control, this is, putting in place a framework of planning and other policies to regulate the pattern and scale of development. These organisations need to be imaginative, well thought out and practical, rather than simply restrictive. They must be implemented fairly, consistently and with vigour.
- Cooperation, this is, recognising that the search for sustainable development, has an international dimension. That is, the rich and the poorer countries of the world need to work together to secure a more equitable use of resources.

## Partnership and Responsibility

Formulating policy and planning for sustainable heritage centres in Jamaica should incorporate the government, the private sector, the non profit sector and community leaders. While it is the primary role of the Jamaican government to enact and enforce laws and maintain order, the government has been involved in the tourism sector over the years, especially in the areas of marketing and promotion. Apart from this, the government equally has responsibility for providing services such as water supply, electricity, sewage disposal, police and fire protection, all on which the survival of tourism destinations depend. Understanding these multifaceted roles of government requires that governmental agencies such as TPDCo and JTB are not left out during planning and policy formulation for any heritage centre.

The largest capital injection in tourism in Jamaica has been through the private sector. These capital injections need to be safe-guarded as investments made in hotels is costly, and should tourists decide to go elsewhere, it is practically impossible to move the physical plants. Also, much of the economic benefit derived from business investment and employment creation; the growth of tourism at a community level; and the infusion of sustainable practices will come through the responses of the private sector tourism operators. The involvement of the private business sector in tourism in Jamaica cannot be overemphasised and hence cannot be left out at policy formulation and planning stage for heritage tourism development in the country.

The non profit sector such as religion, health and professional organisations have not received prominence in tourism in Jamaica. According to Knechtel (1985), the non profit sector holds great promise for tourism expansion, especially in developing countries. His contention is that rather than inviting the large multinational companies to invest outside capital and labour, local talent can be harnessed for many indigenous and small scale tourism developments. This is because the goal is less for profit than for ideologies, many cultural benefits can accrue from non profit tourism development.

The Circle K and Rotaract annual convention could be expanded to attract more youth from other parts of the world. Their inclusion will also allow the youth of the country to take active part in the success of tourism in the future. The Rastafarian religion in Jamaica, through the influence of 'late Right Honourable Nesta Bob Marley', could attract thousands of pilgrims to the country. If their functions are further developed, it could grow into festivals similar to the Moslems' pilgrimage to Mecca and Medina or the Christians pilgrimage to Jerusalem. Incidentally, many historic sites such as the birth place of Bob Marley and Marcus Garvey may be included as part of the product offering.

The role of community leaders during policy formulation and planning need not be over emphasised. While the tourism industry aims at marketing the community resources, the community should take an active and leading role from the inception as the decisions made would affect them both presently and in the future. It may be well argued that, on the one hand, part of the community may be receptive to tourism development because of anticipation of economic gain, and on the other hand, some part of the community may antagonise any form of tourism development due to its negative social, economic, cultural and environmental costs. Spring break and nude weddings in Jamaica are the two most recent examples where there arose a lot of public and community outcry. Who knows what these may bring to the future of tourism in Jamaica?

With the inclusion of all the stakeholders at the planning and policy formulation stage for heritage tourism in Jamaica, likely negative impacts or costs can be anticipated from such development and predictions made for curbing or reducing them.

Apart from meeting all the necessary considerations, some ten principles behind the approach to sustainable tourism policy and planning put forward by Bramwell (1996) need to be emphasised. The approach emphasises that natural and human resources should never be allowed to be damaged catastrophically or irreversibly, and more generally, should be managed within limits and in ways considered to be sustainable. The principles to the approach are:

- The approach sees policy, planning and management as appropriate and indeed essential responses to the problems of natural and human resource misuse in tourism.
- The approach is generally not anti-growth, but it emphasises that there are limits to growth.
- Long term rather than short term thinking is necessary.
- The concern of sustainable tourism policy and planning are not just environmental, but are also economic, social and cultural.
- The approach emphasises the importance of satisfying human needs and aspirations which entails a prominent concern for equity and fairness.
- All stakeholders need to be consulted and empowered in tourism decision-making, and they also need to be informed about sustainable development issues.
- Putting the ideas of sustainable tourism into practice means recognising that in reality there are often limits to what will be achieved in the short and medium term.
- An understanding of how market economies operate, of the cultures and management procedures of private sector business and of public and voluntary sector organisations, and of the values and attitudes of the public is necessary in order to turn good intentions into practical measures.

- There are frequently conflicts of interest over the use of resources, which means that in practice trade-offs and compromises may be necessary.
- The balancing of costs and benefits in decision on different courses of actions must extend to considering how much different individuals will gain or lose.

It would seem that if the principles, conditions and objectives stated are adopted by Jamaica's heritage tourism planners, it is likely that they will be able to positively move from where they are to where they intend to be. However, formulating sustainable tourism strategy is the key to achieving the principles, conditions and the stated objectives. Lane (1994) asserts that there are four keys to success in producing sustainable tourism strategies. Firstly, it is important that the person or team formulating the strategy is skilled not only in tourism development but also in economic, ecological and social analysis. Secondly, wide consultations amongst all interest groups are essential. These consultations will include trade and business, transport, farmers, administrators, and the custodians of the natural and historic assets of the area. Thirdly, openness has a very special role to play. Tourism relies more than any other industry on local goodwill, that is, the ability of the locals to make holiday makers feel welcome. Fourthly, the strategy making process should not be a once-only affair. It has to be an evolving long-term enterprise, able to cope with changes and able to admit to its own mistakes and short comings. It should be the beginning of a partnership between business, government, and cultural and conservation interests.

## CONCLUSION

The concept of sustainable tourism sees conventional tourism as an eternal triangle of forces, with host communities and habitats, visitors and tourism businesses in an unstable relationship. In Jamaica today, the growth requirements of tourism has led to the domination of host areas such as Ocho Rios and Montego Bay by visitors and tourism businesses. The aim of sustainable tourism for heritage centres therefore, is to bring the opposing forces of the triangle into equilibrium for the benefit of all.

For the local community, sustainable tourism should provide carefully planned economic growth that will provide satisfying jobs without dominating the local economy. It must not abuse the natural habitat and traditional values and societies should be maintained. The benefits of tourism should be diffused through many communities and not concentrated in one section of the island. There must be limit to growth and such growth should be gradual.

For the industry, there should be a responsibility accepting, that is, developers should consciously agree that some form of tourism activity are not acceptable in some areas. Development must be carefully tailored to the communities involved and the need for cooperation between the tourism industry and the planning authorities should be recognised. For the visitors, it should provide a good value with harmonious and satisfying experience. The host community and the visitors should be on equal terms. The goal therefore begins with sound policy and proper planning both at the local and national levels.

## REFERENCES

Bramwell, B. 1996. *Tourism Policy and Planning, First Serial Rights*. Sheffield: Sheffield Hallam University.

Gunn, C.A. 1994. *The Purpose of Tourism Planning, Basics, Concepts, and Cases*. 3rd edn. Washinton DC: Taylor and Francis.

Inskeep, E. 'Environmental Planning for Tourism'. *Annals of Tourism Research* 14(1987).

Jafari, J. 1982. 'The Tourism Market Basket of Goods and Services'. In *Studies in Tourism Wildlife Conservation* eds. T.V. Singh, J. Kanr and D.P. Singh. Metropolitan Books.

Lane, B. 1994. *Sustainable Rural Tourism Strategy, A Tool for Development and Conservation*. Clevedon: Channel View Publication.

Matheison, A and G. Wall. 1982. *Tourism, Economic, Physical and Social Impacts*. Hallow: Longman.

Mill, R.C. 1992. *The Tourism System, An introductory Text*. New Jersey: Prentice Hal.

Owen, R.E., S.F. Witt and S. Gammon. 1993. 'Sustainable Tourism Development in Wales, From Theory to Practice'. *Tourism Management*.

# 13

# NO NOOK OF GROUND SECURE FROM RASH ASSAULT? ECOTOURISM, HERITAGE TOURISM AND THE JAMAICAN MAROONS

Elizabeth Thomas-Hope

## ABSTRACT

*The active consideration of proposals by Jamaican government agencies to encourage heritage tourism by opening up the Cockpit Country (an ecologically sensitive area and home to the Maroons), raises questions about the manner in which this unique aspect of Jamaica's cultural and environmental heritage is to be exploited. The Maroons, the descendants of runaway slaves, secured treaty rights to land from the colonial authorities in the eighteenth century, were able to retain better their cultural traditions because of their inaccessibility. Tourism literature illustrates the difficulties and dangers in the development of heritage sites unless careful safeguards are put in place. It also raises questions about authenticity and leads to the suggestion that much more consultation both with the Maroons themselves, as well as anthropologists, historians and ecologists, needs to take place before this unique cultural and ecological heritage is developed by tourist entrepreneurs.*

## INTRODUCTION

The Maroons of Jamaica — descendants of runaway slaves — still remain in small communities in the Cockpit country and the Blue and John Crow mountain ranges. They have retained their sense of identity as Maroons, based on pride in their ancestors' resistance to enslavement, a retention of identity made possible by their physical isolation and continued mastery of their environment. Maroon culture, as it is understood by the Maroons themselves (as well as society at large), is based on adherence to ancestral ways of life and technologies, on secrecy concerning the philosophies, beliefs and symbolic meaning of life, death and the afterlife, and on relationship with and reverence for the environment. Maroon culture, therefore, cannot remain authentic and survive the outward migration of its people and the inward penetration of modern culture.

The inroad of modern tourism, and with it the potential for foreign tourist flows into the areas and communities, will hasten this process and bring the additional risk of the maroon legacy becoming corrupted by fakism and gimmickry, as folklore and souvenirs are packaged as products for the industry. This underlines the importance of capturing what remains now of Maroon authenticity so that it will properly inform and be reflected in the heritage which is preserved. If there is no continuity of people or their material culture (buildings, artifacts and the like), even if the continuity is only present in remnants of the true past which is to be captured or reconstructed, then authenticity will be lacking. Thus, we need to ensure that those who are still part of that culture will contribute to its transition from living culture to Maroon heritage — and subsequently gain through the economic opportunities which could be derived from the appropriate absorption into the wider development of Jamaica's national heritage tourism.

As the Jamaican tourist industry develops further into the realm of ecotourism and heritage tourism, Maroon people and culture have much to offer in philosophical and practical ways to that development. This contribution could be through the conservation of the ecosystem and preservation of culture. The opportunities which tourism could bring will largely depend on the full appreciation of the processes — both ecological and cultural/societal — which will occur. The implications of ecotourism and heritage tourism will be determined by both the type and qualitative aspects of the industry and also by the volume or quantitative aspects. There is an important, even an urgent, need for pro-active policies and careful planning, so that the transition from authentic and living culture to heritage and tourism resource and product are appropriately understood and managed for sustainability.

While both the John Crow and Blue Mountain ranges and the Cockpit country are sensitive ecological zones in Jamaica, the latter is especially sensitive and important. The potential environmental and ecological impacts of tourist development in the karst hills of the Cockpit country alone are vast (Eyre, 1989 and 1995). This area of Jamaica contains many of the endangered endemic species: thirty-seven of the forty-eight types of unique amphibians and reptiles that live in Jamaica, like the yellow boar snake, are found in this region. It is home to many species in danger of becoming extinct, such as the Jamaican Giant Swallowtail butterfly, as well as three-quarters of the nearly 100 species of the island's birds. It is famed for its biodiversity with over 100 different species of plants. Its caves are the habitat of bat colonies with three types of bats found no where else in the world (Balfour Spence, 2000). It is the source of some of Jamaica's most important rivers. In short, any development such as that proposed under the 'Jamaica 2000 Millennium Project' (Office of the Prime Minister, Government of Jamaica, September 1999) and the 'Cockpit Country Conservation Project' (2000) have to look very carefully at all aspects of the situation.

This chapter concentrates on the cultural issues, for the current generation has no excuse for being ignorant of cultural prostitution for short-term economic gain. William Wordsworth, the nineteenth century English poet, wrote scathingly of the growing invasion of tourists into his native Lake District nearly two centuries ago: 'Is there no nook of ground secure from rash assault?' Our senses and our information base are now so much greater that it should be possible to avoid the kind of cultural destruction inflicted on islands such as Hawaii. Yet the contemporary environmentalist, Jonathan Porritt, is still sufficiently alarmed to pose the question: 'How many hellholes are we prepared to create on the way to paradise?' (Quoted in Croall, 1995).

## THE JAMAICAN MAROONS
### Background

Some African slaves of the Spaniards took to the hills at the time of the British conquest (1655), forming the nucleus of the first Maroon communities in Jamaica (Campbell, 1990). From fragmentary data, it appears that there were at least three main groups of Maroons with recognised leaders under the Spanish. They settled in the hills of present day St. Catherine, Clarendon and Manchester. After 1655 were added new bands of Africans who resisted enslavement after arrival in Jamaica and who found refuge in the mountainous, forested interior, and regularly raided the plantations. After nearly a century of intermittent warfare against the 'rebellious Negroes', treaties were signed by the British colonial authorities with Jamaica's Leeward Maroons in 1738/39 and with the Windward Maroons in June 1739. The peace treaty, which was signed, resulted in the Maroons gaining recognition, self-government and a significant amount of land in different parts of Jamaica.

### Contemporary Maroon communities and culture

The current Maroon settlements in the Blue and John Crow Mountains and the Cockpit Country (figure 1) are directly linked to the areas of the earliest hideouts of the runaway slaves that escaped during the Spanish occupation and the British invasion. Two distinct areas of settlement developed — the Windward Maroons in the east (Blue and John Crow Mountains) who originally settled Nanny Town, Moor Town, Charles Town and Scotts Hall and the Leeward Maroons in the west (Cockpit Country) who originally settled Maroon Town and Accompong. Perhaps the most significant community was Nanny Town, located in the most inaccessible and hostile area of the Blue Mountains and led by one of Jamaica's National Heroes — Nanny. Today, the main Windward Maroon communities are Moore Town and Charles Town in Portland, Scotts Hall in St. Mary and Hayfield in St. Thomas. The

Leeward Maroon communities are Maroon Town in Trelawny and Accompong in St. Elizabeth.

The land given to the Maroons at the time of the signing of the treaty in the eighteenth century was not taxed by the Jamaican Government and, to this day, no Maroon is allowed to sell any portion of it to a non-Maroon. Each clan owns a section which is inherited by succeeding generations. Only the Maroon settlement of Hayfield is not part of treaty lands, but instead, was purchased by a wealthy Maroon for his grand children. Although there exists only one title for the property, the land is divided up for use by Maroon families, many of whom moved from Moore Town.

A significant effect of the peace treaty was that the Maroons were brought into close contact with the Jamaican society. This, combined with their increasing participation in economic activity with non-Maroon communities, resulted in what has been referred to as the 'creolisation' of the Maroon culture, especially of their language. On the other hand, the Maroons have maintained some aspects of the original culture and lifestyle of their African ancestors largely as a result of the continued inaccessibility of their settlements.

The Maroons have come from varying ethnic backgrounds: Koromantes (mainly Akan slaves from the Gold Coast [Ghana], and Ga, Adangme and Ewe slaves from neighbouring areas); Non-Koromantes (from the slave coast —Volta to Benin); Creoles (descendants of Africans born either on the plantations or in the Maroon settlements); and Indians (Arawaks; and Mesquito Indians brought in by the Spaniards and British from Central America).

The culture, which was consolidated under conditions of physical inaccessibility, rebelliousness, attack, defense and self-sufficiency, resulted from the fusion of traditions from the various groups. The more distinctive aspects of the Maroon culture included the following:

1) A political organisation/structure with its government machinery consisting of the colonel (head of the political hierarchy), his cabinet consisting of a secretary, a major and a captain, and a council;
2) An economy which evolved from wild hog hunting and fishing to agriculture;
3) The retention of practices, traditions and beliefs, in particular rituals; and
4) The use of music and dancing associated with healing, birth and death, which have their roots in the original Maroon culture.

## Legal Status and Government

The Maroons still hold a unique position in Jamaican society. This stems from the fact that the Jamaican Government has to recognise the terms of treaties signed between the British and the Maroons in 1739. These terms included not only the granting of lands but also the life tenure of Maroon chiefs or colonels. This has recently changed in the Accompong community where colonels are now elected by ballot and hold office for five years, but in Moore Town the leader retains his post for life. The smaller Maroon towns also have colonels who are chosen by elections about which outsiders are not consulted. Community affairs in Accompong and Moore Town are directed by the colonel and a council of thirty-two and ten members respectively, who are appointed by him. The colonel's approval or permission is sought in all matters. He in turn may seek advice from his councillors or any individual of his choice. Since 1966, colonels have been farmers and teachers. It is important for them to have a very thorough knowledge of Maroon history and heritage. He and the council settle disputes and, by Clause 12 of the Treaty signed with the British, the Maroons were given full power to inflict any punishment they think proper for crimes committed among themselves, the death penalty the only exception. This still holds true today. The Jamaican police cannot arrest a Maroon within the latter's territory.

In Moore Town, no leader has ever sought office — each was taken unawares when asked to accept the position and on every occasion there was election by acclamation. The current colonel, Col Harris, recalled his surprise at his nomination which was due to the fact that as a young man he had courageously involved himself in lessening the influence of 'the Dancer man' tradition, as he thought it did more harm than good (Bedasse and Stewart, 1994).

## *Maroon Identity, sense of heritage and perception of change*

Colonel Harris wrote in his article 'The Maroons and Moore Town' (1993) that it was most important to understand that the African slaves brought language, culture, and 'extra-sensory attributes from Mother Africa' some five centuries ago. These survived the vicissitudes of existence in what was once a 'strange land' — a rugged and inhospitable environment — and they were dedicated to the preservation of all that was best in their past. Though extremely poor in monetary terms, the Maroons refused to be mendicants or ciphers in the political game. They recognised their 'vast potential for the greater good of humanity' and awaited some 'decent' assistance in the development of their assets (Bedasse and Stewart, 1994).

The Maroons' traditional approach to natural resources on their lands had always been one of conservation and preservation, but Colonel Harris expressed the view that environmental education amongst his young people was lacking but that they were prepared to learn. This situation perhaps resulted from the reluctance on the elders' part to divulge secrets to the younger generation who sometimes ridiculed them, thus allowing a great tradition of conservation to become endangered.

With changing times, outside cultural penetrations and high economic costs, the council members realised that the Maroon community needed to embark on projects which embrace sustainable development. Consequently, they have sought dialogue with the National Parks and Conservation Areas and expressed a desire for the beginning of new partnership. Colonel M.L. Wright (1993) states,

> Maroons in former times were skilled in bush medicine, and even today some use the different (bush) herbs of the land for medicinal purposes. The roots and barks of trees are also used to make Maroon drinks, which are always available at moderate costs to visitors. Most Maroons still honour and respect their Heritage Treaty and customs. However, a small minority of males are desirous that these should cease and the Accompong Maroons should now forfeit these privileges and customs and be totally merged into the tax-paying population of Jamaica. Such a suggestion will always be defeated by well thinking Maroons for it would dash to nought what past Maroon warriors — men women and even children risked their lives so desperately and arduously to obtain.

Within the Maroon communities of Jamaica many traditions seem to have been discontinued. The heroes of the resistance are still revered and celebrated. Celebration days re-enact folkloric scenes from the past, but rituals and some customs have become in danger of extinction because they are no longer being passed down to a younger generation. The beliefs and practices of groups and individuals have been kept secret for centuries, and the elders have voiced their displeasure at the efforts of the young who try to copy their music and dancing. They find the vocal sounds 'too English'. The elder Maroons would rather see the death of a tradition than allow it to be treated with disrespect (Bedasse and Stewart, 1994).

Customs regarding resource-use have also changed, due largely to external influences. Hunting wild boar for 'jerk' made popular by the Maroons is now done only on very special occasions because the destruction of the forest and hunting has made the animal scarce. Pollution of the rivers has destroyed much of the fish life – fishing and the eating of the 'hog nose' fish were a much enjoyed custom accompanied by story telling. These fish, which were once endemic to Jamaica, have disappeared.

Communication methods have changed and given way to 'modern' methods (some of which are now proving highly inadequate). The Abeng (cow horn) is still used to communicate special messages to the community and the drums are also still used for celebrations. The old Jamaican Maroons remember their own creole which is now used only to communicate with ancestral spirits but which was probably their everyday speech until the early part of this century. Jamaican Maroon creole is extremely conservative in its English component. The same Maroon populations have also retained some African speech as well.

## AUTHENTICITY AND MAROON HERITAGE

The authenticity of the surviving Maroon communities and culture is based on the persistence of many practices and beliefs handed down through the generations in the oral tradition. The evidence is that the number of persons who still genuinely participate in and are entrusted with the Maroon secrets is now rapidly diminishing. Certainly, the opening up of the Blue and John Crow Mountains National Parks to tourism will rapidly erode the remaining elements of the authentic culture.

The importance of the past to the Maroons is derived from belief in the significance of place; the celebration of ethnic roots and a victorious military record. Their sense of the past validates their present location in the inaccessible settlements of the Cockpit Country and Blue and John Crow Mountains. Their identification with ethnic roots and a history of victory over oppressors enhances their identity and serves to enrich their culture and sense of tradition. The past totally validates the present. But there is a tension, especially seen among the young, between the past and the present. For them, the past is an embarrassment in the present and there is a strong temptation to dispossess the past by selling it to the first bidder in the eco-tourist business. With the loss of pride in the past is likely to occur a reduced sense of worth.

It is not feasible to 'sell' living culture without losing its authenticity and, in the case of the Maroons, without becoming the image of primitive curiosity. Soon traditional practices become acts played out for tourist consumption and payment and the practitioners become actors. This is already occurring in Accompong as the elders dress up in 'African' robes and perform ritual ceremonies as a spectacle for the regular arrival of foreign tourists. Already the authenticity of Accompong Maroon culture has begun to give way to heritage tourism. A small museum houses a number of artifacts, many of which are or were common to households throughout Jamaica. Thus Maroon culture to be absorbed into heritage tourism will have to be re-constructed for tourist consumption and the method of this re-construction will determine its success. Above all, it will be important that in the involvement of surviving Maroon culture as a resource for tourism full cognisance is taken of the image that will be portrayed. It is in their favour that Maroons believe in their own historical successes and, as a result, retain a strong positive sense of identity.

This past, and their pride in the past, has been tremendously important to the Maroons. There is much to be learned from this both with regard to the significance of heritage to the rest of Jamaican society and as an indication of the sensitivity which has to be exercised if all that has been gained by Maroon identity is not to be lost after the current generation of elders has passed away.

First, this must be constructed for Jamaicans — not the tourists. Heritage is rarely neutral. If it is reconstructed only for its own sake — because it is the past or history — then it will not be relevant to anyone, least of all the Maroons. It has to be 'domesticated', not politicise it. Heritage is selective and it makes important statements about the identity, which a people wish to create, and the memories which they wish to preserve. Nevertheless, it can be successfully used to purge the bitter memories of the past for it can emancipate from the tyranny of the past (Lowenthal 1985). The gentrification of history can be just as dangerous as the tourist packaging of it. In this age of post-modernism the people themselves — in this case the Maroons — must represent themselves. In the conservation of history, as well as of nature or the ecosystem, we must preserve the ordinary as well as the spectacular, for only then can the ordinary people find support and enrichment of their culture. But, they must be aware of what it is they are representing; seek guidance and not rely only on the oral tradition and memory. It is important to remember (and for the Maroons this will be the challenge) that the authenticity of their past, like all histories, is reconstructed for heritage. Still, they must be there to benefit not only from the advantages of the knowledge of their identity of which they are so proud, but also to benefit from the economic results of the absorption of their historic localities into the circuit of ecotourism and the absorption of their history into the national heritage.

## TRADITIONAL CARIBBEAN TOURISM, ECOTOURISM AND HERITAGE TOURISM

The critique made nearly a decade ago still needs to be kept in mind:

> The peoples of the islands of the Caribbean have in the past undergone repatriation and colonisation. Tourism is a key industry for them now, but, in many instances, this new situation is essentially an old one of colonisation and/or exploitation. Often, an island will present an exotic version of the European culture of its old colonisers to the present day tourists from that same country (Boniface and Fowler, 1993).

'Sun, sea and sand tourism' is the image the travel industry has developed for the Caribbean tourist business. A foreign airline advertisement is recorded as having promoted Caribbean vacations with bill-boards showing a half-dressed woman discarding her clothes with the words: 'Take off.... for the Caribbean' (cited in Barry et al 1984).

A foreign-based hotel chain advertises the Caribbean as an 'antidote to civilisation':

> the notion of primitive societies and systems charming or quaint because they have withstood change: 'Visit a plantation with its original 18th century splendour and running much the same way for hundreds of years' (Barry et al, 1984).

Sensuous, unprogressive and primitively curious are the images constructed abroad of the Caribbean as the 'other', which it unwittingly grasps as the identity of the region and by which marketers endeavour to sell the products in a mass tourist market.

'Exotic' tropical islands, like the concept of the Orient, is predominantly a European invention. To the Westerner, wrote Edward Said, the Orient was always 'like some aspect of the West' (Said, 1978). The exotic speaks through the European imagination and creates positional superiority. Above all, where there is exoticism there can be no real dialogue (Sachs, 1976). Exoticism and the industry with which it is associated is a signal of North American/European power over the Caribbean; a cultural hegemony reflected in the way each perceives themself in relation to the other.

Now that the past has been popularised by tourism, and ecotourism and heritage tourism have been placed on the agenda, one must beware that heritage tourism does not rob the society of a meaningful past. Tourism has the tendency of leaving a people 'surrounded by relics' one can barely relate to, or understand, or feel is theirs. Tourist culture hardly feels like something that is theirs. As tourism has tended to remove the sea and sand from the real Jamaica in the more popular resort areas, so it could have a similar impact upon the ecosystems and the relics of cultural heritage. Appropriate management of the impact is essential if heritage is not to be de-authenticised and finally even become alienating.

The apparent economic gains now have to be measured and balanced against the ability of both environment and society to retain their integrity and thus, in the long run, even retain a tourist industry. How do the Maroons relate to these issues? The successful inclusion of Maroon culture in heritage tourism will depend upon the ability of the Maroons and the managers of this tourism to effectively guide the transition from living culture to heritage. The historical characterisation of the Maroons has been established from the perspectives of the planters and their hostility towards the 'barbaric rebels' that challenged the existence and peace of the planter class (Bryan Edwards, 1793; and R.C. Dallas, 1803). Otherwise, there has been the portrayal of the Maroons, as in Carey Robinson's book (1969), as a groups of primitive and uneducated peoples who successfully challenged the powerful and sophisticated.

There has been only a few works done on the Maroons based on accurate and in-depth evidence either of a historical or anthropological nature (Campbell, 1990; Patterson, 1970; Price, 1973; Zips, 1999). There is the risk that the Maroons could become absorbed into the tourist product as primitive curiosities and people caught, through their lack of sophistication and traditional beliefs, in a time capsule which has withstood the influences of modernisation and change.

The authenticity of Maroon culture can become part of national heritage in a dignified way, depending totally upon the manner in which it is packaged for tourist consumption. The Maroons have to be protected from the temptations and the dangers of selling their culture in a sensational and 'cheap' form. Further, they have to be protected against the inroads of tourist operators for whom heritage may be viewed as a means to quick tourism returns, with the commodity a phoney product packaged for the industry. The input of the historian, the anthropologist and environmentalist in association with the Maroons themselves, would seem the best method of presenting heritage in an interesting, authentic and at the same time sensitive and carefully constructed way. To do otherwise would be to open up at least the possibility of a Disneyland-style theme park, which, while it may attract certain visitors, would be fatal to Maroon heritage. While, as one author put it, 'Disneyland tells us that faked nature corresponds much more to our daydream demands', it can also destroy any cultural authenticity (Eco, 1986, p.44).

Insightfulness and appropriate management of this developing component of Jamaica's tourism are essential to its sustainability. Further, the Maroons will require wise counsel in the transition from living culture to national heritage, for, at that stage, there will occur a different relationship with the symbolism which has provided them with the positive self identity and pride in their ancestry, which has been theirs for more than three centuries.

## CONCLUSION

It is important to be cautioned that should ecotourism and heritage tourism alter the traditional product or resource and consequently, the location of the industry from coastal zone to mountainous and forested interior, then even greater disasters to their prospect of achieving sustainable development will occur. Thus, the challenge to the tourist industry of Jamaica and the potential danger to the future of the Maroons, whether as authentic communities or national heritage, will be determined by the paradigmal shift which can be brought about in the whole conceptualisation and character of the tourist industry.

One of the main factors which will determine the nature of the future of tourism in Jamaica will be the realisation that the long-run economic benefits from tourism will be conditioned by the ability of eco-system and society not only to survive, but to make positive contributions to the success of the tourist industry itself. Ecotourism and heritage tourism are challenged to create and manage a new genre of tourist industry (Shaw and Williams, 1994). If they fail to do this then in the future they will find that not only the coastal region has been polluted and eroded, but so too will be the mountain eco-systems and the remaining elements of heritage.

Tourism is selective and has to be. But Jamaica's culture is critical to national development and it is important that Jamaicans make the final selection of what to show and how to show it. Paradise constructed from an image of the uncivilised, primitive and unchanged, the sensual and the charismatic, is even more demeaning than the other side of paradise — the hardship, poverty and degradation — which development seeks to overcome.

# REFERENCES

Agorsh, E. K. 'Archaeology and the Maroon Heritage in Jamaica'. *Jamaica Journal* 24, no. 2 (1994).

Agorsh, E. K. ed. 1994. *Maroon Heritage:Archaeological, Ethnographic and Historical Perspectives*. Kingston: Canoe Press.

Barker, D. and B. Spence. 'Afro-Caribbean Agriculture: A Jamaican Maroon Community in Transition'. *Geographical Journal* 154, (1988): 198-208.

Barry, T., B. Wood and D. Preusch. 1984. *The Other Side of Paradise: Foreign Control in the Caribbean*. New York: Grove Press.

Bedasse, J. and N. Stewart. 1994. 'The Maroons of Jamaica: One with Mother Earth'. Case Study Document for the Nature Conservancies Workshop: 'Traditional Peoples and Biodiversity Conservation in Large Tropical Landscapes'.

Bilby, K., M. 'Religious Change Among the Jamaican Maroons: The Ascendance of the Christian God within a Traditional Cosmology'. *Journal of Social History* 20, no. 3, (1987): 463-484.

Boniface, P. and P. J. Fowler. 1993. *Heritage and Tourism in the 'Global Village'*. London, Routledge.

Campbell, M.C. 1990. *The Maroons of Jamaica 1655-1796:A History of Resistance Collaboration and Betraya*. New Jersey: Africa World Press.

*Cockpit Country Conservation Project*. 2000. Unpublished report, Kingston.

Croall, J. 1995. *Preserve or Destroy: Tourism and the Environment*. London, Calouste Gulbenlkian Foundation.

Dallas, R. C. 1803. *The History of the Maroons*. London: T.N. Longman and O. Rees.

Eco, U. 1986. *Travels in Hyper-Reality*. London: Picador.

Edwards, B. 1793. *The History, Civil and Commercial, of the British Colonies in the West Indies*. 2 Volumes. Dublin: Luke Whit.

Eyre, L.A. 1989. 'Slow Death of a Tropical Rain Forest: The Cockpit Country of Jamaica, West Indies'. In *Environmental Quality and Ecosystem Stability* Vol. IV-A *Environmental Quality* eds. M. Luria, Y. Steinberger, and E. Spanier. Jerusalem: I.S.E.Q.S. Publication.

Eyre, L.A. 1995. 'Cockpit Country: A World Heritage Site'. In *Environment and Development in the Caribbean: Geographical Perspectives*, eds D. Barker and D. F.M McGregor. Kingston: The Press University of the West Indies.

Government of Jamaica. 1999. 'Jamaica 2000 Millennium Project'. Unpublished draft, Kingston: Office of the Prime Minister.

Harris, C.L.G. 1993. 'The Maroons and Moore Town' Maroon Cultures. Washington DC: Smithsonian Institute.

Kopytoff, B.K. 1973. 'The Maroons of Jamaica: An Ethnohistorical Study of Incomplete Polities'. Ph.D. dissertation, University of Pennsylvania.

Lowenthal, D. 1985. *The Past is a Foreign Country*. Cambridge University Press.

Miller, David J. 1998. 'Invasion of the Cockpits: Patterns of encroachment into the Wet Limestone Rainforest of Cockpit Country, Jamaica'. In *Resource Sustainability and Caribbean Development* eds. D.F.M McGregor, D. Barker and S. Lloyd Evans. Kingston: The Press University of the West Indies.

Patterson, O. 'Slavery and Slave Revolt: A Sociological Analysis of the First Maroon War 1655-1740'. *Social and Economic Studies* 1970.

Price, R. 1973. *Maroon Societies*. New York, Anchor Books.

Robinson, C. 1969. *The Fighting Maroons of Jamaica*. Kingston: William Collins and Sangster.

Sachs, I. 1976. *The Discovery of the Third World*. Boston: MIT Press.

Said, E. 1978. *Orientalism*. New York, Pantheon Press.

Shaw, G. 'Culture and Tourism: the Economics of Nostalgia'. *World Futures* 33, (1992): 199 – 212.

Shaw, Gareth and A.M. Williams. 1994. *Critical Issues in Tourism: A Geographical Perspective*. Oxford: Blackwell.

Spence, B. 2000. *Cockpit Country Conservation Project: Land Management Report*. Unpublished report, Environmental Foundation of Jamaica.

Wright, M.L. 1993. *The Accompong Town Maroons*. Maroon Cultures. Washington DC: Smithsonian Institute.

Zips, W. 1999. *Black Rebels: African Caribbean Freedom Fighters in Jamaica*. Kingston: Ian Randle Publishers.

# -14-

# FROM SUGAR TO HERITAGE TOURISM IN THE CARIBBEAN: ECONOMIC STRATEGIES AND NATIONAL IDENTITIES

Grant H. Cornwell and Eve W. Stoddard

## ABSTRACT

*This chapter surveys a project on the relationship between the history of plantation sugar production and contemporary tourist strategies in the Caribbean, analysing how the ruins of former plantations, especially windmills, reflect national identity in such societies as Barbados, Cuba, St. Kitts, and Tobago. The ruined sugar mill is a cultural icon in representation of Caribbean tourism, on resort stationery, websites, cocktail coasters, and tourist art. Since Caribbean plantation production was enmeshed in an early form of globalisation, its history should be of interest to visitors from all those societies that have evolved its matrix of economic relations, including West Africa, Asia, Europe, and the Americas. But heritage tourism must not celebrate from a Eurocentric perspective, the plantation era. As Caribbean states develop strategies for tourism based on sustaining the natural environment and affirming the nation's post-colonial cultural heritage, there is the need to ask how the story of sugar can be told without reinscribing colonial desire and Eurocentric viewpoints.*

## INTRODUCTION

This chapter is an introductory overview of an extensive research project on the relationship between the history of plantation sugar production and slavery and contemporary tourist strategies in the Caribbean. The researchers are especially concerned with how the ruins of former plantations, and windmills in particular, represent national identity and national history in different societies, including Barbados, Cuba, Martinique, Mustique, St. Croix, St. John, St. Kitts, Saint Lucia, St. Vincent, and Tobago.

Slowly, over the last half century, the Caribbean has been dismantling its social and economic base of monocrop sugar agriculture, a base that caused the creation of plantation slavery, which brought together European masters and African forced labourers for hundreds of years in an environment alien to workers, owners, and crop. The economic base which has replaced monocrop sugar production is tourism. Polly Patullo notes in her study of Caribbean tourism that 'When tourism overtook sugar as the major foreign-exchange earner it pitched the Caribbean into a new historical phase' (Patullo, 1996).

The Caribbean region, with close ties to both North America and Europe, has for a century been identified with sun, sea and sand tourism. During the twentieth century, as many nations of the Caribbean emerged from colonialism, the kind of tourism that flourished was a very direct evolution from plantation relations. Even economically, for the most part, just as sugar-based agriculture produced crops for consumption by those outside the region, so the tourism industry developed to serve consumers outside the region. On this model, white wealthy northerners descend during their winter months on the latest fashionable and exclusive island, to be served and waited on by Black Caribbean people. In most cases, the owners and managers of tourist facilities are white, sometimes local, sometimes expatriates. This pattern of development is subject to rapid shifting of markets driven by the opening of the latest resort, the shifting opinions of Northern tour operators and travel writers, or the trends set by a global elite. As markets shift, previously prosperous resorts and other facilities spiral downward. Now the rise of cruise ships makes possible much faster changes in trends and much smaller investments in island economies.

Over the past decade most governments have been working toward newer models of tourism based on sustaining the natural environment and affirming the nation's cultural heritage in a post-colonial context. Thus, the question becomes how can a country effectively serve its own peoples' interests while operating a successful tourist industry? On a strictly economic level, the ownership and surplus accumulation from the many businesses related to tourism, and or tax revenues from them, must accrue in a greater proportion than heretofore to the nation where tourism is located. Beyond that, just and sustainable tourism needs to respect and preserve the natural environment and the local culture of a place.

The idea behind ecotourism and heritage tourism is that nations can build on and maintain their most valuable resources in a symbiotic relationship with a thriving tourist industry which will be environmentally and economically sustainable and supportive of local cultural and national identities. If tourists come not for a generic week of beaches and rum drinks, but for a stay on a culturally distinctive island, it will be in the interest of the tourism industry to protect natural landscapes and to showcase national culture. This will foster research into local history and recovery of submerged cultural traditions and links, especially to Africa but also to India and to the indigenous peoples who inhabited the region before the European conquest.

# NATIONAL IDENTITIES AND THE CONSTRUCTION OF HERITAGE

In the combined processes of decolonisation and modernisation, the challenge for many Caribbean societies has been to define for themselves what their heritage and their history are all about. The cultural hegemony of European values under colonialism perpetuated a view that the Creole cultures, including languages, religions, histories, foods, and oral traditions, were inferior to European standards. In the second half of the twentieth century many Caribbean nations, but not all, gained independence from their former colonial masters. Each nation has its own unique layers of history, influenced by how the island was settled, who colonised it, what shape slavery took and how long it lasted, what kinds of rebellions there were against slavery, how and whether independence was achieved and consequently what kinds of narratives have been constructed about the past and about national identity.

In the English-speaking Caribbean, these range from St. Kitts and Barbados as the 'Mother Colony' and 'Little England', respectively, to Trinidad's sense of itself as a 'Callaloo Society'. In the case of Cuba, the struggles for emancipation and independence have been constructed as proto-revolutions anticipating the 1959 Revolution, whereas Puerto Rico, Martinique, St. John and St. Croix, to name places remain territories or departments of the US and France. Extinction of native peoples, forced abduction from Africa, the plantation system, chattel slavery, and European colonisation are common features of the Caribbean heritage, but so are slave rebellions, struggles for independence, ground provisions, African-based religions, music, dance, folklore, proverbs, the colour-class hierarchy, the Black Power movement, indentured labour of Asian immigrants, Caribbean Christianity, and so forth. Which elements do any particular nation choose to represent its history and its heritage? Whose stories get told, for what audience, and how?

In 'Narrating the Nation', acknowledging his debt to Benedict Anderson, Homi Bhabha describes the nation as essentially ambivalent:

> (Anderson) contests the traditional authority of those national objects of knowledge — Tradition, People, the Reason of State, High Culture, for instance — whose pedagogical value often relies on their representation as holistic concepts located within an evolutionary narrative of historical continuity. Traditional histories do not take the nation at its own word, but, for the most part, they do assume that the problem lies in the interpretation of 'events' that have a certain transparency or privileged visibility (Bhabha, 1994).

In the Creole nations of the Caribbean region, this is all the more true. Histories and historic monuments can be narrated from a Eurocentric view about forts and naval battles and famous US and European heroes who were born or raised on

Caribbean islands and in plantation great houses. For example, visitors to Nevis can visit the Alexander Hamilton museum, on the site where he was born, or the Horatio Nelson museum, commemorating 'Britain's greatest naval hero', the British admiral who was married on Nevis to Fanny Nisbet, a member of the local sugar plantocracy. At both museums there are interpretive installations on sugar and slavery, but both presume that the persons worthy of naming are the white men who played large roles in colonial struggles to create the New World, and that it is the lives of these persons that would be interesting to North American and European tourists. On St. Kitts, Brimstone Fortress has been designated a 'World Heritage Site', and most tourists to the island are channelled there during their visit. The interpretive video tells of the history of the fort, of the struggles between the French and the British for St. Kitts, and of the battles fought. It also tells of the century of slave labour required to build the massive stone fort, but the narrative thrust is Eurocentric; it focuses on the history of European struggles and achievements in controlling the Caribbean.

The history of the Caribbean can also be told from an Afrocentric perspective or a Creolisation perspective or as narratives of struggle for liberation from various forms of oppression. It is instructive to consult the history texts of the CXC syllabus, which is the basis of the school curriculum throughout the contemporary Caribbean. The three volumes in the Caribbean Certificate History series are titled *Arawaks to Africans, Emancipation to Emigration,* and *Development and Decolonisation.* The narrative strategy of these texts quite intentionally seeks to develop regional and national identities that replace Eurocentrism.

The project of heritage tourism is to build upon and foster regional and national identities of independence. Hence, it is asked in this project *Who does the history of sugar belong to? How can its story be told without reinscribing plantation relations and Eurocentric values?* The risk is great, since the archival history of the colonial era is the collected documents of those who wrote about it at the time, and those can easily yield up a Eurocentric viewpoint if they are not read against the grain. While there is not a body of slave narratives as resources, historians have to rely on statistical records and the remnants of material culture, as well as oral histories, to avoid reinscribing exclusively the points of view contained in the texts of white planters, naval captains, or estate managers.

## NARRATING THE CULTURE OF SUGAR

For nations that still grow sugar cane in large quantities, there are additional questions about its economic viability and its cultural meaning. Sugar *is* the history, the environment, and the cultural heritage for many Caribbean societies at the same time that it represents an enforced creoleness, a forced indigenisation serving the interests of the metropole. In an essay analysing 'sugar realism' in three Caribbean novels, Joseph Lockard writes that:

Sugar acts as an elemental, incomprehensible force that governs the islands. Life begins, flows through, and ends with sugar. The high, arching canes over the field trails are the birth canals of communal history. Sugar cane is parent, brutal sustenance, and death embodied in a unitary source (Lockard, 1995).

Yet while sugar imbues every aspect of the environment in the novels he interprets, novels set in Haiti, Martinique, and a fictitious Anglophone island, what Lockard finds in the novels is 'a common anti-sugar sentiment. Sugar cane cultivation was the original sin that demanded the enslavement and importation of Africans to the Caribbean islands, and in these narratives it continues as a near-unredeemable source of social degradation' (Lockard, 1995).

In the Anglophone Caribbean there has been strong sentiment for decades from progressive academics and intellectuals to eradicate sugar from the region, either because of its economic weaknesses or because of its associations with a degraded colonial past. However, in interviews, the authors have not necessarily found the same sentiment in nations where sugar is still produced. What they have found, even on the part of working-class people, is a profound ambivalence.

On the one hand, many will articulate a sense of nostalgia for the rhythms of sugar production and the contours of the sugar cane covered landscape. Sugar dominated the nature and the culture of sugar islands, it set the schedule of work and festivals, it determined the structure of social relations for generations. Inevitably, therefore, there is a deep sense of attachment to its associated lifeways. At the same time, sugar invokes a memory of slavery, tellingly, especially in younger generations. Some want to disassociate themselves utterly with that history and would prefer to destroy all vestiges of it. Others see its contemporary traces and, thus, want to remember the history of sugar as a foundation for anti-colonialist resistance.

While one might assume that the presence of sugar cane diminished from the 1950s onward as its economic importance decreased, in fact the amount grown and processed actually increased on most islands, so its social and cultural resonances did not diminish (Ramsaran, 1989). For example, while Barbados shifted its economy from near total reliance on sugar in the 1940s to an early investment in tourism, as of 1968 about half the cultivable land was in sugar and about 25 per cent of the labour force was employed in the sugar industry. There are still three factories operating, but one can see the land being bought up for luxury housing developments, much of it for expatriates.

One Barbadian grandmother told one of the authors nostalgically how, when she was growing up, each house had its own small plot of cane and its own small family sugar mill for crushing the juice out of the cane. Even the young, professional and politicised members of her family, now in their thirties, spoke of the way the harvest continues to shape the festivals (Cropover and attendant events) of the summer months in Barbados. Everyone interviewed in Barbados seemed cognisant of the price of sugar, the dates when the processing of the crop would be finished, and so forth.

## ST. KITTS

In many ways, St Kitts appears to be a society completely defined by sugar production even today. Though sugar represents less than 5 per cent of the GDP and a small and declining percentage of the workforce, the economy, politics, and processes of sugar production remain at the centre of national consciousness. The reasons for this are clear and many. First, sugar has been at the centre of Kittitian history for 350 years. The ancestral stories of every family, of whatever race or class, are woven into the history of sugar on St. Kitts and Nevis.

Second, in the 1970s the government of St. Kitts and Nevis nationalised the sugar industry, and bought the central processing factory and all sugar lands. This action was a defining moment in the development of Kittitian national identity, and it continues to have formative reverberations. As a national industry there is a very material sense in which sugar production is of interest to every citizen.

Third, the entire landscape of St. Kitts is a compelling reminder of the place of sugar in Kittitian history and culture. Cane fields circle the island in a broad apron that divides the sea from the central mountain ranges, and these fields are punctuated by dozens of former sugar estates, many with the remnants of mills and factories still intact. There is a railroad, built in the early 1900s solely for the purpose of transporting cane to the central processing factory that circles the island and frequently crosses the main road. In a section called 'Cultural Patrimony' of the *St. Kitts and Nevis Tourism Master Plan*, the report states:

> Planners must look at landscape not only as a natural attraction, but also as a cultural vista. The green vistas of St. Kitts and Nevis are not just pretty; heritage lies behind what the viewer sees (Bacci, 1993).

This observation is quite consciously available to Kittitians from all walks. Sugar remains a very visible dimension of Kittitian culture, and the lifeways associated with sugar continue to inform Kittitian national identity.

## TRINIDAD

In Trinidad, on the other hand, where the Afro-Trinidadian national identity, at any rate, is de-linked from sugar production because of the 150-year role of Indo-Trinidadians in the sugar industry, national festivals are not connected with sugar, and there is more awareness of oil prices and their role in the national economy than of sugar. Sugar seems to be viewed more instrumentally as an industrial, agricultural crop for export than as the all-pervasive arbiter of the national calendar that it still is in St. Kitts or Barbados. Trinidad has a very intentionally created national rhythm of festivals based around the religious holidays of the major religions in the country, including Hindu, Christian, Muslim, and African-based, along with more strictly national holidays like Emancipation Day, Indian Arrival Day, and Independence Day. This reflects a very conscious choice to build an imagined community in which 'all o' we are one', and where ethnic heritage is seen as a stream contributing to a very mixed national identity.

Perhaps because Trinidad has a performance-based cultural heritage, which is always on the move, in comparison to other Caribbean nations, there is relatively little in the country in the way of material memorialisation of the past. There are few traces of typical plantation houses such as one finds in Louisiana or St. Kitts and Nevis or Barbados. And Trinidad is not a tourist destination except for the very specialised clientele who come for Carnival or bird watching. Trinidad, thus, can be placed at one end of a continuum of approaches to heritage, particularly the heritage of plantation sugar production.

Trinidad is a society that enacts creolisation, the constant process of negotiating and performing various identities, on the move with a vibrant oral tradition, studying the pasts that comprise its present, but really lacking in nostalgia. Whereas other countries have monarchs and national heroes or monuments on their currency, Trinidad has oil rigs; this speaks to its forward motion and its resistance to physical memorialisation of the past. Tobago has been designated a tourist economy for the two-island nation, and in Tobago the authors found a completely different situation, more similar to that of Antigua, St. Croix, or Barbados, though on a very small scale.

## CUBA

Among other Caribbean nations, at the other end of the spectrum, are those that have created or restored monuments to represent the past. These range ideologically from restored great houses filled with luxurious Eurocentric antiques and paintings to Cuba's massive sculptures in two different locations, one of a slave rebellion and one called "The Monument to the Runaway Slave', which will form part of UNESCO's route of the slave. Cuba's contemporary national identity is constructed as a narrative of revolution, and the struggles of African slaves for freedom holds a major symbolic role in the creation of the revolutionary state. The fight for the end of slavery and the settlers' struggle for independence from the colonial domination from Spain are represented as linked so that the whole nation, across the spectrum of colour and ethnicity, can at least in theory share in the narrative of slave emancipation as central to the nation's identity.

The monument to the runaway slave, created in 1997 by Alberto Lescay in Santiago del Prado de El Cobre, is a vertical bronze figure, 9 meters high, set in a huge iron cauldron used for boiling cane juice. The cauldron is meant to symbolise Nganga, a receptacle for the attributes of spirits in the Congo religion. Thus, in its representation of what is considered the first successful slave uprising in Cuba, when enslaved Africans working in the copper mines finally defeated Spanish troops and gained their freedom after a series of struggles between 1731 and 1800, the monument incorporates a material remnant of the sugar industry but transforms its meaning from a metonymic signifier of sugar's relation to African slavery to a symbol of the spiritual bonds between the African diaspora in the New World and their ancestral past in Africa. Thus, in the Cuban revolutionary context, a piece of equipment from a sugar factory which is often used decoratively as a planter in other Caribbean settings, is imaginatively used to embody the tragedy, the resistance, and the positive spirituality of a past embedded in forced exile, brutal enslavement and plantation sugar production.

The other sculpture, at Triumvirato, in Matanzas Province, is part of a preserved plantation house and garden that also distinctively reflects the Cuban national narrative. At the site there is a plantation house that serves as a small museum of slavery, and tells the story of the first slave uprising and houses some of the material implements used to restrain and torture slaves. Outside in the immediate vicinity of the house are two ancient, sacred trees, important in the practice of Afro-Cuban religious practices. But the most striking feature of the site is the sculpture representing the first Cuban slave rebellion.

As with all the sites the researchers interpret in the project, this contemporary sculpture tells as much about today's Cuban national identity as it does about the past it represents. It is comprised of three bronze, larger than life, human figures, the one in the middle a woman and on either side of her a man with a weapon frozen in the act of slashing an invisible opponent. The woman is having her shackles cut off. The figures are mounted on a kind of graduated concrete base that abstractly represents a mountainous hillside, perhaps suggesting the uphill climb to freedom. The posture of the man lowest down on the platform is also literally lowest to the ground as he is crouched down with his machete raised as if to kill someone already on the ground. The woman stands in a posture of the newly free from chains, with arms outstretched, while the highest perched man holds an aggressive pose more akin to contemporary images of revolutionary assertion, standing with one arm upraised. Yet the two male figures, powerful and angry as they look, also look worn out and exhausted from hard labour. The roles of these three figures in a historic slave revolt are well developed in a narrative of the revolt told and re-told in popular culture. Tourists visiting the museum have ready access to this story.

## BARBADOS

Barbados, unique among the Anglophone Caribbean countries for being colonised exclusively by Britain, has a national identity of stability. It claims the third oldest parliament in the world, dating from 1639. It has always had a majority of women in its population. Hilary Beckles argues that Barbados had less armed rebellion than comparable islands because in the eighteenth century, the height of plantation sugar slavery, Barbados slaves exhibited 'patterns of collective behaviour characterised principally by limited protest and the seeking of socioeconomic concessions from masters' (Beckles, 1988). He speculates that the strong military defense available around Barbados allowed planters to 'liberalise their individual plantation control systems', leading to a system in which there was great stratification among the slaves themselves. However in 1816, the uprising known as Bussa's Rebellion occurred and Bussa is now an emblem of liberation, his bronze statue with arms extended, broken chains hanging from them, present as one whizzes around the roundabout that bears his name. But the history Beckles narrates and interprets is more a history of continuity than of revolution and that can be felt in the culture of Barbados.

Barbados has done an interesting job of representing the past of plantation sugar production both for tourists and for Barbadians. Considering the continuity of British ties through colonialism and into the present, Barbados has done a very even-handed job of representing the past at all levels of society, from great houses to chattel houses, from the sugar factory to the sugar labour force. Of course one could critique the representation for its very evenhandedness, for its failure to criticise the plantocracy or the British colonial heritage. But it cannot be criticised for omitting the past of the Black working classes. Barbados has a 'Sugar Trail' which incorporates five sites:

1. a 300 year old Jacobean style great house, St. Nicholas Abbey, built in the 1650s and surrounded by a working sugar plantation and abandoned windmill,
2. a restored windmill,
3. a modern working sugar factory,
4. The Sugar Museum which houses old machinery and tells the story of how sugar was produced, from its introduction to the New World, the slave trade, the use of animal-powered and wind mills, to steam-driven machinery,
5. the Mount Gay rum factory.

The museum was created by a white man, Sir Frank Hutson, who was chiefly interested in conserving the machinery used to process cane as he saw sugar production diminishing in Barbados. However, the museum gives a full representation of the labourers' roles, under slave conditions and afterward. In fact as one enters the building, there is a sign stating that, 'This museum is dedicated to the sugar machinery of the past, and to the hundreds of workers . . . working to produce sugar into the twentieth century, when modern technology replaced them'.

There is something a bit odd in this statement, which on the one hand is dedicated to the labour force, but on the other hand places human workers on an equal footing with the old machinery and the new technology, although there is a hint of nostalgia at the replacement of labourers with technology. The reference to 'hundreds' is also odd given the fact that at emancipation there were roughly 82,000 slaves in Barbados. Not all of these were working in sugar, but that's one year out of centuries of sugar production. There is a similarly neutral statement under 'The Sugar Story' about 'How the European and African peoples from vastly different cultures serviced the plantation system of the 17th-19th centuries'.

The Barbados National Trust flyer for the sugar museum is titled "The Sugar Museum: St. James: 'A Sweet Experience'. It begins:

> Follow the sugar trail into the beautiful Barbadian countryside to the yard of Portavale, a sugar-cane grinding factory. Here in a restored sugar 'Boiling House', you can trace the story of one of the most fascinating commodities on the world market. The National Trust's Museum tells the colourful story of the people, the innovations, and the triumphs and disasters during the development of the sugar industry in Barbados.

While in some respects this representation of sugar and slavery seems incredibly depoliticised, on the other hand, the information within the museum is comprehensive about the slave trade and demographics of plantation society. There is a pyramidal diagram of the layers of Barbadian society with a line between the Poor Whites and the Free Blacks and Mulattos. There is a lot of information about Agro-economy, slave labour, sugar technology, machinery, and shipping, as well as information about labour conditions post-emancipation, the exodus to build the Panama Canal, and the development of labour movements. So the museum attempts to present a comprehensive and factual picture of sugar production, which neither romanticises the plantation era nor participates in a rhetoric of anti-colonialism. It is a valuable resource both for tourists and for Barbadian citizens and school children to learn about the history of sugar and its role in the creation of their nation.

The tour guide for the modern factory is an older Black Barbadian man who worked in the factory for many years. This point is significant because in many of the sites we have visited, it has been white descendants of the planter class or expatriates who staff historical societies and museum sites. While these people have good intentions in preserving archival records and restoring historical sites, they do tend to be interested in telling the stories from what is implicitly the coloniser's perspective, thus reinscribing in national monuments the colonial rather than the independent national construction of local history. The Barbados National Museum has the same kind of inclusive collection, ranging from Plantation House Period Rooms to the African Gallery, though the collection is slanted somewhat toward colonial interests. On a broader scale, the tourist or the Barbadian citizen can visit a range of historical sites, including several plantation great houses to Tyrol Cot Heritage Village, which includes the nineteenth century West Indian Palladian home of national hero Sir Grantley Adams and his son, the second prime minister of independent Barbados, a replica of an 1820s slave hut, a 1920s chattel house museum, a working blacksmith's shop, and a circle of chattel houses serving as crafts shops.

Most interesting for this project is the Morgan Lewis windmill in Barbados. Along with Betty's Hope in Antigua, this is one of a small number of fully operational windmills left in the Caribbean. One can go up inside the windmill and see how the machinery is operated. The placards make clear how dangerous the mill could be to the labourers feeding it with cane. The only bizarre feature of the mill is its complete disconnection from the kind of setting it would have functioned in. It is surrounded by a cattle farm. Compared to other islands like St. Croix, Tobago, St. Kitts, and Antigua, Barbados has relatively few ruined windmills in evidence. A few have been incorporated into private homes, but many have probably been cannibalised for stones or even knocked down to make way for further arable land or housing developments. Surprisingly, considering how thoughtfully developed the heritage tourist sites are, there appears to be no comprehensive survey of remaining ruins. In fact in 1995 the National Trust sponsored 'The Amy Nicholls Mill Competition' which asked competitors to 'research and record information about remaining mill sites on our island'.

## SUGAR ESTATES AND HERITAGE TOURISM: THE CASE OF ST. KITTS

By contrast, a number of other islands, including St. Croix and St. Kitts, have had inventories compiled and assessments done of all extant windmills, under the auspices of the Organisation of American States (OAS). For over a decade, St. Kitts and Nevis has been pursuing a strategy of heritage tourism development very intentionally. Given the history of these islands, and the physical and cultural legacies of sugar production, heritage tourism in St. Kitts and Nevis means translating a heritage of sugar, slavery, and a plantation economy into a tourism attraction. This politically and ethically fragile project is being pursued with care and thoughtfulness. In 1993, the Government of St. Kitts and Nevis commissioned a study funded by the OAS to chart a course for tourism development. The report, called the *St. Kitts and Nevis Tourism Master Plan,* makes a direct connection between the decline of sugar as an economic base and the re-appropriation of the nation's sugar heritage as a tourism development strategy.

As already noted, a prominent feature of sugar heritage is the island landscape. The report notes:

One of the beauties of St. Kitts, and a drawing card for tourism, is the island's great expanse of green cane fields. The Government, which owns most of the agricultural lands, must consider the aesthetics of future land use. The vistas alone are particularly inviting: the open green expanse of sugar cane blending into the dark green of the mountain forest. St. Kitts has a large area of agricultural land devoted to sugar cane cultivation extending almost from the sea to the 1000 ft contour. The visual effect is one of startling beauty (Bacci 1993).

This landscape has important cultural significance. The ecology of the island was transformed under colonialism, and the look of the land has not changed for centuries. While the tranquillity of the sweeping emerald vistas belies the violence and labour it took to create it, citizens and visitors alike appreciate its distinctive aesthetics.

Since all arable land was divided into sugar estates roughly 300 acres in size, and since prior to 1920 each estate had its own sugar mill and processing factory, the landscape is dotted with the remnants of estate yards. Smoke stacks and mill ruins evenly punctuate the landscape. Some of these estate yards have been renovated as private homes or plantation inns, but most either lie in ruins or are actively in use as the industrial organising centres of the St. Kitts Sugar Manufacturing Company. Many tourists, utterly unaware of the history of St. Kitts, are curious, even perplexed about the colonial stonework architecture rising up through the fields. In an interview, one tourist remarked with a relieved confidence that he determined that the stone towers dotting the landscape — i.e. the ruins of seventeenth and eighteenth century windmills – were silos used to store the sugar. Clearly, this heritage architecture needs to be interpreted for visitors. The *Master Plan* recognises this:

> The countryside is dotted with the stonework remains of sugar plantation houses, mills, and chimneys. Many of these historic landmarks are disappearing. Tourism planning must structure a way by which this heritage can be preserved and enhanced for tourists and citizens alike (Bacci, 1993).

In 1998, the Government of St. Kitts and Nevis commissioned a follow-up study of the 'heritage sites' of St. Kitts and Nevis, again funded by the OAS. The report, called the *St. Kitts Heritage Site Management Project*, catalogued all potential heritage sites and ranked them by their historical significance and preservation integrity. In the report, 'heritage sites' are defined as 'places of historical, cultural and natural significance bequeathed from past generations of a nation to their living descendants. They are distinctive physical landmarks that help a people understand and define their national experience and national identity' (Tyson and Bacci, 1998). Of the 254 sites catalogued, 110 are former sugar plantations. The report recommends that these sites be protected, preserved, and in some cases carefully restored. To foster heritage tourism, the report specifically recommends that

A St. Kitts Sugar Industry Museum should be established as soon as possible at the Estridge Estate Yard, which has by far the best surviving complement of sugar plantation buildings on St. Kitts. The museum would document the history of the sugar industry on St. Kitts. Interpretive elements would include guided tours, displays and exhibits, signs and cultural demonstrations. The museum would provide a much needed tourism attraction and educational resource in this part of the island (Bacci, 1998).

The authors are greatly concerned with the complex and sedimented meaning of former plantations, and elsewhere we explore the semiotics of these ruins in depth (Stoddard and Cornwell, 2001).

The renovation and interpretation of former sugar estates to serve heritage tourism development must keep the human dimensions of sugar history in the foreground. As the *Master Plan* notes,

> Heritage is not building and history alone. Heritage is also people, life styles, customs, and traditions. Tourism planning should focus on ways in which the Kittitian and Nevisian culture can become a part of the visitor's experience. . . To think of the development of tourism in St. Kitts and Nevis without taking into account the cultural wealth would be a serious mistake. Yet this added enjoyment of the tourist must occur without jeopardising the integrity of the life styles of individuals and the community (Bacci, 1993).

The discourse of heritage tourism includes an implicit critique of earlier tourism development strategies that ravaged the cultures and ecologies of long-established Caribbean destinations. The *St. Kitts and Nevis Tourism Master Plan* pays as much attention to the ethics of heritage tourism development as it does to the economics. The authors write,

> There is a vital need to take into consideration the culture and cultural legacy of the islands in the early stages of tourism development. It is important to develop a tourism product that blends with local lifestyles, revitalises positive local values, stimulates local traditions and customs, and enhances pride and dignity. A strategy of heritage tourism can do this (Bacci, 1993).

Elsewhere, in a section titled "National Goals", the *Master Plan* articulates a set of objectives for heritage tourism in St. Kitts and Nevis. What is distinctive is that each point balances a concern for economic development with a concern for human development. The objectives are:

- To achieve sustained growth in tourism without adversely affecting the country's cultural heritage
- To structure tourism investment policies to secure local capture of tourism income
- To provide new opportunities for productive and satisfying local employment at acceptable and equitable income levels
- To develop new sources of income from tourist receipts to assist in the preservation of historical and natural resources.
- To assure that tourism product development works to achieve the appropriate blend of interaction between tourists and citizens so that the tourist's experience is enriched through local contact without jeopardising citizen rights and integrity.
- To encourage public sensitivity to tourism and tourist needs and to encourage friendly and cordial interaction with the tourist (Bacci, 1993).

The researchers applaud the ethical thrust of the report, but are less sanguine about the prospects for heritage tourism. One of the most distinctive features of heritage tourism is its educational dimension. When the heritage being taught is that of sugar and colonialism, honesty demands a careful analysis of the history of slavery, and of the racialised economies of past and current Caribbean societies. It is a challenge not yet met to develop a tourism 'product' that simultaneously attracts tourists without alienating them *and* honestly treats the colonial legacies of suffering and injustice.

## CONCLUSION

Thus far, in this research the authors have analysed nations where ruined mills are silently incorporated into restaurants or romanticised into honeymoon suites at plantation hotels. They have seen them incorporated into luxury homes for expatriates and in a few instances made into museum or monument sites. However, in the past few years a new phenomenon has occurred on the Caribbean landscape and that is the creation of fake ruined windmills. The ruined sugar mill is becoming a cultural icon throughout the Caribbean; it can be found on resort stationery, websites, cocktail coasters, and tourist art. New mega-hotels employ ersatz mills in their architectural design. One of them is the Tobago Hilton and Plantations, a vast luxury complex that is changing the character of tourism in Tobago, and another is the Saint Lucia Hyatt Regency. Decoding this icon reveals deeply contested narratives of the history of sugar in the Caribbean. In some cases, former plantations have become museums interpreting the history of sugar and slavery. In other cases, the tourist industry romanticises this history in a narrative of 'colonial charm', recreating in labour practices the racial, ethnic, and class divide of the plantation economy. In so far as sugar mills are appropriated as icons, beacons of colonial nostalgia, they attract as they construct a clientele drawn by desire to participate in imagined community of white privilege.

It is one thing to preserve as a memorial a ruined former windmill in order to show the technology through which sugar was produced in the past by slave labour. School children studying Caribbean history can visit it to learn their own history and outsiders can be reminded of the past that created the unequal world in which we now live, in which Britain's industrial revolution and cultural institutions were funded with capital and profits from the slave trade and sugar and in which Africa was dealt a blow from which it has not yet recovered.

A fake mill incorporated into a multinational chain hotel, however, is a different thing, especially when the hotel restaurant is named the Sugar Mill and the stationary and cocktail napkins are emblazoned with stylised ruined windmill towers and a perky palm tree. The clientele who consume these images are by and large not the descendants of the sugar cane workers who reside in the Caribbean or the diaspora, but rather people who look like and perhaps have benefited indirectly from the planter class. So what messages are these northern consumers receiving when they dine in sugar mill restaurants and stay in buildings meant to invoke plantation great houses? What kind of representation of history is this? People don't stay in restored barracks at German concentration camps, but in several places they stay in restored slave quarters or windmills. It is commonplace to see ads for experiencing the luxury of colonial times.

Thus, as the ruins at each site is read, the researchers examine the links, metaphorical and literal, between its past and its present, and ask the following questions:

- Who owns and controls the use and meaning of the site?
- How is the meaning, both past and present, represented?
- How are specific artifacts and architectural elements employed in the representation?
- Is the history of the mill and plantation told and from whose perspective? For what purpose?
- Who consumes its meaning?
- Who does the labour?
- What is made visible and invisible?

Remembering the history of slavery and the post-Emancipation plantation system, whether worked by Afro- or Asian Caribbean people, is especially fraught, troubling for persons on both sides of the plantation divide. Yet it is an important part of the Caribbean heritage. Since Caribbean plantation production was enmeshed in an early form of globalisation, its history should be of interest to visitors from all those societies that have evolved its matrix of economic relations, including West Africa, Asia, Europe, and the Americas. But as tourism continues to replace sugar, it is essential that new patterns of heritage tourism be created that do not simply recreate or celebrate from a Eurocentric perspective the plantation era.

The most important variable is the narrative point of view enacted in the presentation of the ruins. Empowering the people of each nation to own and shape the story encoded in the plantation ruins is a step toward resisting the reinscription of colonial relations as has happened in many tourist sites around the region. On a practical level, leaving post-colonial politics aside, if tourism is to be sustainable in the Caribbean, each nation needs its own distinctive story, its niche, what marketing consultants call a 'brand'. When tourists visit Europe, they do not blur together Buckingham Palace with Versailles the way many North American tourists lump the whole Caribbean region into sun and sand. Part of the reason is that many of us in the world, even in North America, have inherited a national identity that springs from European lineage. Like the colonised people of the Caribbean did, we study European history, languages, and literatures in school. So if heritage tourism in the region is to benefit both the recovery of local histories and cultures and the economics of tourism, both prospective tourists and local Caribbean peoples have to value what is to be found in various Caribbean nations.

The case studies the authors are doing suggest that there is a wide range of possibilities for the ways the stories of slavery and contemporary nationhood can be told, and for the most part, the people of the region are now learning their own histories and traditions, music and literatures, religions and festivals. However, the prospective tourist populations in North America and Europe need the same kind of education. Tourists will come looking for heritage if they have read novels from the region or studied its thought and histories. As US professors, this is something we can do to promote the Caribbean as a destination with important and varied cultures and artifacts. A typical US student wrote after taking a Caribbean literature course:

> Overall, I learned that the Caribbean is much more than beautiful waters and beaches, but a culture that has struggled through slavery, colonisation, poverty and the mixing of so many backgrounds. Music, food, and dance is important to so many of the people. And most of all, each island has its own history and story.

This is the kind of potential tourist who will seek out heritage tourism rather than an all-inclusive enclave, who will not necessarily follow fads that abandon one island for the latest hot place, but will seek out various destinations based on what they have to offer in the way of history and culture.

# REFERENCES

Bacci, M.E. 1993. *St. Kitts and Nevis Tourism Master Plan*. Washington DC: Organisation of American States.

Beckles, H. 1988. *Afro-Caribbean Women and Resistance to Slavery in Barbados*. London: Karnak House.

Beckles, H. 1998. *Bussa: The 1816 Barbados Revolution*. Vol. 2 of *Rewriting History*. Barbados: University of the West Indies Department of History.

Bhaha, H. 1994. 'Narrating the Nation'. *Nationalism*. New York and London: Oxford University Press.

Lockard, J. 'Sugar Realism' in Caribbean Fiction'. *Journal of Commonwealth and Postcolonial Studies* 1 no. 2, (1995): 80–103.

Patullo, P. 1996. *Last Resorts: The Cost of Tourism in the Caribbean*. London: Cassell.

Ramsaran, R. 1989. The Commonwealth Caribbean in the World Economy. London: Macmilllan.

Tyson, G. and M.E. Bacci. 1998. *St. Kitts Heritage Site Management Project*. Washington DC: The Organisation of American States.

Stoddard, E. and G.H. Cornwell. 2001. 'Reading Sugar Mill Ruins: "The Island Nobody Spoiled" and Other Fantasies of Colonial Desire'. In *Early Modernity and Europe's Race for the Globe, ed.* Mita Choudhury. Special Issue of *South Atlantic Review* 65, no. 2.

# 15

# 'COME TO JAMAICA AND FEEL ALRIGHT!': MARKETING REGGAE AS HERITAGE TOURISM

Carolyn Cooper

## ABSTRACT

*This chapter examines reggae music as a cultural/heritage tourism attraction in Jamaica. The author briefly traces the roots of reggae and examines its impact on tourists visiting Jamaica. The chapter also presents a review of the influence of Bob Marley on the development and popularising of reggae. While the use of this art form as a promotional tool was not accepted initially, reggae has developed and evolved to occupy a distinctive place in the Jamaican culture. The author also discusses the development of events such as the Reggae Sumfest and Reggae Sunsplash that were created to attract tourists to the island in the off-peak periods. These events enjoyed some measure of success and have helped to make reggae widely accepted as a part of international culture.*

## INTRODUCTION

The turn of phrase 'heritage tourism' appears to be somewhat of an oxymoron, a yoking of contradictory terms for rhetorical effect. Indeed, the etymology of the word 'oxymoron' reveals it to be a fusion of the 'sharp' (oxy) and the 'dull, foolish' (moron). It is not proposing that 'heritage' is the 'sharp' element of the contradiction; and 'tourism' the 'dull' and 'foolish.' It is not the intention of the author to antagonise those sharp entrepreneurs who have a vested interest in the tourism enterprise nor to lull the heritage experts into a false sense of complacency. Unimaginative marketing of 'culture' can become a rather dull business. However, it is essential to interrogate the term 'heritage tourism' in order to disclose some of the ways in which the project of conventional 'sun and fun' tourism often does function in direct opposition to the grand objectives of heritage conservation.

# HERITAGE TOURISM

In an essay entitled 'Heritage Tourism and the Myth of Caribbean Paradise', Rex Nettleford argues that:

> Cultural tourism to many people is, in any case, a camouflage for 'touristic culture' which any West Indian who is serious about his heritage and the integrity of its authenticity and autonomy would not wish to adopt. And understandably so! For where cultural tourism works best is when the culture genuinely belongs to the host people, where it is very much in place, active, alive and available in normal circumstances for their guest (visitors) to enjoy.

> Is the Caribbean thus blessed? Some feel not. For one thing, visitors do not normally come, and are not encouraged to come, to the region to "soak up" its culture. The marketing strategies have themselves been soaked in something called 'Paradise' (Nettleford, 1993).

In the specific case of reggae, the unpacking of the concept 'heritage tourism' helps to clarify ways in which the culture of reggae is often appropriated as commodity, as undervalued currency in the tourism enterprise. 'Heritage' as the collective cultural legacy of a people is not often a high priority on the list of 'must do' activities for the 'sun and fun' tourist. Indeed, tourism is often packaged in travel brochures as 'escape' from the everyday anxieties of real living. Tourism is, thus, popularly conceived as leisure a willing suspension of normal intellectual activities. Rest and relaxation become overwhelming preoccupations of the somewhat mindless tourist.

In the Caribbean, this unflattering representation of the not quite moronic tourist finds its highest literary expression in Jamaica Kincaid's 1998 polemical antitravelogue, 'A Small Place'. Kincaid examines the tourist industry in Antigua, and, by extension, in the wider Caribbean, as yet another neocolonialist project that replicates the exploitative power relations of institutionalised underdevelopment. Tourism disfigures the native with the markings of the exotic. But Kincaid also constructs tourism as a disempowering project for the visitor. She painstakingly exposes the grotesque body of the innately ugly tourist as a legible sign of the diseased body politic from which s/he issues. Everyday, communal rituals that ordinarily define the tourist's sense of home and identity eventually become an oppressive trap from which escape becomes essential.

Addressing the archetypal tourist directly, Kincaid catalogues in fine detail the gradual process of degeneration from 'whole person' to parasitic feeder on the suffering of the world. In delineating this process of transformation, Kincaid clearly intends to call into question notions of 'normalcy'. She dislocates the tourist on foreign soil, dispossessing him/her of the presumed power and freedom that travel affords. Touring becomes a temporary panacea for the ills of home; it is not a permanent solution to the problem of endemic meaninglessness to which the tourist must inevitably return:

> ...at home on your street, your church, in community activities, your job, at home with your family, your relatives, your friends you are a whole person. But one day, when you are sitting somewhere, alone in that crowd, and that awful feeling of displacedness comes over you, and really, as an ordinary person you are not well equipped to look too far inward and set yourself right, because being ordinary is already so taxing, and being ordinary takes all you have out of you, and though the words 'I must get away' do not actually pass your lips, you make a leap from being that nice blob just sitting like a boob in your amniotic sac of the modern experience to being a person visiting heaps of death and ruin and feeling alive and inspired at the sight of it; to being a person lying on some faraway beach, your stilled body stinking and glistening in the sand, looking like something first forgotten, then remembered, then not important enough to go back for; (Kincaid, 1993).

In Kincaid's biting critique of tourism even those activities that one might ordinarily dignify with the label 'heritage tourism' are themselves undermined. Archaeological tourism as much as the beachedwhale variant is satirised. The ruins of ancient civilisations that are sanctimoniously celebrated in tourist catalogues as the shared cultural heritage of the world become in Kincaid's revisionist polemics, mere 'heaps of death and ruin' which function to make the smug tourist feel 'alive and inspired'. The escapist act of visiting ruins does not inspire any profound reflection on the meaning of the cultural signposts that the selfsatisfied tourist reads with such casual narcissism. Everything is entertainment; pure and simple.

## THE CULTURE OF REGGAE

Given this neocolonialist cultural politics of 'sun and fun' tourism as the ready supply on demand of colourful local entertainment, one would expect that reggae music would function as valuable cultural capital in Jamaica's tourist industry. After all, reggae music is a uniquely Jamaican product that has become a world-class trademark. But the paradox emerges that reggae as background music is an acceptable tool of the tourist trade; reggae as cultural heritage definitely puts a spanner in the works. The culture of reggae encodes the whole history of oppression and exploitation of the masses of the Jamaican people. Hardcore reggae is a music of political resistance. In the words of Bob Marley's 'One Drop' from the Survival album, reggae music is 'a rhythm resisting against the system'.

The etymology of the word 'reggae' confirms its downmarket origins in urban revolt against the stark class contradictions of post independence Jamaican society. The 1967 *Dictionary of Jamaican English* defines the pseudolatin 'reggae' as 'a recently estab[lished] sp[elling] for *rege* (the basic sense of which is *raggedsee regerege* with possible ref[erence] to ragtime music (an early form of American jazz) but referring esp[ecially] to the slum origins of this music in Kingston'. 'Regerege' is defined first as 'rags, ragged clothing'; its secondary meaning is 'a quarrel, a row'. The dictionary entry invites readers to compare 'regerege' with 'ragaraga' which is defined in the nominative as 'old ragged clothes'; as adjective, it means 'in rags, ragged' and as verb, it means 'to pull about, pull to pieces'.[1] Reggae's metaphorical rags clearly signify the workingclass origins of this musical manifestation of a querulous, ragaraga politics of resistance to appropriation by 'Babylon system'.[2]

In the early years of the evolution of reggae music, there was no need on the part of the masses to fear that their distinctive urban sound, with all its weight of oppression, would be appropriated by Babylon. It is popularly believed that government institutions such as the Jamaica Tourist Board made it a firm policy not to use reggae music to advertise Jamaica. This ragaraga music certainly did not conform to the image of Jamaica that was being constructed for tourist consumption. The new nation's motto, 'Out of many, one people', served to consolidate an idealised view of Jamaica as a multiracial paradise in which all would feel welcome. One love. Apocalyptic reggae lyrics that evoked the imminent collapse of Babylon could not be allowed to penetrate the consciousness of the carefree tourist.

By the 1970s, references to reggae begin to creep into the print ads of the Jamaica Tourist Boards.[3] A series of advertisements published in 1977 features a variety of scenes, all with the same written text: 'A Jamaican welcome. It's as warm as our sun on your shoulders. As heartfelt as our reggae music. As friendly as our waterfalls'. Notice the way in which reggae is naturalised as part of the background scenery. Like the warm sun and the friendly waterfalls, heartfelt reggae is part of the soothing island ambience. Reggae music thus, becomes the perfect auditory accompaniment to a restful vacation. Nothing of the disturbing message of roots reggae music remains. Adulterated Jamaica Tourist Board reggae is thus, essentially elevator music taken to the great outdoors.

## REGGAE SUNSPLASH

The increasing use of references to reggae in Jamaica Tourist Board advertisements of the late 1970s clearly coincides with the emergence in 1978 of Reggae Sunsplash. This international reggae music festival, a private sector initiative, was designed to showcase reggae music as an aesthetic and cultural experience — as 'heritage' — not as mere background muzak for more laidback touristic activities. Commenting on the cultural significance of Sunsplash, Rex Nettleford argues that:

> Perhaps the best example of popular identification with the tourism product by way of heritage promotion is the development of Sunsplash, the reggae festival that attracts certain visitors to Jamaica for that reason and no other, to share in the heritage of

popular music which is the creation of the people of Jamaica and now deemed as natural to it as are the sun, the sand and the sea (Nettleford, 1993).

Nevertheless, the strong tourist oriented element in the conception of the Sunsplash product meant the institutionalising of contradictions. It could be argued that the naturalisation of reggae as part of Jamaica's landscape of sun, sand and sea served to attenuate the conscious ideological elements in the heritage of reggae. The very name of the festival, Sunsplash, cunningly evoked sun and sea, essential ingredients in the success of the more conventional tourist product. The primary objective of Reggae Sunsplash was to fill up empty rooms in Montego Bay hotels during the low occupancy summer season by providing an attractive musical package for visitors. Entertaining the natives was a fortunate byproduct. Reggae Sunsplash, thus, brought together both the reggae connoisseur and the usual 'sun and fun' tourist from abroad; Reggae Sunsplash also generated a domestic tourist market of local reggae fans who made the annual trek to Montego Bay to 'play tourist'.

Roger Steffens, founding editor of *The Beat* magazine, and coauthor of *Bob Marley: Spirit Dancer* epitomises the foreign reggae connoisseur for whom Reggae Sunsplash was far more than 'sun and fun' tourism. In 'Memories of Sunsplash' Steffens recalls that:

For my part, 1981s Tribute to Bob Marley remains my favourite and most indelibly imprinted Splash. The venue in that long distant day was the 'mudsplash' site of Montego Bay's Jarrett Park, a soccer stadium that seemed a veritable United Nations once I got past the shoving sweating mob jamming the few entrances. At the time I wrote that once one joined the slowly surging masses of people who jammed the darkened infield, you could mix with tall blondes from Finland, English colonials from Kenya, Africans from Sierra Leone and Dakar, hippies from the Bronx, ska revival singers from Birmingham, England street hustlers up from Kingston for a quick week's killing, dapper police with dictatorial bearing, little kids selling peanuts, record producers from Hollywood looking for acts to sign, fans from all over the States who'd saved for months to come down for a week that felt like the latest, and largest, international reggae convention. Even the Japanese and Australians were there.

Today, 13 years onward, those descriptions remain apt (Steffens 1996).

What remains particularly 'apt' is Steffens's provocative representation of the local reggae fans — the Jamaican massive — as 'the shoving sweating mob jamming the few entrances'. It is true that Jamaican crowds are notoriously unruly. But the distance Steffens seems to establish between the dehumanised 'mob' outside and the 'veritable United Nations' of particularised people inside the concert venue underscores the social contradictions that the Reggae Sunsplash festival has not

*226*

been able to quite resolve. These are the very social contradictions that characterise Jamaica's cultural heritage.

The transgression of social class boundaries that massive, tourist oriented public events like Sunsplash and, more recently, Jamaica Carnival seem to facilitate is purely illusory. The border crossing between Jamaica and home that the tourist makes is analogous to the crossing of social class barriers within Jamaican society itself. The otherness of uptown and downtown is temporarily effaced in a carnival of displacement somewhat like the Trinidad original, which is itself being imported into Jamaica as an experiment in intra regional crossfertilisation. But, ideological tensions between the predominantly uptown Jamaica Carnival and the largely downtown Sunsplash, around the public representations of sexuality, for example, reproduce the social class conflicts that only appear to be mediated by these ritual events. In Jamaica Carnival, downtown 'slackness' becomes permissive uptown 'licence'. The freedom of the middleclass to parade its nakedness in the streets is a symbolic acting out of its usual position of social superiority, literally at centre stage. Indeed, the increasing cost of participation in both Jamaica Carnival and Reggae Sunsplash reduces workingclass aspirants to the role of mere spectators who find themselves on the periphery of a new decentering drama of social dominance. The people can indeed become alienated from mass marketed forms of indigenous cultural expression that are reconstituted for tourist consumption: Steffens's 'shoving sweating mob jamming the few entrances'.

Reggae Sunsplash has been a major success for most of its 17-year history. Mike Jarrett, in an article entitled 'Welcome to the Greatest Reggae Festival on Earth', traces the evolution of the festival, noting the changes of venue over the years that indicate Sunsplash's fluctuating fortunes. Of the second staging of the event in 1979 Jarrett notes that:

> The Jamaica Tourist Board had more time to promote the festival and the economy of Montego Bay discovered, in a tangible way, the true value of the Reggae Sunsplash and the awesome power of Reggae. For when negative press stories about the political situation in Jamaica were leaving hotel rooms empty, even during the traditional high season. Reggae Sunsplash pulled them in (Jarrett, 1994).

In 1993, after years of increasingly strained relations between the Reggae Sunsplash promoters, Synergy Productions Ltd., and the Montego Bay power brokers, the festival venue was changed to the Jam World entertainment centre in Portmore, St. Catherine. The festival received overwhelming support that year, particularly from Kingstonians. It may have been the novelty of the Jam World venue, as well as a matter of local pride; Reggae Sunsplash had been ousted from Montego Bay in order to accommodate a Montego Bay-based competitor, Reggae Sumfest.

In anticipation of another 'boom' staging of the event in 1994, Mike Jarrett noted in that year's *Reggae Sunsplash* magazine that '1993 marked a significant turning point for this internationally famous festival. That was the year when, on being relocated to Kingston, the Reggae Sunsplash changed character, from 'a tourist event that Jamaicans attend; to a Jamaican event that tourists attend' (Jarrett, 1994). This optimistic revalorization of the tourist : Jamaican ratio in the Sunsplash mix proved premature. Sunsplash 1994, held again at Jam World, was a financial disaster. The consolidation in Montego Bay of a tourist oriented Reggae Sumfest, designed to fill the cultural and economic vacuum created by the withdrawal of Sunsplash, proved to be formidable competition for the 'Jamaicanised' Sunsplash. Sunsplash failed to draw the crowds that Sumfest did.

For 1995, Reggae Sunsplash was relocated from its peri urban setting to a more conventionally touristy location. A *Sunday Gleaner* story, headlined 'Sunsplash Rebounds' raised a number of issues of direct relevance to the author's argument that there are cultural contradictions at the very heart of the project of marketing reggae as heritage tourism. Meeting tourism objectives often requires bowing to sun, sand and sea imperatives:

> Synergy had elected to abandon Portmore's Jam World Entertainment Centre (where the show has been held for the past two years) indicating that without a beach and other attractions, Jam World fails to attract the usual heavy support from tourists.

> At the same time, many locals who once cherished the idea of driving out of town to the festival while it was in Montego Bay, abandoned the event when it moved to Jam World, saying it lacked the excursion element.

> 'Sunsplash does better as a tourist event, and it got its powerful image while it was in Montego Bay', Burke admitted (*The Sunday Gleaner* 26/2/95).

The Sunsplash case study seems to confirm that the original 'excursion element' in the reggae festival is essential for both international and domestic tourists. The role of the domestic tourist, particularly the Kingston-based reggae fan, in the success of both Sunsplash and Sumfest complicates the author's reading of the cultural politics of heritage tourism. For if the domestic tourist does, indeed, prefer to consume the commoditised reggae package in a tourist setting, rather than in the more familiar Jam World backyard, then 'excursion' reggae tourism must be acknowledged as one kind of resolution of the contradictions that inhere in heritage tourism.

## REGGAE AS A MARKETING TOOL

In Jamaican culture there is a long established tradition of going on 'outings', particularly at major holiday seasons. These outings, usually one-day excursions, are often to beach destinations. These events are always accompanied by music, be it the saintly hymns of church outings or the secular sounds of ungodly gatherings. The excursion element in the original Sunsplash package clearly synchronised with local cultural practices. The week long, out of town reggae festival concept was a fortuitous consummation of a long 'heritage' tradition of both beach and music-oriented recreational activities. Unlike participation in the regular dancehall sessions held in Kingston, annual reggae excursions to resort destinations allow the native the freedom to play tourist.

Jamaica Kincaid's vitriolic extended essay, 'A Small Place', describes the symbiotic relationship between the native and the tourist, emphasising the native's longing to become tourist:

> That the native does not like the tourist is not hard to explain. For every native of every place is a potential tourist, and every tourist is a native of somewhere. Every native everywhere lives a life of overwhelming and crushing banality and boredom and desperation and depression, and every deed, good and bad, is an attempt to forget this. Every native would like a rest, every native would like a tour. But some natives — most natives in the world — cannot go anywhere. They are too poor. They are too poor to go anywhere. They are too poor to escape the reality of their lives; and they are too poor to live properly in the place where they live, which is the very place you, the tourist, want to go — so when the natives see you, the tourist, they envy you, they envy your ability to leave your own banality and boredom, they envy your ability to turn their own banality and boredom into a source of pleasure for yourself (Jamaica Kincaid 1988).

The primary target of Jamaica Tourist Board advertisements is, naturally, the international, not the domestic tourist market. But the common excursion expectations of these markets, as demonstrated in the Reggae Sunsplash case study, suggests that the sophisticated marketing of authentic local heritage tourism can work. The use of reggae in Jamaica Tourist Board advertisements of the late 1980s and 1990s seems to more closely approximate the function of the music in everyday Jamaican society than in the earlier advertisements.

## 'ONE LOVE' ADVERTISING CAMPAIGN

The controversial 'One Love' advertisement of the 1990s exemplifies the promotion of reggae as cultural heritage, not mere background music. Indeed the message of the revolutionary 1970s advertisement, 'We're more than a beach, we're a country', seems to have penetrated the marketing strategies of the 1990s with respect to reggae. But not without resistance from some conservative elements in Jamaican society.

In a cynical article entitled 'Tourism Madness', *Gleaner* columnist Dawn Ritch savages the 'One Love' advertisement:

I understand the Jamaica Tourist Board's (JTB's) television commercial was vetted and approved by the Cabinet of Jamaica. Everybody knows that the slogan is 'One love, one heart, come to Jamaica and feel awright'. I haven't seen the commercial, but reports are that it has flora, fauna and Dunn's River. A more perceptive comment from a veteran hotelier however, is that the ad seeks to promote Jamaican culture through the use of reggae music, and a Rastafarian musician flashing his locks on stage. The hotelier said, "The Rasta has white teeth, red gums, looks exactly like a gorilla[4] and the Tourist Board would be well advised not to show it in the Mid West to white farmers who want what every other Caribbean destination is promoting . . . not culture, but sun, sea and fun. The problem with the Jamaican authorities is that the moment they hear reggae, their hearts begin to beat faster and market sense flies out the window".

Even when reggae was hot, the JTB never used it. Now when the posses have created a perception in the American mind that reggae plus Rasta plus drugs means violence, we have a national commercial which reinforces that perception. It may appeal to some corners of the North East, and reggae fans everywhere, but we don't need advertising to bring that market here. They come anyway (Dawn Rich, 1991).

In his witty response to Dawn Ritch, entitled 'War, Recession and Gorillas — Tourism madness indeed!', Rex Nettleford (1991) identifies himself as 'one who qualifies for being a gorilla.' From that perspective he reveals the rank racism and stark class prejudice that inform Dawn Ritch's second hand account of the 'One Love' advertisement:

For the bottomline we are expected to keep lying to the visitors (from the Mid West and the South Ms Ritch insists) that there are no black people in Jamaica. And if we admit that there are, they are to be seen merely as smiling waiters, barmen, skulleryboys, chambermaids, beach pimps, entertainers, or musclebound lifesavers, with a few 'Uncle Toms' scattered all over the properties as second tier managers or some 'uppity niggers' stashed away in faroff Kingston where such presumptuous things as daring to govern a country, writing columns for newspapers, or running a University, other education institutions and businesses, are pursued without much success despite the kind efforts of the IMF (Nettleford, 1991).

So we come full circle, back to the oxymoron, 'heritage tourism.' The message of Bob Marley's 'One Love', appropriated by the Jamaica Tourist Board to project a nonthreatening image of a unified Jamaica, is undermined in the eyes of Dawn

Ritch's anonymous hotelier informant by unsettling images of black bestiality. The preferred image of Jamaica occurs, for example, in a post-hurricane Gilbert advertising feature in the *Toronto Star* of Saturday January 21, 1989. The seven feature columns are entitled 'All-inclusive happiness'; 'Jamaica does it for you again and again'; 'Accommodation to suit every whim'; 'Blue skies are your only limit when rediscovering Caribbean'; 'Hollywood lands in paradise'; 'Phoenix rises from the ashes after Hurricane Gilbert's fury;' 'An upbeat mood to this island in the sun'.

References to reggae in this advertising feature are nonthreatening: 'Jamaica attracts visitors from every walk of life. From reggae aficionados and lovers of tranquillity to the young of heart who simply wish to dance all night; tourists come and come again in Jamaica'; Yet more reassurance:

'So unlock your senses and abandon yourself to adventure. Give in to the rhythms of the country, the pulsating beat of reggae music and the sound of waves hitting shore. Let them revive your spirit and soothe your soul'.

In the following text, reggae, like calypso and soca becomes generic island music:

'We started with Reggae. Club hopped to Calypso. Then switched to soca music. It was new to me. But that's Jamaica. Different kinds of music are all a part of it. It was almost morning when we finally headed for our hotel. And I had the most difficult decision of my vacation. To bed? or to beach?'

In this familiar tourist world of sun and sea there are exotic, smiling Rastas. No frightful, red gummed gorillas. Of Negril it is said: 'This is where you'll find Rick's Cafe, the most popular spot to watch the sun go down, and a number of small, very informal restaurants, many of them vegetarian and run by Rastas who are always ready to share a smile and to "reason" with interested visitors'. It is ironic that Negril, though positioned in this tourist advertisement as a laid back leisure spot, does, in fact, function as the unofficial reggae capital of Jamaica. Even more so than Kingston, in terms of the regularity of scheduled reggae concerts. There are several reggae concerts held every week in Negril: at Kaiser's Cafe, MX3 and Central Park, for example. Internationally known reggae acts, like Yellowman, the Mighty Diamonds, Dillinger who might appear to be dormant based on their absence from the national reggae circuit, frequently perform in Negril. Jamaicans from the south coast and the West do support these events which give them the opportunity to play tourist. [5]

The most fascinating statement in the entire *Toronto Star* advertising feature is the opening paragraph of the article entitled 'Accommodation to suit every whim:' 'It seems perfectly natural in this country of astounding variety and contrast, where the Bob Marley Museum sits cheek by jowl on the same stretch of road as the prime minister and the governor general's residences, that visitors find just as much diversity in accommodation.' This facile naturalisation of social contradictions is a familiar theme in sun and fun tourism advertising. 'Astounding variety and contrast' cannot be allowed to astound; they become 'perfectly natural' and therefore unquestionably safe. Indeed, the social distance Bob Marley appears to have travelled from Trench Town to Hope Road cannot itself be accommodated in this simplistic ordering of things.

## CONCLUSION

It is essential to note that Bob Marley's original 'One Love' lyrics do not unequivocally affirm the 'out of many oneness' of the Jamaica Tourist Board's versions of local social reality. The original lyrics actually interrogate this artificial oneness. The three chorus (cited parenthetically), somewhat optimistically chants 'one heart, one love'. Bob Marley, the lead singer, seems less certain:

> There is one question I'd really love to ask (one heart)
> Is there a place for the hopeless sinner
> Who has hurt all mankind just to save his own?
> Believe me (one love)
> What about the 'one heart'? (one heart)
> What about the 'let's get together and feel alright'?
> In the unquestioningly positive Jamaica Tourist Board versions we hear:
> Feel Jamaica move you
> Warm Jamaica touch you.
> Hear Jamaica singing
> See Jamaica smiling.
> Feel Jamaica's magic
> Hear Jamaica's music
> Come to Jamaica and feel alright.

At the celebratory reggae concert to mark Bob Marley's 50th birthday that was held on the grounds of the Bob Marley Museum on February 6, 1995, Mrs Fay Pickersgill, Director of the Jamaica Tourist Board, accepted from Mr Neville Garrick, Chairman of the Bob Marley Foundation, a token of appreciation of the support of the Jamaica Tourist Board in the promotion of the event — a framed Bob Marley poster. In her brief acceptance speech Mrs Pickersgill acknowledged the fact that Bob Marley had made the work of the Tourist Board exceptionally easy. Around the world, Bob Marley, reggae and Jamaica are synonymous.

Despite the contradictions that are foregrounded in my reading of reggae as heritage tourism, this tribute from the Director of the Jamaica Tourist Board does confirm an essential truth. Reggae music, as disseminated by Bob Marley, is an authentic manifestation of Jamaica's resonant cultural heritage. Marley's apocalyptic message music, however adulterated by the sun and fun priorities of the marketing experts within the tourist industry, is, nevertheless, a resounding affirmation of the remarkable creativity of the Jamaican people. This is the cultural heritage that Jamaicans can afford to share. It is a renewable resource that cannot be totally consumed; not even by the most voracious tourist.

## REFERENCES

Jarrett, M. 1994. 'Welcome to the Greatest Reggae Festival on Earth'. *Reggae Sunsplash Magazine*.

Kincaid, J. 1988. 'A Small Place'. NY: Farrar Straus Giroux.

Rex Nettleford. 1993. 'Heritage Tourism and the Myth of Caribbean Paradise'. In eds. D. Gayle and J. Goodrich. *Tourism Marketing and Management in the Caribbean*. London & New York: Routledge.

Ritch, D. 'Tourism Madness'. *The Sunday Gleaner*. January 13, 1991.

Rex Nettleford. 'War, Recession and Gorillas (Tourism Madness Indeed!)'. *The Gleaner*. January 16, 1991.

Steffens, R. 'Memories of Sunsplash'. *Reggae Sunsplash Magazine* (1994).

The Sunday Gleaner. February 26, 1995.

## NOTES

1. Professor Hubert Devonish, Head of the Department of Language, Linguistics and Philosophy, University of the West Indies, Mona, Jamaica explains that in Jamaican creole there are a number words formed from the consonants, r and g/k which share essentially the same meaning of ragged and connote disorder and deviation from the habits of respectability. Words such as tegereg (related to the English tagandrag, meaning 'of our belonging to the rabble'); regjegz (described in the *Dictionary of Jamaican English* as probably reduced from the English 'rags and jags', 'jags' meaning 'rags and tatters'; *rogorogo, rokoroko, rugorugo, rukuruku* are defined in the *Dictionary of Jamaican English* as 'basically phonosymbolic .... The basic idea is that of unevenness: hence, inequality of surface (roughness), unsteadiness of movement (up and down, back and forth). As usual in such words, one part of speech may be converted into another, as sense requires without change of form. A. adj.: Rough; uneven; unsteady; shaky; . . . B. vb.: To handle roughly; to shake; to mix; C. sb: A rough thing or action'.
2. In the words of Bob Marley's 'Babylon System' from the 1979 *Survival* album: 'Babylon system is the vampire/ Sucking the children day by day/ Babylon system is the vampire/ Sucking the blood of the sufferers'.
3. I am indebted to Mr Eric Murray, Librarian at the Jamaica Tourist Board, for his ready assistance in locating JTB print and audiovisual ads containing references to reggae.
4. The author was not able to locate in the Jamaica Tourist Board library any ad that fits this description. The one Rastafarian image in the videos I did see was a long shot of a silhouetted Rastaman, carrying a little child on his back. The child appeared to be white. This may be a revised version of the original closeup shot of the 'gorilla'.
5. I am indebted to Dennis Howard, Entertainment Journalist, for this insight.

# 16

# FESTIVAL TOURISM:
# THE CASE OF TRINIDAD CARNIVAL

Keith Nurse

## ABSTRACT

*The contribution of the arts and entertainment to the field of tourism is one that is largely under researched. This is the case even in the sub-field of cultural tourism where the focus is generally on built heritage. This chapter addresses this lacuna. It highlights the role of festivals as a demand-pull for the tourism industry as well as the ways in which tourism generates markets for the arts. The case for festival tourism is made in an economic assessment of the Trinidad Carnival, which is one of the largest festivals in the Caribbean region.*

## INTRODUCTION

Cultural tourism has emerged to be an important innovation and a new source for competitive advantage in the global tourism industry. It is estimated that 37 per cent of all trips have a cultural element (EIU, 1993). Increasingly, it is being appreciated that the relationship between the tourism and cultural industries is such that cultural industries generate demand for tourism while tourism generates additional markets and income for the cultural sector (Myerscough, 1988).

Global tourism trends suggest that there is much scope for growth in festival tourism, which is a sub-component of cultural tourism (Getz, 1997). Changes in the tastes and demographics of international travellers are such that there is greater demand for differentiation in the tourism experience as exemplified in the shift away from high-impact mass tourism towards more environment-friendly and community-oriented travel options (EIU, 1993; McCarthy, 1992). It also appears to be an effective means by which a country can diversify its tourism product in the increasingly competitive world of global tourism.

This chapter analyses the performance and prospects for festival tourism with a specific focus on the case of the Trinidad Carnival. The Trinidad Carnival is selected because it is one of the largest and well-known festivals in the region. It is also that it is one of the better-documented festivals and so allows for some analysis. The chapter starts with a global overview of the experience of festival tourism from an economic standpoint. In the case study, the primary aim is to evaluate the economic impact of the festival.

## THE CARIBBEAN AND FESTIVAL TOURISM

Festivals are public themed celebrations that exhibit the history, worldview, and social and cultural identity of a community (Getz, 1997). Festivals are as old as human civilisation and play an integral role in the development of world society. A critical aspect of festivals is the way in which they facilitate creative expression, allow for social catharsis and bolster the cultural identity and confidence of a people. From this standpoint, festivals can be an important ally in promoting authenticity in the tourism industry as well as fostering a positive socio-cultural impact (Bushell & Jafari, 1996). This is manifest in strong word-of-mouth promotion and the general 'good-feel' that they generate. A sustainable festival tourism strategy is, therefore, reliant on creating a significant psycho-cultural impact.

Festivals have emerged to be an important contributor to the tourism industry throughout the Caribbean. In many territories the peak in tourist arrivals coincides with some event, particularly a musical or carnival festival. This is the case in several territories: Trinidad and Tobago, Saint Lucia, Barbados, Jamaica, St. Kitts and Nevis, Dominica and the Dominican Republic. Festivals throughout the region contribute in a significant way to boost tourism arrivals, visitor expenditures and hotel occupancy rates. Festivals have also made an important contribution because they perpetuate and transplant Caribbean culture and values and influence global culture, media and public opinion. In spite of this contribution to the diversification and the competitiveness of the tourism industry, there has been little or no study of the phenomenon. In most countries there is no published data that measures the economic impact of festivals on the tourism and entertainment economy.

The synergy between tourism and the arts, entertainment or cultural industries is largely under-researched in the Caribbean. This state of affairs can be explained by the fact that the cultural industries have traditionally been viewed as leisure and recreational activities and not as a commercially viable sector. For example, there are few studies of the business and economic aspects of the music and audio-visual sectors. Another problem is that the demand-pull of the cultural industries tends to be excluded if not minimised in analyses of the tourism industry. This is in relation to both the role of the performing arts in providing entertainment in the hospitality sector (that is live performances in the tourism zone: hotels, resorts and restaurants) as well as the contribution of festivals and other events in enhancing the image of a destination.

Another issue is that a large proportion of the literature on cultural tourism is focused on heritage sites (for example, monuments) and the 'high' arts (such as, art galleries and opera). An area that is often neglected is that of live entertainment and popular culture (Hughes, 1996). This observation is of particular significance to the countries of the Caribbean in that many of the heritage monuments are institutions of oppression from the colonial era, for example, military forts, plantation houses and sugar mills where the history of the mass of the population is rendered invisible. On the other hand, the heritage and legacy of the masses is to be found in the popular arts, which embody social protest, affirm social identity and recall psychic memory (Nettleford,1990). The popular cultures of the region embody both celebration and resistance and are sites for the public display, negotiation and contestation of the varied social tensions and struggles of the society against class, race and gender oppression as well as representations of nation and empire (Nurse, 1999).

An important feature of popular culture is that it is a major contributor to global culture through the commodification of the cultural industries. Commodification has facilitated globalisation. This has been applicable to several popular culture art forms from the Caribbean. This is evident in the export success of musical genres like reggae, zouk, calypso, meringue, salsa, dancehall and soca (Nurse, 1997). It is also the case with the large number of overseas Caribbean carnivals (Nurse 1999). It can be argued that Caribbean popular culture, more than any other feature of Caribbean society, has had the greatest influence in advancing the region's position and stature in the global cultural political economy and consequently, the region's popular culture should be central to the cultural and festival tourism initiative.

## THE ECONOMICS OF FESTIVAL TOURISM

Appreciation of the relationship between tourism and the cultural industries has grown with increased attention to the economic importance of the arts. For example, a British study contends that 'the benefits to tourism are the expansion of special interest groups, a new potential clientele, and finally an expanded season as the arts are not dependent on the weather' (Myerscough, 1988: 91). The contribution of the arts to the tourism economy was estimated to be 41 per cent of overseas tourist spending. It is also that arts-related tourists stay 75 per cent longer and spend 64 per cent more per trip (Myerscough, 1988). The study concludes that arts tourism has a promising future because:

- the trade is a new and expanding market;
- it has an up-market profile;
- levels of satisfaction are high; and
- willingness to repeat the holiday or take a short break was high.

The benefits to tourism of the cultural industries have gained in recognition on the other side of the Atlantic. In New York, it was estimated that approximately 40 percent of overseas visitors are cultural tourists, in what is measured to be a $2.5 billion industry (Alliance for the Arts, 1997; McKinsey & Company, 1997). As in the case of the UK cultural tourists who visit New York tend to stay longer, spend more and have a keen interest in the arts, live performances and festivals.

There are some very good economic reasons for embracing the concept of festival tourism. The experience with festivals and other cultural events is that they tend to create a tourism demand that is resilient and less susceptible to economic downturns. Festivals have several key economic and social roles:

- as attractions capable of spreading tourism geographically and seasonally, especially to destinations lacking alternative appeal;
- as animators of sites and other attractions;
- as catalysts for infrastructure development, including urban renewal and heritage conservation;
- as creators or enhancers of destination images; and
- as alternatives to built attractions and high-impact tourism (Getz, 1997).

The economic impact of festivals is also quite significant. One of the better-documented festivals is the Edinburgh Festival in Scotland. The festival, which has multiple events, operated on a budget of £5.0 million and generated income of £44 million in festival related activities (for example, tickets, programmes, merchandise, refreshments at the venues) and £9 million in accommodation, travel and food (Casey et al, 1996). A 1992 study in the UK estimated the total annual income of arts festivals to be £40.6 million of which box office receipts accounted for 43.3 per cent, business sponsorship 16.7 per cent and arts funding bodies 17.2 per cent (Rolfe, 1992: 70).

## TRINIDAD CARNIVAL: AN ECONOMIC IMPACT ASSESSMENT
### Methodology

An economic impact assessment involves an evaluation of the direct contribution of festival tourism on the hotel, airline and entertainment industries. The analysis will specifically look at tourist arrivals, hotel occupancy rates, visitor expenditures, tax revenues and employment. The impact assessment will include a cost-benefit evaluation and an analysis of the division of costs and surpluses.

In tourism studies there are essentially two main approaches to determine the economic impact of tourist-related activities. The most comprehensive approach is based on data derived from an input-output model (Fletcher, 1989). Whereas an input-output analysis can give detailed information about imports, exports, income, sales and employment, when it comes to the tourism sector rarely are these studies disaggregated enough to afford specific information on the expenditures of tourists by sector of the economy, country of residence, type of accommodation, etcetera (Archer, 1996).

When it comes to data on a festival, which occurs at a specific point in time in the tourist calendar then the problems of an input-output analysis become more compounded. Consequently, few studies are able to provide the required detail on tourism receipts. Researchers are thus obliged to select the alternative approach of a visitor survey (Archer, 1996). Most territories conduct annual visitor surveys. However, they tend to be inadequate for the task of festival tourism in that they very often don't allow for the disaggregation of tourism expenditures for a specific event nor does it facilitate differentiation between regular visitors and cultural or festival tourists.

One solution is to administer an exit survey at the time of the festival (Archer, 1996). This is an appropriate approach for festival tourism in the Caribbean because most territories have few exit points and are thus able to capture a representative sample. This approach also solves the attribution problem: how much of the resultant economic flows can be validly attributed to the festival? For example, an input-output model would find it difficult to differentiate spending by locals from visitors or spending by visitors who would have travelled nonetheless. An exit survey avoids the attribution problem and therefore allows for the measurement of the 'new' or 'incremental' expenditure, which is considered equivalent to the earnings of an export industry (Getz, 1997).

The case study uses the exits surveys done by the Central Statistical Office for the years 1997 and 1998. More up-to-date surveys are not available.

## Tourism in Trinidad and Tobago

The tourism industry in Trinidad and Tobago, after several decades of neglect, has experienced steady growth in the 1990s. As table 1 illustrates, stay-over arrivals have increased by close to 80 per cent over the period 1990 to 1998. This upward trend has been matched by an 87 per cent increase in the number of hotel rooms, primarily in Tobago, which is viewed as the holiday destination, while Trinidad is seen as the commercial and business centre. Within the government, tourism is viewed as the key emerging sector and an important element in the diversification of the energy-based economy.

## Table 1.
## Trinidad & Tobago - Tourism Selected Indicators, 1990 – 1998

|  | 1990 | 1991 | 1992 | 1993 | 1994 | 1995 | 1996 | 1997 | 1998 |
|---|---|---|---|---|---|---|---|---|---|
| Arrivals (000's) | 195 | 220 | 235 | 249 | 266 | 260 | 266 | 324 | 347 |
| Hotel Rooms | 2,120 | 2,141 | 2,314 | 2,650 | 2,950 | 3,107 | 3,500 | 3,652 | 3,970 |
| Occupancy Rates (%) | N/A. | N/A | 54 | 55 | 47 | 44 | 46 | 48 | 52 |
| Avg. Daily Exp. (US$) | 97 | 92 | 86 | 54 | 54 | 45 | 65 | 96 | 93 |
| Annual Tourism Exp. TT$M | - | - | - | 433.1 | 512.4 | 427.9 | 647.4 | 792.7 | 1,165 |

Source: Caribbean Tourism Organisation 1999.

The tourist markets in Trinidad and Tobago can be broken down into three broad categories of visitors:

- Business visitors — that is any person (except students) permitted to enter the country for a period of less than one year, mainly on business or to work on a short-term contract.
- Vacation visitor — any visitor who came for holidays or vacation. Trinidad and Tobago nationals resident abroad returning to visit friends and relatives (VFRs) are also included. These visitors are sub-divided into Hotel holiday visitor, Guesthouse holiday visitor and private holiday visitor.
- Other visitor — all other non-residents who are visitors to Trinidad and Tobago and are not classified as vacation or business visitors. This category includes educational, religious and sporting visitors. (CSO, 1998).

Trinidad and Tobago has three distinct tourist seasons based upon peaks in tourist arrivals (see table 2). The first is the carnival season, which runs from the beginning of January until Ash Wednesday, the start of the Shrovetide in the Christian calendar. The second season is referred to as the summer or vacation season, the months of July and August, where a large number of nationals resident abroad return to visit family and friends. The third season is that of Christmas in December.

In each of these peak seasons the majority of visitors are VFRs. This group is indicated by the category, private visits, which accounts for over 50 per cent of the annual stay-over arrivals. February is the month with the largest inflow of total visitor arrivals as well as private, hotel and guesthouse visits. For example, tourist

*239*

arrivals in February 1998 accounted for 12.6 per cent of total arrivals, which is a slight decrease from February 1997 where tourist arrivals accounted for 12.8 per cent of total arrivals as shown in table 2.

## Table 2.
## Monthly Visitor Arrivals, January –December 1997 and 1998

| MONTH | 1997 | 1998 |
|---|---|---|
| January | 27,059 | 25,013 |
| February | 41,649 | 43,740 |
| March | 26,109 | 25,719 |
| April | 25,153 | 29,305 |
| May | 21,225 | 23,697 |
| June | 22,434 | 24,854 |
| July | 33,299 | 33,073 |
| August | 27,190 | 31,329 |
| September | 19,092 | 23,535 |
| October | 20,750 | 25,003 |
| November | 23,385 | 25,284 |
| December | 36,948 | 37,057 |
| **TOTAL** | **324,293** | **347,609** |

Source: TIDCO, Trinidad and Tobago Tourism Statistics 1998.

Table 3 shows visitor arrivals to Trinidad and Tobago by purpose of visit. February has the highest number of hotel, private and guesthouse visits, but the month with the lowest number of business visits. Private visits during the carnival period accounted for 16.3 per cent of total visits as compared to December, which accounted for 13.8 per cent of total visits. In terms of hotel visits the month of February accounts for 11.5 per cent of total hotel visits as compared to the summer and Christmas seasons, which account for 8.2 per cent and 9 per cent of total hotel visits for 1998, respectively.

## Table 3.
## Visitor Arrivals by Purpose of Visit – 1998

|  | Hotel Visit | Private Visit | Business Visit | Guest House | Other | Total |
|---|---|---|---|---|---|---|
| Jan | 4,584 | 9,988 | 6,640 | 1,675 | 2,126 | 25,013 |
| Feb | 6,567 | 29,090 | 4,022 | 2,275 | 1,786 | 43,740 |
| March | 4,817 | 10,715 | 7,400 | 1,226 | 1,561 | 25,719 |
| April | 5,371 | 14,010 | 5,870 | 1,320 | 2,734 | 29,305 |
| May | 4,091 | 9,765 | 6,870 | 957 | 2,104 | 23,697 |
| June | 3,390 | 12,624 | 6,450 | 1,049 | 1,341 | 24,854 |
| July | 3,930 | 20,193 | 4,920 | 1,072 | 2,958 | 33,073 |
| August | 4,721 | 16,461 | 6,010 | 1,594 | 2,543 | 31,329 |
| September | 3,824 | 9,351 | 8,020 | 968 | 1,372 | 23,535 |
| October | 5,330 | 10,670 | 6,370 | 1,088 | 1,625 | 25,003 |
| November | 5,279 | 10,035 | 7,010 | 1,497 | 1,463 | 25,284 |
| December | 5,139 | 24,650 | 4,350 | 1,976 | 942 | 37,057 |
| Total | 57,044 | 177,552 | 73,931 | 16,697 | 22,555 | 347,609 |

Source: TIDCO, Trinidad and Tobago Tourism Statistics, 1998.

## CARNIVAL ARRIVALS

The concept of a carnival visitor is defined as a vacation visitor during the carnival period. There are different ways of determining the carnival period, but the working definition selected by the CSO is the 19 days before Ash Wednesday, the start of the programme of official carnival activities. Based upon this definition the number of carnival visitors for 1997 and 1998, respectively, was 24,947 and 32,071 (see table 4). Approximately half of the carnival visitors come from the US. The UK, Canada, the Caribbean and the Rest of Europe are the next largest source of carnival visitors. The carnival visitor category includes foreign nationals as well as Trinidad and Tobago nationals. Table 5 shows the share between both groups for 1997 and 1998 and illustrates that foreign nationals are a rising share of carnival visitors.

## Table 4.

## Carnival Visitors by Country/Region of Residence, 1997 & 1998

|  | 1997 | 1998 |
|---|---|---|
| Caribbean | 3,410 | 3,853 |
| Central & South America | 1,640 | 1,860 |
| Canada | 3,180 | 4,161 |
| United States | 13,139 | 15,611 |
| UK | 2,143 | 4,197 |
| Rest of Europe | 1,216 | 2,183 |
| Rest of the World | 169 | 196 |
| Total | 24,947 | 32,071 |

Source: Central Statistical Office, Carnival Bulletin 1997 & 1998.

## Table 5.

## Share of Foreign and Trinidad & Tobago Nationals in Carnival Visitors, 1997 & 1998

|  | Foreign Nationals | Trinidad & Tobago Nationals |
|---|---|---|
| 1997 | 72% | 28% |
| 1998 | 78% | 22% |

Source: CSO, Carnival Bulletin 1997 & 1998.

## *Hotel Occupancy*

On average, hotel occupancy levels during the year range between 50 per cent and 60 per cent. However, during the carnival season, hotel occupancy rates increase to between 80 and 100 per cent, and this is so despite the hike in room rates. Most hotels and guesthouses boast of 100 per cent occupancy from one week prior to carnival until three days after the festivities. Hotels and guesthouses are also able to charge above premium room rates. Some of the larger hotels increase room rates by 30 per cent while some of the smaller hotels and guesthouses are able to charge over 100 per cent. Hotels and guesthouses in Trinidad, especially in and around Port of Spain, report that bookings for the carnival period are usually made a year in advance.

Carnival does create an element of destination loyalty. Hoteliers indicate that there is a strong element of event loyalty among customers. The repeat factor for carnival visitors is considered to be very high. It is also suggested that carnival visitors return to visit the destination outside of the carnival season. This is exemplified by the high satisfaction ratings that the festival enjoys.

Table 6 shows that for the month of February, the average hotel visitor spent TT$507.00 per day, a guesthouse visitor spent TT$214 per day, while private home visitor spent only TT$47.00 per day. Average spent on other expenditure amounted to TT$133.00 per day. Data relating to visitor expenditure for the entire year, so as to provide a comparison, were not readily available.

## Table 6.
## Average Daily Visitor Expenditure By Length of Stay and Category of Expenditure, February 1988 (TT$)

| Length of stay (days) | Accommodation, Meals, & Expenditure | | | | Other Expenditure | | | | | Total Avg. |
|---|---|---|---|---|---|---|---|---|---|---|
| | Hotel | Guest House | Private Home | Avg. | Entertain-ment | Land Transport | Shop-ping | Misc. | Avg. | |
| 1 | 606 | 217 | 0 | 468 | 0 | 138 | 346 | 0 | 484 | 952 |
| 2 | 697 | 162 | 52 | 437 | 50 | 112 | 499 | 84 | 745 | 1,182 |
| 3 | 973 | 160 | 74 | 321 | 65 | 36 | 208 | 5 | 314 | 636 |
| 4 | 563 | 318 | 111 | 308 | 108 | 48 | 140 | 18 | 318 | 626 |
| 5 - 7 | 637 | 217 | 87 | 195 | 85 | 34 | 83 | 14 | 219 | 414 |
| 8 -14 | 514 | 269 | 52 | 89 | 58 | 26 | 60 | 13 | 160 | 249 |
| 15 – 30 | 348 | 172 | 42 | 62 | 38 | 20 | 33 | 13 | 107 | 169 |
| 31+ | 386 | 171 | 26 | 41 | 22 | 12 | 17 | 7 | 59 | 100 |
| Total | 507 | 214 | 47 | 84 | 48 | 23 | 47 | 12 | 133 | 217 |

## Visitor Expenditures

With regards to visitor expenditure, it is estimated that for the period, the 6th to the 24th of February 1998, 32,071 carnival visitors spent an estimated TT$88.7 million (see table 7), which is an increase from the previous year. In 1997, 24,947 carnival visitors spent TT$64.5 million during the period 24th January to 11th February. Total estimated visitor expenditure for 1998 amounted to TT $1,165 million. The carnival period accounted for 7.6 per cent of total tourist expenditure for 1998 (see table 8). Carnival arrivals from the 6th to the 24th February 1998 amounted to 32,071, whilst for the entire month of February visitor arrivals stood at 43,740. The carnival festival accounted for 73 per cent of arrivals for the month of February. The 1999 Carnival period (29th January to 16th February) accounted for 74 per cent of arrivals for February. In terms of Carnivals share of total arrivals for 1998, carnival represented 9.2 per cent of total visitor arrivals (see table 8), whilst in 1999 it accounted for 8.8 per cent of total arrivals, a decrease over 1998.

## Table 7.
## Estimated Total Expenditure of Carnival Visitors by Type of Accommodation, 1998

|  | No. of Persons | % | Expenditure on Accommodation and Meals | % | Other Expenditure | % | Total Expenditure | % |
|---|---|---|---|---|---|---|---|---|
| Hotel | 5,032 | 15.7 | 17,858.60 | 48.1 | 4,528.40 | 8.8 | 22,387.00 | 25.2 |
| Guest House | 1,729 | 5.4 | 2,590.00 | 7.0 | 1,556.00 | 3.0 | 4,146.00 | 4.7 |
| Private House | 25,310 | 78.9 | 16,654.00 | 44.9 | 45,554.00 | 88.2 | 62,207.90 | 70.1 |
| TOTAL | 32,071 | 100 | 37,102.60 | 100 | 51,638.30 | 100 | 88,740.90 | 100 |

Source: CSO, Carnival Bulletin 1998.

## Table 8.
## Carnival's Share as A Percentage of Annual Visitor Arrivals and Visitor Expenditure, 1998

|  | Carnival Arrivals | Annual Arrivals | Carnival Share (%) | Carnival Exp. TT$ | Annual Tourist Exp. | Carnival Share (%) |
|---|---|---|---|---|---|---|
| 1997 | 24,947 | 324,293 | 7.7 | 64.5 mn | 792.7 mn | 8.1 |
| 1998 | 32,071 | 347,609 | 9.2 | 88.7 mn | 1,165 mn | 7.6 |
| 1999 | 31,609 | 358,537 | 8.8 | n.a. | n.a. | n.a. |

Source: CSO Carnival Bulletin 1997 & 1998; and TIDCO, Trinidad & Tobago Tourism Statistics 1997 – 1999.

## THE AIRLINE ECONOMY

The airline economy is another area that enjoys significant benefits from Carnival. The airline industry is broken down into three categories: scheduled air carriers, charters, and cargo. There are ten scheduled international air carriers that service Trinidad. These airlines service the major routes outside of Trinidad. The major destinations can be classified as United States (New York and Miami), Canada (Toronto), Europe (London), the Caribbean and South America. BWIA, the national carrier, travels to the majority of these destinations and controls a substantial portion of the travel market. For example, in 1998, total passengers (that is embarked and disembarked) on BWIA amounted to over half a million passengers, as compared to the nearest rival, American Airlines, which accounted for one hundred and seventy thousand arrivals and departures.

The carnival season is viewed as an important source of revenue for BWIA. During the peak seasons BWIA operates at an average of between 85 – 90 per cent capacity, whilst in the off-seasons they operate at 40 per cent or below capacity. The peak seasons for BWIA are the carnival months, January and February, the summer months, July and August and the Christmas season, December. Travel to Trinidad during the carnival months requires several months advance bookings as the airline enjoys close to 100 percent capacity, especially in the two weeks before the festival. In addition, the carnival months account for close to 20 per cent of annual passenger arrivals, as exemplified by 1998 arrivals. The core market for BWIA during the carnival season is the VFRs travelling out of North America.

During the off-season BWIA offers tactical prices, lower fares to stimulate travel during the slow period. Tactical prices are only offered in Trinidad and Tobago. On a year round basis the average tactical ticket price is approximately 20 per cent cheaper than tariff prices. For example, tactical fares for a Port of Spain to London return ranges from US$600 to US$700 as compared to tariff prices that range from US$799 to US$899. In similar terms, a Port of Spain to New York return ranges from US$350 to US$450 in the off-season and rises to US$450 to US$650 in the peak season. During the carnival period and other peak times, BWIA avoids tactical pricing and the fares that apply are the tariff prices.

Another benefit to the airline economy arises from the increased number of flights to Tobago from Trinidad in the two weeks after carnival. The Tobago trip is seen as a rest-up opportunity after the hectic carnival festivities. From a tourism standpoint, visitors are able to enjoy the benefits of a twin island destination, which offers the better of two worlds. There is no data to show the number of travellers to Tobago, but it is considered significant by the airlines and hoteliers in Tobago.

## THE ENTERTAINMENT ECONOMY

The entertainment industry in Trinidad and Tobago is one of the emerging industries with potential to increase foreign exchange earnings, generate employment and enhance a growing tourism product. The entertainment industry includes the music industry, film and video production, commercial theatre and dance, costume design and production, sound, stage and lighting, visual arts and cultural tourism. The foreign exchange earnings of the entertainment sector were estimated at TT$ 267 million in 1995 and $274 million in 1996. These earnings positioned the industry in seventh position among the major export sectors in the Trinidad and Tobago economy (Nurse, 1997).

*245*

The main contributor to the overseas earnings of the sector comes from festival tourism whose share of approximately 67 per cent, is largely a result of visitor expenditures at the annual Carnival festival. The next major source of income is from overseas music performances, generating between 22 – 24 per cent of earnings. Earnings from the recording industry are ranked third (Nurse, 1997).

The entertainment industry in Trinidad and Tobago is intertwined with the National festival, as the entertainment industry is largely a product of Carnival (Nurse, 1997). Trinidad carnival is often associated with three specific art forms, that is, Calypso and Steel pan and Masquerade. Each of these art forms has developed export markets.

The overseas Caribbean carnivals, which number in excess of seventy, are an important feature of the entertainment industry because they account for a large percentage of the year-round work for musical artists and other carnivalists, such as costume designers. These carnivals have grown rapidly since the early 1990s and are now the largest street festivals and generators of economic activity in their respective locations (see table 9). The 'Notting Hill' carnival attracts over 2 million people over two days and generates over £20 million in visitor expenditures. Similarly, the 'Labour Day' carnival in New York earns US$75 million while the 'Caribana' festival in Toronto generates CND$200 million (Nurse, 1998).

## Table 9.
## Economic Impact of Overseas Caribbean Carnivals

| Overseas Carnivals | Estimated Attendance | Tourist Expenditures |
|---|---|---|
| Toronto – Caribana (1995) | 1 million | CND$ 200 million |
| New York – Labour Day (1995) | 2 million | US$70 million |
| London – Notting Hill (1995) | 2 million | STG £30 million |

Source: Nurse 1997.

One of the key features of the entertainment sector is the relatively large share that overseas music performances contribute to overall foreign exchange earnings. Performances are the main economic activity for most recording artists as well as steel pan players. In many ways sound recordings and videos operate as promotional tools for the performance-based activity. The industry is also transnational in that many of the recording artists, music bands and steel pan bands are either overseas or spend a large percentage of their time outside of the country, for example, servicing the Trinidad-style overseas Caribbean carnivals in the US, Canada, the UK and through-out the Caribbean region.

Carnival is a substantial generator of employment in the masquerade bands (also known as 'mas bands'). The carnival period plays a critical role in terms of employment as most of the workers in the 'mas' camps are usually unemployed or self-employed during the off-season and '...as such the industry generates employment in sectors which are not usually engaged by the formal economy' (Burke 1997). Overseas carnivals also provided an avenue of employment for designers. Mas bands such as Barbarossa, Wayne Berkley, Stephen Derrick, Harts and Poison produce costumes for bands in overseas Caribbean carnivals like Miami, New York, London, Toronto and Jamaica. These exports largely involve high-end skills as low-skill workers such as decorators and stitchers are hired abroad.

The entire carnival season, which begins months before the actual two-day street festival, creates thousands of jobs in a host of entertainment-related and down-stream industries. Ground transportation, accommodation, catering, tour operations, security, advertising, handicraft sales and the clothing industry are just some of the sectors that attribute an upsurge in business to the carnival season. In fact, for some people, employment in those fields is seasonal and is created almost entirely because of carnival and lasts for the duration of the festival, demonstrating the undeniable impact of the carnival economy on people's lives.

## ECONOMIC IMPACT ASSESSMENT

A method for measuring the economic contribution and impact of festival tourism is to examine the cost-benefit ratio of public funding of the festival to the visitor expenditure. The available data encompasses the years 1997 and 1998. As table 10 shows, in 1997, the state funding, or government subvention amounted to TT$17.1 million. Visitor expenditures for that year's carnival came to $64.5 million, thereby giving a return of 1:3.76. The year 1998 saw a reduction in state funding, but an expansion in visitor expenditure to $88.7 million for a return of 1:7.36.

## Table 10.
## Economic Impact Assessment, 1997 – 1999

|  | 1997 | 1998 | 1999 |
|---|---|---|---|
| Budget $TTmn | 17.1 | 12.0 | 27.4 |
| Visitor Expenditure $TTmn | 64.5 | 88.7 | n.a. |
| Cost-benefit Ratio | 1:3.76 | 1:7.36 | n.a. |

From the above analysis, it can be concluded that the carnival season has a positive impact on theTrinidad andTobago economy. In terms of tourism expenditure there has been a gradual increase over the years.The hotel and airline industries are the main beneficiaries in that they enjoy excess demand, advanced bookings and premium rates. The benefits also accrue to a wider grouping in the hospitality sector, as there is a marked increase in guesthouse and other kinds of accommodations during the carnival period.

The carnival industry generates income and employment in a number of ancillary sectors through backward and forward linkages. Backward linkages arise when the target sector (tourism) demands inputs from other sectors. For example, the carnival sector demands inputs from the food and beverage sector, and the arts and craft sector.

The other main beneficiary is the entertainment sector, which is intimately linked to the carnival industry. This sector has benefited from increased foreign exchange earnings in terms of merchandise and sound carrier exports, overseas performance and services income and royalty income. In terms of the general economy, the carnival season generates employment, for mas bands and sectors of the economy such as vendors selling crafts, food, and beverages.

## REFERENCES

Alliance for the Arts. 1997. *The Economic Impact of the Arts on NewYork City and NewYork State*. City of NewYork: Arts Research Centre.

Archer, B. 'Economic Impact Analysis'. *Annals ofTourism Research* 23, no. 3, (1996): 704 – 707.

Burke, S. 1998. 'Culture and Economic Development:The Case ofTrinidad Carnival'. M.Sc. Thesis, Institute Social Science,The Hague.

Bushell, R. & J. J. 'Developing CulturalTourism Opportunities'. *Annals ofTourism Research* 23 no. 4 (1996): 954–955.

Casey, B. et al. 1996. *Culture as Commodity? The Economics of the Arts and Built Heritage in the UK.* London: Policy Studies Institute.

CSO. *Tourism Statistics Bulletin*, Carnival 1997. Vol.18. no. 1 (1997). Port of Spain: Central Statistical Office.

CSO. *Tourism Statistics Bulletin*. Carnival 1998 18. no. 2 (1998). Port of Spain: Central Statistical Office.

CTO. 2000. *Main Statistical Report 1999*. Bridgetown: CaribbeanTourism Organisation.

EIU. 1993. *The Market for CulturalTourism in Europe*. London: EIUTravel andTourismAnalyst no. 6.

Fletcher, J. 'Input-OutputAnalysis andTourism Impact Studies'. *Annals ofTourism Research* 16 (1989): 514 –529.

Getz, D. 1997. *Event Management and Event Tourism*. NewYork: Cognisant Communication Corp.

Hughes, H. 1996. 'Redefining CulturalTourism'. *Annals ofTourism Research* 23 no. 3, (1996): 707 – 709.

McCarthy, B. 1992. *CulturalTourism: How the arts can help market tourism products; How tourism can help promote markets for the Arts*. Oregon: Bridget Beattie.

McKinsey & Company. 1997. *You Gotta have ART!: Profile of a Great Investment for New York State.* New York: McKinsey & Company.

Myerscough, J. 1998. *The Economic Importance of the Arts in Britain.* London: Policy Studies Institute.

Nettleford, R. 'Heritage Tourism and the Myth of Paradise.' *Caribbean Review* 16, no. 3 & 4, (1990): 8-9.

Nurse, K. 'The Trinidad and Tobago Entertainment Industry: Structure and Export Capabilities', *Caribbean Dialogue* 3, no. 3 (1997): 13–38.

Nurse, K. 'The Globalisation of Trinidad Carnival: Diaspora, Hybridity and Identity in Global Culture', *Cultural Studies* 13, no. 4, (1999).

Rolfe, H. 1992. *Arts Festivals in the UK.* London: Policy Studies Institute.

TIDCO. *Trinidad & Tobago Tourism Statistics*, 1997–1999. Port of Spain: Tourism and Industry Development Company.

WTO. 1999. *Tourism Market Trends Americas, 1989–1998.* Madrid: WTO Commission for the Americas.

# SECTION 4
# EVENTS &
# SPORTS TOURISM

# 17

# ORGANISING AND MARKETING SPECIAL EVENTS IN THE CARIBBEAN: A GUIDE FOR AMATEUR PLANNERS AND ORGANISERS

A. Denise Gooden, Deon Miller & Howie Prince

## ABSTRACT

*This chapter focuses on how special events are organised and marketed. It is important though that this discussion be placed into its proper perspective. Hall (1992) affirms that although the majority of events have probably arisen for non-tourist reasons there is clearly a trend to exploit them for tourism and to create new events deliberately as tourist attractions. What precipitated this trend? The researchers scanned the global scene to find possible reasons for this growing trend. A compilation of the best practices and recommendations that can be used as a guide by amateur organisers and planners to assist them with the task of organising and marketing special events is provided.*

## INTRODUCTION

This chapter is a study into how events are organised and marketed in the Caribbean. The study takes as its cue, the practices of organisers of special events and attempts to identify the best practices as evidenced from field research into special events that are staged in the region. The study was conducted on two fronts. In the first instance, the researchers combed the literature to compile the varying views of the experts in this field. The question — what are the best practices as described by the experts that the amateur should observe when organising an event? In the second instance, the researchers collected primary data from the field to find answers to many questions related to the practices of organising special events. The study does not pursue the line of cause and effect, but rather looks at correlation between practices observed and the successful organising of events.

This research hopes to provide amateur organisers with tools that they can use when planning and organising special events in their communities or countries.

Additionally, this research:

- Explores the relationship between organisers and other stakeholders of special events namely, participants, sponsors and visitors. It explores how the actions or aspirations of each stakeholder impacts the success of an event.
- Identifies the links between proper planning, marketing and co-ordinating and the success of an event.
- Provides guidelines that can be used as a checklist by organisers and planners of special events.

Many experts in the field have made the link between special events as one catalyst that could lend support to the task of meeting the diverse needs of the 'new tourist', defined by Martin and Munt as the tourist who shares an expressed concern for participation and control of tourism by the local people (Martin and Munt, 1998).

Colin Hall, (1992) in his book '*Hallmark Tourism Events: Impact, Management and Planning*' contends that special events have as their primary objective 'a means by which to place or keep tourism destinations on the tourists map, through the staging of short-termed attractions'. Hall further notes that these events or festivals 'are good medicine for the soul, a glue that galvanises communities together'. Jean Holder of the CTO joins Polly Patullo in agreeing that countries must 'look inside, find their cultural selves and create niche markets around their natural, cultural and historical attributes'. Holder advances further that countries could 'design' and market special events to capture niche markets (Patullo, 1995).

The experts agree that special events can play a significant role in the development of the tourism and hospitality industry. Therefore, much importance should be attached to the organising and marketing of these events to:

1. ensure their success; and
2. maximise the benefits that could be derived by all stakeholders of these events.

It is this important aspect of special events that the researchers now address with the major research question being, what are the key factors involved in organising and marketing successful special events in the Caribbean.

## THE NATURE AND OBJECTIVES OF THE STUDY

This chapter, in the first instance, attempts to capture the essence of this Caribbean mystique. The researchers chose three Caribbean countries and from each selected special events, which are used as 'microcosms' for a study on the key to organising and marketing successful special events.

## The Objectives of the Study

Specifically the study provides the opportunity to:

1. Explore the nature, form and artistic value of our cultural activities, which find expression in the performing or visual arts, festivals and carnivals.
2. Identify these activities which visitors and stakeholders in the tourism industry and the arts classify as worthy of higher pursuit.
3. Examine the organisation and marketing of the events under consideration with the view of identifying and highlighting the best practices and those actions that contribute to the success of events.
4. Develop guidelines that can be used by amateur organisers and planners to successfully organise and market their chosen event.

Many attempts at organising events in the past have ended in failure. This research is built on the premise that failure can be avoided if proper planning procedures are observed. There is really no need to reinvent the wheel. Rather the amateur organiser can learn from the mistakes and success stories of his/her predecessors. This research brings to the table the practices and experiences of the past with a view to influencing the future of the organising and marketing of special events.

## METHODOLOGY
### Research Design and Sampling Techniques

The researchers utilised two main tools to establish linkages and correlation between effective planning and organising and special events. The tools used were three questionnaires and a structured interview.

Three countries were selected from which to draw samples of events for further research. The countries selected were Jamaica, Saint Lucia and St. Vincent and the Grenadines. From these three countries, events were selected from the following categories: carnivals, music and community festivals and a national festival of the arts. A more detailed breakdown reads as follows:

*Carnivals*

- Jamaica Carnival
- Saint Lucia's Carnival

- St. Vincent and the Grenadines' Carnival

*Music and Community Festivals*

- The Yam Festival

*The National Festival of Arts in Jamaica*

## The Sample

A total of 19 questionnaires were administered to organisers of all the events under consideration. For all the festivals studied, members of the organising committees were the main respondents. Additionally, responses were solicited and received from persons who participate in these events, such as 'mas' designers, dancers, musicians and other players and performers. A questionnaire was also administered to visitors who witnessed or attended some of the events under consideration. Finally, some attention was given to the funding aspects of special events. Sponsors and representatives of advertising agencies were interviewed to gauge their reactions to the efforts of funding these events.

## Analysis of Data

The study relied heavily on the collection and analysis of qualitative data. Although there is a fair amount of quantitative analyses resulting from the data generated, it is really the measure of the quality of organising and marketing special events to which the researchers devoted the greatest effort. Since this study looked for correlation between several variables such as organising, marketing, co-ordinating and the success of special events, the questionnaires were constructed to gather information relating to the quality of each variable and the degree of success associated with output in each area.

Secondary data was also collected from several sources. The researchers gleaned from the rather limited field of literature on special events to gather information on how these events are organised and marketed. This information provided a basis from which to crosscheck or compare and contrast the findings from the field research. The researchers also used data collected in the secondary research to assist with the compilation of the organiser's guide / checklist which is the ultimate result of the research.

# DESCRIPTION OF SELECTED EVENTS

## *Carnivals*

### Carnival in Jamaica

Jamaica Carnival is an annual 'stellar event' which 'unites the Jamaican people musically, culturally and socially' (jamaicacarnival.com). This event, now eleven years old, is described by its founder, Byron Lee, as 'a lesson in having fun'.

Carnival, as it is practised around the Caribbean, has become an art in Trinidad which now produces a spectacular show, a standard which other Caribbean countries try to achieve. Even in Jamaica, which historically was not rooted in the carnival tradition, these festivities today enjoy much popularity and wide international appeal with many visits planned to coincide with the event.

Jamaica Carnival started as a private venture headed by Byron Lee and is supported by the Jamaica Tourist Board (JTB) and Jamaica Promotions Limited (JAMPRO). The event provides the subject for an excellent case study to highlight the contrast between a privately organised carnival and the government controlled carnivals of the Eastern Caribbean countries of St. Lucia and St. Vincent and the Grenadines.

### Vincy Mas — Carnival in St.Vincent and the Grenadines

Vincy Mas is a cultural mix of all the carnivals of the Caribbean and traces its origins back to Africa and later to slavery. For many years, the carnival was, like in Trinidad, a pre-Easter affair, but in 1976, the people and government agreed to move it to July not only because of its tremendous growth and popularity but also to give it the opportunity to create its own identity as a spectacular Caribbean calendar event. The carnival holds great appeal for both regional and international visitors and July is the month that now records the highest level of stay-over visitors in the country.

Vincy Mas is organised by the Carnival Development Committee (CDC), a non-profit organisation funded by government.

### Saint Lucia's Carnival

Two weeks to the day after the Vincy Mas, carnival in Saint Lucia comes to a resounding climax. Saint Lucia's carnival was relatively small-scale and more of a pre-Lenten village gala until 1999 when it was transformed into a summer festival.

The carnival has truly come into its own and is now being promoted overseas by the Saint Lucia Tourist Board as an affair with international appeal. The organising board, known as the National Carnival Development Committee (NCDC), is appointed by Cabinet, but also boasts representation from major components of the Carnival, Pan, Mas and Calypso Associations.

## Community and Music Festivals

Jamaica has a rich tradition of music and community festivals and an interesting list emerged from the research. Some of the more nationally recognised festivals are Reggae Sum Fest, the Trelawny Yam Festival, the Air Jamaica Jazz and Blues Festival and the Jerk Festival. Each of these events boasts unique and interesting characteristics and each merits detailed research. However, given the limited scope of this research, the researchers opted to examine only one of these events — the Trelawny Yam Festival.

### The Trelawny Yam Festival

The first Yam Festival was organised by the Southern Trelawny Environmental Agency (STEA), a non-governmental organisation developed out of a community initiative to bring about economic development to the region. The aims of the festival were:

- To highlight the culture and heritage of the area;
- To promote the consumption of yam and the development of value-added by-products;
- To promote economic development by providing an outlet to market products and to explore investment opportunities;
- To provide a source of funding in order that STEA may realise its development goals;
- To promote South Trelawny and the Cockpit Country as an eco-tourism destination.

According to organiser Hugh Dixon, this festival was the first event of its kind to take place in Jamaica and involves a wide range of activities. A wide variety of local dishes are offered including the popular roasted yam and saltfish.

## The National Festival of the Arts in Jamaica

In Jamaica today the word 'Festival' immediately conjures up the picturesque cultural festivities and celebration of the arts that have, for the past thirty-eight years been associated with the celebration of the country's independence. However, according to the Jamaica Cultural Development Commission (JCDC) 'Festival' actually had its origins in the parish of Portland. The success of the Portland Festival was an inspiration to many of the other parishes, which in turn established their own parish festivals.

Today, it is the Jamaica Cultural Development Commission (JCDC) which has responsibility for organising numerous important national events each year and primary among them is the National Festival of the Arts.

The Festival of Arts is a national competition with a well established network islandwide. The competition incorporates almost every aspect of the visual and performing arts including dance, music, drama, traditional folk forms, speech, the culinary arts, the fine arts and photography. The JCDC encourages and supports the process by offering training in the various art forms to prospective competitors. The activities of each annual competition span almost an entire year and start in September with an island wide evaluation of the previous year's work. The competition culminates in July of each year when the top performers showcase their talent through a variety of festivities held in the July/August period such as Mello Go Roun, the Culinary Arts Exposition, the Fine Arts Exhibition and the Best of Festival to name a few.

## EVENT MANAGEMENT AS VIEWED BY THE EXPERTS
### *Arriving at a Definition for 'Special Events'*

Most participants, performers, observers and organisers of special events are able to give a description of what a special event does for them or means to them. To the participant, it is an avenue for involvement in an aspect of life that he or she finds pleasing (Alexander, 1991), while to the performer, it offers an avenue for creative self-expression. To the organisers, special events hold many meanings including community development or the development of the people through their own creative flows; it provides opportunities through which the local people can derive economic and social benefits; it also adds diversity to the local tourism product. But when asked to define special events, some respondents seem to attach little value to this exercise. So the researchers turned to the literature in search of specifics.

Hall (1992) defined a special event as a 'short-term attraction that has as its primary objective a means by which to place or keep tourism destinations on the tourist map'. Hall goes on to say that a special event is a 'major one-time or recurring event of limited duration, developed primarily to enhance awareness, appeal and profitability of a tourist destination in the short or long term. Such events rely for their success or uniqueness, status or timely significance to create and attract attention' (Hall, 1992).

Hall argues that although the majority of events have probably arisen for non-tourist reasons, there is clearly a trend to exploit them for tourism. This is an important link made by Hall in defining the phenomenon and understanding its true nature.

The use of the term 'special events' was popularised by Disneyland in 1955. The occasion was the opening of Walt Disney's theme park in Anaheim, California. Disney's Director of Public Relations, Robert F. Jani, was asked what he called the new programme involving the Parade of Floats during the nights, which had become a major attraction. He replied 'a Special Event'. When the reporter responded by asking what that was, Jani thoughtfully answered with what may yet be the simplest and best definition of a special event — 'A special event is that which is different from a normal day of living'.

A special event can, therefore, be defined as a major one-time recurring moment in time in which rituals and ceremonies, aspects of a peoples' existence is celebrated. These celebrations are useful in enhancing the awareness, appeal and profitability of the area where they occur. The celebrations or events also have the potential to attract tourists.

## Special Events and the Host Community

It would be rather remiss of the researchers if a link was not made between special events and the local communities. Hall advances that a 'primary function of special events is to provide the host community with an opportunity to secure a position of prominence in the tourist market for a short, well-defined period of time' (Hall, 1992). Hall further affirms that these events are celebrations of something the local community wishes to share and which involves the public as participants in the experience. From this, we can infer that special events are the prerogative of the local people. It should be their initiative to develop it. There is the further implication that special events should not be imposed on any community. The people should be the initiators and the public participates at the invitation of the host community.

Special events come in many forms and fashions. Falassi (1987) identifies some of the elements that characterise the spirit of these events:

- A sacred or profane time of celebration marked by special observance (Pre-Lenten carnivals in Trinidad and Tobago and Dominica);
- Annual celebration of a notable person (Bob Marley Day) or event or harvest of an important product (Crop-Over in Barbados);
- A cultural event consisting of a series of performances or fine arts expositions which may be devoted to a single artist or genre (Jamaica National Festival of the Arts);
- A fair;
- Generic gaiety, conviviality, cheerfulness (Jamaica Carnival).

In concluding this chapter, the researchers draw attention to an appeal made by Falassi for more meaningful involvement of the host communities in events planning and organising. Falassi writes 'both the social function and the symbolic meaning of the festival are closely related to a series of overt values that the communities recognise as essential to its ideology and to its social identity, its historical continuity and its physical survival which is culturally what the festival (special event) celebrates' (Falassi, 1987).

## ORGANISING AND MANAGING SPECIAL EVENTS
### *Administration of Special Events*

Goldblatt advances five main functions or five critical stages that must be performed effectively by organisers of special events to ensure the success of the events. These are researching, designing, planning, co-ordinating and evaluating (Goldblatt, 1997).

### *Research*

There is an element of risk in the hosting of an event. The role of research in event planning is to reduce the risk (Goldblatt, 1997). It is important to conduct research prior to the event to ensure that the activities being organised will satisfy the needs of the stakeholders and that they are in keeping with the goals of the organisation. Consumer research will provide the guidelines for developing a product that will capture the interest of the target audience. Non-attendance at an event is a disaster that a careful planning process seeks to eliminate.

Research has indicated that events management professionals are in agreement that adequate time is not being dedicated to research and evaluation of events, and that both money and time would be saved in the long run if greater focus were given to research during the initial planning stage of an event (Hall, 1992).

Hall advises that far too often events are planned without conducting very simple research that may represent the difference between success or failure of an event. The importance of research can be neatly summed up in the six 'P' mnemonic — proper prior planning promotes perfect performance.

### *Design*

Research is the prerequisite to a successful event. Therefore, an event should only be designed following a thorough feasibility study to determine its viability (Goldblatt, 1998). Goldblatt advances that it is important for organisers to maintain their inspiration. He further admonishes that organisers should pay constant visits to the libraries, other events, movies, plays and art galleries, the creative arenas that can help to add interest and variety to an event.

Goldblatt advances further that the event organisers must answer the five 'W' questions:

- Why      Why must this event be held? What are the compelling reasons for this event?
- Who      Who will benefit from this event? Who do you want to attend?
- When     When will the event be held? Is the date/time flexible or subject to change?
- Where    Where is the best location, destination and/or venue?
- What     What elements and resources are required to satisfy the need identified?

Goldblatt asks three questions that organisers of special events must answer before committing themselves and other organisations to staging a special event. These questions are:

- How will the creditors be paid?
- How will you ensure that the key players will work together towards the ultimate goal — the success of the event?
- How will you solicit the support of the powers that be who hold control over some aspect of the event?

All these questions must be considered during the design process. The challenge will be to find creative ways of bridging these gaps.

## The Planning Process

The statement 'failing to plan is planning to fail' may seem a trivial cliché, but many special events fail because they were not planned properly (Alexander, 1991). The first step in the planning process is to establish measurable objectives for the event. Create a written list of objectives to keep organisers within the boundaries of the goals of the organisation. Good objectives also serve as an evaluation tool, a yardstick with which to measure the event's success (Alexander, 1991). The following list is composed of strategies in the planning process as advocated by different writers —

- Establish a realistic budget showing projected income and expenditure (Hall, 1998);
- Plan the event around a central theme (Alexander, 1991);
- Select date and timing of the event carefully (Goldblatt ,1998);

- Plan carefully when selecting a venue. Site inspection is critical (Goldblatt, 1998);
- Consider carefully the rate or tempo at which the event will progress from conception to completion;
- Test and review the plans regularly;
- Use the 'gap analysis' technique to identify and close gaps before staging the event.

The planning process prepares the blueprint for the coordination stage during which the plans are implemented.

## Coordination

Coordination refers to the minute by minute activities being effectively carried out. Goldblatt describes the coordination process as the 'resumé' or 'event order' the event managers use to ensure that all necessary tasks are fulfilled and that the fulfilment of each task follows a logical sequence. Following on Goldblatt's lead, it can be inferred that the core functions of coordination are:

- Identifying all tasks to be accomplished
- Establishing a logical sequence for the fulfilment of each task
- Matching resources — human and material — to effectively accomplish each task

Goldblatt was emphatic in his prognosis that coordination begins with sound rationale and regulation and an approach to decision making that emphasises timeliness and production scheduling 'without which (the events manager) may never find the right road or navigate so poorly that your event is hopelessly lost before you even begin' (Goldblatt, 1998).

Other coordination strategies worth considering include:

- Delegation of responsibilities;
- Crisis management;
- Risk management;
- Time management.

## Evaluation

Watts argues that events evaluation is 'vital to each and every event, large or small'. An evaluation should be carried out at the end of the event (summative) as well as throughout the event (formative). Watts also has a term for evaluation that goes on throughout the entire event. He calls it controlling and monitoring (Watts, 1998). There should be criteria established for the events evaluation process. One set of criteria should measure the outputs (hard criteria), the tangible and quantitative elements such as deadlines, performance specifics, specific quality standards, cost requirements and resource constraints. The soft criteria process measures the intangibles and qualitative characteristics such as positive image, staff commitment, total quality and ethical conduct.

Evaluation should be measured against the objectives of the organisation and the event. If an objective is to attain 20 per cent attendance over the last year, then at the end, the evaluation should measure this standard. Watts advances fifteen 'C's' to remind us of the evaluation procedures and this is captured in the chart as shown in table 1.

## Table 1.
## The Cs of Event Evaluation

| | |
|---|---|
| Compulsory | It must be done for every event, large or small. |
| Concise | It should be no longer than necessary. |
| Concurrent | It should take place during the event and continue after it. |
| Constant | Throughout the event and even in the earlier planning stages, consider how to evaluate the success. Evaluation should take place all the time. |
| Customised | Although there may be an existing checklist for evaluation, each project should have an additional set of criteria to match its own unique objectives. |
| Consulted | Evaluation involves seeking the opinions of as many relevant groups as possible, e.g., participants, officials, VIPs, sponsors. |
| Canvassed | Canvass opinion, do not wait for it to be given; just because customers don't actively complain, it doesn't mean they're happy. |
| Circulated | Circulate among people to gather opinions; circulate the debrief document as widely as possible, to help everyone involved build for the future. |
| Customer focused | Whatever the nature of the customers, they must all be asked for an evaluation through means like exit surveys. |
| Colleague based | All staff, paid or voluntary, should be involved in evaluating their part within the event. |
| Collected | Care should be taken to collect appropriate information. |
| Catalogued | Record information in an appropriate way and file it for reference. |
| Complete | It should cover all aspects of the event from before the arrival to after departure. |
| Communicated | It should be communicated to all relevant parties, explaining how the debrief is conducted and reporting its findings. |
| Copied | Successful evaluation methods should be reused on future projects in order to repeat their success.' |

Source: Watt 1998

# MARKETING OF SPECIAL EVENTS
## *Matching Needs with Products*

Watts (1998) notes that in order to achieve organisational goals there must first be a determination of the needs and wants of the target market. The target market is defined as the set of actual and potential buyers of the product. Kotler agrees with this point of view when he states that the fundamental principle in marketing is the importance of the customer and everything must be done with the customer in mind (Kotler, 1999). The first step to marketing an event should therefore involve researching the prospective customer to find out what his needs are and to determine if the product matches those needs.

## *Target Groups*

For marketing to be effective it must be clear at whom it is aimed. For many events the audience might be drawn from demographic groupings based on age, academic levels and so on. A good marketing plan will clearly identify the target market. For a particular event it may be necessary to identify additional targets such as potential participants, spectators, sponsors and staff. Different marketing strategies may be required to attract the attention and support of this varied group. The action plan should be to identify each group's needs and devise a marketing strategy to meet those needs.

## *Advertising*

Goldblatt (1998) notes that an effective and cost effective advertising plan will make the difference between the success or failure of an event. Since advertising is in most cases expensive, the marketing manager has to choose the medium that best suits the event, bearing in mind the overall objectives. A successful advertising campaign should:

- Make people aware of the event;
- Make persons knowledgeable on relevant event details;
- Encourage a spirit of participation;
- Let the public know that the event is worthwhile;
- Build an interest for future events;
- Promote the image of the event;
- Attract people to the event (Goldblatt, 1997).

## Media Relations and Publicity

Media relations and publicity is an area that should be given much focus and should run alongside an advertising campaign. One secret to good media relations is imagination and attention to detail. Another is remaining positive about the event. For an event to attract attention, press releases should be interesting and should also be brief, succinct and clear.

It is quite clear that organising and marketing special events require serious planning and much effort. For these events to be successful, management practices must be adhered to. These include, but are not limited to, the process of research, design, planning, marketing, co-ordinating and evaluating. Organisers should view the challenge of carrying out these functions as a process for the acquisition of skills that ensure successful event planning. While it should be considered an asset to have professionals with these skills on board, the organisation is more empowered when all its members make it their objective to become multi-functional.

## SUMMARY AND ANALYSIS OF FINDINGS

Following is the analysis of the questionnaires/interviews administered to –

- 19 organisers/planners of special events in three Caribbean countries;
- 19 visitors at these special events;
- 13 participants/performers at these special events;
- 18 sponsors of these events.

Given the limited length of the study and the numerous questions to be analysed, the researchers decided to analyse the findings in categories, rather than on a question-by-question basis. In order to achieve this, the questions from all four questionnaires were divided into eight main categories and the related findings compared and analysed.

## Aims, Goals and Objectives

The findings indicated that many of these special events such as the carnivals of the Eastern Caribbean and the Jamaican National Festival of the Arts have been a part of Caribbean life for several decades, while others such as the Jamaica Carnival and community festivals in Jamaica are relatively new developments. Notwithstanding, the objectives of all these events are very similar.

The pioneers who spearheaded the development of these special events in the Caribbean had as their main objectives the:

- Preservation and celebration of our cultural heritage;
- Celebration of our independence;
- Financial gain;
- Promotion and development of the arts;
- Development of local artistic talent;
- Community development.

Although these special events have maintained the ability to evoke national pride and promote the arts, cultural heritage and community development, a new dimension was introduced over the last ten years as many of these special events are now being recognised and promoted as tourist attractions. This confirms Hall's contention that although special events may have their origins in the celebrating of local festivities, their potential as tourist attractions are now being exploited.

Most of the respondents (89 per cent), however, have indicated the need for constant review of the objectives of the events. Such a move may become necessary to:

- Increase market share as festivals grow;
- Satisfy market demand;
- Facilitate regional and international participation;
- Take advantage of intra-regional cultural exchange and job opportunities for entertainers.

Evidence of this was gathered, for example, from St. Vincent's and Saint Lucia's decision to move out of the shadow of Trinidad and Tobago's carnival, thereby facilitating growth and expansion not only of the carnivals themselves, but also widening the scope for participation of their Caribbean neighbours as players or performers.

## Visitor Satisfaction and Support

Public support for special events ranged in description from fairly good (20 per cent) and good (27 per cent) to excellent (40 per cent) based on the perception of the organisers. There is a direct correlation between what the organisers perceive and what was actually recorded by the Visitors' Survey. Figure 1 shows the visitors' ratings of the events studied.

## Figure 1:
## Visitor Ratings of Special Events

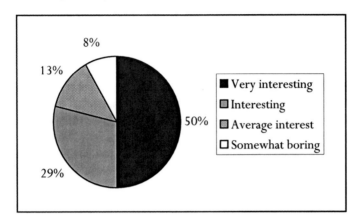

Almost 80 per cent of the visitors polled reported having a good experience (interesting — 29 per cent) and very interesting (50 per cent). The result vouches for the international appeal that Caribbean festivals and events are generating and the prognosis for their continuing usefulness to tourism development is encouraging. 89 per cent of them vowed to return to the country specifically to be a part of the event in question, with the same percentage indicating that they would recommend it to their friends.

However, there is much work to be done. Of the two who vowed neither to return nor to recommend the event to a friend, one was dissatisfied with the level of organisation, and also said that the event was 'boring', while both complained of harassment by the local people. Though 11 per cent may appear a relatively small dissatisfaction rate, the ripple effect of the adverse publicity that these customers can generate could be damaging.

The importance of local support should not be underplayed as sustainability of these events depends heavily on local patronage. In addition, the value and impact of domestic tourism is now receiving some recognition in the Caribbean and special events are excellent avenues through which the full benefits from the growth of domestic tourism could be realised.

## BENEFITS TO STAKEHOLDERS AND LINKAGES TO OTHER SECTORS

The research indicated that there are many beneficiaries of special events. All the organisers interviewed reported that special events are important to the country mainly for the reasons given in figure 2.

# Figure 2:
# Reasons given for the importance of special events

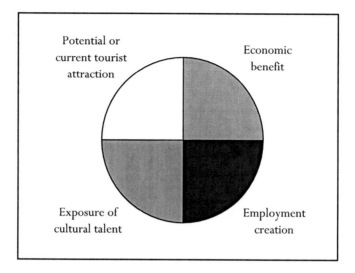

The organisers also indicated that special events provided the opportunity for linkages with —

- Agriculture;
- Craft and food processing industries;
- Traders and caterers;
- The entertainment industry.

Performers also agreed that although many events are seasonal, 38 per cent of the performers who take part in the events consider themselves to be professionals. Special events therefore provide the opportunity for many professional performers to earn professional fees. However, these same performers gave only a 33 per cent rating for satisfaction of current rates of payments as in many instances many receive only small honoraria for their services. Special events offer a good platform for new talents, but more importantly, it provides linkages to other sectors.

## *Administration*

According to the majority of the organisers interviewed, the following five areas should be key factors in event administration:

- Openness to new ideas for growth and development;
- Modification / Upgrading of event based on feedback;
- Focus on efficiency and on streamlining the administrative functions;
- Focus on making the event viable;
- Focus on the cultural and educational aspects of the event.

The event mangers indicated the following functions are critical to organising a special event:

- Personnel management;
- Financial management;
- Volunteer coordination;
- Fundraising;
- Marketing/Promotions;
- Logistical coordination;
- Safety and security management.

In addition, the interviewees:

- Recognised the need for more trained event managers and 66 per cent agreed that the total number of trained event managers is inadequate
- Pointed to the heavy reliance on volunteers (81 per cent)
- Agreed that the spirit of volunteerism still exists in communities (73 per cent)
- Noted the prevalent trend to target people with specific skills, experience and track records as volunteers.

Most organisers felt that there was a need to establish more companies that specialise in events management (88 per cent). This recommendation has implications for volunteerism and community involvement and raises the question of the high cost of outsourcing. However, in assessing performance, 47 per cent of the organisers polled indicated that paid professionals do not perform more efficiently than volunteers, while 35 per cent said they did, and 18 per cent remained undecided. These responses seem to imply that though there is a need for professional event managers, these experts sometimes lack the required experience. A mix of experienced volunteers and professional event managers who pool their experience and expertise could, therefore, make up a good team.

## Logistics and Operations

The following represents some of the logistical concerns and problems of event organisers.

Venue selection is critical and is based mainly on:

- ease of access for vehicular and human traffic;
- high carrying capacity;
- availability of ample parking (90 per cent ranked as important);
- available funding.

Other issues that were highlighted, but not raised in questionnaire included:

- security of venue;
- affordability of venue;
- essential services such as water and electricity.

The critical observation was the problem of over capacity. Of the organisers polled, 82 per cent reported hosting events in venues that were too small. This begs the question, how should carrying capacity be determined? There is a clear need for research and training in this area.

The need for adequate funding and sponsorship also arose as organisers sometimes felt obliged to select smaller, but less costly venues due to budgetary constraints. More importantly, however, the research indicated that there is a lack of venues suitable for the performing arts in terms of size, acoustics, type of stage and number of changing rooms.

The problems associated with over subscribing were:

- Refunding;
- Negative impact on image of organising body;
- Limited facilities especially toilets;
- Frequent fights among audience/spectators;
- Vandalism — broken facets, chairs and other equipment;
- Logistical breakdowns.

Some organisers indicated that it was difficult to co-ordinate the procurement and installation of some of the required facilities, with stage, light, sanitary facilities and display booths being the most difficult to procure. Other facilities that they are frequently required to provide include:

- Medical and emergency post;
- Interpretation / Information centre;
- Police post;
- Changing rooms;
- Shuttles.

In addition to the above, the organisers are sometimes hard-pressed to provide equipment such as:

- PA system (82 per cent)
- Office equipment (58 per cent)
- Generators (11 per cent).

The cost of renting equipment/facilities was cited as most critical burden on the organisation. In fact, a few of the more experienced organisers did not consider the procurement and installation of equipment a challenge, as they are very familiar with the procedures. The real challenge was in allocating the limited funding, which could allow inefficiencies to creep into the system, such as late installation of lighting/sound due to down payment being made to the contractors after the specified deadline date.

## Marketing

An effective marketing programme should include:

- the total marketing mix with focus on product development;
- careful pricing strategies;
- strategic distribution to the target market; and a
- good promotional plan.

Most of the events seemed to have a good promotional plan, but there was little evidence of a strategic marketing approach being undertaken. When asked how they would determine the target market for these events, only 26 per cent of the respondents alluded to market research, while 31 per cent of the respondents indicated that there was no need to target new and specific markets because of the presence of a large local traditional market. Interestingly, up to 60 per cent of the organisations utilise the services of professional advertising agencies.

The organisers recognise the linkage between these events and the tourism sector and 100 per cent of them viewed the events as having a strong potential to be developed into attractive tourism products. There is cause for concern as 95 per cent of the organisers cited insufficient funding as a major problem inhibiting the effective execution of their marketing, with 73 per cent of them lamenting the high cost of advertising via the mass media.

## *Funding*

As indicated earlier, many of the organisers polled spoke of the inadequacy of funding for events. The interview administered to sponsors was therefore devised to be used as an instrument to determine the preferences of sponsors and guidelines in seeking sponsorship.

Table 2 summarises the main reasons why sponsors are likely to become involved with an event. This information is useful in assisting events organisers/planners in understanding what drives the corporate community.

## Table 2.
## Reasons why Sponsors become involved in Special Events

| Reasons | Responses |
| --- | --- |
| To enhance image as good corporate citizens | 60% |
| To increase company visibility and profile | 50% |
| To increase sales of products | 40% |
| To promote the company's image | 35% |
| To provide support for community based tourism | 10 % |

Sponsorship of events in all the categories under study has been almost evenly distributed except in Jamaica, where there seems to be a greater preference for sponsorship of music and community festivals. Interestingly over 65 per cent of the sponsors polled indicated a strong interest in supporting/sponsoring sporting events, with cricket and football being more likely choices for sponsorships. Notwithstanding, the future augers well for the support to events already receiving sponsorship as all the sponsors polled indicated that they would continue to sponsor the special events with which they are now affiliated.

Interestingly, the vast majority of the respondents indicated that future sponsorship would always be predicated on the proportion of corporate budget available for that purpose and that they are more likely to sponsor events when:

- When proper plans including objectives and budgets for the event is presented;
- When there appears to be a good fit between corporate objectives and the objectives of the event;
- When the organising committee demonstrates its ability, seriousness and commitment to the event by:

    a) Having a cadre of capable personnel to manage activities related to the event.
    b) Having a good track record for organising this or similar events.

- When requests for sponsorships arrive early enough to facilitate long-term corporate planning.

## Evaluation

Seventy-four per cent (74 per cent) of the organisers interviewed stated that they conducted evaluations on visitor satisfaction and sought regular feedback from all the stakeholders and that these findings were incorporated into the planning of future events. They also indicated a preference for the use of surveys, focus groups, and to a lesser extent, participant observation as evaluation tools. However, when asked to express their views on the key elements for successful event management, only one of the organisers highlighted the value of ongoing evaluation of the product to the development of the event. This apparent contradiction is cause for concern as organisers may still not be using evaluation as a useful management tool, but are regarding it instead as an important academic exercise.

## CONCLUSION

There is conclusive evidence from this research that all special events share some common characteristics. They all seem:

- To have their origins in a celebration of some importance to the host community;
- To thrive on community involvement and volunteerism;
- To provide valuable outlets for creative expressions;
- To provide income generation and employment opportunities;
- To be exploited as tourist attractions.

Organisers, who were successful in the past, embraced the management principles of researching, designing, planning, co-ordinating and evaluating as tools to assist the process. This was corroborated by the field research as well as by the organisers polled. There is also general agreement that all events should begin with a good plan that sets out clear goals and objectives. Writers on the subject as well as the organisers polled agreed that the planning process is critical to the success of the event. Another critical strategy identified is the evaluation process. Regular feedback aids in monitoring the progress of an event.

A recurring theme throughout this study was the inadequacy of funding to undertake many of the vital functions. In particular, promotions and the installation of the infrastructure necessary to host the event were the areas most affected.

# RECOMMENDATIONS

The scope of this study does not allow the researchers to elaborate on the findings as comprehensively as they would wish. One major observation is that most Caribbean countries lack centres and theatres suitable for the performing arts and other major events. This is one area that ought to be addressed given the extent to which the people of these countries focus on cultural expression and also the fact that special events have the potential to become a viable industry.

In addition, there are a few other observations that the researchers hope the amateur organiser/planner may find useful. The essence of these observations is captured in the following checklist. The researchers wish to emphasise, however, that no checklist of this nature should be considered an exhaustive tool for directing the planning and organising of special events. Each event is unique and its uniqueness must be taken into consideration when organising an event. The checklist, which follows, was informed by both the field and desk research that formed part of the research process.

## *The Checklist*

1. Carry out a feasibility study to ensure the viability of the event.
2. Draw up a good plan which contains clear goals and objectives, a provisional budget, and as much details as possible on how the goals and objectives will be achieved.
3. Ensure that the event has widespread support of all key stakeholders in the host community.
4. Carry out detailed market research to match your product to potential markets.
5. After you know what the customer needs, find creative ways of satisfying these needs.
6. Pay attention to details in the design of the event.
7. List all the tasks to be undertaken and all the skills required to accomplish each task.
8. Ensure that there are enough personnel to manage all the tasks identified.
9. Seek volunteers, especially those with skills that you have identified as critical to the process.
10. Establish a logical sequence for the fulfilment of each task.
11. Involve as many of the stakeholders as possible in the planning process.
12. Establish linkages with other sectors within the community by offering opportunities for meaningful participation such as avenues for sales of products.
13. Consider the five W's — why, who, when, where, what.

14. Prepare site inspection checklist.
15. Select venues carefully and conduct site inspection.
16. Manage time carefully. It is a key factor to success at event coordination.
17. Establish a structured form of conducting ongoing as well as summative evaluations.
18. Consider the fifteen C's of events evaluation.
19. Establish a plan for marketing the event. Pay attention to how promotional material will be distributed. Remember, good public relations result in cost effective promotions.
20. Consider ways to involve sponsors in your advertising campaign.
21. Establish good relations with the media and make information readily available to them. Plan ways to facilitate the media during the event.
22. Consider the safety of the customer and put all possible measures in place to make him/her feel safe. Work with the local police, fire and medical services to achieve this goal.
23. When approaching prospective sponsors, go well prepared, armed with elaborate plans. Research the company to try to find out their own goals. Make sure that the event can advance their corporate goals.
24. Collect feedback from as many persons as you can and use their feedback to improve your plan.
25. Plan to enjoy yourself while providing a fulfilling and memorable experience to all who attend the event.

## REFERENCES

Alexander, P. 1991. 'Managing Festivals and Tourism Events'. A booklet based on and adapted from *Building a Festival: A Framework for Organisers*. Arkansas Department of Parks and Tourism.

Angulu, D. and N. Dacres. 2000. T. Warner-Arnold and G. Yearwood, G. 'The Marketing and Planning of Special Events — Generating Intra-regional Travel'. M.Sc. thesis, University of the West Indies, Jamaica.

Cuffe, M. 2001. Interview of Byron Lee on 'My Place'. January.

Falassi, A. 1987. *Time out of Time: Essays on the Festival*. Alburquerque: University of New Mexico Press.

Getz, D. 'Special Events'. *Managing Tourism* no. 338.40, (1994): 122 – 130.

Getz, D. 'Event tourism and the authenticity dilemma'. *Global Tourism: the next decade* no. 338.48, (1994): 313–329.

Goldblatt, J. J., 1997. *SPECIAL EVENTS – Best Practices in Modern Event Management*. New York: John Wiley & Sons.

Goldblatt, J. J. and Sapovitz, F. 1999. *Dollars and Events – How to succeed in the Special Events Business*. New York: John Wiley & Sons, Inc.

Hall, C.M. 1992. *Hallmark Tourist Events: Impacts, Management and Planning*. New York: John Wiley & Sons, Inc.

Haksever, C., R. Render, R. Russell and R. Murdick. 2000. *Service Management and Operations*. New Jersey: Prentice Hall, New Jersey.

Kotler, P., J. Bowen and J. Makens. 1998. *Marketing for Hospitality and Tourism*. New Jersey: Prentice Hall.

Mayfield, T.L. 'Development of an instrument for identifying community reasons for staging a festival'. *Travel & Tourism Research Association* 33, no. 3, (1995): 37 – 44.

Martin, M., and J. Munt. 1998. *Tourism and Sustainability: New Tourism in the Third World*, London and New York: Routeledge.

Patullo, P. 1996. *Last Resorts*. London: Cassell.

JTB. 2001. 'Tourism Statistics'. Kingston: Jamaica Tourist Board.

'Trelawny 2000 Yam Festival – Celebrating Yam'. *The Weekend Observer*, Thursday, April 20, 2000.

'Trelawny 2000 Yam Festival – About the Southern Trelawny Environmental Agency', *The Weekend Observer*, Thursday, April 20, 2000.

Watt, D. C. 1998. *Event Management in Leisure Tourism*. Essex: Addeson Wesley London Limited.

*www.jamaicacarnival.com.*

# 18

# 'I AM NO TOURIST':
# THE ENGLISH CRICKET FAN AS
# CARIBBEAN TRAVELLER

Hilary McD. Beckles

## ABSTRACT

*In this chapter the author examines the impact of cricket on the culture of the West Indies, with particular reference to Barbados. The author presents an account of the test match between the West Indies and England at Kensington Oval, 1994 and examines the responses of the 'locals' and the 'foreigners' to this event. While the match boosted tourist arrivals to the island and generated foreign exchange, there were mixed reactions as some locals felt disenfranchised by the over 6,000 English fans who arrived for the match. The author explores this issue against the backdrop of cricket in the postcolonial Caribbean society and its importance in the culture of the West Indies.*

## INTRODUCTION

The cricket fan has recently emerged as a new addition to the global tourist traffic. To the casual observer of the Caribbean tourism industry the appearance of this 'product' has been sudden and spectacular. Within the regional cricket community this travelling supporter of the visiting team has attained a striking visibility. Their presence has added a new and generally enriching feature to the crowd culture of the game.[1]

There are moments, however, during play when the changing fortunes of the teams generate some tension between foreign fans and local crowds. Yet, these visitors are keen to readily admit that they experience a greater sense of personal safety, enjoyment, and social acceptance from West Indians sitting in the cricket stands than lying on hotel sands.

Mostly from England, and attracted to the region to enjoy and celebrate cricket culture, these travellers are loathe to consider themselves tourists in the dominant tradition of an industry that promotes itself with imageries of 'sea and sun'. Rather, they espouse a new identity and iconography that are consistent with the discourse of cultural redefinition in the postcolonial space.

An opportunity to examine these developments was presented in 1994 when the English cricket team visited the West Indies to play at Kensington Oval in Bridgetown, Barbados. It was a historic event for several reasons, but not least of which was the new 'tourism' context within which the game was designed and played. For the first time the domestic West Indies cricket culture was visibly laid naked as a new-look tourism product by the forces of financial and communications globalisation.

It was a process not without its contradictions and ironies. The cash nexus, long suppressed by social codes and notions of cricket as high culture, swept all before it as tourism stakeholders celebrated the 'new ball game'. The images of the new tourism product surrounded the conservative cricket fraternity, particularly the administrators and spectators. Traditional local patrons cringed at the hiked up prices of tickets, the overwhelming presence of visitors, and protested that cricket officials had turned their backs on the local in pursuit of the global. Tourism officials, on the other hand, celebrated their acquired status as major players in the new ball game.

Media stories were dominated by talk of the latest tourism revenue stream. But everywhere on the island the one-sided competition between local and 'foreign' patrons for tickets took centre stage. Cricket culture was integrated by global tourism forces and the notion of the foreign cricket fan as a lucrative market find generated considerable excitement among hotel managers, airline carriers, government officials, and local entrepreneurs.

## CRICKET, TOURISM AND THE WEST INDIAN SOCIETY

The spectacular arrival of 6,000 English cricket fans to watch the game turned upside down the tradition on the island of open and easy access to a seat at the cricket venue. Local cricket fans feared dispossession by tourists, and argued that the globalisation of their cricket was part of a trend to appropriate hard won cultural rights. The visitors were not left without a response. Whose game is it anyway, they wanted to know, and entered the cricket space with a definite sense of confidence and belonging.

The question invokes an important interpretation of the origins and development of popular culture in West Indian history. West Indians have claimed that cricket has been fundamentally transformed by their hand, and that any English claim to an authenticity must be viewed as imperialist. The Sri Lankans, in very recent times, made a similar claim with respect to developments in the one-day version of the game. Aside from claims of cultural ownership, cricket fans as tourists expressed an important aspect of the paradigmatic shift in global tourism.

The shift from colonial to nationalist perspectives on development in the Caribbean posited both tourism as industry and cricket as popular culture. The former was considered the dominant force in the generation of new wealth and higher levels of economic growth. The latter emerged as the principal cultural expression of a globally competitive identity. The West Indies as a postcolonial space became identified principally with these manifestations. Yet for most of the period no direct and interactive relation was established between them for mutual growth and sustainability.[2]

The seemingly undeveloped relationship between cricket culture and tourism has, therefore, been disrupted by challenges posed by triumphal neo-liberal capitalism that seeks to redefine value in terms of revenue to be derived from the commodification process. Cricket is being untangled from political links with hegemonic nationalist ideologies. As such it is increasingly being made available to the international market through on site tourist access and by global television.[3]

The economic decline of the regional economy, and its dependence for sustainability upon North Atlantic financial institutions, have facilitated the search for new forms of income generation. One result is that organised culture has found centre stage in innovative development strategies. In addition, the imperative of finding new linkages between old and new market initiatives is serving to facilitate the industrialisation of cricket culture.

The ideological assertion of market penetration into this traditional area of culture has had the effect of polarising popular opinion. On the one hand, the discussion of economic survival is taking place in an atmosphere that seeks to legitimise a range of hitherto unexplored forms of economic activity. On the other hand there is a counter charge of subversion and appropriation by the market of things culturally sacred that reside at the core of national identity. The power of this perception is to be found in the popular belief that the globalisation of West Indies cricket in the form of direct linkages with the tourism sector constitutes a process of cultural decline and dilution.[4]

## KENSINGTON OVAL, 1994
### Benefits for the Stakeholders

When, in April 1994, the English cricket team and its mass support arrived in the West Indies at Barbados, the encounter released a frenzy of ideological debates that placed in clearer perspective an understanding of the new role of tourism in cricket culture. The match highlighted the multi-layered cultural meaning of postcolonial sport as an indigenous cosmology with respect to cultural ownership and territoriality. In addition, the game publicly raised issues pertaining to the critical features of cricket and its relations to cultural rights and national identity.

The background is important and should be recalled. In a document released by the Central Bank of Barbados entitled 'Review of 1994 and the Prospects for 1995', there are references to the 'good' news that followed the 'bad' news they and other West Indians had earlier experienced. It contained a financial statement released to the press, part of the bank's normal communication with stakeholders, concerning indices of national economic performance. It stated:

> Economic recovery in Barbados gained momentum during 1994. Real GDP expanded by an estimated 4 per cent, compared with about 0.6 per cent in 1993. The export sectors together grew twice as quickly as the rest of the economy . . . Tourism was again the main engine of growth, expanding by 11 per cent ... The upturn in the UK market has been attributed to an influx of cricket fans, cheaper fares, additional charter flights and intensified marketing.[5]

In the final section of the release, subtitled 'Prospects for 1995', it is stated that 1995 is expected to be a less buoyant year. Overall economic activity is projected to grow by only about 2 per cent, as the major foreign exchange earning sectors are likely to be less dynamic than in 1994. Although tourism will again be the leading sector, 'activity will not be as strong in the absence of the special event which took place in 1994'.[6]

The good news was the enormous financial success of the special event mentioned; the influx of cricket fans from England occasioned by a tourism marketing blitz of the West Indies vs. England Test match. The 6,000 English spectators, delivered to the island by a host of charter companies, descended upon the Kensington Oval in Bridgetown, was hailed as a major success story in the tourist sector.

The bad news was that the English team, 3-0 down in the five-match series, won the game, defeating the West Indies in a convincing display before a massive 'home' crowd. The English victory was historic in proportion. The last occasion that England had defeated the West Indies at Kensington Oval was in 1935.

This kind of spectator migration and participation had never happened on this scale before. It was a first for English fans, West Indian supporters, cricketers, administrators, tourism officials, and the overall culture of West Indies vs. English contest. On the surface all was well.

Occupying the high ground of civic exchange, 'locals' and 'foreigners' were embraced by the theatrical grip and magic of a cultural practice that had assumed new tourism dimensions and ideological expression. Beneath the surface, however, a new cricket world was being created. Furthermore, ideological representation, aspects of post modern philosophical discourses, and social reactions to postcolonial cultural globalism were being examined, fashioned, and legitimised. It was cricket at its ideological best.

## Post-match Analysis

On Friday 15 April, two days after the 'special event', a letter over the name of P. Francis, appeared in the *Barbados Advocate* with the headline 'When Kensington looked like Lord's'. A photograph showing 'a sea of English supporters' over a caption which asked 'Is this really Kensington Oval?' accompanied the letter. In the opening paragraph the author sets a surreal stage for a discussion on cultural possession and celebration, identity, and the ethnic politics of heritage:

> Last weekend I went to Kensington Oval to watch the Fourth Cable and Wireless Test Match. Upon arrival, I fell into a trance! I dreamt that all the stands had been painted in various shades of white . . . Then someone pinched me and I came to the realisation that I had not been dreaming — this was real! It is estimated that on the first day, approximately 80 per cent of the spectators were English supporters; on the second day over 70 per cent, and on the third over 65 per cent. By the third day many of them, with the help of the sun, had turned from lily white to brown or lobster-red.[7]

On being 'pinched' into consciousness the author asked the question, 'what does all this mean?'

The search for meaning, it is argued here, should begin with a recognition that fundamental changes are taking place in postcolonial Caribbean cricket, and that these changes have origins within North Atlantic capitalism as well as in the cultural contradictions endemic to the anticolonial project.

The constituent elements within these processes can be identified as follows: (1) the globalisation of postcolonial mass culture by international capital; (2) the willingness of former imperialist societies to consume the cultural products of former colonies as quality offerings; (3) the postcolonial social acceptance that cultural identity and heritage ownership transcend national political boundaries; (4) the inability of West Indian nation states to achieve sustainable development; and (5) the extreme vulnerability of these new states with respect to neo-imperial cultural and economic penetration and domination.

## The Return of the English

The arrival in Barbados of 6,000 English cricket supporters in early April 1994 to witness and celebrate an encounter on the cricket field was in essence a technology-aided, postcolonial, multicultural communication. Barbados was (re)claimed by these tourists as an idyllic and privileged part of their own heritage; and cricket, the Barbadians believe, is England's lasting gift to them — a nexus more binding than the discarded chains of earlier slave plantations. These cricket fans, as tourists, were going 'back' home to the 'old country — their own 'South', as the Americans would say — to a place where many cultural things remained in a primate and immensely recognisable form.

In Barbados, English fans were 'away at home' engaging 'their' clever natives in an orgy of heritage mania that continues to be misunderstood by both sides as an ideological contest. The journey to Barbados by the English had little to do with the tourism of the foreigner. As far as these 6,000 were concerned, they could have been at Old Trafford in Manchester or at Lord's in London.

In the colonial period, Barbados, or as the natives call it 'Bimshire', was never keen to bite the English hand, and remained in many ways a 'shire' for sure. Many of the English fans that made the quarter-day trip across the Atlantic considered the journey no more than an internal journey on the cultural terrain of a holistic heritage. It was essentially a reassertion of cultural right, and a subversion of retreating nationalist self-definitions. But it was also an accommodation of sorts, recognition that things had changed in order to remain the same.

Cultural globalisation, however, is a very contentious political business. Stuart Hall has argued that it is always contested since it necessitates a powerful struggle for space, and because many people have multiple cultural identities that are continuously being reconstructed under the impact of diverse political discourses.[8]

During the five-day cricket encounter, locals were divided along much the same cerebral lines as they have been for the past 30 years. But it was not just an additional opening. It was one that moved closer to the heart of the matter. It exposed the spirit of a people whose location at a centre of the periphery has shaped all around and within them. The nerve-ends of cultural ownership and dispossession were touched and the reaction was predictable.

## Cricket in the Post-colonial West Indies

The Kensington Oval is designed to accommodate 11,000 clients comfortably. During the course of a well-hyped and exciting Test match capacity crowds of locals have given the venue its well-known reputation as a place of ease and peace. Six thousand English fans reconfigured the clientele and loud cries of dispossession were heard long before the match commenced.

Locals claimed that their cricket, a product shaped and refined by their sweat and tears over 100 years of a degrading apprenticeship, was being appropriated by international capital — with local agents — and removed from their reach. Talk of cultural disenfranchisement filled the airwaves as angry, excluded spectators recounted pitiful tales of trying to purchase tickets to enter the Oval. Anger led to despair among traditional consumers who, in an act of desperation, called for a national boycott of the game.

Calypsonians, politicians, intellectuals, and other shapers of public opinion, were called upon to assist in resisting the process of perceived cultural alienation. Tourism, they said, was at it again.

When, in the 1970s, for example, elements within the government section of the Barbados tourism industry indicated a desire to close certain beaches to the public in order to improve the comfort and consumption of tourists, a local calypsonian (The Mighty Gabby) produced a song whose chorus rang out: 'Dat beach is mine, I can bade dey anytime, despite what you say, I gonna bade dey anyway'.

The song became a national call to ideological arms, the most popular of its generation, and any policy of hotels' privatisation of public beaches government may have had, was buried in the sand of popular protest. Barbadians now spoke about winning the battle at sea and losing the war on land. Tempers flared and the politics of cultural heritage tourism raged.

The letter by P. Francis had located the predicament of local cricket supporters within a developmentalist paradigm that juxtaposed social exclusion and financial globalisation:

> He [local spectator] has been denied the opportunity to witness a Test match being played in his own backyard. Why? Because the almighty dollar (or pound, in this case) is more important than the desire of locals to participate in a West Indian affair — an occasion to render not just moral, but physical support to our fine cricketers . . . There is something wrong in our society if we believe that our welfare is always inextricably entwined in something foreign — currency or otherwise. Various sectors of the economy will certainly benefit substantially from the influx of visitors to our shores, but at whose expense?[9]

The dispossessed local spectators, Francis tells us, had also gained the sympathy of some dispossessors, many of them expressing 'surprise at the extent' of the displacement of local spectators.

## The demand

The size of English market demand for the event was reported in the local press as evidence of 'the intensified sports-tourism drive by the Barbados Tourism Authority (BTA) paying off'. During the 18 months leading up to the tour, the BTA's marketing efforts were spread across the United Kingdom.[10]

This included co-operative efforts with travel agents, schools, and cricket clubs. Some tour operators, such as Airtours which has established a strong presence in Barbados, did some individual marketing. The Fred Rumsey Travel Group also played an important role in market preparation. The BTA claimed that it 'spent considerable sums of money' in promoting 'the island as a cricketing destination' and the returns on that investment were finally being realised.[11]

By the end of March reports were appearing in the local press that only the lowest category of tickets were available for sale to residents. The implication was that the prime seats were presold in England by agents who had bulk purchased from the Barbados Cricket Association (BCA), acting in collaboration with the WICBC.

When the BCA announced on 8 February that tickets would go on sale at its premises, those who entered the market were told that the comfortable seats had been presold to English agents. Some Barbadians reported phoning to England desperately trying to purchase tickets. A black market developed and ticket prices were inflated by over 400 per cent.

The global demand for access, highlighted by English tourist consumption, drove many locals out of the market and led to a redesigning of the traditional ethnic and class character of the clientele. The BCA, shot onto the export market, confronted local consumers with a new policy that required ticket purchase for all five days. Pre-match panic set in, and many in the financially secure income groups purchased the remaining match tickets while spectators with less cash waited eagerly to see how events would unfold.

Strapped for cash for most of its turbulent history, the BCA argued that its position was based upon rational market responses that would work to the overall benefit of Barbados and West Indies cricket. Working class patrons, the traditional core of cricket spectators, were placed in an unfavourable relationship to the market, and scrambled for access to the recently covered, but still very basic, poorman's stand — known as the bleachers. A scenario of race and class, local and tourist, emerged with respect to consumption, an indication of the pervasiveness of the globalisation process.

Barbadians were convinced that for most of the match they were outnumbered by English tourists. B.C. Pires' column in the *Daily Nation*, 15 April, entitled 'Spot the Bajan: New Game at Kensington' began: 'You could have played spot the Bajan at the Kensington Oval during the fourth Test -and lost'.

The ground, he said, was 'swamped with potbellied, lobster-pink, tattooed Englishmen who hung Union Jacks upside down and sang football songs and made England feel like they were playing at Wembley'.[12] All told, there were 89 Union Jacks waving on the first day compared with 12 Barbadian flags and three West Indies flags. 'When the English batsmen came on there was a deafening roar, Pires states, 'and Bajans were hushed in Barbados'.[13]

Sports columnist for the *Barbados Advocate*, Barry A. Wilkinson, presented attendance figures that support those of P. Francis. He reported being 'extremely surprised at the large numbers of Englishmen'; it was 'the first time' he had seen 'so many white patrons watching a match at Kensington'. On Friday 8 April, the first day of the Test, he informed readers that 'the crowd appeared to be approximately 70 per cent English'.

During the weekend more locals came on stream and the ratio fell to 'an estimated 60 per cent' on the Saturday, rising again to 'about 65 per cent' on Sunday. Monday was the rest day, and on Tuesday when England's grip on the game intensified it went up again to about 75 per cent where it remained the following day. Barbadians, Wilkinson concluded, 'had been deprived of an opportunity to see their West Indies team in action'.[14]

The *Sunday Sun* (10 April) agreed that 'the British [tourists] greatly outnumbered their Barbadian counterparts'. Malcolm Marshall, legendary West Indies fast bowler, commented in his *Daily Nation* column that 'West Indians were outnumbered by English supporters', and Oliver Jackman, distinguished Barbadian diplomat, lamented the 'prodigious display of rapaciousness on the part of the WICBC, in cahoots with the BCA', that 'kept thousands of Barbadian cricket lovers out of Kensington'.[15]

The game was played, however, in an atmosphere which, though charged by some unease due to the unfamiliarity of developments, was cordial and according to police reports largely incident free. Eric Lewis, satirical writer for the *Barbados Advocate*, stated that he was not surprised by the 'historic moment' which witnessed more 'foreigners' at the Oval than locals. The reason he gave was that on the first day of the match he saw 'a woman driving an old car', a phenomenal event in Barbados where 'only we men drive vehicles which are tetanus traps'.[16]

## The impact of the media

The local and international press expressed fascination with the event and photographers especially revelled in capturing the colourful social event. Roving microphones recorded the opinions of spectators and the print media made splendid copy of narratives. When asked about the atmosphere in the packed stands, Tony Grandison, a Barbadian, said: 'It's all right and I think that we all have a healthy respect for each other'. He added that he appreciated the concerns local Barbadian cricket fans have as a result of their inability to purchase tickets in their home.

William Blades, another Barbadian, was also not too bothered by the British takeover: 'There are more British people sitting where I am than local people but I still know that we [West Indies] will win the game'. Asked how he felt about the extra loud cheers for England's achievement on the field, Blades said: 'They've come to support their team and we have come to support ours and that's the way it is'.[17]

Briton, David Rake, said the 'invasion' of the famous cricket ground by his countrymen was 'no big thing' since Britons of Caribbean origin always came out in their numbers to support the West Indies team: 'It reminds me of the 1970s. We English always used to be outnumbered whether we were playing at Lord's or Old Trafford', Rake said.

An ardent West Indies fan, a black Englishman from Leeds, said he was not happy about the English predominance in the stands: 'They shouldn't have allowed them to buy all of the tickets in advance like that. Later this year or whenever Pakistan or India come here they will be encouraging local fans to come out and support cricket, but for now it is as though they are telling blacks we are not important', he added. [18]

The massive English presence, noted Tony Cozier, the distinguished Barbadian cricket commentator and analyst, 'emphasized how beneficial sport can be to our tourism — and, consequently, our shaky economies'. The 'presence of thousands of free-spending England supporters', he added, 'sent Central Bank's indices soaring'[19]. The Nation's Marilyn Sealy described the event as 'the million-dollar Test match'.[20] WICBC's executive secretary, Steve Camacho, is reported to have said that 'it is undoubtedly the best performance ever at Kensington'. This was confirmed by the executive secretary of the BCA, Basil Matthews.[21]

'Local businesses and small entrepreneurs', the press reported, 'cashed in on the crowds by setting up several stalls outside the Oval and by throwing their bars open to the celebrating Brits'.[22] Hired car operations, restaurants, duty free stores, hotels, liquor shops, food vendors, souvenir stalls and banks, all reported record sales for the month of April, while the 'outcry of hundreds of disappointed locals who were unable to purchase tickets' was drowned in the flow of gallons of rum and beverages.[23]

Cozier explained the predicament of local cricket supporters. While he sympathised with Barbadians who 'consider a seat at the cricket as part of their birthright', and were angered that English tourists 'occupied so much space', he also recognised that they 'cannot have their cake and eat it too. You either want tourism or you don't'.[24]

Popular perceptions of alienation, furthermore, were deepened by the maintenance of WICBC policy provision that matches should not be televised for viewers in countries where the match is being played. Locals, then, were not only 'blocked out' but 'blacked out' with respect to the consumption of their cultural event.

Transnational television networks, hooked up by satellite facilities, beamed the match into households across the world. English supporters in England could also watch every moment of the fascinating encounter. Only Barbadian homes that were equipped with satellite dishes, however, could participate in this global viewership. Those without a 'dish', or a 'ticket', resorted to archaic transistor technology and agonised in the embrace of radio.

Tourists, then, had an all-round advantage. They could tan on the benches at the Oval in Barbados or sit in an armchair before a television in England. West Indian cricket culture had become a global commodity, but not readily available to the villager who claimed to have produced it. The international division of labour had taken another twist. Barbadians could, however, watch five minutes of televised highlights of the previous day's play during the evening news, compliments of multinational media carriers such as Sky Television and Trans-world Communications.

The editorial leader of the *Daily Nation* on Monday 18 April was not satisfied with these developments. The WICBC was painted by the paper as 'the last remaining bastion of power without responsibility'. It is a 'very strange decision', the editor stated, that the locals should be refused TV viewing facilities when the match was presold in England. The editorial continued:

> But the whole thing does not just end at counting the millions the Board makes by the sensible policy of preselling much of the Oval. There are people living here in Barbados who, as a direct consequence of the Board's decision, will be unable to attend the game. Their exclusion is foreseeable . . . We have certainly reached the stage now where, as a community, we will not meekly be shut out of what's going on . . . . We expect that the BCA representatives on the WICBC will appreciate our argument and use their influence to ensure that never again will the WICBC sell out the seats and still black out its potential patrons.[25]

Barry A. Wilkinson also ended his column in the *Advocate* (Friday 15 April) with a warning to cricket officials. 'Do not repeat this folly in the future,' he said. 'Our players need their supporters just as much as England or any other team would need theirs'.[26]

In all of this West Indians had little time to reflect on the feelings of English crowds who since the 1950s were called upon to absorb their unashamed support for the West Indies at English Test match venues. The behaviour of the West Indies cohort at England's Kensington Oval is now legendary; located in Brixton — the heart of London's black community — it has witnessed West Indian calypsonians and revellers basking in English defeats.

The English stiffened their upper lips, complained about the noise, but generally tolerated West Indian bacchanal. The tables were now turned, and the 'cricket chicken' had come home to roost. The English, after years of exposure to the calypso culture, were now behaving like West Indians at the rendezvous of their victory.

Against this background the English team arrived in Barbados with a local press showing little mercy. 'West Indies set to keep England sliding', 'England not good enough', and 'Into the Lion's Den', screamed the *Barbados Advocate* in headlines on 8 April — first day of the test.

On the 14th, however, these headlines gave way to 'West Indies Surrender', 'England Break the Jinx', 'English Resilience and Character Paid Off' and 'England — Simply Triumphant!' Gayle Alleyne began a column in the *Daily Nation* — on the 14th: 'A white flag went up over Kensington Oval at 2:54 p.m. yesterday as the West Indies' cricket fortress surrendered to the persistent enemy'.[27]

The English media, not surprisingly, did not take the charge of the West Indian press lying down. They had their own style of communications warfare, fashioned by centuries of ideological terrorism in colonial parts, to direct against representatives of West Indian cultural claims.

The battle of the subtext had begun with weapons more precise and destructive than those used on the field of play.

The 'smart missiles' used by English journalists in the assault at Kensington struck at the centres of West Indian cultural sensibilities. They targeted its postcolonial sense of historical identity, moral authority, and the intellectual worth of its cultural heritage. In short, the 'thinking bombs' were designed to obliterate the West Indian voice which spoke possessively and eloquently of its culture now projected so confidently as global fare.

The attack was led by Ian Wooldridge, an English journalist on the London *Daily Mail*. His account of the tour up to the Barbados Test was designed to prepare English supporters for the trip to Barbados. It was also published in the Barbados press soon after their arrival. Wooldridge was less than subtle in his rejection of West Indian notions of cultural sophistication.

In a Naipaulian sort of way he suggested that the West Indies — outside its persisting and proliferating criminal subcultures — is a place of nothingness. He insisted upon recognition of a 'boundaries dispute' between West Indies and English cricket culture, and indicated the side and direction from which the barbarians were coming.[28]

The tourist brochure spiel that promoted the Barbados Test, Wooldridge argued, was designed to inveigle English fans to the island, since it did not tell them that the 'Caribbean is a very tough place', 'born of imperial and freelance piracy, funded by slavery and now riddled with drugs'. Neither did it tell them that the 'West Indies are beating all hell out of a thoroughly honourable England team' because the islands' team is made up of 'back street' boys for whom cricket is the only 'passport to a better life'.

'There isn't much literature here', he states, and the West Indian male can pull himself 'out of the back streets' only by being 'pretty smart' at cricket.[29]

During the week of the Test, the 'Wooldridge Affair', as it became known, dominated the media. Barbadians of all shades took umbrage at Wooldridge's pejorative tone and insinuations. Writer and literary critic, John Wickham, in his *Daily Nation* column, 'People and Things', dealt with the issue at length. For him, the Wooldridge intervention was 'loaded with transparent innuendo designed to induce a sense of inferiority in the West Indian psyche'.[30]

Joel Garner, former West Indies Test cricket star, suggested that the background to the matter has to do with a persistent ideological posture adopted by some in England who believe that 'they are better than the rest'. 'Having savoured the pleasantries of our island, often this is how we are repaid,' Garner stated. 'We should encourage our visitors', he added, 'to interact with the locals for there is a wider interest at stake'. In summary, Garner informed readers that 'there is a cultural gap to be bridged' and that 'much of the fear born out of ignorance can be abated and removed by mutual celebration of cricket's achievement'.[31]

According to Louis Brathwaite, sports analyst for the *Barbados Advocate*:

> Wooldridge was trying to scare off his countrymen from coming to this island paradise, but despite his pathetic efforts thousands of them are watching the current Test . . . They have been mixing without any fear with people from throughout the Caribbean and farther away, and are not only thrilled by the cricket action, but have been eating and drinking as heartily as any local person.[32]

Sports analyst for the Caribbean Broadcasting Corporation (CBC), and writer for the *Daily Nation*, Andy Thornhill, advised Wooldridge that when he sees West Indian cricketers he should not think in terms of emissaries of a subcultural criminality, but he should see a reflection of the rest of us.

## CONCLUSION

England's surprising devastation of the West Indies side cut deeper than the 208 runs chasm of victory. When in 1950 West Indians defeated England at Lord's, their first Test victory against England on their turf, West Indians held a mass fete on the grounds. The bacchanal was led by Lord Kitchener and Lord Relator whose calypso 'Cricket Lovely Cricket' is now legend.[33]

It was a moment of liberation for the West Indian — a conquest in the nascent anticolonial struggle. England in Barbados repaid in full all the items on the cultural invoice. Now, unencumbered, the sounds of celebration filled the island under the canopy of dozens of Union Jacks carried by '6,000 plus skimpily clad, sun-baked bodies'.

Kensington (1994) and Lord's (1950) were therefore, linked on a terrain of cultural heritage made possible by the accumulative logic of postcolonial global capitalism. There was an understanding that the ritual on both sides had become, in fact, one cultural expression.[34] When the 'white flag went up over Kensington it meant that the West Indies' cricket fortress surrendered to the present enemy', the battle was over, and the victors celebrated in customary style:

> Spraying champagne and beer, a buoyant sea of Union Jack-waving Englishmen converged on the pavilion steps to pay homage to their newest heroes. 'Swing Low, Sweet Chariot', bellowed the jubilant fans who then crafted a new version of 'Jingle Bells': 'Jingle bells, jingle bells, / England all the way, / Oh what fun it is to beat the Windies today'. Hugging, shouting, jumping and, a few, even kissing total strangers, they savoured the rare and historic occasion.[35]

Simon Daw, an English supporter, managed somehow to say to a journalist: 'I had a marvellous five days at Kensington — and I will be back'. John Toppin, a rejected Barbadian summed it up: 'The fat lady is singing the Beatles now'.[36]

Former minister of sports in the Barbados government, the legendary West Indies fast bowler, Wes Hall, was philosophical and looked at a bigger canvas: 'We have lost a Test match, but the sports-tourism fusion has won. Thousands of sports enthusiasts will remember Barbados and tell their family and friends about the wonderful time they had here'.[37]

Peter Roebuck, former English cricketer, now journalist, examined the process and event — the selling of West Indies cricket as cultural tourism — and summarised, with a touch of irony, 'West Indies cricket must watch this cultural Yorker'.[38]

## REFERENCES

Alleyne, G. 'West Indies surrender'. *Daily Nation*, April 14, 1994.

————. 'Barbados Test a good catch: tourism'. *Barbados Advocate*. April 4, 1994.

Beckles, H. 1995. *An Area of Conquest: Popular Democracy and West Indies Cricket Supremacy*. Kingston: Ian Randle Publishers.

Blenman, R. 'Sports tourism paying off'. *Daily Nation*. April 7, 1994.

Brathwaite, L. 'Author attempts to belittle our cricketers'. *Sunday Advocate*. April 10, 1994.

Cashman, R. 'Cricket and colonialism: colonial hegemony and indigenous subversion'. In J.A. Managan, ed. *The Cultural Bond: Sport, Empire and Society*. London: Frank Cass.

Central Bank of Barbados. 1994. 'Review of 1994 and the prospects for 1995'.

Chris Searle. 'Race before wicket: cricket and the white rose'. *Race and Class* 31 (1990): 343-55.

'Friendly rivals in the stands'. *Daily Nation*. 11 April 1994.

Cozier, T. 'Lara: the icing on series to savour'. *Sunday Sun*. April 24, 1994).

Cummings, C. 'The ideology of West Indian cricket'. *Arena Review* 14, no. 1(1990): 25-32.

Francis, P. 'When Kensington looked like Lord's'. *Barbados Advocate*. April 15, 1994.

Garner, J. 'On the Wooldridge issue'. *Sunday Advocate* April 10, 1994.

Hall, S. 1981. 'Cultural studies: two paradigms'. In *Culture, Ideology and Social Process: A Reader* ed. T. Bennett. London: Open University Press.

Jackman, O. 'One for the history books'. *Sunday Sun*. April 17, 1994.

James, C. L. R. 1963. *Beyond a Boundary*. London: Hutchinson.

Lewis, E. 'Historic moment'. *Barbados Advocate*. April 15, 1994.

Mandle, W. F. 'Cricket and Australian nationalism in the nineteenth century'. *Journal of the Royal Australian Historical Society* 59, no. 4 (1973): 225-46.

Mangan, J.A. 1989. *Pleasure, Profit, and Proselytism*. London: Frank Cass.

Manning, F. 'Celebrating cricket: the symbolic construction of Caribbean politics'. *American Ethnologist* 8, no. 3 (1981): 616-32.

Marshall, M. 'Tetley too bitter for Windies'. *Daily Nation*. April 14, 1994.

Marshall, M. 'Tourism still holds the upper hand'. *Daily Nation*. April 14, 1994.

Pires, B. 'Spot the Bajan: new game at Kensington' *Daily Nation*. April 15, 1994.

Roebuck, P. 'WI cricket must watch cultural yorker'. *Sunday Sun*. April 10, 1996.

Sealy, M. 'Match hauls in $1 million'. *Weekend Nation*. April 15, 1994.

'The view from Silly Point'. *Daily Nation*. April 13, 1994.
Thornhill, A. 'We won't be sidetracked'. *Daily Nation*. April 13, 1994.
Wilkinson, B. A. 'Lack of support for Windies'. *Barbados Advocate*. April 15, 1994.

## NOTES

1. The author was an observer of this event, and conducted the interviews that inform this analysis.
2. Richard Cashman, "Cricket and Colonialism: Colonial hegemony and indigenous subversion" (1989).
3. Christine Cummings, 'The ideology of West Indian cricket', *Arena Review* 14, no. 1(1990): 25-32; W. F. Mandle, 'Cricket and Australian nationalism in the nineteenth century', *Journal of the Royal Australian Historical Society* 59, no. 4 (1973): 225-46; Frank Manning, 'Celebrating Cricket: the symbolic construction of Caribbean politics', *American Ethnologist* 8, no. 3 (1981): 616-32; Chris Searle, 'Race before wicket: cricket and the white rose', *Race and Class* 31(1990): 343-55.
4. C. L. R James, *Beyond a Boundary* (London: Hutchinson, 1963). For a critique, see Helen Tiffin, 'Cricket, literature and the politics of decolonisation: the case of C.L.R James's, in *Liberation Cricket:West Indies Cricket Culture*, edited by H. Beckles and B. Stoddart (Kingston:Ian Randle Publishers; Manchester: Manchester University Press), 356-70.
5. Central Bank of Barbados, 'Review of 1994 and the prospects for 1995' (1994): 1-2.
6. Ibid, 5-6.
7. P. Francis, 'When Kensington looked like Lord's', *Barbados Advocate*, 15 April 1994.
8. Stuart Hall, 'Cultural studies: two paradigms', in *Culture, Ideology and Social Process:A Reader*, edited byTony Bennett (London: Open University Press, 1981), 19-37.
9. P. Francis, 'When Kensington looked like Lord's'.
10. See Rose Blenman, 'Sports tourism paying off', *Daily Nation*, 7 April, 1994.
11. 'Barbados Test a good catch: tourism', *Barbados Advocate*, 4 April, 1994.
12. B. Pires, 'Spot the Bajan: new game at Kensington', *Daily Nation*, 15 April 1994.
13. Ibid.
14. Barry A.Wilkinson, 'Lack of support for Windies', *Barbados Advocate*, 15 April 1994.
15. Malcolm Marshall, 'Tourism still holds the upper hand', and 'Tetley too bitter for Windies', *Daily Nation*, 14 April 1994; Oliver Jackman, 'One for the history books', *Sunday Sun*, 17 April 1994.
16. Eric Lewis, 'Historic moment', *Barbados Advocate*, 15 April 1994.
17. Comments reproduced in 'Friendly rivals in the stands', *Daily Nation*, 11 April 1994.
18. Ibid.
19. Tony Cozier, 'Lara: the icing on series to savour', *Sunday Sun*, 24 April 1994.
20. Marilyn Sealy, 'Match hauls in $1 million', *Weekend Nation*, 15 April 1994.
21. Ibid.
22. Ibid.
23. Ibid.
24. Tony Cozier, 'Lara: the icing on series to savour'.
25. Editorial, *Daily Nation*, 18 April 1994.
26. *Barbados Advocate*, 15 April 1994.
27. See *Daily Nation*, 14 April 1994; Barbados Advocate, 18 April 1994.

28. See 'The view from Silly Point', *Daily Nation*. 13 April 1994.
29. Ibid.
30. Ibid.
31. Joel Garner, 'On the Wooldridge issue', *Sunday Advocate*, 10 April 1994.
32. Louis Brathwaite, 'Author attempts to belittle our cricketers', *Sunday Advocate*, 10 April 1994.
33. Andi Thornhill, 'We won't be sidetracked', *Daily Nation*, 13 April, 1994.
34. Gayle Alleyne, 'West Indies surrender', *Daily Nation*, 14 April 1994.
35. Ibid.
36. Ibid.
37. Ibid.
38. Peter Roebuck, 'WI cricket must watch cultural yorker', *Sunday Sun*, 10 April 1996.

# 19

# SPORTS TOURISM EVENTS: A MEASURE OF THE BENEFITS OF STAKEHOLDERS IN BARBADOS

Gale Yearwood

## ABSTRACT

*As a result of increasing competition for visitors as the number and variety of destinations increase and even the traditional source markets seek to encourage domestic tourism, a sports tourism programme and a number of other events were developed and are marketed by the Barbados Tourism Authority in an effort to rejuvenate, enhance and diversify the product in a very competitive marketplace. This chapter measures the benefits of sporting events in an effort to determine the most beneficial events to the stakeholder. Two factors that influence the benefits include the means of finding out about the event and the length of advance notice given to the stakeholders. The results of this study show the events that are more beneficial and recommendations are made to increase the level of benefits received by the stakeholders in the Barbados tourism industry.*

## INTRODUCTION
### Importance of Tourism to Barbados

Tourism became the mainstay of the Barbados economy after the 1950s when a fall in the price of sugar on the world market as well as increasing costs in the production encouraged the government of the day to seek to diversify the economic base of the island. Hence tourism was chosen since it utilised resources that were already plentiful on the island; the natural resources of sun, sea and sand, and a labour force consisting of many that were unskilled and under-employed.

Today tourism is the country's main foreign exchange earner and provides jobs for over 12, 000 persons or some 9.8 per cent of the workforce. It also contributes 16 per cent of the island's Gross Domestic Product. In 1998 the country recorded some 512, 397 long-stay visitors and an estimated tourist expenditure of 1.4 billion Barbados dollars. (BTA 1999)

## Challenges that the island faces in the marketing of its tourism product

Barbados is no different from other destinations in that, during the last two decades, it has been facing increased competition from other countries within the region and indeed the world. Faced with the failure of other sectors of their economies, many other Caribbean islands have turned to tourism as a generator of foreign exchange, employment provider and contributor to Gross Domestic Product. The tourism product of these islands is indistinguishable from that of Barbados — all are marketing the sun, sea and sand type of tourism.

## Competition

East Asia and the Pacific is the fastest growing region of the world in terms of tourism arrivals and with the Pacific islands offering sun, sea, and sand tourism, that region can be seen as being in competition with the Caribbean which was the traditional warm-weather destination. A number of destinations have also opened in Africa and even though many of these do not offer the same sun, sea and sand product as the Caribbean, they are competitive since they offer warm-weather vacation activities. Traditional source markets such as the United Kingdom, Canada and the United States of America are also seeking to capitalise on the economic opportunities being offered by the growth of tourism worldwide, by encouraging their nationals to engage in domestic tourism. These countries too can be considered as competition for Barbados.

Faced with this competition, as well as the fact that the island is considered a mature destination, Barbados has sought to rejuvenate and differentiate its tourism product by renovating its hotel plant, construction of new facilities, staging of special events and catering for a number of niche markets. Sports tourism has emanated as an avenue for diversifying the tourism product. The sports tourism programme serves this purpose well as it consists of both the staging of special events and the targeting of niche markets.

## Growth of Sports Tourism in Barbados

During the last two decades there has been an increase in the number of sports clubs, teams and groups visiting Barbados to participate in various disciplines, chief among them are cricket and field hockey. An increase in the area of field hockey prompted the Barbados Men's Hockey Association to encourage 'Hockey Tourism' in 1980.

The fulfilment of two main objectives were the focus of a firm commitment made by the government in 1987:

- To further the development of sports in the country in order to enhance the performance of Barbadian athletes in the regional and international arenas.
- To reinforce the sports tourism concept, which has helped to reduce seasonality in the tourism sector, sustain development over the traditionally slow summer months and to boost tourism earnings.

The portfolios of sports and tourism were merged into one ministry in order to facilitate this development. The Barbados Tourism Authority has launched a vigorous campaign to promote Barbados as a sporting destination internationally.

According to the Green Paper on Policies, Proposals and Programmes in the Tourism Sector prepared by the Ministry of Tourism (1999), sports tourism is one of the fourteen subject areas which is part of a Policy Document which will ultimately become the National Tourism Policy for Barbados. According to this document, sports tourism will be used as a means of fostering closer interaction between locals and visitors, and enhancing international publicity for Barbados. One of the strategies for achieving this objective is to utilise sports as a means of encouraging travel to Barbados by participants and spectators.

## RESEARCH
### Significance of the research

Since Barbados has joined many other countries in pursuing the sports tourism market, it is necessary to ascertain if the perceived benefits to the major stakeholders, for example, hotels, restaurants & bars and car rental agencies are being met. This chapter seeks to assess the benefits that will accrue to the main stakeholders and will further show how effective the sports tourism programme has been in realising the objectives that have been set out by the Ministry of Tourism in the Green Paper on Tourism. If the stakeholders are not realising the benefits of the sports tourism events then it will be necessary to evaluate the events themselves, their planning and marketing with a view to redesigning the sports tourism programme so that it is more effective in realising its goals.

### Problem Objective

To assess the direct benefits that key sectors of the hotel and tourism industry derive from sport tourism events.

*Specific Objectives*

- To ascertain which event(s) are perceived by the stakeholders as providing the most benefit.
- To ascertain the events(s) which are perceived by the stakeholders as being of the least benefit.
- To ascertain specific events which are perceived as being the most beneficial to the various categories of stakeholders.

## The Definition of Sports tourism

Sport derives its root definition from disport meaning to divert oneself. It carried the original implication of persons diverting their attentions from rigours and pressures of everyday life by participating in the mirth and whimsy of frolic.

Sports tourism refers to different sports, that throughout history, have been the source and/or principle reason for travel relative in distance according to the lifestyle epochs of history (Zauhar, 1995). In ancient times the Greeks and Romans travelled to watch and participate in sporting events. Gibson (1998) has proposed a working definition of sports tourism as follows:-

Leisure-based travel that takes individuals temporarily outside of their home communities to play or watch physical activities or to venerate attractions associated with these activities.

Gibson further states that there are three types of sports tourism:

1. active sports tourism — which refers to participation in sports away from the home community;
2. event sports tourism — which refers to travel to watch sports events such as the Olympics, World Cup Football and Wimbledon tennis; and
3. nostalgia sports tourism — refers to visits to sports' halls of fame, famous sporting venues and to meet sporting celebrities.

Today sport is regarded as the world's largest phenomena and tourism is considered by many to be the world's largest industry. As such the contacts between sport and tourism have increased dramatically. Zauhar (1995) has further stated that the mutual benefits for both are perceptible and the relationship is very compatible.

The term sports tourism has been coined to better understand the use of sport as a touristic endeavour. In the last decade there have been philosophical and entrepreneurial developments that contribute to such a marriage.

Sports tourism events are sports activities that attract tourists of which a large percentage are spectators. Furthermore, sports tourism events have the potential to attract non-resident media, technical personnel, athletes, coaches and other sports officials.

# METHODOLOGY
## Research Design

Since information was needed directly from the various stakeholders, a structured questionnaire was deemed the ideal tool for the collection of the data. This allowed the respondents to choose specific responses, which led to an easier analysis of the data.

### Selection of events to be studied

The main events chosen are those that have been promoted by the Barbados Tourism Authority as part of its sports tourism programme. Most of the events chosen have been established for some years and are for the most part annual events. The occasional events such as the regional championships in many events have also been measured since one of Barbados' objectives is to become the premier sports tourism destination for the region and each year a growing number of regional sports championships are held in the island. It is important that the significance of hosting these events be measured. The events measured are:

1. Sandy Lane Gold Cup – billed the Caribbean's premier horse race, this event is held the first Saturday of March each year. It is organised by the Barbados Turf Club.
2. International Cricket – Barbados hosts at least one test match and one One-Day International each year. These matches are usually held between January and May and are organised by the West Indies Cricket Board.
3. Regional Cricket - this includes the four-day Busta Cup championship and the limited-overs Red Stripe Cup.
4. Sir Garfield Sobers International Schools' Cricket Championship – held in July each year, this event is organised by the BTA and has been held since 1986.
5. Banks Hockey Festival – this event has been held since 1985 and takes place the last week of August.
6. Board-surfing – the Soup Bowl competition which is held annually in early November attracts amateur surfers from eight countries. The event is organised by the Barbados Surfing Association.

7. Run Barbados Series – held in December each year, it began in 1982 and includes a marathon and a 10K race.
8. Occasional Events – each year Barbados hosts a number of regional championships in various sporting disciplines e.g. basketball, tennis, football, volleyball, swimming etc. The mix differs each year as different countries usually host these events each year.

## *Selection of subjects to be surveyed*

Subjects to be surveyed were chosen for the various sub-sectors of the tourism industry and, given that the questionnaire was to be conducted via the telephone, the subjects were selected from the yellow pages listings. It was assumed that the subjects to be studied were businesses and would therefore have telephone contact.

The questionnaire was administered to managers/owners of the restaurants, tour companies, car rental agencies and smaller hotels and guest-houses, and to the reservations manager in the larger hotels. For analysis there are four main categories:

- Accommodation – 6 hotels and 2 guesthouses;
- Transportation – 4 ground tour operators, 3 taxi operators and 2 car rental agencies;
- Food and Beverage – 7 restaurants and bars;
- Other – 2 souvenir shops.

Some of the questionnaires were also emailed to the respondents and these were chosen based on them having an email address.

## *Measurement*

### *Variable identification*

The level of benefit accruing to the subject from each event was measured. This was a subjective study since the respondent indicated the level of the benefit. Other variables that were identified were the length of time before the staging of the event and the method by which the stakeholders found out about the event.

### *Variable operationalisation*

The variable of benefits to the organisation was operationalised according to the following:

- No benefit to the organisation as a result of the event;
- Some benefit to the organisation as a result of the event;
- Lots of benefit to the organisation as a result of the event;

The length of time before the staging of the event that the stakeholders found out about the event was operationalised as follows:

- Less than a month;
- One to three months – more than a month but less than three months;
- Three to six months – more than three months but less than six months;
- Over six months.

The method by which the stakeholders found out about the event was operationalised as follows:

- Media – radio, television, newspaper et cetera.
- Barbados Tourism Authority.
- Barbados Hotel and Tourism Association (BHTA) – the trade association of the tourism stakeholders.
- The event planner.
- Other – travel agents, participants, spectators (when reservations are made).

## Data Collection Methods

Data was collected primarily through the administration of a questionnaire which consisted of a mix of closed and open-ended questions. Other data was collected from the Barbados Tourism Authority, the Barbados Ministry of Tourism and the Internet.

## Limitations of the Research

- The sample sizes were small in the case of the accommodation, transportation and food & beverage sectors and maybe a survey of the population would have been more effective.
- The airline and marine stakeholders were not part of the sample.
- A test match was occurring in Barbados at the time that the survey was done and this may have influenced some persons' choice as to the event that was most beneficial.
- Some sub-sectors such as the taxi drivers were reluctant to complete the questionnaire.

- There is no information from the event planners themselves to ascertain if the event was planned as a tourist generator.
- Not all sports tourism events were covered by this research, as there are some other sports events that have been developed over the last few years and are not very well known.

## SPORTS TOURISM AND SPORTING EVENTS

In the early years sporting events were considered part of special events and therefore, were researched on that basis. With the growth of sports tourism, sporting events are now being researched as sports tourism events, for example the Centre for South Australian Economic Studies in Adelaide investigated the impacts of the Adelaide Grand Prix as a special event in 1986 (Burns et al, 1991). Getz (1991) has stated that two other major sporting events in Australia have been analysed in depth yielding valuable insights into the links between events and tourism. These events were the 1987 America's Cup defence in Perth/Fremantle and the 1985 World Cup of Athletic in Canberra.

Zauhar (1995) has done research on the historical perspective of sports tourism in which he investigated the extent to which various sports have been intermingled with tourism throughout history leading to the identification of the status of sports tourism. Zauhar's paper was limited by the fact that the secondary historical data and documentation were limited to documents in the English language and that the societal conflicts, national crises, international wars and their impacts on sports tourism were not studied. The paper further states that throughout history man and woman have been impelled to travel because of sport — the motive, drive or the concern. In effect in the last decade or so there has been an increasing participation in a wide variety of sporting activities.

Pigeassou (1997) has stated that dynamic articulation, which has not stopped developing itself between sport and tourism, found itself on the constant movement of adaptation and transformation, which bore into each one of its social intervention spheres. By acquiring an economic value from its different facets and by increasing its symbolism, the fields of sports grew and met other activity sectors such as bodily leisure, the show and event or even adventure. In the same way the search for development of new products and new markets pursued a constant extension and adaptation towards strong sectors or economic niches such as sports declinations.

Pigeassou has also stated that the development of sports tourism appears as a support vector for the development of tourism, a solution for local development of tourism and an economic opening. Sports tourism does not create new utopias but relies on demand.

Getz (1991) has developed a topology of event tourism, which includes sporting events. These events can be categorised into a hierarchical arrangement according to their origin and impact — local events drawing local people at the bottom and mega-events at the top because of their capacity to motivate large-scale domestic and foreign travel. In the case of Barbados, only International cricket including Test Matches and One-Day Internationals can be considered to be mega-events.

Steve Tow (1994) of the Hillary Commission prepared a paper for the Journal of Sports Tourism on the benefits of sports tourism to New Zealand. In this paper Tow stated that the sports and leisure industry makes the following social and economic impacts:

- It supports 23,000 full-time jobs.
- It contributes NZ$1.6 billion to the economy.
- It pays NZ$300 billion in taxes each year.
- It involves 300,000 volunteers contributing NZ$200 million worth of time each year.
- Club memberships total 1.4 million persons.
- Local Government invests NZ$300 million in sports and leisure each year.

The paper prepared by Tow has also stated that there are a number of reasons why a country would want to host sporting events:

- To generate economic activity.
- To give athletes home advantage.
- To provide or promote a country's sport or sports.
- To recruit or train volunteers.
- To upgrade and establish new facilities.

The paper concluded by mentioning that there were huge opportunities for New Zealand and all tourism destinations to boost revenue by promoting sports tourism.

The Sports Tourism International Council (STIC) research unit has conducted research to identify the number and percentage of sports tourism activities listed by tourism boards/agencies worldwide and also to calculate the contribution of sport tourism activities to the overall tourism industry. The study found that 34 per cent of all tourism activities listed in the schedules were devoted to sports tourism. The Caribbean had one of the highest percentages of number of days of listed sports tourism activities.

Sports activities were also rated and major games, such as the Olympics and the World Cup, were top rated. Among the top-twenty sport tourism events were such activities as ballooning, kite flying and wind surfing. The study concluded that sports tourism was reinforced as a significant part of the overall tourism activity spectrum.

Zauhar and Kurtman (1997) have also indicated that in the age of easy inter-regional and international travel, sports events are able to generate substantial recurrent gatherings of people. The historical and religious pilgrimages have been replaced by modern international flows to such rites as the Olympic Games, the World Cup, national championships, cup finals and even smaller events.

Zauhar and Kurtman have further stated that Guttman believes that the mega-structures (sports facilities) of large cities are not only there for symbolic reasons but also to enhance the economic dominance of the city through the movement of transients between cities. They have also stated a number of positive economic impacts associated with sports tourism:

- Construction/renovation of facilities;
- Creation of employment;
- Cultural exchanges;
- Specific services;
- Regional awareness;
- Commercial activity.

Sports tourism strengthens the regional-community traditions and values. Sports to a large degree provide the stimuli for local entrepreneurs, civic leaders and the community at large for more touristic-oriented skills and sensitivities.

STIC Research Unit (1994) has indicted through research that tourism sport generated 25 per cent of the tourism receipts in urban centres in North America.

Sofield and Sivan (1994) have conducted some studies in the evolution of the Hong Kong Dragon Boat Races from a cultural festival to an international sport. The Dragon Boat Races were used to diversify the Hong Kong tourism product and to become an added attraction.

According to Butler (1980) as quoted by Scofield and Sivan (1994), in the context of the Tourism Destination Life Cycle, the stages of consolidation and decline may be pointed in the direction of rejuvenation by a mix of actions such as the opening of new resort areas, renovation of old hotel plant and the construction of new facilities (theme parks, convention centres etc.) and the staging of special events in conjunction with a planned advertising campaign to appeal to different market segments. Hence, sports tourism events can be used to rejuvenate mature destinations like Barbados.

Townley (1993) suggests that since the 1990s the growth of money in sport has been exponential. The catalysts for this growth have been television, travel, education and wealth. The purity of sport is its unpredictability. That is the factor that distinguishes it from many other forms of entertainment.

## SPORTS TOURISM IN THE CARIBBEAN

Most of the research carried out in the Caribbean in the area of sports events and sports tourism have focused on cricket, which is a dominant sporting event.

Adrien (2000) has stated that tourism will be the nucleus around which services are developed…policies should be directed towards diversifying the tourism product to introduce retirement tourism, health tourism, convention tourism & sports tourism, in general and cricket in particular. A 1998 Caribbean Tourism Organisation (CTO) study on the impacts of the test match in April 1998 in Barbados indicated that there were 8,300 visitors for cricket of which 6,474 were from the United Kingdom. These visitors stayed an average of 10 days in the hotels and spent US$24 million.

Poon (1993) has stated that for the new tourist the sun is still a necessary factor in vacation pursuits, however the sun is not sufficient to satisfy their expectations. The new tourists are more adventurous, they like sport and want to be active. For many the vacation is an extension of their normal lives and they use the time whilst on vacation to take part in activities which they wish they had more time for in their normal lives…many of these activities include sporting activities.

Poon has quoted the 1991 Bahamas Ministry of Tourism Stopover exit survey that stated that 30 per cent of all visitors to the family islands in The Bahamas claimed that they were attracted to the island by the sporting activities. According to the CTO (1999) sporting teams generate large blocks of movement across the Caribbean and span the gamut of national representative teams involved in regional competitions, to school groups to private social clubs and organisations on a weekend tour. The study, which looks at intra-regional travel for a number of reasons, among them sporting events, states that the number of spectators travelling with a team may be as high as 50 per cent of the number of competitors in some sports. The study cites specific examples such as the Aquatic Centre International in Barbados that attracts 650 persons annually. Other events such as regional lawn tennis competitions, volleyball, hockey and net-ball also generate significant travel as each sports involves between 200 to 300 persons including competitors, officials and team supporters.

## SUMMARY AND ANALYSIS OF RESULTS

### The Events

*Sandy Lane Gold Cup*

Fifty-eight per cent of the respondents indicated that the event was of no benefit to their organisation. None of the respondents indicated that the event gave them lots of benefit, however 42 per cent did derive some benefit from the event.

*304*

## International Cricket

This event was proven to be the most beneficial to the respondents with fifty-four of them indicating that they derived a lot of benefit. A further 38.5 per cent indicated that they received some benefit from this event and just 7.7 per cent of the respondents indicated that the event was of no benefit to them.

## Regional Cricket

Ninety-six per cent of the respondents stated that they derived little or no benefit from the event. Interestingly only one respondent from the accommodation sector indicated that it received a lot of benefit from that event.

## Sir Garfield Sobers

Eight per cent of the respondents, who were from the food & beverage sector, indicated that they benefited a lot from the event. Sixty-five per cent of the respondents indicated that the event was of no benefit to them whilst a further 26.9 per cent indicated that the event was of some benefit to them.

## Banks Hockey Festival

Half of the respondents indicated that the event was of no benefit to their organisations. A further 42.3 per cent indicated that the event was of some benefit to their organisations. The respondents (7.7 per cent) that indicated that their organisations derived lots of benefit from the event were from the food and beverage sector.

## Board Surfing

Eighty-five per cent of the respondents indicated that their organisations derived no benefit from the event. Three respondents did derive some benefit, two of then from the accommodation sector and the third being from the transportation sector.

## Run Barbados Series

Sixty-two percent of the respondents indicated that the event was of no benefit to their organisation. Thirty-five per cent found that the event was of some benefit while just 3 per cent said that the event was very beneficial.

*Occasional Events*

Fifty-four per cent of the respondents found the occasional events to be of no benefit to their organisations. Sixty-eight per cent of the respondents from the transportation sector stated that they did derive some benefit from the event. Twelve per cent of the respondents indicated that they received lots of benefit from the island hosting occasional events. The benefits of these events to the different sectors are shown in figures 1, 2, 3, 4, 5.

## Figure 1.
## Events and their benefit to the Accomodation Sector

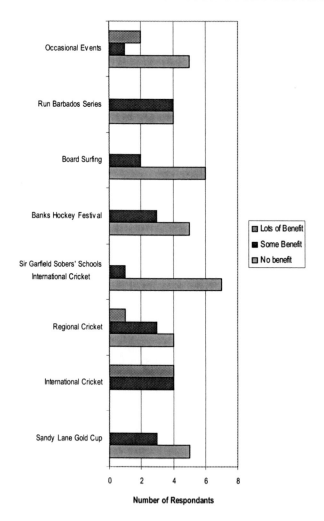

# Figure 2.
# Sports Events and their benefit to the Transportation Sector

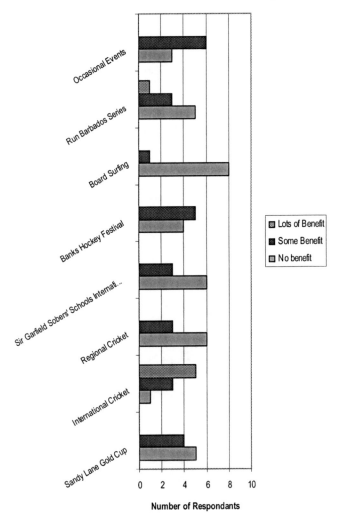

# Figure 4.

## Sport Events and their benefit to the Food and Beverage Sector

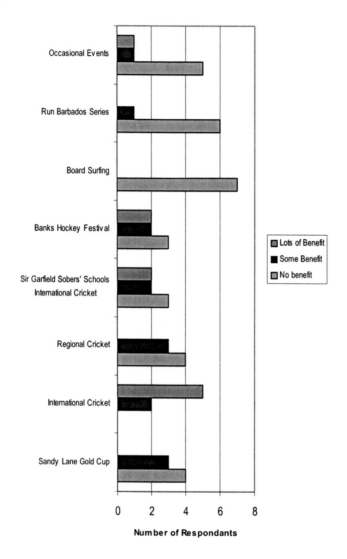

## Figure 5.
## Summary of all sectors

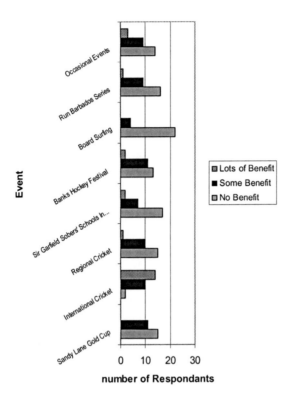

*Other Data*

*Means of Finding out about the Event*

38.5 per cent of the respondents indicated that they found out about the event from the media. Under one third (30.7 per cent) of the respondents indicated that they found out about the event from the event planner. Only 11.6 per cent found out about the event through the BTA and none of them found out about the event through the BHTA. Nineteen point two per cent of the sample indicated that they found out about the event by other means than the event planner, BTA, BHTA or media. In most cases they found out that the event was occurring when a reservation was made.

## Length of advance notice of the event

More than half (65.4 per cent) of the respondents found out about the event less then three months before the actual event with 19.2 per cent of all respondents finding out about the event less than a month before the event was to take place. With regard to the hotels 50 per cent of them had less then three months notice before the actual event.

## Analysis of the Findings

Most of the sporting events being pursued by the Tourism management team for Barbados do not accrue benefits to the stakeholders. This can be seen by the large numbers of respondents who indicated that the events were of no benefit to them. Some of the stakeholders, for example, the taxi operators and some ground transportation companies commented that they did not know when sporting events were taking place. This can be proven by the number of respondents who stated that they usually find out about sports tourism events when reservations are made.

In the case of the hotels, late notice is not conducive to maximisation of the benefits of the sports tourism event, since hotels need to plan months in advance. If there is no event on the horizon to fill the hotel rooms, properties will turn to tour operators and tour wholesalers in order to have their rooms sold. Lack of advance notice about the event also means that the stakeholders are not in a position to pool with stakeholders from other sub-sectors to prepare packages.

Some of the respondents have also stated that they were not able to benefit from the sporting event because the markets from which the visitors came were not lucrative to them. Taxi operators indicated that they found that the visitors who came for cricket often used public transportation rather than taking taxis. Other stakeholders also indicated that because of the age group that some events catered for, the participants and spectators were often unable to use their services. This was the case of the car rental companies and the restaurants and bars where board surfing and the schoolboys' cricket competitions were concerned.

The benefits that some accommodation properties derived from the event were highly dependent on whether or not the participants were staying on the property. Since the arrival figures for some events were small, the benefits remained within a small group of stakeholders. There are other properties that are not interested in the sports tourism programme because tour operators are keeping them operating at full capacity and they are therefore not dependent on sports tourism events.

There were other respondents who indicated that they benefited most from other areas of the sports tourism programme such as the hosting of teams who train on the island during the winter and the teams that visit the island to take part in friendly competition with local teams. This has some implications for the tourism management teams as it indicates that more emphasis should be placed on these areas of the sports tourism programme rather than on the planning and marketing of sports tourism events.

One area of the sports tourism events that this study did not consider was the benefit to the destination as a whole. There are some events that the stakeholders stated that they did not derive a lot of benefit from, however the country as a whole benefits. The sample indicated that stakeholders do not derive lots of benefit from events such as the Sandy Lane Gold Cup and windsurfing. However, the country is able to gain from exposure though the media as these events are usually recorded by ESPN and other television companies and trade magazines. This type of exposure to the destination on the whole may be more beneficial to the destination in the long run than the benefits distributed to a few stakeholders.

On average most events were found to be of some benefit, which indicates that they are successful at meeting some of the goals set by the tourism management team, using the sports tourism programme as a tool for diversifying the tourism product and minimising periods of low tourism arrivals. There is however a problem with the communication of these events to the stakeholders and this could be part of the reason why the events are not as beneficial to the stakeholders as they could be.

This would indicate that there is a problem with the internal marketing of the sports tourism events. If businesses in the accommodation and food and beverage sub-sector do not know about an event well in advance then those businesses will be disadvantaged when it comes to forecasting and budgeting for the event. Organisations that are not properly informed about an event are unable to properly plan for the event in such a way as to maximise the benefits of that event to the organisation. The industry stakeholders are also not able to provide extra benefits such as special rates, happy hours and vouchers for the visitors who attend these events.

Therefore, one of the reasons why certain events do not benefit the stakeholders is that they are not informed about the event and thus, are not able to market themselves to the spectators and participants of that sporting event.

The reason for the success of the international cricket could be contributed to the fact that the event is organised and marketed by the West Indies Cricket Board, a professional organisation. This event is also well marketed by that institution and itinerary of the tour is usually known months in advance giving the stakeholders ample time to plan for the event.

## RECOMMENDATIONS

In order to increase the benefits of the sports tourism events in Barbados to the stakeholders, the following recommendations are being made:

- The BTA and the Ministry of Tourism in Barbados, as part of the country's tourism management team should ensure that all concerned parties are involved in the planning, marketing and operation of successful sports tourism events. Since the events are developed with support from the Ministry of Tourism and the BTA, these agencies are in a position to comply with the above. If any of the parties are not involved then the event will fail to realise its goals.
- The BHTA must play its role as the voice of the stakeholders informing the event planners of the importance of being in close communication with the stakeholders when the sporting events are being planned. The industry stakeholders can be informed and kept up-to-date on the sports events through the monthly newsletter of the association, special bulletins and association meetings.
- Packages can also be prepared with other stakeholders so that the industry, on the whole, benefits from the events. For example, car hires can be part of the package as well as tours to attractions and shopping trips. This type of packaging calls for all the stakeholders to work together so that all can benefit.
- The event planners should also be trained in the planning and marketing of an event as a tourism generator. It takes highly skilled persons to plan, organise and implement successful tourism events and the planning of tourism sporting events are no different. While the event itself will attract the target market, the planning and organising of the event will determine its success. This training should also seek to improve the communication between the planners and the stakeholders and could be implemented by the Ministry of Tourism, the BTA and the BHTA. Event planners could also be sent to seminars and conferences on event planning since there are international bodies that have been formed to promote special events tourism.
- Given that a number of the hotels in Barbados are small hotels which are in many cases owner operated, these properties especially need the support of the tourism management team for guidance in the way to exploit the sports tourism programme. Since not all hotels will be catering for the same market, it will be necessary to make a list of the properties that best suit each event.
- The tourism management team should also consider if it is necessary to have many small events which do not attract visitors and hence, do not spread their benefit or to have fewer but better organised events which can attract larger numbers and hence, benefit a larger number of stakeholders. Tourism marketing dollars and other resources may be better spent on a few large successful events rather than lots of smaller events.

# CONCLUSION

While there is recognition that as a mature destination there is a need for diversification and rejuvenation of the tourism product and that the sports tourism programme is an excellent choice for fulfilling both of these needs, some care must be taken to ensure that the programme is properly developed so as to meet the stated goals and to benefit both the stakeholders and the country as a whole. This chapter has shown that sports tourism events which are promoted as part of the sports tourism programme are not as effective as they could be in meeting the goals set out for that programme in the Green Paper for Tourism in Barbados.

The chapter has also shown that there are weaknesses in the programme between the tourism management team, the event planners and the stakeholders and as such, many stakeholders do not reap the benefits of the sports events. These weakness which include lack of communication and at times poor communication between the tourism management team, the event planners and the stakeholders, will have to be improved before the full benefits of the staging of sports tourism event can be realised.

# REFERENCES

Adrien, P. 2000. 'Cricket: A Viable Industry, 2nd Annual Conference, Alternative Development in the Eastern Caribbean: The Roles of the Services sector'. Barbados, University of the West Indies. Sir Arthur Lewis Institute of Social and Economic Development.

Barbados Tourism Authority. 1999. Key Tourism Indicators of Barbados.

Burns, J.P.A. Hatch, J.H. and T.J. Mules. *Adelaide: Journal of Sport & Social Issues* 15, no. 1 (1991).

Caribbean Tourism Organisation. 1999. *Caribbean Intra-Regional Travel Market Study*. Bridgetown: Caribbean Tourism Organisation.

Getz, D. 1991. *Festivals, Special Events & Tourism*. New York: Van Nostrand Reinhold.

Gibson, H. 'Sports Tourism: Rules of the Game'. *Parks & Recreation* 34, no. 6 (1998).

Gibson, H 1999. 'Wide World of Sports Tourism'. *Parks & Recreation*.

Gratton, C. and T. Kokolakaki. 1997. 'Financial Games'. *Sport Management*, (1997).

Guttman, A. 'Sports Spectators from Antiquity to the Renaissance'. *Journal of Sport History* 2, no. 1, (1981). Penn State University Press.

Ministry of Tourism. 1999. *Green paper on Policies, Proposals and Programmes in the Tourism Sector*. Barbados.

Pigeassou, C. 1997. *Sport Tourism: The Emergence of Sport into the Offer of Tourism. Between Passion and Reason*. An Overview of the French Situation and Perspectives.

Poon, A. 1993. *Tourism Technology & Competitive Strategies*. United Kingdom: CAB International.

Ritchie, J. 'Assessing the impact of Hallmark Events: Conceptual and Research Issues'. *Journal of Travel Research* 23, no. 1 (1984).

Sofield T.H.B. and A. Sivan. 'From Cultural Event to International Sport – The Hong Kong Boat Race'. *Journal of Sport Tourism* 1, no. 2 (1994).

Sports Tourism International Council Research Unit. 'Sports as an Economic Generator', *Journal of Sports Tourism* 1, no. 2 (1994).

Sports Tourism International Council Research Unit. 'Sports Tourism Categories Revisited'. *Journal of Sports Tourism* 2, no. 3 (1995).

Tow, S. 'Sports Tourism – the benefits'. *Journal of Sports Tourism* 2, no. 1 (1994).

Townley, S. 'Some Legal Issues Associated with International Sports Marketing'. *Sports Marketing Quarterly* 2, no. 2 (1993).

Zauhar, J. 'Historical Perspectives of Sports Tourism., *Journal of Sports Tourism* 2, no. 4 (1995).

Zauhar, J. and J. Kurtzman. 'A Wave In Time —The Sports Tourism Phenomena', *Journal of Sports Tourism* 4, no. 2 (1997).

# BIBLIOGRAPHY

Abel, Thomas. *Ecosystems, Sociocultural Systems, and Ecological-Economics for Understanding Development: The Case of Ecotourism on the Island of Bonaire, N.A.* Gainesville, FL.: University of Florida, 2000.

Adams, Vicanne. 'Tourism and Sherpas, Nepal: Reconstruction of Reciprocity', *Annals of Tourism Research* 19 (1992): 534-554.

Adrien, P. 'Cricket: A Viable Industry'. 2nd Annual Conference, Alternative Development in the Eastern Caribbean: The Roles of the Service Sector. Cave Hill: Sir Arthur Lewis Institute of Social and Economic Development, University of the West Indies, 2000.

Agorsh, E.K. ed. *Maroon Heritage: Archaeological, Ethnographic and Historical Perspectives.* Kingston: Canoe Press, 1994.

Agorsh, E. K. 'Archaeology and the Maroon Heritage in Jamaica'. *Jamaica Journal* 24, no. 2 (1994): 2-9.

Alexander, M. R. 'Farmer turns to Agro-tourism'. The *Detroit News*, 1999.

Alexander, P. 'Managing Festivals and Tourism Events' *A booklet based on and adapted from Building a Festival: A Framework for Organisers*, Arkansas Department of Parks and Tourism *http://www.msue.msu.edu/imp/modtd/33530075.html.*

Alleyne, G. 'West Indies surrender'. *Daily Nation*, April 14, 1994.

Alliance for the Arts. *The Economic Impact of the Arts on New York City and New York State.* New York City, NY: Arts Research Centre, 1997.

Anderson, D. and M. Leiserson. 'Rural Non-Farmer Employment in Developing Countries'. *Economic Development and Cultural Change* 28, no. 2 (1980): 227-248.

Andreason, A. R. *Marketing Social Change: Changing Behaviour to Promote Health, Social Development and Environment.* San Francisco, CA: Jossey-Bass Publications, 1995.

Angulu, Doreen et al. 'The Marketing and Planning of Special Events - Generating Intra-regional Travel'. MSc thesis, University of the West Indies, Mona, 2000.

Archer, B. 'Economic Impact Analysis'. *Annals of Tourism Research* 23, no. 3 (1996): 704–707.

Bacci, M.E. 'St. Kitts and Nevis Tourism Master Plan'. Washington, DC.: Organisation of American States, 1993.

*Barbados Advocate.* 'Barbados Test a good catch: Tourism'. April 4, 1994.

Barbados Tourism Authority. 'Key Tourism Indicators of Barbados'. Bridgetown, Barbados, 1999.

Barker, D. and B. Spence. 'Afro-Caribbean Agriculture: A Jamaican Maroon Community in Transition'. *Geographical Journal* 154 (1988): 198–208.

Barkin, D. 'Ecotourism: A Tool for Sustainable Development in an Era of International Integration?' *Contours* 8, no. 2 (1993): 9–11.

Barry, T., B. Wood and D. Preusch. *The Other Side of Paradise: Foreign Control in the Caribbean.* New York: Grove Press, 1984.

Beckles, H. *Afro-Caribbean Women and Resistance to Slavery in Barbados*. London: Karnak House, 1988.

Beckles, H. ed. *An Area of Conquest: Popular Democracy and West Indies Cricket Supremacy*. Kingston: Ian Randle Publishers, 1995.

Beckles, H., 'Bussa: The 1816 Barbados Revolution', *Rewriting History*, vol. 2 Cave Hill: University of the West Indies, Department of History, 1998.

Bedasse, J. and N. Stewart. 'The Maroons of Jamaica: One with Mother Earth'. Case Study Document for the Nature Conservancies Workshop: 'Traditional Peoples and Biodiversity Conservation in Large Tropical Landscapes, 1994.

Belisle, Francois J. 'The Significance and Structure of Hotel Food Supply in Jamaica'. *Caribbean Geography* 1 (1984): 219–233.

Belisle, Francois J. 'Tourism and Food Imports: The Case of Jamaica'. *Economic Development and Cultural Change* 32, no. 4 (1984): 819–842.

Bélisle, F. J. 'Tourism and Food Production in the Caribbean'. *Annals of Tourism Research* 10 (1983): 497–513.

Benjamin-Trotman, L. Seminar on Comprehensive Tourism II in Fiscal Year 1996, Country Paper. Georgetown, Guyana: Ministry of Trade, Tourism and Industry, 1996.

Bentick, K. 'Sustainable Tourism in Guyana: New Initiatives'. Proceedings of the First Conference on Sustainable Tourism Development. Dominica: Caribbean Tourism Organisation, May 21-24, 1997.

Berle, Peter A.A. 'Two Faces of Eco-Tourism'. *Audubon* 92, no. 2 (1990): 6.

Bhaha, H. 'Narrating the Nation'. In *Nationalism,* eds. J. Hutchinson and A.D. Smith. London: Oxford University Press, 1994, 306–12.

Bilby, K. M. 'Religious Change Among the Jamaican Maroons: The Ascendance of the Christian God within a Traditional Cosmology'. *Journal of Social History* 20, no. 3 (1987): 463–484.

Blenman, R. 'Sports tourism paying off'. *Daily Nation* April 7, 1994.

Boniface, P. and P. J. Fowler. *Heritage and Tourism in the 'Global Village'*. London: Routledge, 1993.

Boo, E. 'Eco-tourism: The Potentials and Pitfalls —Two Country Case Studies'. World Wildlife Fund Publications, 1990.

Bookbinder, M.P. et al. 'Ecotourism's support of biodiversity conservation'. *Conservation Biology* 12, no. 6 (1998): 1399–1404.

Boxill, I. 'Overcoming Social Problems in the Jamaican Tourism Industry'. In *Tourism in the Caribbean* eds. I. Boxill and J. Maerk. Mexico: Plaza y Valdex, 2000.

Boza, M. 'Costa Rica National Parks'. In *Fundación Neotropica*. San José, 1998.

Bramwell, B. 'Tourism Policy and Planning, First Serial Rights'. Sheffield: University of Sheffield, 1996.

Brandon, Katrina and R. Margoluis. *The Ecotourism Equation: Measuring the Impacts* New Haven, CN: Yale University Press, 1996.

Brandon, Katrina. 'Basic steps towards encouraging local participation in nature tourism Projects'. In *Ecotourism*, eds. E. Donald, Lindberg, Kreg and Hawkins, 134–151. Washington DC.: International Ecotourism Society, 1993.

Brathwaite, L. 'Author attempts to belittle our cricketers'. *Sunday Advocate*, April 10, 1994.

Brotherson, F. 'The Politics of Tourism in a Caribbean Authoritarian State: Cooperative Republic of Guyana'. *Caribbean Affairs* 3, no. 2 (Second Quarter 1990): 38–55.

Brown, M.T. and R.C Murphy. In *Emergy Synthesis Perspectives, Sustainable Development, and Public Policy Options for Papua New Guinea. Final Report to the Cousteau Society,* S.J. Doherty and M.T.

Brown eds., 3D1–3D27. Gainesville, FL: Centre for Wetlands, University of Florida, 1993.

Bryner, G.C. *Gaia's Wager: Environmental Movements and the Challenge of Sustainability*. Lanham, MD: Rowman & Littlefield Publishers, 2001.

Bull, A. *The Economics of Travel and Tourism*. Harlow, UK: Longman Publishers, 1995.

Burke, S. 'Culture and Economic Development: The Case of Trinidad Carnival'. MSc thesis. The Hague: Institute of Social Science, 1998.

Burns, J.P.A. et al. *Journal of Sport & Social Issues* 15, no. 1.

Busby, G. and S. Rendle. 'The transition from tourism on farms to farm tourism'. *Tourism Management* 21, no. 6 (2000): 635–642.

Bushell, R. 'Developing Cultural Tourism Opportunities'. *Annals of Tourism Research* 23, no. 4 (1996): 954–955.

Butler, R.W. 'The Concept of the Tourist Area Cycle of Evolution: Implications for the Management of Resources'. *Canadian Geographer* 24 (1980): 5–12.

Campbell, L. M. 'Ecotourism in rural developing communities'. *Annals of Tourism Research* 26, no. 3 (1999): 534–553.

Campbell, Mavis C. *The Maroons of Jamaica 1655-1796: A History of Resistance Collaboration and Betrayal*. Trenton, NJ: Africa World Press, 1990.

Casey, B. et al. *Culture as Commodity? The Economics of the Arts and Built Heritage in the UK*. London: Policy Studies Institute, 1996.

Cashman, R. 'Cricket and Colonialism: Colonial Hegemony and Indigenous Subversion?' In *The Cultural Bond: Sport, Empire and Society London* ed. J.A. Mangan. London: Frank Cass Publishers, 1992.

Central Bank of Barbados. 'Review of 1994 and the prospects for 1995'. Bridgetown, Barbados, 1994.

CEPAL. Summary of Economic Survey of Latin America and the Caribbean, 1998–1999.

Chambers, Robert. *Whose Reality Counts? Putting the first last*. London: Intermediate Technology Publications, 1997.

———. *Challenging the Professions: Frontiers for Rural Development*. London: Intermediate Technology Publications, 1993.

Charles, H. 'Opening Address', Regional Agro-tourism Conference. Trinidad and Tobago: IICA, 2000.

Clarke, J. 'Marketing structures for farm tourism: beyond the individual provider of rural tourism'. *JOST* 7, no. 1 (1999): 26–47.

Clayton, A. 'Sustainable Tourism: the agenda for the Caribbean'. *Worldwide Hospitality and Tourism Trends* 1, no. 2 (2000): 60–78.

Cox, L. J. and M. Fox. 'Agriculturally based leisure attractions'. *Journal of Tourism Studies* 2, no. 2 (1991): 18–28.

Cox, L. J. et al. 'Does Tourism Destroy Agriculture?' *Annals of Tourism Research* 22 (1994): 210–213.

Cozier, T. 'Lara: the icing on series to savour'. *Sunday Sun*, April 24, 1994.

Cresser, Hugh. 'Environmental Management: A New Dimension to Tourism Training'. In *Tourism and Hospitality Education and Training in the Caribbean*, ed. C. Jayawardena. Kingston: The University of the West Indies Press, 2002.

Crick, Malcolm. 'Representations of International Tourism in the Social Sciences: Sun, Sex, Sights, Savings and Servility'. *Annual Review of Anthropology* 18. Palo Alto, CA: (1989) 307–344.

Croall, J. *Preserve or Destroy: Tourism and the Environment*, London: Calouste Gulbenlkian Foundation, 1995.

Crouch, G.H. and S. L. Wood. 'Eco-tourism 101'. *Business and Economic Review* 47, no. 2 (2001): 19–21.

CSO. *Tourism Statistics Bulletin, Carnival* 18, no. 1. Port of Spain, Trinidad and Tobago: Central Statistical Office, 1997.

CSO. *Tourism Statistics Bulletin, Carnival* 18, no. 2. Port of Spain, Trinidad and Tobago: Central Statistical Office, 1998.

CTO. Caribbean Tourism Statistical Report 1999–2000. Bridgetown, Barbados: Caribbean Tourism Organisation, 2001.

CTO. Main Statistical Report 1999. Bridgetown, Barbados: Caribbean Tourism Organisation, 2000.

Cuffe, M. Interview of Byron Lee on 'My Place', January, 2001.

Cummings, C. 'The ideology of West Indian cricket'. *Arena Review* 14, no.1 (1990): 25–32.

D. W. Knight Associates. A Study of Agri-Tourism in Newfoundland Labrador, 4-6. Canada: The Department of Forest Resource and Agri-foods, Newfoundland & Labrador, 1999.

*Daily Nation*. 'Friendly rivals in the stands'. April 11, 1994 (Comments reproduced).

*Daily Nation*. 'The view from Silly Point'. April 13, 1994.

Dallas, R.C. *The History of the Maroons*. London: T.N. Longman and O. Rees, 1803.

de Kadt, E. *Making the Alternative Sustainable: A Lesson From Development For Tourism*. Discussion Paper, no. 272. Brighton: Institute of Development Studies, 1990.

Denman, R. M. and J. Denman. *The Farm Tourism Market: a Market Study of Farm Tourism in England*. London: English Tourist Board, 1993.

Devas, E. 'Hotels in the Caribbean'. *Travel and Tourism Analyst* 2 (1997): 57–76.

Dieke, P. 'Tourism and Development Policy in the Gambia'. *Annals of Tourism Research* 20 (1993): 423–449.

Drumm, A. 'New approaches to community-based eco-tourism management: Learning from Ecuador'. In *Eco-tourism: a guide for planners and managers*, eds. K. Lindberg, M.E. Wood and D. J. Engelburn, 197–213. North Bennington: Eco-tourism Society, 1998.

Duffy, R. 'Shadow players: Eco-tourism development, corruption and state politics in Belize'. *Third World Quarterly* 21 no. 3 (2000): 549–565.

Eagles, P. F. 'Understanding the Market for Sustainable Tourism'. Information available at: *www.ecotourism.org*.

*Eastern Voice* 2, no 2. (May, 1999). 'Obtain Sustainable Development through Environmental Protection'.

Eco, U. *Travels in Hyper-Reality*. London: Picador Publishing, 1986.

Economist. *Pocket World in Figures*. London: Profile Books, 1999.

Edwards, B. *The History, Civil and Commercial, of the British Colonies in the West Indies*. 2 vols. Dublin, Ireland: Luke White Publishers, 1793.

Edwards, S.N. et al. *Comparative Study of Eco-tourism Policy in the Americas, 1998*. Moscow, ID: University of Idaho, 1998.

EIU. 'The Market for Cultural Tourism in Europe'. *Travel and Tourism Analyst* no. 6 (1993).

English Tourist Board. *Tourism and the Environment. Maintaining the Balance*. (London: ETB, 1991).

Eyre, L.A. 'Cockpit Country: A World Heritage Site'. In *Environment and Development in the Caribbean: Geographical Perspectives*, eds. D. Barker and D.F.M. McGregor, 259–270. Kingston: The University of the West Indies Press, 1995.

Eyre, L.A. 'Slow Death of a Tropical Rain Forest: The Cockpit Country of Jamaica, West Indies'. In *Environmental Quality and Ecosystem Stability Vol. IV- A Environmental Quality* eds., 599 – 606. M. Luria, Y. Steinberger and E. Spanier. Jerusalem: ISEQS Publications, 1989.

Fagence, M. 'Rural and village tourism in developing countries'. *Third World Planning Review* 20, no. 1 (1998): 107–118.

Falassi, A. *Time out of Time: Essays on the Festival*. Alburquerque: University of New Mexico Press, 1987.

Fennel, D.A. *Eco-tourism: An Introduction*. London: Routledge, 1999.

Fernandez, B.P. and Graham L.B. 'Sustainable Economic Development through Integrated Water Resources Management in the Caribbean'. Paper presented to the 11th Water Meeting. Montevideo, Uruguay, June 15 –18, 1999.

Fernandez, B.P. Proposal for Integrated Water Resources Management for the Caribbean, Food Security and the Environment. Rome, World Food Summit, November 13–17, 1996.

Fernandez, B. and Graham, L. B. 'Sustainable Economic Development through Integrated Water Resources Management in the Caribbean'. *COMUNIICA* 14 (2000): 39–43.

Fleischer, A. and D. Felsenstein. 'Support for Rural Tourism: Does it make a Difference? *Annals of Tourism Research* 27, no. 4 (2000): 1007–1024.

Fletcher, J. 'Input-Output Analysis and Tourism Impact Studies'. *Annals of Tourism Research* 16 (1989): 514 –529.

Francis, P. 'When Kensington looked like Lord's'. *Barbados Advocate*, April 15, 1994.

Freitag, T.G. 'Tourism and the transformation of a Dominican coastal community'. *Urban Anthropology* 25 no. 3 (1996): 225–258.

Ganga, Gobind. 'Ecotourism in Guyana: Implications for Sustainable Development'. Working Paper no. 12. Turkeyen, Guyana: University of Guyana, Institute of Development Studies, 1994.

Garner, J. 'On the Wooldridge Issue'. *Sunday Advocate*, April 10, 1994.

Getz, Donald. 'Event tourism and the authenticity dilemma'. *Global Tourism: the next decade*, class no. 338.48 (1994): 313–329.

————. 'Special Events'. *Managing Tourism*, class no. 338.40 (1994): 122 – 130.

————. *Event Management and Event Tourism*. New York City, NY: Cognisant Communication Corp, 1997.

————. *Festivals, Special Events & Tourism*. New York: Van Nostrand Reinhold, 1991.

Gibson, H. 'Wide World of Sports Tourism'. Parks & Recreation, (1999).

————. 'Sports Tourism: Rules of the Game'. *Parks & Recreation* vol. 34, issue 6 (1998).

Goldblatt, J. J. and F. Sapovitz. *Dollars and Events – How to succeed in the Special Events Business*. New York: John Wiley & Sons, 1999.

Goldblatt, J. J. *Special Events – Best Practices in Modern Event Management,* New York: John Wiley & Sons, 1997.

Golding, S. The Potential of Eco-Tourism in Jamaica. MSc thesis. Mona: University of the West Indies, 2000.

Goodrich, J. N. eds. *Tourism Marketing and Management in the Caribbean*, 143–166. New York: Routledge, 1993.

Gould, K. A. 'Tactical Tourism'. *Organisation & Environment* 12, no. 3 (1999): 245 – 262.

Government of Jamaica. Jamaica 2000 Millennium Project., Kingston: Office of the Prime Minister, 1999, unpublished.

Gratton, C. and T. Kokolakaki. 'Financial Games'. *Sport Management* (1997).

Green Globe. 'Green Globe 21- About Us'. (2001). Available at: *www.greenglobe21.com*.

Grekin, J. and S. Milne. 'Community based tourism: the experience of Pond Inlet'. In *Tourism and Native Peoples*, eds. R. W. Butler and T. Hinch, 76–106. London: Thomson International, 1996.

Gunn, Claire A. *The Purpose of Tourism Planning, Basics, Concepts, and Cases*. 3rd Edition. Washington DC.: Taylor & Francis, 1994.

Guttman, A. 'Sports Spectators from Antiquity to the Renaissance'. *Journal of Sport History* 2, no. 1 (1981): 5–27.

Haksever, C., R. Render, R. Russell and R. Murdick. *Service Management and Operations*. Upper Saddle River, NJ.: Prentice Hall Publishing, 2000.

Hall, C.M. *Hallmark Tourist Events: Impacts, Management and Planning*. New York: John Wiley & Sons, 1992.

Hall, Kenneth O., J.S. Holder and C. Jayawardena. 'Caribbean Tourism and the Role of the UWI in Management Education'. In *Caribbean Tourism: Visions, Missions and Challenges*, ed. C. Jayawardena. Kingston: Ian Randle Publishers, 2005.

Hall, S. 'Cultural studies: two paradigms'. In *Culture, Ideology and Social Process: A Reader*, ed. T. Bennett, 19–37. London: Open University Press, 1981.

Harris, C.L.G. 'The Maroons and Moore Town's Maroon Cultures'. Washington DC.: Smithsonian Institute, 1993.

Harrison, D. *Tourism and the Less Developed Countries*. London: Belhaven Press, 1992.

Hernandez, Gina. An Analysis of the Strategies for Eco-tourism Development in the Dominican Republic. MSc thesis. Mona: University of the West Indies, 2000.

Hernandez, G.B. et al. Eco-tourism – Myth or Reality? MSc thesis. Mona: University of the West Indies, 2000.

Heskett, J.L. *Managing in the Scarce Economy*. Boston, Mass.: HBS Press, 1986.

Holder, J.S. 'The Pattern and Impact of Tourism on the Environment'. In *Environmentally Sound Tourism Development in the Caribbean*, ed. F. Edwards. Calgary: The University of Calgary Press, 1987.

Holder, Jean. 'Marketing Competitiveness in a New World Order: Regional Solutions to Caribbean Tourism Sustainability Problems'. In *Practising Responsible Tourism* eds. L.C. Harrison and W. Husbands, 145–173. Ontario: John Wiley & Sons, 1996.

Holder, Jean. 'Regional Solutions to Caribbean Sustainability Problems'. Presented at the Caribbean Conference on Sustainable Tourism, Punta Cana Beach Resort, Dominican Republic, November 29 – December 2, 1995.

Holder, Jean. *Some Ideas for Tourism Change in a Changing World*. Bridgetown, Barbados: Caribbean Tourism Organisation, 2001.

Honey, M. *Eco Tourism and Sustainable Development*. Washington DC.: Island Press, 1991.

Horwich, R. H., D. Murray, E. Saqui, J. Lyon and D. Godfrey. 'Eco-tourism and Community Development: A View from Belize'. In Eco-tourism: A Guide for Planners and Managers. Vermont: The Eco-tourism Society, 1993.

Hudson, B. 'Paradise lost: a planners view of Jamaican tourist development'. *Caribbean Quarterly* 42, no. 4 (1996): 22–31.

Hughes, H. 'Redefining Cultural Tourism'. *Annals of Tourism Research* 23, no. 3 (1996): 707–709.

Fernandez, Basil and Graham, Barbara. 'A Synthesis of Country Reports on Water Resources Management in the Caribbean'. Castries: Inter-American Institute for Cooperation on Agriculture, 1999.

IICA. 'Diversification of the Saint Lucian Agricultural Economy through Agrotourism'. A joint endeavour of the Florida State University, The Florida Association of Voluntary Agencies for Caribbean Action and the Inter-American Institute for Cooperation on Agriculture, 1999.

IICA. 'Performance and Prospects for Caribbean Agriculture'. Inter-American Institute for Cooperation on Agriculture, 1999.

Inskeep, E. 'Environmental Planning for Tourism'. *Annals of Tourism Research* 14, no. 1 (1987): 118–135.

Issa, John and Chandana Jayawardena. 'All-Inclusive Business in the Caribbean'. In *Caribbean Tourism: People, Service and Hospitality*, ed. C. Jayawardena. Kingston: Ian Randle Publishers, 2002.

IUCN - The World Conservation Union. 'Vision for Water and Nature. A World Strategy for Conservation and Sustainable Management of Water Resources in the 21st Century'. Gland, Switzerland: IUCN-The World Conservation Union, February 7, 2000.

Jackman, O. 'One for the history books'. *Sunday Sun,* April, 17, 1994.

Jafari, J. 'The Tourism Market Basket of Goods and Services'. In *Studies in Tourism Wildlife Conservation*, eds. T.V. Singh, J. Kanr and D.P. Singh. London: Metropolitan Books, 1982.

James, C.L.R. *Beyond a Boundary*. London: Hutchinson, 1963.

Jarrett, M. 'Welcome to the Greatest Reggae Festival on Earth'. *Reggae Sunsplash* Magazine, 1994.

Jayawardena, C. and A. Crick. 'Human Resource Management in Jamaica Responding to Challenging Times'. In *International Human Resource Management in the Hospitality Industry*, eds. S. M. Hofmann, C. Johnson and M. M. Lefever, 113–128. Lansing MI: Educational Institute of the American Hotels and Motels Association, 2000.

Jayawardena, Chandana and H. McDavid. 'Implications of Agro-Tourism in the Caribbean'. In *Agro-tourism – A Sustainable Approach to Economic Growth*, ed. P. Collins. Trinidad and Tobago: Inter-American Institute for Co-operation on Agriculture.

Jayawardena, Chandana. 'An Analysis of Tourism in the Caribbean'. *Worldwide Hospitality And Tourism Trends* 1, no. 3 (2000): 122–136.

————. 'Community Tourism: Applying the Lessons in the Caribbean'. In *People and Tourism: Issues and Attitudes in the Jamaican Hospitality Industry*, eds. H. Dunn and L. Dunn. Kingston: Arawak Publishers, 2001.

————. 'Harmonising the Tourist Needs and Country's Expectations from Tourism Industry'. In *Tourism, Hoteliering and Hospitality Education*, ed. C. Jayawardena, 28-31. Colombo, Sri Lanka: Vijeya Publications, 1993.

————. 'Strategic Planning and Management in the Caribbean Tourism: Recent Research by Graduate Students'. *Journal of Education and Development in the Caribbean* 5, no.1 (2001).

————. 'Tourism and Hospitality Education and Training in the Caribbean: An Analysis of Recent Initiatives'. Paper presented at the Pan-American Confederation of Hospitality and Tourism Schools (CONPEHT) Conference, Cuba, April 2001.

————. 'Tourism and the Community: Challenges in the Caribbean'. In *People and Tourism: Issues and Attitudes in the Jamaican Hospitality Industry*, eds. H. Dunn and L. Dunn. Kingston: Arawak Publishers, 2001.

————. 'Tourism vs. Community: Direction, Purpose and Challenges of Caribbean Tourism'. Paper presented at the 26th Annual Conference of the Caribbean Studies Association, St Maarten, May 2001.

————. 'Tourism Trends in the World and the Caribbean'. Conference paper presented at The Millennium Tourism Trends Conference, Centre for Adult Education, North – East of Finland, September 1999.

Jenkins, J.M. and E. Prin. 'Rural landholder attitudes: the case of public recreational access to "private" rural lands'. In *Tourism and Recreation in Rural Areas*, eds. R. Butler, C.M. Hall, and J. Jenkins, 179-196. Chichester: John Wiley & Sons, 1997.

*321*

Johnson, D., J. Snepenger and S. Akis. 'Residents' perceptions of tourism development'. *Annals of Tourism Research* 21, no. 3 (1994): 629–642.

Journal of Sports Tourism - *http://www.mcb.co.uk/journals/jst/issues.htm.*

JTB. *Tourism Statistics*. Kingston: Jamaica Tourist Board, February, 2001.

Kambon A. 'Placing Women and Youth within the Framework of an Agro-tourism Strategy'. Proceedings, Regional Agro-tourism Conference. Trinidad and Tobago: IICA, 2000.

Kincaid, J. *A Small Place*. New York, NY: Farrar Straus Giroux Publishers, 1988.

Koch, E. 'Ecotourism and rural reconstruction in South Africa: reality or rhetoric?' In *Social Change and Conservation: environmental policies and impacts of national parks and protected areas*, eds. K.B. Ghimire and M.P. Pimbert, 214-38. London: Earthscan Publications, 1997.

Kopytoff, B. K. 'The Maroons of Jamaica: An Ethnohistorical Study of Incomplete Polities'. PhD diss. University of Pennsylvania, 1973.

Kotler, P., J. Bowen, and J. Makens. *Marketing for Hospitality and Tourism*. Upper Saddle River, NJ.: Prentice Hall Publishers, 1998.

KPMG. *An Agro-Tourism Strategy for Nova Scotia, Nova Scotia Agriculture and Marketing*. Nova Scotia, Canada: KPMG Management Consultants, 1996.

KPMG. Intra-Regional Travel Market Study, Caribbean Tourism Organisation. Bridgetown, Barbados: KPMG Management Consultants, 2000.

Lane, B. 'Sustainable rural tourism strategies: a tool for development and conservation'. *JOST* 2, nos. 1&2 (1994): 102–111.

————. *Sustainable Rural Tourism Strategy, A Tool for Development and Conservation*. Clevedon: Channel View Publication, 1994.

Lawrence, S. 'Macro-economic conditions and sustainable agriculture and rural development'. (1999). Available at: *http://www.fao.org.sard.*

Lewis, E. 'Historic moment'. *Barbados Advocate*, April 15, 1994.

Lockard, J. 'Sugar Realism' in Caribbean Fiction'. *Journal of Commonwealth and Postcolonial Studies* 1, no. 2 (1995): 80–103.

Lowenthal, D. *The Past is a Foreign Country*. Cambridge: Cambridge University Press, 1985.

MacDonald, C. 'Agro-tourism – New Dimensions of Industrialisation in the Caribbean'. Proceedings Regional Agro-tourism Conference. Trinidad and Tobago: IICA, 2000.

Mader, R. 'Eco-tourism Research and promotion on the web: experiences and insights'. *International Journal of Hospitality Management* 11, nos. 2 & 3 (2001): 78–79.

Mader, R. 'Latin America New Ecotourism: What is it?' Available at: *http://www.planeta.com.madder(1999-2000).*

Madramootoo C.A. *From a Green to a Blue Planet*. Montreal: McGill University, Brace Centre for Water Resources Management, 1999.

Mandle, W. F. 'Cricket and Australian nationalism in the nineteenth century'. *Journal of the Royal Australian Historical Society* 59, no. 4 (1973): 225–46.

Mangan, J.A., ed. *Pleasure, Profit, and Proselytism*. London: Frank Cass Publishers, 1989.

Manning, F. 'Celebrating cricket: the symbolic construction of Caribbean politics'. *American Ethnologist* 8, no. 3 (1981): 616–32.

Marshall, M. 'Tetley too bitter for Windies'. *Daily Nation*, April 14, 1994.

————. 'Tourism still holds the upper hand'. *Daily Nation*, April 14, 1994.

Mason, D. and S. Milne. 'Linking Tourism and Agriculture: Innovative Information Solutions Technology Solutions'. In *Agro-tourism - A Sustainable Approach to Economic Growth*, ed. P. Collings, 27–42. Port of Spain: Inter-American Institute for Co-operation on Agriculture, 2000.

Matheison, A. and G. Wall. *Tourism: Economic, Physical and Social Impacts*. New York: Longman House, 1982.

Mayfield, T.L. 'Development of an instrument for identifying community reasons for staging a festival'. *Travel & Tourism Research Association* 33, no. 3 (1995): 37–44.

McCarthy, Bridgett. 'Cultural Tourism: How the Arts can help market tourism products; How tourism can help promote markets for the Arts'. Portland, Oregon: American Association of Museums, 1992.

McCool, S. 'Linking Tourism, the Environment, and the Concept of Sustainability: Setting the Stage'. (1995). Available at: *www.ecotourism.org*.

McDonald, D. and J.B. Zeiger. 'Eco-tourism: Wave of the future'. *Parks & Recreation,* 32, no. 9 (1997): 84 – 92.

McElroy, J. L. and K. de Albuquerque. 'An Integrated Sustainable Eco-tourism for Small Caribbean Islands'. Indiana Centre on Global Change and World Peace, Occasional Paper no. 8 (1992).

McElroy, J. L. and K. de Albuquerque. 'Sustainable Small-Scale Agriculture in Small Caribbean Islands'. *Society and Natural Resources* 3 (1990): 109–129.

McHardy, Pauline. 'Planning for Sustainable Tourism Development'. Paper presented at the Second Annual Educators Forum of the Caribbean Tourism Human Resource Council, Antigua, 2001.

McIntyre-Pike, D. 'Country Style Community Tourism'. *Jamaica Profile*. Kingston: Tourism Product Development Company, 1999.

McKinsey and Company. *You Gotta have ART! Profile of a Great Investment for New York State*. New York: McKinsey and Company, 1997.

Meredith, M. 'Sorry Tales From the Swamp'. *Sunday Express*, section 2, (2000): 4.

Midmore, P., N. Parrott and A. Sherwood. 'Integrating Agriculture and Tourism in South Pembrokeshire: A Review of Marketing Opportunities'. Aberystwyth, Wales: University of Wales, Welsh Institute of Rural Studies, 1996.

Mill, R.C. and A. M. Morrison. *The Tourism System: An Introductory Text*. Englewood Cliffs, N J: Prentice Hall Publishing, 1985.

Miller, David J. 'Invasion of the Cockpits: Patterns of encroachment into the Wet Limestone Rainforest of Cockpit Country, Jamaica'. In *Resource Sustainability and Caribbean Development*, eds. D.F.M. McGregor, D. Barker, and S. Lloyd Evans. Kingston: The University of the West Indies Press, 1998.

Ministry of Tourism and Sport. The Ten Year Master Plan for Sustainable Tourism Development. Kingston: Ministry of Tourism and Sport, 2001.

Ministry of Tourism. Green paper on Policies, Proposals and Programmes in the Tourism Sector. Bridgetown, Barbados: Ministry of Tourism, 1999.

Momsen, J. Henshall. 'Caribbean Tourism and Agriculture: New Linkages in the Global Era'. In *Globalization and Neoliberalism: The Caribbean Contextm*, ed. Thomas Klak. Lanham, Maryland: Rowman & Littlefield, 1998.

Munt, I. and Mowforth, M. *Tourism And Sustainability: New Tourism in the Third World*. London: Routledge Publishers, 1998.

Myerscough, J. *The Economic Importance of the Arts in Britain*. London: Policy Studies Institute, 1988.

Nettleford, Rex. 'Heritage Tourism and the Myth of Paradise.' *Caribbean Review* 16, nos. 3&4 (1990): 8–9.

————. 'War, Recession and Gorillas (Tourism Madness Indeed!)'. The *Gleaner,* January 16, 1991.

Noel, C. 'Developing the Linkage Between the Tourism and Agricultural Sectors'. Proceedings, Regional Agro-tourism Conference. Trinidad and Tobago: IICA, 2000.

Nurse, Keith. 'The Globalisation of Trinidad Carnival: Diaspora, Hybridity and Identity in Global Culture'. *Cultural Studies* 13, no. 4 (1999): 661–690.

————. 'The Trinidad and Tobago Entertainment Industry: Structure and Export Capabilities'. *Caribbean Dialogue* 3, no. 3 (1997): 13–38.

O'Connor, E. 'Rural tourism as a farm diversification option for small farmers'. In *Tourism on the Farm*, ed. J. Feehan , 73–82. Dublin, Ireland: University College, Dublin, Environment Institute, 1996.

Obermair, K. *Future Trends in Tourism.* Vienna: University of Vienna, 1999.

Odum, H.T. *Environmental Accounting: Emergy and Decision Making.* New York: John Wiley & Sons, 1996.

O'Ferral, A.M. 'Tourism and Agriculture on the North Coast of the Dominican Republic'. *Revista Geográfica* 113 (1991): 171–191.

Olsen, B. 'Environmentally sustainable development and tourism, lessons from Negril, Jamaica'. *Human Organization* 56, no. 3 (1997): 285–93.

Oppermann, M. 'Farm tourism in New Zealand'. In *Tourism and Recreation in Rural Areas*, eds. R. Butler, C.M. Hall and J. Jenkins, 225–238. Chichester: John Wiley & Sons, 1997.

Organisation of American States. Reference Guidelines for Enhancing the Positive Socio-cultural and Environmental Impact of Tourism. Washington DC, 1984.

Owen, R.E., S.F. Witt and S. Gammon. 'Sustainable Tourism Development in Wales, From Theory to Practice'. *Tourism Management* 14 (1993): 463–474.

Paris, J. and C. Zona-Paris. *100 Best All-Inclusive Resorts of the World.* Guilford, CT: The Globe Pequot Press, 1999.

Patterson, Orlando. 'Slavery and Slave Revolt: A Sociological Analysis of the First Maroon War 1655-1740'. *Social and Economic Studies* 19, no. 3 (1970): 289–325.

Pattullo P. *Last Resorts: The Cost of Tourism in the Caribbean.* Kingston: Ian Randle Publishers, 1998.

Pigeassou, C. 'Sport Tourism: The Emergence of Sport into the Offer of Tourism. Between Passion and Reason. An Overview of the French Situation and Perspectives'. *Journal of Sport Tourism* 4, no.2 (1997). Available at: http://www.mcb.co.uk/journals/jst/archive/vol4no2/welcome.htm.

Pigram, John. 'Planning for tourism in rural areas: bridging the policy implementation gap'. In *Tourism Research: Critiques and Challenges*, eds. David Pearce and Richard Butler, 156–174. London: Routledge, 1993.

Pires, B. 'Spot the Bajan: new game at Kensington'. *Daily Nation,* April 15, 1994.

Poon, Auliana. 'Addressing the Challenges —Towards a European Union Program of Support to the Dominica Ecotourism Sector'. Proceedings of the First Annual Sustainable Tourism Development Conference, Dominica, May 21–24, 1997.

————. 'All-inclusive resorts'. *Travel and Tourism Analyst.* 6 (1998).

————. *Tourism Technology & Competitive Strategies.* Oxfordshire: CAB International, 1993.

Pourier, M., Bestuurscollege van het Eilandgebied Bonaire en de Regeringen van de Nederlandse Antille en Nederland, Kralenkijk, 1992.

Price, Richard. *Maroon Societies.* New York: Anchor Books, 1973.

Ramsaran, R. *The Commonwealth Caribbean in the World Economy.* London: Macmillan Publishers, 1989.

Reingold, L. 'Identifying the elusive eco-tourist'. In *Going Green*, a supplement to *Tour and Travel News*, October 25, 1993.

Report of the Caribbean Regional Workshop, Vision 21. Port of Spain, Trinidad and Tobago September 29–30, 1999.

Ritch, D. 'Tourism Madness'. *The Sunday Gleaner*, January 13, 1991.

Ritchie, J. 'Assessing the impact of Hallmark Events: Conceptual and Research Issues'. *Journal of Travel Research* 23, no. 1 (1984): 2–11.

Robinson, C. *The Fighting Maroons of Jamaica*. Kingston: William Collins and Sangster, 1969.

Roebuck, P. 'WI cricket must watch cultural yorker'. *Sunday Sun*, April 10, 1996.

Rolfe, H. *Art Festivals in the UK*. London: Policy Studies Institute, 1992.

Rovinski, Y. 'Private reserves, parks and eco-tourism in Costa Rica'. In *Nature tourism: managing for the environment*, ed. T. Whelan, 39-57. Washington DC.: Island Press, 1991.

Ryan, C. Recreational Tourism: A Social Science Perspective. New York: Routledge, 1991.

Sachs, I. *The Discovery of the Third World*. Boston, Mass: MIT Press, 1976.

Said, E. *Orientalism*. New York: Pantheon Press, 1978.

Sealy, M. 'Match hauls in $1 million'. *Weekend Nation*, April 15, 1994.

Searle, Chris. 'Race before wicket: cricket and the white rose'. *Race and Class* 31 (1990): 343–55.

Severin, F. O. 'Community Development'. Paper presented to the students of MSc Tourism and Hospitality Management, University of the West Indies, Mona, 2001.

Shaw, G. 'Culture and Tourism: the Economics of Nostalgia'. *World Futures* 33 (1992): 199–212.

Shaw, G. and A.M. Williams. *Critical Issues in Tourism: A Geographical Perspective*. Oxford: Blackwell Publishing, 1994.

Sherman, P.B. and J.A. Dixon. 'The economics of nature tourism: determining if it pays'. In *Nature Tourism: Managing for the Environment*, ed. T. Whelan. Washington DC.: Island Press, 1991.

Shiklomanov I.A. World water resources: modern assessment and outlook for the 21st century. Russia: Federal Service of Russia for Hydrometeorology and Environmental Monitoring, State Hydrological Institute, 1999.

Shores, John N. 'The Challenge of Eco-tourism: A Call for Higher Standards'. (1999). Available at: *www.planeta.com*.

Simmons, D.G. 'Community Participation in Tourism Planning'. *Tourism Management* 15, no. 2 (1994): 98–107.

Sinclair, Donald, (consultants) et al. 'Tourism Policy (Guyana)'. Turkeyen, Guyana: University of Guyana, Division of Caribbean and Tourism Studies, 1999.

Sirakaya, E., V. Sasidharan and S. Sonmez. 'Redefining eco-tourism: The need for a supply-side view'. *Journal of Travel Research* 38, no. 2 (1999): 168–172.

Sofield T.H.B. and A. Sivan. 'Form Cultural Event to International Sport – The Hong Kong Boat Race'. *Journal of Sport Tourism* 1, no. 2 (1994): 21–33.

Spence, B. Cockpit Country Conservation Project. Land Management Report. Kingston: Environmental Foundation of Jamaica (unpublished), 2000.

Sports Tourism International Council Research Unit. 'Sports as an Economic Generator'. *Journal of Sports Tourism* 1, no. 2 (1994).

Sports Tourism International Council Research Unit. 'Sports Tourism Categories Revisited'. *Journal of Sports Tourism* 2, no. 3 (1995).

Springer, B. 'Towards a Regional Policy for Agro-tourism Linkages'. Proceedings, Regional Agro-tourism Conference. Trinidad and Tobago: IICA, 2000.

*325*

Sproule, K.W. 'Community-Based Ecotourism Development: Identifying Partners in the Process'. Prospect Park, PA: Wildlife Preservation Trust International, 1995.

Sproule, K.W. In *The Ecotourism Equation: Measuring the Impacts*. New Haven, Connecticut: Yale University Press, 1996.

*Stabroek News.* 'Promoting Tourism'. Editorial, May 23, 2000.

Steffens, R. 'Memories of Sunsplash'. *Reggae Sunsplash Magazine* (1994): 27.

Stoddard, E. and G.H. Cornwell. 'Reading Sugar Mill Ruins: "The Island Nobody Spoiled" and Other Fantasies of Colonial Desire'. In *Early Modernity and Europe's Race for the Globe*, ed. Mita Choudhury. Special Issue of South Atlantic Review 65, no. 2 (2001).

*Sunday Gleaner*, The. (February 26, 1995): IA & 3A.

Taylor, B.E., J.B. Morison and E.M. Fleming. 'The Economic Impact of Food Import Substitution in the Bahamas'. *Social and Economic Studies* 40, no. 2 (1991): 45–62.

Tefler, D.J. and G. Wall. 'Linkages Between Tourism and Food Production'. *Annals of Tourism Research* 23, no. 3 (1996): 635–653.

Thomas, C. 'Product Innovation: Reflecting on the Prospects for Agro-tourism in the Caribbean'. Proceedings, Regional Agro-tourism Conference. Trinidad and Tobago: IICA, 2000.

Thornhill, A. 'We won't be sidetracked'. *Daily Nation*, April 13, 1994.

TIDCO. Corporate Report. Available at: *www.tidco.co.tt/corporate/report/tourism*.

TIDCO. Trinidad and Tobago Tourism Statistics, 1997–1999. Port of Spain: Tourism and Industry Development Company, 1998.

Torres, R. 'The Linkages Between Tourism and Agriculture in Quintana Roo, Mexico' PhD diss., Dept of Geography, University of California. Available at: *http://www.ntrnet.net/~skilli/dissert.htm*, 1996.

Tosun, C. 'Limits to Community Participation in the Tourism Development Process in Developing Countries'. *Tourism Management* 21, no. 6 (2000): 613–633.

Tow, S. 'Sports Tourism – the benefits'. *Journal of Sports Tourism* 2, no. 1 (1994).

Townley, S. 'Some Legal Issues Associated with International Sports Marketing'. *Sports Marketing Quarterly* 2, issue 2 (1993).

Tyson, G. and M.E. Bacci. Saint Kitts Heritage Site Management Project. Washington DC: The Organisation of American States, 1998.

UNDP. Human Development Report. United Nations Development Programme, 1994.

United Nations Environment Programme. 'International Year of Eco-tourism'. Available at: *www.world-tourism.org*.

USAID. *Caribbean Regional Program-Assistance Strategy 2000-2005*. Washington DC: United States Agency for International Development, 1999.

Wahab S. and J.J. Pigram. *Tourism Development and Growth: The Challenge of Sustainability*. New York: Routeledge, 1997.

Waldrop Bay, H. 'Greening the Caribbean'. *Successful Meetings* 47, no.1 (1998): 107– 108.

Wallace, G.N. *The Ecotourism Equation: Measuring the Impacts*. New Haven, CN: Yale University Press, 1996.

Watt, D.C. *Event Management in Leisure Tourism*. Essex, England: Addeson Wesley London Limited, 1998.

WCED. *Our Common Future: The World Commission on Environment and Development*. Oxford: Oxford University Press, 1987.

Weaver, D. *Ecotourism in the Less Developed World*. New York: CAB International, 1998.

Weaver, D. 'Alternative to Mass Tourism in Dominica'. *Annals of Tourism Research* 18 (1991): 414–432.

Weech, P. Case Study Water Resources in The Bahamas. Water Resources in the Context of the imperatives of Tourism Industry in The Bahamas. Nassau, Bahamas, 1999.

*Weekend Observer*, The. 'Trelawny 2000 Yam Festival – About the Southern Trelawny Environmental Agency'. April 20, 2000.

*Weekend Observer*, The. 'Trelawny 2000 Yam Festival – Celebrating Yam'. April 20, 2000.

West, P. C. and S.R. Brechin. *Resident Peoples and National Parks: Social Dilemmas and Strategies in International Conservation*. Tucson, AZ: University of Arizona Press, 1991.

Western, D. 'Defining eco-tourism'. In *Eco-tourism: A Guide for Planners and Managers*, eds. K. Lindberg and D.E. Hawkins. North Bennington, VT: The Eco-tourism Society, 1993.

White, D. Social Marketing: A Strategy for Eco-tourism Development in Jamaica. MSc thesis. Mona: The University of the West Indies, 2000.

Wilkinson, B.A. 'Lack of support for Windies'. *Barbados Advocate*, April 15, 1994.

Wilkinson, P. F. 'Strategies for Tourism in Island Microsta'. *Annals of Tourism Research* 16 (1989): 153–177.

Wilkinson, P.F. Caribbean cruise tourism: Delusion? Illusion? *Tourism Geographies* 1, no. 3 (1999): 261–282.

Williams, P. 'Farm Based Tourism and Leisure: A Step Further'. East Essex: Nuffield Farming Scholarship Trust, 1994.

Wood, M. E. 'Ecotravelling into the Century'. Article from the *Greenmoney Journal*, 1997.

Wood, R.E. 'Caribbean cruise tourism: globalisation at sea'. *Annals of Tourism Research* 27, no. 2 (2000): 345–370.

Wright, M.L. *The Accompong Town Maroons, Maroon Cultures*. Washington DC: Smithsonian Institute, 1993.

WTO. *Tourism Market Trends Americas, 1989-1998*. Madrid: World Tourism Organisation Commission for the Americas, 1999.

WTTC, APEC Tourism Working Group. 'The Economic Impact of Travel and Tourism Development'. London: World Travel and Tourism Council, 1998.

Yearwood, S. The Role of Education and Training in Eco-tourism in Belize. MSc thesis. Mona: The University of the West Indies, 2000.

Zauhar, J. and J. Kurtzman. 'A Wave In Time – The Sports Tourism Phenomena'. *Journal of Sports Tourism* 4, no. 2 (1997).

Zauhar, J. 'Historical Perspectives of Sports Tourism'. *Journal of Sports Tourism* 2, no. 4 (1995).

Zips, W. *Black Rebels: African Caribbean Freedom Fighters in Jamaica*. Kingston: Ian Randle Publishers, 1999.

## ELECTRONIC SOURCES

*www.campfire-zimbabwe.org.*

*www.eco-tourism.org*, Eco-tourism Statistical Fact Sheet.

*www.greenbuilder.com.*

*www.interconnection.org.*

*www.jamaicacarnival.com.*

*www.kiskeya-alternative.org.*

*www.planeta.com.*

*www.tourismconcern.org.uk.*

# CONTRIBUTORS

## EDITOR

Chandana Jayawardena, DPhil, FHCIMA, is Professor in Hospitality and Tourism Division, Niagara College, Canada and Past President of Hotel & Catering International Management Association, UK. He was the first Academic Director — MSc in Tourism and Hospitality Management of the University of the West Indies. He has co-authored/edited nine books.

## AUTHORS

Thomas Abel, PhD, is an ecological anthropologist and currently an NSF International Postdoc Fellow, conducting research on ecotourism in Taiwan. His interests include complex systems theory and ecological economics. Recently he co-edited a special issue of *Conservation Ecology* titled *Human Ecosystems: the Integration of Anthropology and Ecosystem Sciences*.

Ibrahim Ajagunna, M.Sc., MHCIMA, is the Head, the Tourism and Hospitality Management Department at the Excelsior Community College, Kingston, Jamaica. He was educated at the Federal Polytechnic, Idah, Nigeria, the University of Technology, Jamaica and Sheffield Hallam University, UK. He has over ten years work experience in the hospitality industry.

Hilary McD. Beckles, PhD, is a Professor and Pro-Vice Chancellor for Undergraduate Studies, UWI. He has published widely in the areas of Caribbean Slave Societies, Gender and Colonialism, and West Indies Cricket History and Culture. Among his books are two volumes of *The Development of West Indies Cricket* (Pluto 2000).

Ian Boxill, PhD, is the Head and a Senior Lecturer in the Department of Sociology, the UWI, Mona campus. He has published extensively in the areas of development, culture, ethnicity and tourism. He is involved in a major tourism research project, which includes Mexico and most of the Caribbean countries.

Carolyn Cooper, PhD, is a Senior Lecturer and Head, Department of Literatures in English, the UWI, Mona Campus, Jamaica. She is also the Coordinator of Reggae Studies Unit of the UWI. She has published widely in a range of topics.

**Grant H. Cornwell**, PhD, is the Professor and Chair, Philosophy Department, St. Lawrence University, New York, USA. With Eve Stoddard, he has published most recently Global Multiculturalism: Comparative Studies in Race, Ethnicity, and Nation (Rowman and Littlefield 2001) and Globalizing Knowledge: Connecting International and Intercultural Studies (AAC&U 1999).

**A. Denise Gooden**, MSc, lectures in the joint degree programme in Hospitality & Tourism Management of the UWI and UTech, Jamaica. She was in the second cohort of graduate students of the master's degree in Tourism and Hospitality degree at the UWI. She also studied in France and Germany.

**Dennis R. Gordon**, PhD, is a Professor of Political Science and Executive Director of international Programs at the Santa Clara University, USA. His research interests include environmental policy in the Caribbean. His scholarship has been honoured with annual awards from the American Political Science Association and the America Historic Association.

**L. Barbara Graham**, PhD, works with Inter-American Institute for Co-operation on Agriculture. She has over 17 years experience in development projects working with the Food and Agriculture Organisation and IICA. In recent years she has published in journals on issues of sustainable development and the environment.

**Macsood Hoosein**, MS, is Guide Training Coordinator at Iwokrama, Guyana. He has   experience in protected area management in Guyana and Costa Rica and developing and teaching courses in wildland management and in environmental interpretation. Among his recent publications are the Iwokrama ranger training manual and two educational publications on biodiversity.

**Eritha Huntley**, MSc, is a Lecturer in the School of Hospitality and Tourism Management, University of Technology, Jamaica. She has previously lectured at Northern Caribbean University, Jamaica and was a Research Assistant at the University of the West Indies, Mona. Her research interests include sustainable development and human resource management.

**Vindel Kerr,** MBA, is a Business Consultant & Corporate Trainer and a DBA candidate at the Manchester Business School, England. He has authored over 30 articles and papers spanning corporate governance, business strategy and agricultural technology transfer, and one book, *Corporate Governance Beyond the Boardroom*, forthcoming.

**David Mason**, MSc, is a Senior Lecturer at Victoria University, Wellington, New Zealand specialising in database design and ecommerce applications. He has extensive consultanty experience internationally and is the author of numerous articles and books on information systems implementation. His research interests are adoption and application of ICT and community informatics.

**Hilton McDavid**, DSc, is a Lecturer in Operations management at the UWI. He co-ordinated the Operations Management and quantitative techniques course and is the research supervisor in Eco-tourism of the UWIs Masters degree programme in Tourism and Hospitality Management. His current research interests include Agro-tourism and Eco-tourism.

**Dionne Miller**, MSc, is an Operations Officer of the Civil Aviation, Jamaica. Her academic interests include environmental protection and sustainable tourism development. She holds a Masters of Science degree in Tourism and Hospitality Management at the UWI.

**Simon Milne**, PhD, is Professor of Tourism and Associate Dean - Research in the Business Faculty, Auckland University of Technology. He coordinates the New Zealand Tourism Research Institute (www.tri.org.nz) and also holds appointments at Derby University and McGill University. His research focuses on creating stronger links between tourism and surrounding economies.

**Keith Nurse**, PhD, lectures at the Institute of International Relations, UWI, Trinidad and Tobago. His current research area is cultural industries. He is the author of *The Caribbean Music Industry* and *Festival Tourism in the Caribbean* and co-author of *Windward Islands Bananas: Challenges and Options under the Single European Market.*

**Willard Phillips**, MSc, is a Policy Analyst at the Caribbean Regional Centre on the Inter-American Institute for Co-operation on Agriculture (IICA) in Trinidad and Tobago. He is currently completing his Doctoral dissertation in Agricultural Economics at the University of the West Indies, St. Augustine Campus, Trinidad & Tobago.

**Howie Prince**, MSc, is National Disaster Coordinator, National Emergency Management Office (NEMO), St. Vincent & the Grenadines. Formerly, he was the Administrative Manager, Department of Tourism and Programme Producer for the Ministry of Education St. Vincent & the Grenadines. He is also a Consultant / International Trainer in Disaster Management.

**Donald Sinclair**, MPhil, is Coordinator of the Division of Caribbean and Tourism Studies at the University of Guyana. He served as Chairman of the Guyana Tourism Advisory Board and as Special Assistant to the Minister responsible for Tourism. He is currently a Director on the Guyana Tourism Authority.

**Tricia Spence**, MSc, is a former Research Assistant in the Department of Management Studies, the UWI, Mona Campus, Jamaica and a recent graduate of the International Business Management Programme. She is also an accomplished actress and broadcaster. Recently she assisted in the writing of 7 papers on tourism in the Caribbean.

**Elizabeth Thomas-Hope** DPhil (Oxon) is the James Seivright Moss-Solomon (Snr.) Professor of Environmental Management and Head, Department of Geography & Geology, UWI. Her publications include: (co-edited with Ivan Goodbody) *Natural Resource Management for Sustainable Development in the Caribbean* (Canoe Press, UWI 2002) and *Caribbean Migration* (UWI Press 2003).

**Eve Walsh Stoddard**, PhD, UCLA, is the Professor and Chair, Global Studies Department, St. Lawrence University, Canton, New York. With Grant Cornwell she has published most recently *Global Multiculturalism: Comparative Studies in Race, Ethnicity, and Nation* (Rowman and Littlefield 2001) and *Globalizing Knowledge: Connecting International and Intercultural Studies* (AAC&U 1999).

**Graham Watkins,** PhD, is acting Director General of Iwokrama, Guyana. His has experience in natural resource management in aquaculture, ecotourism, fisheries and wildlife in Ecuador and Guyana. He is an ex- Naturalist Guide of Galapagos National Park and has a number of publications in wildlife, community resource management, and training.

**Gale Yearwood**, MSc, is the Senior Research Officer, Ministry of Tourism, Barbados. She obtained a master's degree in Tourism and Hospitality Management, with distinction, from the UWI (Mona). She has a first degree in Hotel Management from the Centre for Hotel & Tourism Management in Nassau, Bahamas.

## OTHER CONTRIBUTORS

**Allison Atkinson**, MBA, is the Administrative Assistant for the M.Sc. in Tourism & Hospitality Management Programme, UWI, Mona Campus. She has had seven years working experience in the travel industry, airline industry and hotel industry.

**Samuel B. Bandara**, BA (Hons), ALA, has served the library of the UWI, Mona Campus, Jamaica since 1977. Currently he is the Acting Deputy Campus Librarian. His main academic interest is in Caribbean bibliography. He is the author of 'Literature of Caribbean Tourism' (Caribbean Finance and Management, 7, 1993).

**Anthony Clayton**, PhD, is the Alcan Professor of Caribbean Sustainable Development at the University of the West Indies. He holds Visiting Professorship at the Sir Arthur Lewis Institute for Social and Economic Studies, the University of Surrey and the University of Edinburgh. He has published widely on Sustainable Development.

**Kenneth O. Hall**, PhD, is Pro Vice Chancellor and Principal of the Mona Campus, UWI. A historian and former Deputy Secretary-General of CARICOM, has recently published three books on Caribbean regional integration. He is Chairman of the Scholarship Committee of the Caribbean Tourism Organisation Michael Manley Scholarship Fund.

**Richard Kotas**, MPhil, Hon. D.Lett., FHCIMA is the Emeritus Professor and previously Director, School of Hotel Management, Schiller International University. Prior to that he lectured hotel management at the University of Surrey, UK for nearly 30 years. He has conducted seminars in 13 countries, published 15 books and over 50 articles.

**Richard Teare**, PhD, FHCIMA, is Principal and Chief Executive, IMCA, President, Revans University —The University of Action Learning and Chief Learning Officer, IMCA Socrates, UK. His publications include 19 co-authored and edited books and more than 150 articles and book chapters on aspects of service management, marketing and organisational learning.

# INDEX

Printed in the United States
85850LV00004B/37-78/A